Graham Campbell McInnes was born in London in 1912. His mother was the indomitable Angela Mackail, later famous as the novelist Angela Thirkell, his father the singer James Campbell McInnes. His brother Colin MacInnes (his preferred spelling) also became a well-known novelist and social commentator.

After her divorce from McInnes, Graham's mother married an Australian, George Thirkell, who formally adopted the boys. The Thirkells sailed from England in 1919, living first in Hobart before a loan from Angela's cousin Stanley Baldwin enabled them to buy a house in Melbourne. Graham was educated at Scotch College and won a scholarship to Melbourne University, where he met his future wife Joan Burke, and in 1933 gained a first class degree in History. He then set off for Canada to find his father, whom he had not seen for fifteen years. From 1938–41 McInnes was the art critic for the Toronto paper *Saturday Night*, and an extra-mural lecturer for Toronto University; from 1942–8 he worked for the Canadian National Film Board. At the age of thirty-six he switched to a diplomatic career, spending four years in Ottawa before postings to New Delhi and then Wellington. Later he attended the Imperial Defence College and served in the Canadian High Commission in London from 1959–62, finally as Minister. After a period as Canada's first High Commissioner in Jamaica he became the permanent Canadian delegate to UNESCO in Paris and was made Ambassador in 1969.

Graham McInnes wrote articles, art books and novels such as *Lost Island* (1954) and *Shushila* (1957), but his lasting fame rests on his classic series of memoirs: *The Road to Gundagai* (1965), *Humping My Bluey* (1966), *Finding a Father* (1967), all to be published by The Hogarth Press, and culminating in *Goodbye Melbourne Town* (1968). He died in Paris in 1970.

THE ROAD TO GUNDAGAI

Graham McInnes

New Introduction by Robertson Davies

THE HOGARTH PRESS
LONDON

TO THE MEMORY OF
MY MOTHER
AND
TO NELL AND BASIL HALL

Published in 1985 by
The Hogarth Press
40 William IV Street, London WC2N 4DF

First published in Great Britain by Hamish Hamilton Ltd 1965
Copyright © The Estate of Graham McInnes 1965
Introduction copyright © Robertson Davies 1985

All rights reserved. No part of this publication may be reproduced, stored in a retrieval system, or transmitted in any form, or by any means, electronic, mechanical, photocopying, recording or otherwise, without the prior permission of the publisher.

British Library Cataloguing in Publication Data
McInnes, Graham
The road to Gundagai.
1. McInnes, Graham   2. Diplomats——Canada——Biograpy
I. Title
327.2'092'4   JX1730.A59
ISBN 0 7012 0593 8

Printed in Great Britain by
Cox & Wyman Ltd
Reading, Berkshire

INTRODUCTION

In the obituary of Graham McInnes which appeared in *The Times* of London on March 2nd, 1970, is the comment, 'his admirers consider him superior as a writer to his more famous brother.' Now that both men are dead and the last books of Colin MacInnes may be considered, this opinion gains in weight. Graham McInnes's reputation as a writer rests not on his novels, but on four volumes of what purported to be autobiography, of which *The Road to Gundagai* is the first. But in what sense are they autobiography? Under examination now they look more like works of literary art, resting on fact certainly, but not bound by fact. These books have many of the characteristics of fiction.

This is not to suggest that they falsify anything, but rather that they are written with qualities of perception and selectivity that are uncommon in autobiography, which usually says, 'Look at me.' McInnes's books say 'Look *with* me,' and that is what makes all the difference. He is the showman, not the hero, centre stage.

What does he ask us to look at? The Australian city of Melbourne, to begin with, as it was during his boyhood and youth. His birthplace was London, and he became a Canadian, at last that country's ambassador to UNESCO; his work as a diplomat took him all over the world and his writer's eye and gift for synthesis accompanied him wherever he went, but to those who knew him he was always a Melbourne man.

In this respect McInnes was lucky, for Melbourne is a city of architectural dignity, planned to be a capital, handsomely placed on the shores of Port Phillip Bay and rich in trees, parks and gardens. People call it old-fashioned, and certainly it is not the bustling Americanized city Sydney has become, but the old-fashioned quality rises from a reserve that is reassuring rather than chilling. This is the heart of the city McInnes shows us, in cunningly chosen detail, but he also tells us of the Melbourne suburbs where people like his stepfather, George Lancelot Allnutt Thirkell, lived the unassuming suburban life so rasping to the sensibilities of his mother. Every great city has several stages, on which are acted portions of its drama; the suburbs are usually the scene of comedy or melodrama. In Malvern, S.E.4, at some distance from the noble heart of Melbourne, Angela Thirkell, granddaughter of Burne-Jones, daughter of the eminent Professor Mackail, cousin of Stanley Baldwin, cousin of Rudyard Kipling, sister of Denis Mackail the well-known novelist, acted out the wry comedy of the second of two bad marriages. It might have been a comedy by Ibsen, even by Strindberg, but it was also shot through and through with that very English sense of class and snobbery which is the rheumatoid arthritis of English society. There is no country without snobbery, but the English people have raised snobbery into the realm of metaphysics.

The two bright-eyed observers of this cruel comedy were Graham and Colin McInnes, arbitrarily re-named Thirkell, but both with the mark of their father, James Campbell McInnes, strongly upon them. Campbell McInnes was a great singer, one of the finest of Edwardian England, who combined in his heroic figure the qualities of an interpretative artist of the first rank with the ungovernable temperament of a Highland Celt. The dark side of Campbell McInnes was apparent in both boys, and in Colin it raged destructively. In Graham it was for the most part controlled, though his anger could be frightening; it is the tension demanded by that control that gives his writing its special, vivid quality. Art has roots in whatever the artist can do to reconcile the opposites in himself, and in Graham, a warm, generous, merry man was at all times battling with a thrawn, angry man who longed to overturn tables and shout at fools. The reconciliation of these opposites was bought at a great price, but in return for the price came his enviable gift of supple and evocative prose.

Graham's sense of comedy was doubtless a legacy from his mother. Her novels, which won her a wide popular reputation, were deft, ironic, brilliant in their reminders of Jane Austen and Anthony Trollope, without ever rising to the level of either author. The books were the best part of her life; her private world was embittered and bleak. But the deeper strain in Graham came from that dark enchanter his father who could, in the course of a short German *lied*, evoke an atmosphere that was both desolating and uplifting. In a lifetime of listening to singers, I have never heard another who sang *Der Dopplegänger* as he did. Even in his last years, when a rackety life and heroic boozing had robbed his voice of most of its splendour, his art was magnificent, and to hear him sing the Christus role in Bach's *St. Matthew Passion* was to be lifted to a new understanding of tragedy. Like all true bards he was part enchanter and part charlatan, and in this latter phase his mode of thought and speech was sardonic.

The sardonic man and the ironic woman could not maintain their union for long. She told her children that she had discarded James because of his cruelty, but of the nature of this cruelty we know nothing. It is well-attested, however, that when he had delighted an Edwardian house-party by his singing in the drawing-room, he might crawl up on the roof and stalk about precariously, shouting insults and throwing bottles at the spectators below. This is social disgrace, which to Angela Mackail might have been worse than a few buffets from that giant's hand. It is also comedy of the Dionysian, Rabelaisian order – a kind of comedy Angela Mackail was utterly incapable of encompassing, but which her son Graham well understood.

Small boys may not seem to take much notice of what their elders do, but we know that they understand a great deal. The disappointment and bitterness of the Thirkell marriage was taken in at the pores by Graham and Colin, and after Angela Thirkell died, Colin wrote an article about her, titled 'Mum's the Word', that caused some scandal. Men are not supposed to speak so of their mothers. But that article does not go as far in showing us what Angela Thirkell really was as does the portrait in this book, which is moderate in tone but clinically accurate in detail. Does it tell all? No, it does not. In 1966 Graham wrote to me:

About my mother: I don't know what kind of impression this portrait created. The critics seemed to think it was detached and compassionate, which was the impression I tried to convey. There again I set out not to say *all* of what I believed in my mind or felt in my heart but what it seemed to me was *just* that I should say: right in taste, appropriate? I search for a word. I could not stomach the received Angela Thirkell image; but neither did I give full rein to my memory. The reason for that was that, in spite of everything, I loved her. I couldn't help it, though she was so awful!

There speaks an artist, and it is not the painter of miniatures on simulated ivory that was his mother, but the artist of large dimension that was his father. Colin wrote of his mother from a bitterness still childish in spirit; Graham wrote of her with maturity and something kept in reserve; even so, the picture is all we can endure. The original version of this book ran to 178,000 words and he wrote to me, 'When I looked at the first draft in cold print I was appalled at myself.' He cut it to the book you hold in your hand. What the angry man wrote the artist had the grace to amend.

In *The Road to Gundagai* Graham writes of childhood. In the later books he told of youth and love, of the search for the discarded James Campbell McInnes and finally of Melbourne, dear and embracing. This first book has the freshness and tangible quality that rises not from an accumulation of detail, not from total recall, but from choices made by an artist and assembled with the skill that conceals art. In the letter quoted above he wrote of this book, 'What you read is (cliché, I fear) emotion recollected in tranquility. At least that is my belief.'

He chose Wordsworth's phrase, I am sure, with full recollection of the definition that contains it: 'Poetry is the spontaneous overflow of powerful feelings; it takes its origin from emotion recollected in tranquility.' But is *The Road to Gundagai* a spontaneous overflow of powerful feeling? Not quite; see with what art the feeling has been channelled and the effect it leaves upon us, when we have read. He might, with greater justice to himself, have quoted Whitman:

> . . . *this is no book.*
> *Who touches this touches a man.*

Robertson Davies, Toronto 1984

AUTHOR'S NOTE

It is customary to append a disclaimer to the effect that the characters bear no resemblance—save the wildly co-incidental—to persons living or dead. I can make no such claim. To those who know the Australia of forty years ago which I describe, it will be evident that this account is peppered with the names of real people, many of whom are still happily with us. To them may I express the hope that if they recognize themselves as having been seen through a glass, darkly, they will also concede that the glass is rose coloured. My especial thanks are due to my friend Mr. J. Barton Hack of Melbourne and to Mr. Frank Perry, Librarian at State Parliament House, Melbourne, for help in tracking down elusive facts relevant to this, to me, dim yet glorious age. The research is theirs; any errors are mine.

I have to make the following acknowledgments. Reproduced by permission of Allans Music (Aust.) Pty. Ltd., Melbourne, owners of the copyright: *The Bugles of England* (words by J. D. Burns, music by L. C. M. Donaldson); *Australia Will be There* by W. W. ('Skipper') Francis; *On The Road to Gundagai* (words and music by Jack O'Hagan); *Back to Croajingalong*, by Pat Dunlop; *Hustling Hinkler* (original title *Lucky Lindy*) by L. W. Gilbert, Australian lyrics by Jack O'Hagan. *Lucky Lindy*: lyric by L. Wolfe Gilbert, music by Abel Baer; copyright 1927/copyright renewal 1955 Leo Feist, Inc., New York. Rights for Great Britain controlled by Francis, Day & Hunter, Ltd., London. Used by permission. *She Was Just a Sailor's Sweetheart*: by Joseph Burke: copyright 1923/copyright renewal 1957, Leo Feist, Inc., New York. Rights for Great Britain controlled by Francis, Day & Hunter, Ltd., London. Used by permission. *Who*: by Otto Harbach & Oscar Hammerstein: copyright 1925 by T. B. Harms Co; used by permission. *Yes We Have No Bananas*, used by

The Road to Gundagai

permission of the Lawrence Wright Music Co., Ltd. *Over There*, by George M. Cohan: copyright 1917/copyright renewal 1945 Leo Feist, Inc., New York. Rights for British Commonwealth except Canada controlled by Chappell & Co., Ltd., London. Used by permission.

My efforts to trace the copyright owners of some of the other songs mentioned here may have been unsuccessful and I apologise if I have unwittingly trespassed in this respect.

Graham McInnes

CONTENTS

I	The Last of England	13
II	A Capital Ship for an Ocean Trip	22
III	Van Diemen's Land	35
IV	This will be the Place for a Village	59
V	Four Grace Street, Malvern, S.E.4	72
VI	Good Old Scotch, We'll Ever Sing	89
VII	The Emigrant Vessel	113
VIII	Policemen and Lepers	121
IX	Up the Country	133
X	We are Scouts of Toorak	154
XI	Prahran Doctors and The Spis Orpheus	187
XII	The Lady Help	202
XIII	Central 434, Please	219
XIV	Up rode the Squatter Mounted on his Thoroughbred	243
XV	Angela (Sui Generis) Thirkell	264
XVI	The Bugles of England	280

ILLUSTRATIONS

Angela McInnes, London 1915. From a charcoal portrait by John S. Sargent

James Campbell McInnes, with his wife and sons, Bournemouth 1915

The author with his maternal uncle, Denis Mackail, London 1913

Margaret Mackail (Burne Jones), with her grandsons, Graham and Colin McInnes, London 1918

George Thirkell with Graham and Colin McInnes, Sheffield 1919

Family group, 4 Grace Street, 1925

Angela Thirkell, Melbourne 1925. From the drawing by Thea Proctor

MAPS

Part of Greater Melbourne

The Western District and Eastern Ranges

There's a track winding back
To an old-fashioned shack
Along the road to Gundagai;
Where the blue gums are growing
The Murrumbidgee's flowing
Beneath that sunny sky;
Where my Daddy and Mummy are waiting for me,
And the pals of my childhood once more I shall see.
For no more will I roam
When I'm headed straight for home
Along the road to Gundagai.

— JACK O'HAGAN

PART OF GREATER MELBOURNE

1 Domain & Botanical Gdns. 2 Federal Government House 3 Flemington Racecourse.
4 Flinders Street Rly. Stn. 5 Melbourne Grammar School 6 Naval & Military Club
7 Princes Bridge Rly. Stn. 8 Scotch College 9 Sir Charles Hotham Hotel
10 Spencer Street Rly. Stn. 11 State Government House 12 'The Works' A.
13 'The Works' B. 14 1st Toorak Troop H.Q. 15 Victoria Docks
16 Wesley College 17 Xavier College 18 4 Grace Street

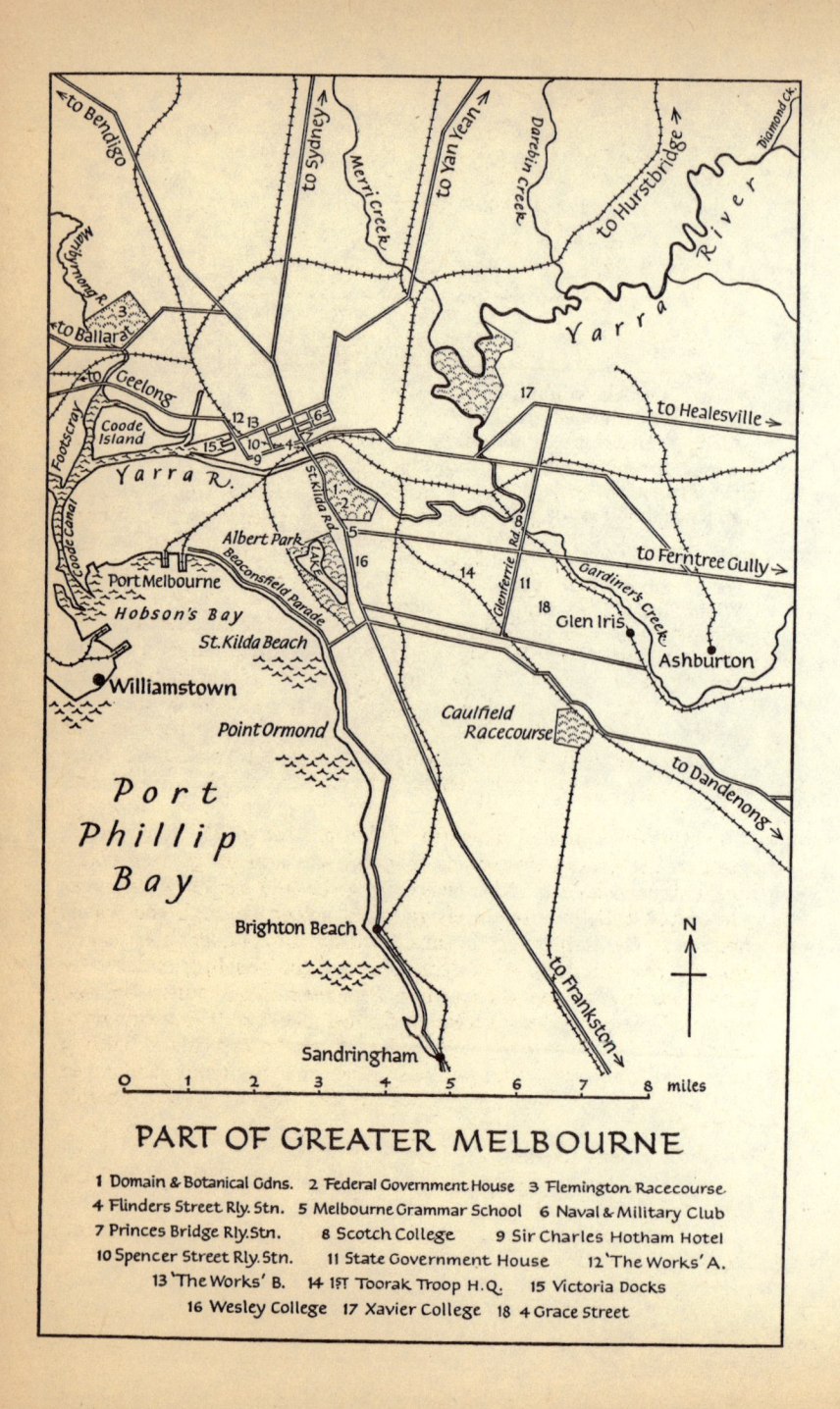

Chapter One

THE LAST OF ENGLAND

O N this blazing February day a hot pungent wind brought aromatic scents to our nostrils after seven weeks at sea. I struggled over the blistering sands, shod in highly unsuitable English boys' sandals, and felt a calamitous sense of loss. Where were the white chalk cliffs? Where were the coarse shingle, the diagonal concrete groynes with their threaded green slime and seaweed, the slippery chalk rocks over which one lurched with a shrimping net? This had been the prospect from Rottingdean, framed by distant views of the Palace Pier three miles away in Brighton, and broken by an impressive row of cyclopean stone piles from the abandoned Maritime Railway. This was the only 'seaside' I knew and it had always been backed, befriended, or overhung—depending on the skittish changeability of damp grey English skies—by towering chalk cliffs at least eight hundred feet high.

But Cottesloe Beach! The sun melted the tar on the road and it stuck to the unsuitable sandals. The sea was a series of deep translucent unbelievable blues. It was Nile green and sapphire blue over white sand and limestone reefs soft and golden through the water; amethyst blue where reefs sank swiftly into underwater caves; emerald blue flung in great scarves above the shoaling underwater sands; cobalt blue and then ultramarine further out where the sun sputtered and sparkled so that it flashed like fire. Far away on a limitlessly distant horizon was a low hump-backed island with a lighthouse. The sky was whiteish-blue and luminous and arced like a blazing shield: heroic Australia, heroic Greece, heroic Gallipoli.

'Don't go out too far!'

A censorious well-worn rubric and I barely heard it. 'Sharks' the voice added matter-of-factly.

At once the bright sea rang with alarm, indeed with horror. Sharks! Better the land.

The Road to Gundagai

The blinding beach died abruptly in low nondescript scrub, indescribably old and tired. Beyond rose stiff trees with ghostly greyish trunks and long leathery leaves dangling listlessly in the heat. When the antipodean sirocco stirred them, they sent out a strange and daring perfume of eucalypt and hinted at a world beyond; a scented oven, hot without menace. The sky and the beach and the sea shimmered and shook in an intense blue-white light and induced a powerful thirst. I whined for a drink until our English nurse, Mabel, dispensed a grudging penny. Across the blazing sand and over the bubbling tar road among the scrubby bushes stood a wooden shed with its front hooked up. In its somnolent depths lurked a sun-yellowed female face.

'Whatcher want, sonny?'

'A drink please.'

'Well, what about a spider?'

First sharks, now spiders; perhaps other demons lurked in the olive-grey scrub. The woman gave a laconic glance.

'New around here ain't you? Thought so. Pommy eh?' I shook my head.

'Course you're a Pommy! Straight off the boat from Home. "Coom out on the Arse-over; bin out a moonth all but three weeks." I can tell. You just try a spider. You'll love it.'

She swivelled on her seat in the heated gloom, yanked from the icebox a bottle of ginger beer and unscrewed the rubber top with a magnificent pop and a small cloud of smoke. She reached for a thick yellow glass and poured in the ginger beer. While the foam sizzled she pulled a wooden scoop from a pail of water and dipped it below the counter with a twist and a grunt. It came up with an enormous dollop of ice-cream which she dropped into the ginger beer.

'There's your spider.' She shoved a straw into the sulphurous bubbling mess. I drank with the ecstasy of revelation and forgot at once about sharks and heat and tiresome Mabel; and also about payment.

'That'll be tuppence,' the woman said sharply.

'A penny's all I've got.'

She nodded with a tired air. 'Then I'll have to be satisfied with that, won't I sonny?' She swept the penny into her apron. 'Pay me next time you come back.'

'But we're not coming back; we're going on to Melbourne.'

'Off with you now!' and her laughter pursued my puzzled steps back across the boiling tar and the blistering sand to the warm waters of the Indian Ocean into whose shallows I flopped exclaiming 'I've just drunk a spider, Maybie.'

The Last of England

'Don't be volegar' was her automatic response, eliciting at once from my brother and me a chorus shouted in unison: 'Don't be volegar or I'll shoot you with a revolever.' Shrieking we fell back into the shallow sparkling water—neither of us could swim—while Maybie's lips pursed in disapproval.

Mabel Baden had come from Kilburn-and-Brondesbury, in the anonymous railway-threaded north-west of London, to accompany my Mother to Australia as a 'Lady Help'. The phrase reflected with paralyzing accuracy her mode of speech and outlook on life; and her rows of semi-detached red brick houses with tudor gables and clerestory window of stained glass like vitrified mucous, were duplicated endlessly in the little houses she saw as the sunsoaked day closed. There'd been no sharks and after splashing joyfully for a couple of hours, after making railways and evanescent harbours in the firm wet sand, after a tea of sandy sandwiches and bottled Kola Beer foaming sweet and sticky into paper cups, we packed and started back. A huge blood-red sun was sinking behind Rottnest Island and the wonderful peace of exhaustion lay on us all. The sunburn with its nights of pain barely assuaged by liberal lavings of coconut oil, lay ahead.

We padded happily across the cooling sand. The tar no longer bubbled on the beach road. At the small wooden station our sandals made a hollow clomp on the platform as we waited impatiently for the little narrow-gauge train. The station was decked out with cheerful coloured enamel advertisements: *Griffith's Tea, Hutton's Hams are the Best, Iron Jelloids, Carter's Little Liver Pills, Kiwi Boot Polish, Monkey Brand Won't Wash Clothes.* The breeze now was from the sea, but wherever it died, the dry scented pungency of the eucalypts floated back again, as if we were in the middle of a gigantic herb garden. Presently with a high toot the little train approached, drawn, I noticed with the engine spotter's eye, by a 0-6-0 tank locomotive. Fussed over by Maybie we clambered into a cattle box with facing wooden seats and glassless windows—second class in the State Railways of Western Australia in those days—and clattered slowly back to Fremantle where we boarded our home for the past seven and the next two weeks, the S.S. *Friedrichsruh*, and went happily to our friendly bunks.

Sometime during the night the *Friedrichsruh*, 9,700 tons and crammed with Australian soldiers returning from Gallipoli, Flanders and the Somme, grumbled out from between the Fremantle breakwaters and set her head south to round the Leeuwin on her way to Melbourne. As we fell asleep the damp sea wind whispered through the porthole scoop, but the tiny cabin smelled of sand and sassafras, of boronia and the flowering gum, and of the great grey continent beyond. Down from the promenade deck floated the familiar and highly romantic strains of *The Missouri Waltz*.

* * *

The voyage really began when Mother asked me whom I would like her to marry. This request was not so odd as it sounds. My father had suddenly disappeared after one or two scenes of towering violence of which I had been the frightened spectator. He was a giant with a troubled stormy visage, a huge black moustache and a deep rumbling voice which filled me with fear and admiration. His name was James Campbell McInnes and he was a baritone of distinction in Edwardian days and a fine Bach singer. He married Mother when he was thirty nine and she was twenty one. The difference in ages and in temperaments was too great for the marriage to last and it finally crashed to the ground in 1917. Mother divorced my father for cruelty and he went roaring off with the Royal Flying Corps and to a subsequent career in Canada which, though constructive and creative, never attained the level to which he might legitimately have aspired. In later life my father believed that his relationship with my mother had ruined his career, and though he never blamed her—in fact scarcely ever spoke of her—he was also very far from blaming himself. He attributed the disaster to Fate and in this he was probably right, if Fate includes the marriage of two totally incompatible persons.

My father left an ex-wife with two boys aged five and three and a girl who died of pneumonia before the year was out and whose death was blamed on my father by my mother's family, though by implication rather than overt statement. We all went to live with my maternal grandparents, Professor and Mrs. J. W. Mackail at their house in Pembroke Gardens, and though I have since lived in Canada, Australia, India, New Zealand, Jamaica and at many addresses in London, the formula 6 *Pembroke Gardens, London W.8* for many years conjured up a mythical home. After my grandmother's death in 1953 the mythical home was devoured with insatiable rapacity by expanding London and though the house still stands there are six doorbells under the 'Kensington Italianate' portico.

While living at 6 Pembroke Gardens I had the last childhood sight of my father. Surrounded, as we were, by my grandfather's Greek and Latin books and his plaster casts of Caesar, Vergil and the Horse of Silene from the Parthenon, and by my grandmother's collection of Burne-Jones paintings, which she had inherited from the artist, who was her father, the possibility of such a meeting

The Last of England

seemed unlikely. But it happened, and was almost the last time Mother ever mentioned my father, at least until I reached the age of reason and perhaps of importunate enquiry. It was on a summer afternoon on Kensington High Street between Warwick Road and Earl's Court Road. An indeterminate and certainly unmemorable Nanny (not dear old Barbara Parsons who left us to marry Sid Brown, the stationmaster's son, and to live in Spalding) was pushing a perambulator containing my brother, while I lagged beside trailing an old umbrella on the sidewalk, to a perpetual hurrying chant from the Nanny.

Out of nowhere burst my father whom I hadn't seen since his inexplicable banishment. He wore the forage cap of the R.F.C. and looked frighteningly unfamiliar, but I naturally ran to him when he called. There ensued an unseemly wrangle between him and the Nanny who, even to my six year old eye, was clearly under instructions not to let us talk to him. In the end she hurried us away down Earl's Court Road and the last I remember of my father was his waving to us from the corner of the High Street, a lonely giant in a strange hat. I was much disturbed by this incident and often dreamed about it. When, many years later, I met my father again in Canada, he asked me what had been my last memory of him. I told him that it was of having seen him in a forage cap on Kensington High Street. He was deeply gratified and though at the time his gratification seemed to me excessive I can now understand why he felt as he did.

Upon returning to 6 Pembroke Gardens I rushed in to mother, full of excitement, to tell her the startling news. Her response was chilling. She said that she did not ever want to hear about my father again, and she went on to ask if I knew why she had sent him away. When I shook my head she said:

'You remember Reuben?'

Of course I remembered Reuben. Mother had been reading aloud to us from Anna Sewell's *Black Beauty* and Reuben was the drunken coachman who allowed Black Beauty to go lame through failing to notice that he had a sharp stone embedded in the frog of his hoof.

'Dadda was like Reuben and I had to send him away.'

I accepted this explanation and for many years thought no more about it. During those same many years my father made no attempt to get in touch with either my brother or myself and when I eventually sought him out at his home in Toronto, he was the most surprised of men.

Within six months of this incident on Kensington High Street Mother was engaged; within nine she was married for the second

The Road to Gundagai

time. Her new husband was Captain George L. A. Thirkell, a sapper in the Australian Imperial Forces, the A.I.F. The courtship took place at Wilsford Manor, near Amesbury in Wiltshire, where my mother, accompanied by her two boys, had gone to spend some weeks with my grandmother's friend Pamela, Lady Glenconner. Wilsford was a little boy's dream: a farm with pigs and chickens and cows; an enormous garden enclosed with scented hedges and topiary shapes; the Wiltshire Avon to paddle in, and a long field at the bottom of which ran a small branch railway line. From the railings of the iron fence one had the immense exhilaration of waving frantically at passing trains which emerged briefly with a cotton-wool clanking from a leafy glade and sped into oblivion while cows tossed their heads in the deep summer pasture and horses capered and snorted in simulated fright.

Wilsford was near the edge of Salisbury Plain and somewhere on this cool and windswept immensity, with its surprisingly deep skies and its distant glimpses of the fingers of Stonehenge, Australian troops were in training. In our childish games we emulated them. One day in a simulated battle game my brother agreed that he was dead and that we should build him a coffin. Beside the cowshed were stacked piles of slates for repairs to the roof of the stables and outhouses. We began the floor of the coffin with neatly arranged slates. When the question of an appropriate bonding material arose, there was the handy and constantly replenished supply of fresh cow manure. We were happily engaged in patting this mess into place when a gig rounded the corner putting us to flight and shattering the carefully aligned slates before the driver could bring his horse to a stop. We were so distraught at the destruction that we didn't notice who was in the gig until a man's voice said in a strange twangy lilt: 'Come on now, be a soldier.' High above the shattered tiles and cow manure was a handsome captain with dark brown hair and freckles in the irises of his eyes. Next to him sat mother and she was smiling and red faced and not angry with us, which filled me with wonderment.

'Well Thirk,' she said, addressing the soldier, 'these are the "Helen's Babies" I was telling you about.'

'Budge and Toddie, eh?' said Thirk.

'You'll have to put up with them,' said mother laughingly. 'Boys, go and get that disgusting mess off under the tap and then come and say hello to Thirk.'

We saw a good deal of Thirk during the next few weeks. He brought flowers to mother and twice took us over to a primitive airfield near Stonehenge where we saw with awed wonder single engined fighters land and take off. The red, white and blue R.F.C. target on

The Last of England

the fuselage and wings sailed through the air as by a miracle and I found my hand in Thirk's. Thirk also brought us chocolate, lifted my brother off the ground by his head, much to our delight and mother's half fearful protests; and when we found that his name was George Lancelot Allnutt, and that he didn't mind if we called him Walnut, and furthermore promised to introduce us to his brother, whose name was Robert Mowbray Winston, and his father whose name was Robert Anthony Claude, we were completely spellbound.

Nevertheless, it didn't occur to me that mother would wish to marry Thirk, principally I suppose because I couldn't grasp the concept of divorce and was still thinking that my own father might some day come back. So that when in due course mother asked me whom I would like her to marry, my immediate reply was 'Uncle Denis'. This brought a shriek from mother, because Uncle Denis was her brother and, like all those whose lives are planned from irresponsibility for the children of others, a firm favourite in the nursery.

'I can't marry Uncle Denis,' said mother, 'who else?'

'Well, Thirk, I suppose.'

So Thirk it was. How a young Australian bachelor soldier of twenty-six could have been so bewitched as to take on a divorced woman older than himself and with two children is something that will have to be examined later. How a woman, after one disastrous marriage, could embark so soon on a second may be explicable, though a paradox. My grandfather used to say that Thirk wooed mother by tales of 'anthropophagi and men whose heads do grow beneath their shoulders'. Or he may have used simpler and more cogent methods. The marriage was at any rate a daunting burden, assumed by mother for womanly reasons and by Thirk with the nonchalance of an incurable optimist. But its principal and immediate effect was that of having once more a man in the house. Not his own house, for we were all now living at 6 Pembroke Gardens. Nor his own children; and no doubt he was feeling his way. But a man. In any case life became more exciting and less predictable.

Suddenly we all left 6 Pembroke Gardens for an idyllic life in Sheffield. The name of this sturdy West Riding city does not at once conjure up an arcady; but on the edges of Sheffield lay some of the most dramatic country in England, with a wild moorland beauty and a steep contrast of crag and fell with rich verdant valleys. Once again we had the luck to live near a railway and this time it was such as to make us the envy of our fellows.

We were lodgers in a boarding house run by a Mr. and Mrs. Isitt. It was called 'Sunnyside' and stood dourly in dressed grey stone on

The Road to Gundagai

a street in the village of Totley overlooking the deep cutting that led to the entrance of the Totley Tunnel. All boys knew that the Totley Tunnel was exceeded in length only by the Severn Tunnel in the whole of Britain. In those days it ranked with the Woodhead as the main route between Sheffield and Manchester, and the traffic was considerable. To watch it we had an eyrie of unexampled excellence. This was the aqueduct in which the Totley Brook was carried across the railway about three hundred yards before the tunnel entrance. To paddle in the waters of the aqueduct high above the railway and to interrupt paddling for the passage of a train beneath was sheer bliss. During a seemingly endless summer the bliss continued even onto the Derbyshire moors. We went picnicking among the gorse and dry stones high up in the fells, and it was a rare landscape which did not contain, somewhere on the horizon, one of the ventilating shafts of the Totley Tunnel. They rose on the moors like blackened martello towers roofed with wire mesh against the depredations of boys and birds. At picnics we would keep our eyes peeled for the dramatic puff of smoke which told of the passage far below in the earth of a train labouring up the tunnel grade from Totley to Grindleford. They fascinated mother too who used to say, having been educated in a classical household, that they were like the angry snorts of Pluto as Persephone escaped his clutches to return to Demeter. We took this as it came.

For Thirk, who had made such delights possible by his decision to pursue what the A.I.F. called Non-Military Employment at the research laboratories of Brown Firth Steel Company, our admiration and thanks were unbounded. He was a metallurgical engineer by profession, and if this calling meant such an ecstatic summer, then we would all be metallurgists when we grew up. And when Thirk —whom we were now tentatively beginning to call Dad at mother's suggestion—said his Non-Military Employment was really Non-Military Enjoyment, he rose even further in our estimation.

We returned to London in the late Autumn and barely were the Christmas festivities over—including a ride in a 'Zeppelin' at Derry and Tom's—than we were told that we were off shortly to the antipodes.

'Then we'll ride to school on ponies?'

'Yes sonny, they all ride on ponies.'

Oh guileful Thirk-Ulysses! How quickly you sent me rushing to my atlas and though in the end, I went to school in Australia by tramcar, there were in the holidays, to be fair, rides both on and behind ponies. I pored over the maps and a ghastly compendium entitled *The Parents' Book: Answers to Children's Questions*, until I got sidetracked from Australian place names and gulfs and bays to

The Last of England

structure of matter: molecules, atoms and electrons. My brother delivered, standing on the nursery table, a long set speech on germs which tickled the grown-ups. I was told to stop reading and he to stop talking.

'Bedtime now.'
'But Mother, it's so early.'
'We're leaving for Australia tomorrow.'

Chapter Two

A CAPITAL SHIP FOR AN OCEAN TRIP

PADDINGTON at seven on a January morning is not calculated to uplift the spirit, despite the noisy bustle, the bright lights pricking the foggy cavern and the clangorous shunting of tank engines. We were what Mother called 'journey proud' and unable to eat. Not surprisingly, by the time Mother, Thirk, my brother Colin, Mabel Baden (alias Maybie) and myself were all safely tucked into a first-class carriage (a great, indeed an indecent luxury for which the Australian Government had paid) along with suitcases and striped carpet bags, we began to clamour for food. The train was bowling up the Kennet Valley and we were told—by Thirk this time—to wait. He was starting to exert his authority. Poor fellow, he'd been surrounded for months by the alien brood; but I sulked in a corner until Swindon when he relented and Mother produced oranges, ginger biscuits, and other messily unsuitable English snacks for the journey.

It will be apparent that we were not going to Australia in the usual direction via Tilbury, but were heading away from it and into the West Country. At Devonport the S.S. *Friedrichsruh*, a German reparations ship allotted by the Allies to the Australian Government, awaited us. Since we were on a troop train there were interminable delays. We dozed after a thermos lunch somewhere near Taunton, awoke to the Priest-and-Clerk tunnel near Dawlish and were finally decanted at Plymouth Hoe, on a black, dreary winter afternoon with the sun already set. The *Friedrichsruh* was anchored in Devonport Roads and we had to go out in a tender, an unforeseen and alarming process. We were herded like sheep down a narrow gangplank into an open well deck and, once there, wedged like pilchards among trunks and crates, while suitcases, baskets and bedrolls hurtled through the air like a stream of meteorites from the dock above to be caught, or not, by nonchalant stevedores. Outside the mole the sea was choppy and poor Maybie was sick all over Mother's sealskin coat. Mother bore this with great fortitude but

A capital Ship for an Ocean Trip

the awful smell was nearly our undoing. Fortunately we soon came under the lee of the *Friedrichsruh* and in calmer water the tender heaved up and down until strong hands grabbed us and we went up the side and into a fairyland of lights.

The *Friedrichsruh* deserves a special word as possibly the most exasperating ship that ever put to sea. Though she was a floating paradise to the children on board, she tried the grown-ups sorely and at times must have frightened them as well. Mother has written of her career with laconic wit, under the thin disguise of the *Rudolstadt** and a brief summary of her iniquities may suffice.

Though the *Friedrichsruh* had been turned over by the Germans as part of reparations, that thorough and painstaking people had assured that her new owners would not learn her ways without difficulty. In doing so they showed a streak of crude but mordant humour. It was early discovered, through a couple of scalded backsides, that the Germans had connected the steam pipes with the lavatories so that he who pulled the chain received a sharp reminder of Teutonic ingenuity. It was then found that the lavatory effluent had, with infinite labour, been connected to the boilers. Harassed mothers, wishing to do the daily baby wash, found the laundry tanks filling with a nauseating red-hot swill. From this it was an easy step to the discovery that almost all the hot and cold taps and the salt and fresh taps had been switched so that no one knew what would come out of what.

Maybie drank half a tumbler of salt water from a tap labelled 'fresh'. Thirk, to our secret delight, was mildly scalded when he turned the cold shower tap on full, and we learned a small but rich vocabulary of 'Digger' expletives. But the Germans had not been content to tamper with the plumbing; they had also monkeyed with the electrical connections. I received from a bell push a shock that sent me reeling. I cracked my head smartly on the edge of the bath and lay on the terrazzo floor shrieking 'Oh mother, mother, come and see me before I die!' This disgraceful exhibition brought Thirk at the run. He felt my head and brusquely told me not to be a fool. However, Mother had 'words', according to Maybie, with the Captain; and by the time we were abreast of Gibraltar most of the major connections had been traced and the misleading labels corrected. Meanwhile we discovered that we were small enough to squeeze underneath the lavatory doors and bolt them on the inside before squeezing out again. As we had access to both men's and women's lavatories we were able to cause much annoyance before the merriment palled.

* *Trooper to the Southern Cross* by Leslie Parker (pseudonym of Angela Thirkell) Faber & Faber, 1934.

The Road to Gundagai

Added to these German monkeyshines and childish jokes, the *Friedrichsruh* was abnormally slow, even for a troopship. She clanked along at about twelve knots and sometimes, for no apparent reason, hove to in the open sea. We were told there was trouble with the condensers but when we pressed Thirk more closely all he would say was 'What they need is a wigwam for a goose's bridle' which was his way of shutting us up. In the Indian Ocean, we circled aimlessly for several hours and it was plain from the worried looks of the grown-ups that something was wrong. During the course of that long afternoon the Orient liner *Osterley* bore down and hove to at a respectable distance. The *Friedrichsruh* ran up a black ball near the masthead; the grown-ups looked serious and for once our eager enquiries were met with a peremptory order to shut up. What really alarmed me was to find, upon raising my eyes from R. M. Ballantyne's *Coral Island*, that the deck was deserted. I rushed round to the port side there to discover all the Diggers and most of the passengers and ship's company attending a band concert. Surely the ship would capsize from this horrifying unbalance? But on my way to warn the Captain, I was halted by a wonderful display of signal flags hoisted on the *Friedrichsruh's* halyards. An answering flutter of bunting came from the *Osterley* half a mile across the sea, and she steamed on her way leaving us gyrating, though not hopelessly, in the vicinity of the Cocos-Keeling Islands. Satisfied that all was well, I joined the band concert and to the blissful strains of *The Blue Danube* on the euphoniums and trombones, lost all interest in the ship's plight. By the time the concert ended we were steaming merrily forward at our customary twelve knots.

It was rumoured among the passengers that our ship had once been a yacht belonging to Kaiser Bill. I was quite ready to believe this. Never having been on board a ship before, the fittings in the 'lounge', into which we were sometimes allowed to penetrate, seemed of truly Byzantine magnificence and variety. But I suspect they were really quite ordinary and that a more sophisticated eye would have found little to remark, except with a twist of the lip, in the mahogany veneer settees, the mirrors with heavy gilt-encrusted edges, the lamps in the shape of Rhine Maidens and the lampshades of pink cretonne with glass bobbles depending from the corners. The dining room was a grave disappointment. It crossed with width of the ship and had portholes on each wall. There was an aisle down the middle from which long tables stretched like fish-bones, and at an increasingly fearsome cant, towards the portholes. These tables were so narrow that we could, and often did, lean forward and hoist into position by grasping the opposite edge,

A capital Ship for an Ocean Trip

though this manoeuvre usually generated an abrupt 'Don't be volegar' from Maybie.

The food, being a change from the nursery food of 6 Pembroke Gardens, was of course Lucullan, and we looked forward with rare eagerness to each meal. Favourite on the menu was mildly curried minced lamb, misread by my brother as 'minced liar'. This we had even for breakfast along with porridge, bread-and-jam and, as we neared the tropics, guavas and mangoes. Fresh limes for squeezing into nectarine drinks were always on the table and though we had to have our meals early, this brought grand opportunities for sky-larking, including such time-tested chestnuts as putting generous spoonfuls of salt into an unsuspecting neighbour's glass, unscrewing the top of the pepper caster for Maybie's special benefit, or lowering the fiddles in rough weather so that cutlery and crockery slid to the floor with a gratifying clatter. After her first memorable voyage to Australia, the *Friedrichsruh* was refitted, refurnished and renamed, and as a ship of the former Orient Line she rendered sedentary service during the Twenties before being broken up. She must have carried unique memories with her to the knacker's yard.

The *Friedrichsruh* was primarily a troopship, returning about eight hundred Diggers to their homes in Australia. We knew that the Army was in charge because Thirk had presented us all to a Colonel with red tabs and also because every trunk, suitcase and valise in our cabins had a big white label: 'Commonwealth of Australia. Australian Imperial Forces. Repatriation and Demobilization'. What we did not know, but which gradually seeped through to us by shipboard rumour, was that this group of eight hundred men contained a hard core of extremely tough eggs and trouble-makers, many of whom had seen the inside of civilian as well as military jails. We were aware of the not altogether goodnatured contempt with which the Diggers, who were herded together in the lower decks, regarded the officers and their wives and families who had the run of the ship. During afternoons the Diggers emerged from their cramped quarters to sun themselves and splash about in small canvas swimming pools in the fore and aft welldecks. Playing games on the promenade deck or the poop we overlooked them and it was difficult not to stare at the mass of half naked soldiery with its suggestion of surging strength barely contained by army discipline. Often they shouted at us in goodnatured banter, 'Howsit up in the dress circle, dig?' 'Come on down and we'll show ya how ter play two-up.' Sometimes the banter took on a ribald note. My brother scored a tremendous success when in response to the bawdy query 'Hey, Snowy, have your balls dropped yet?' he threw his parti-coloured rubber ball down among the soldiers in the

The Road to Gundagai

well-deck, who roared their approval before throwing it back. 'There's a bonzer kid!' a black-browed giant shouted. Not being gifted with so extrovert a temperament I was less popular. I stared too often and my look must have been unconsciously prideful for one man shouted up, 'Lookin' us over, the young barstid' and when I turned away another man called out 'Go and get yourself a tart.' I reported this remark to Mother, without being aware of its import. She looked solemn and spoke to Thirk who said he would speak to the Colonel. This didn't make me any more popular with the Diggers.

But there was a darker side. We were expressly forbidden, under pain of unnamed penalties, to go below our own deck; and even the promenade deck was abruptly curtailed by a wooden grille reinforced by steel bars with the sign 'Other Ranks Only. No Entry. Military Police'. Behind this grille we could see soldiers, clad only in shorts and gym shoes, prowling about like caged tigers; and from the close-packed crowd came a constant low, menacing murmur which rose sometimes to a roar as a fight broke out or an officer smashed a Two-up school. There was also 'The Clink'. This was on the lowest deck in the bowels of the ship and we never saw it. But the phrase 'He's in the clink', or 'That bloke'll end up in the clink' filled us with fearful expectation. Thirk was quick to spot this and the threat—half bantering—of 'A stretch in the clink' was enough to bring us to heel. I don't suppose the proportion of real bad hats was greater than that in any other similar group of men. But the snail-like pace of the *Friedrichsruh*, the interminable length of the journey, the cramped quarters, the miserably small ration of beer and above all the oppressive heat, stirred the men to a frenzy and when the ship hit port violence erupted like a volcano.

The fact that in the whole of that endless seven week voyage to Australia, we docked only twice, and then because of the urgent necessity of coaling, was due entirely to the dangerous and indeed violent indiscipline of this large body of semi-imprisoned veterans. Port Said and Colombo were the only ports at which the *Friedrichsruh* tied up and both had cause to regret it. At Port Said the Diggers went ashore and after a riotous evening of drinking, beat up every Egyptian in sight including the police. They milled through the *suq* fighting and smashing up little stores until the Military Police got them under control and back on board. Because of the disturbance we were not allowed to go ashore and spent much of the day watching 'coolies', as they were called, climbing antlike up the ship's gangplanks in an endless stream, each with his sack of coal on his shoulders. Their work-chant with its strange cadences and glottal shifts in key kept us for hours rapt in contemplation at the rail, returning to the cabin covered in a fine film of coal dust.

A capital Ship for an Ocean Trip

We were six hours late leaving because of the riots, and missed a convoy through the canal. At the Colonel's request the captain sent a wire to Aden saying that we would not be calling there. Poor Aden, if only it knew what it had missed.

The military police at Colombo had been warned and it was thought that this would be sufficient. The officers and their families and the Diggers, except for a few hard cases who were held on board, all went ashore in launches. Our family spent the day at Mount Lavinia. In this heavenly palm-fringed retreat innumerable emaciated little boys and girls darted sinuously from behind trees accosting us, hand outstretched, with the woeful cry: 'Penny, penny, no mother, no father; penny, penny.' My tender heart was stricken at these entreaties and I thought very ill of Thirk who kept repeating 'Come on now, buzz off. Buzz off or I'll get the police.' We returned to the ship towards nightfall, with a coconut, to secure which a Sinhalese boy had literally walked straight up a palm tree with the aid of a noose; and a model catamaran which kept us quiet for hours and, from this point of view, was one of Thirk's better investments.

The ship was strangely quiet and one of the officers greeted Thirk with, 'Well I'm glad *somebody's* back.' We went down to the stifling little cabin and fell asleep among bits of the catamaran. It turned out that on shore, while we had been at Mount Lavinia, the Diggers had run wild. After a good deal of heavy drinking they had roamed the commercial area near the Grand Oriental Hotel in bands of six to ten singing and shouting and with rough goodnature overturning stalls and pushing chaprassis off their bicycles. The police managed to prevent undue violence or looting, and patiently pressed the gangs towards the water's edge. But when this strategem became clear to the Diggers, by now somewhat fuddled, their anger rose, and a minor Sinhalese official who endeavoured to address them from a rickshaw was tossed into the harbour, rickshaw and all, to be fished from the shark-infested waters by the port police with a boat hook. The Diggers roared and cheered at this exploit, but the fat was in the fire, for the official's father was a big noise in the Ceylon Government. While the Diggers stood in a milling crowd, joshing the fellow on his fortunate escape, and one or two friendly drunks fell into the harbour trying to recover the rickshaw and in turn had to be fished out, someone telephoned military headquarters.

This time a company of Gurkhas showed up and assisted the M.P.'s to get the men into boats. Some of the more persistent rowdies were clapped in handcuffs and by five in the morning they were all back on board. There was a fearful official hullabaloo and

The Road to Gundagai

the Australian Government subsequently paid compensation to the doused official. Meanwhile courts of enquiry were held on board, the ringleaders were put in the clink, and the rest were told that no one would be allowed ashore at Fremantle, except those who were to be demobbed in Perth. Further, the ship would not call at Adelaide and there would be an armed guard to meet us on the dock at Port Melbourne. The announcement was greeted with angry roars, ironic cheers, cat-calls and much blasphemy. There was some fear among the women passengers that the men might 'take over the ship' and we children were warned not to speak to them. It was at this particularly delicate moment that I chose to obtrude myself odiously into the centre of things.

A group of us were playing quoits when one of them, as quoits will, rolled along the deck and came to rest against the wooden grille barricading the diggers' area. I ran to catch it but it was snatched from my grasp by a bronzed hairy arm and I looked up to see the same Digger who had teased me earlier in the voyage about 'getting a tart'. He was a thickset nuggetty fellow with a blue chin and quizzical eyes and was clearly prepared to enjoy a game of cat-and-mouse with the superior little English boy. He held the quoit out to me and as I grabbed at it he snatched it deftly away. After this had happened two or three times I grew angry.

'Give me my quoit,' I said.

'Say, please,' said the Digger in mincing mimicry.

'It's mine,' I cried, 'give it to me.'

'Tut, tut, the naughty temper,' said the Digger.

I stamped my foot. 'Give it to me or I'll tell my father!' (it was in that moment that Thirk ceased to be Thirk and became Dad.)

The Digger had now been joined by two or three cobbers and this threat amused them greatly. The Digger wriggled his big bottom and, brandishing the quoit with grotesque effeminate parody, said, 'Girls, girls, toss your curls.' There was a titter from behind the bars. I lost my temper. 'My father's a Captain!' I shouted at the top of my voice, 'and you're only a common Digger!'

There was a moment of awful silence in which I could hear my heart pumping. It was followed by an explosion of oaths of which the only one I understood was 'You bloody little barstid, just wait till I get hold of you, I'll wring your bloody little neck.' Great arms grasped at me through the cracks in the grille; snarls of disapproval rose to a roar as I fled back along the deck, down the companion way and into the cabin where I threw myself on the bunk and burst into tears.

Within about fifteen minutes Thirk came into the cabin. One can dimly imagine to what pressures he had been subjected. But

A *capital* Ship for an Ocean Trip

though he looked grim his voice was kindly. He sat down on the bunk.

'Well young feller-me-lad,' he said, 'you've got yourself into a pretty pickle.'

'I'm sorry, Dad, I'm sorry,' I said blubbing all over the sheets. 'I didn't mean to be rude.'

'That's all right, but you'll have to *say* you're sorry.'

'Oh I will, I will.'

'Wait a minute, sonny, it's not going to be easy. You've got to get up there, go through the barricade and apologize to Mulligan in front of the other Diggers. They're his friends.'

I was silent: a Daniel going into the lion's den without his courage.

'Do you think you can do it?'

I lifted a stained face but said nothing. I didn't know if I could do it.

'If it makes it any easier,' said Dad, 'think of it this way. You're doing it for me as well as yourself. My name's mud with the Diggers.'

He looked shrewdly and kindly at me and I could see the freckles in his irises twinkle. I smiled feebly.

'You'll do it,' he said.

'Yes, I'll do it now.'

'That's the spirit that won the war!'

I clambered out of the bunk and he took my hand, but I withdrew it and marched forward to my fate. In the end it was not as terrible as I had feared. Dad and a lieutenant unlocked the barricade and I went through. The Diggers were silent and hostile. I faced a crowd of blonde giants with marmalade fuzz on their chests; the heroes, some of them, of Gallipoli, Villers-Brettoneux, Passchendaele, Mons and the Ancre. I swallowed hard, went up to Mulligan and said in a loud quavering voice.

'I'm very sorry, sir, for what I said, and I'll never say it again.'

'I should bloody well think not,' was all Mulligan said. I waited. Someone said, 'Come on Nugget, the kid's apologized.'

'Can I go sir?' I asked.

Mulligan looked me full in the eye for the first time. 'You can go to buggery as far as I'm concerned.'

'Yes sir.'

'And don't call me sir,' he growled.

'Okay snowy, vamoose,' said a kindly Digger and off I went.

My apology was not without beneficial results, principally in the direction of Sergeant Corcoran. This dry and laconic man had been instantly pounced upon by Mother as a likely part-time tutor for

The Road to Gundagai

two boys out of school in the middle of term for a probable period of at least two months. She had been attracted by the fact that Corcoran lacked the more outrageous diphthongs of what, at that early time, she still called the Orsetrylian Accent. He proved to be an excellent teacher of elementary arithmetic and geography and I owe to him not only a continuing interest in geography but also whatever feeble apprehension I still have of mathematical processes. Each morning after breakfast Corcoran would gather my brother, myself and three other companions into a corner of the vacant dining saloon and set up school for two hours. During that interminable voyage he taught us our multiplication tables, fractions, and decimals, and gave us a basic grounding in Australian geography and natural resources. Corcoran was a lean hooknosed Queenslander, and he was a firm but fair taskmaster. He played no favourites and he never let us out of school one minute earlier than the prescribed hour. He easily handled both my brashness and the fact that I was a quick learner.

One day he opened an atlas of Australia and asked us to point out the six state capitals. I was the only one who knew them all, but as usual, overreached myself by a running commentary which included the observation that Sydney was about halfway up the coast of New South Wales and Brisbane about an inch north of the Queensland border. He let me go on until I had misread Spencer Gulf as Serpent Gulf and had endeavoured to recoup my losses by observing that Cape Byron might as well be called Cape Shelley or Cape Keats. At this point he closed the atlas and said 'What's nine times eight?' I was dumbfounded—and dumb. 'Seven times nine?' Silence. 'All right. Thanks for your contribution to the geography. Now study your nine times and your eight times tables till the bell goes.'

I was thus not exactly a favourite with Sergeant Corcoran who, as he was fond of telling us, had no time for 'skites', that is, boastful know-it-alls. But my apology to Mulligan won his approval and it was through this that I learned of the Corcoran who existed outside school hours. When he gathered up his books the morning after the Great Incident, he said 'You did well to be honest with Mulligan. I admire a man (Man! My chest practically burst open) who can admit he's wrong. Like the Greeks,' he added inconsequentially. We looked mystified. He leaned across the table, his huge beak of a nose poised over us. 'The Greeks knew about the stars, too; would you like to see the stars, really see them?' We nodded expectantly. 'Then come up on the boat deck after tea tonight,' he said, 'and we'll talk about them. I'll fix it with your Mum.'

In the tropics at one stride came the dark and by the time of our

A capital Ship for an Ocean Trip

rendezvous with Corcoran on a raft behind one of the lifeboats, the stars had indeed rushed out, together with a very full, low-slung muskmelon moon by the light of which Corcoran was cutting the corns on his feet. This was an amazing sight and for some time completely banished from our minds all interest in the stars. Corcoran used scissors, a knife and a razor blade and shaved and skirted the great nodules on his toes with skill and panache, while we craned over him, half hoping, half fearing that he would misjudge a stroke and that the corn would be sheared off like a poppy head leaving a gory mess behind. I had seen an advertisement for an ointment which, by means of persistent use, made it possible to lift a corn right out with the finger and thumb. I was sceptical of this and was delighted to find my disbelief confirmed by Corcoran.

'That's all me eye and Betty Martin,' he said slicing away deftly in the moon-soaked light. 'Don't you believe all you read in the papers. The stuff they try to sell you! That's acid, boys, that's all it is, acid. Burns right into your flesh. You use that stuff and you end by lifting off a toe, not just a corn. No, the best way to keep 'em under control is with this little tool.' He brandished the knife aloft and it glinted in the moonlight. 'Course it's even better not to get 'em in the first place.'

'How did you get yours, Sergeant Corcoran?'

'Ah, that's a long story. Me mother squeezed me into dainty little shoes when I was a nipper. Don't ever let your Mother do that to you. Those sandals now, that's the kind of footwear for kids.'

He went on to apologize for the smell. 'But boys, that's not corns; corns are dried up little things like old men sitting on a roadside in the sunset. What you smell is what they call trench feet. That's what you get from standing with your feet in slime and mud in the trenches in Flanders. Cold too; sometimes you'd stand in wet muddy boots and wear stinking socks for days at a time.' He gave a sardonic laugh in the night. 'And then they wonder why your feet start to rot and stink like an old manure pile. Well, that's that.'

He folded his clasp knife, wrapped the razor blade in waxed paper, put it carefully in his shirt pocket and started to pull on his socks and gym shoes.

'Now boys, what about the stars?'

'Tell us some more about your trench feet,' we begged.

Sergeant Corcoran laughed. 'No, we've had enough about feet for one night.'

'Tomorrow night then, promise?'

'All right, I promise. Now come up here on the bench while I

The Road to Gundagai

show you a few stars, though it's by way of being a pity the moon is so bright. Well here goes.'

This was rather like Millais' painting of 'The Boyhood of Raleigh' with a boy smuggled into the crook of each shoulder and another crouched on the deck while the Ancient Mariner expounded his geography of the velvet night. The moon was hidden now behind the *Friedrichsruh's* single yellow smokestack; tropical breezes whispered in the guy wires; the lifeboat davits were silvery green swans' necks on the port side and curved grey ghosts on the starboard side. Phosphorescent cream swelled from the prow far below; the wake spread out like Pegasus' tail; and overhead the sky was lit like a Cairene lamp with thousands of stars. Up to this time the only constellation I had been taught was The Great Bear, and now that we were approaching the equator I did not know where to look for it. But Corcoran, like the guide who takes you down a familiar street and suddenly opens your eyes to the dramatic and the unfamiliar, plucked his way through the heavens, and as his slow Australian drawl beat comfortably upon the deep of the night, the stars began to arrange themselves into wonderful patterns.

During the nights that followed he showed us Cassiopeia hunched in her eternal chair, Orion straddling the heavens with his club and his belt and his dangling sword, the Pole star disappearing over the Northern horizon, Perseus and Andromeda, Castor and Pollux and then, with a throb in his voice, the Southern Cross, always a puzzle to us with its fifth star, and the Pointers that led to the faint south polar star. The Milky Way was a great band of luminous cloud studded with countless points of light. He showed us Venus, Mars, Saturn and Jupiter, and perhaps most frightening of all The Black Cloud of Magellan, that pit darker than the darkest sky which raised its ebony horse's neck against the faint lustre of the Southern Cross. Corcoran spoke of all these mysterious bodies in a slow matter-of-fact voice, but he also imparted to us a little basic mathematics for the solar system, and a few simplified versions of the Greek myths and legends about the stars. We felt the depth and mystery of the universe, and began for the first time to be teased by the problem of infinity and awed by the problem of eternity. But Corcoran linked these mysteries to the familiar and we felt on easy terms with the stars and the planets because we believed that we knew who they were and what they were doing.

Somewhere between Colombo and Fremantle I fell in love, for the second time. The first time had been with a figure of Britannia on a War Bond poster in London and I had been much put out to overhear the temporary nameless Nanny say *sotto voce* to a friend 'Look at the boy *admiring* that poster.' But this time it was real flesh and blood, the daughter of the Colonel who was, I suppose, in her early twenties but who seemed to me to be the embodiment of Guinevere, Circe, my Mother, my Aunt Clare, Freya and Dido. I mooned about in the vicinity of this goddess whenever she came to her deck chair. I lay on my belly on the deck with my chin cupped in my hands and gazed up at her. I twisted about the awning stanchions on one foot waiting for her to speak to me. I even went as far as to lean over the back of her chair and was disconcerted by the very odd, not to say carnivorous, appearance which lower teeth present when they are seen in the guise of uppers. I must have been a perfect bloody nuisance, but the girl never told me to go away and never uttered a cross word. The end of the affair came by quite another means and the agent was a Captain Wright of the A.I.F. Wright had first commanded our attention, indeed our awe, by beating my stepfather in an officers' wrestling match. Consequently when he beckoned me over to his side of the deck one morning I was not disposed to refuse. I presented myself at his deckchair, and looked respectfully at his large florid face and the scar on his neck —a legacy of the Somme that still showed livid yellow. The Captain harrumphed.

'How would you like to do something for me?'

'Yes sir.'

'You know Miss Mills?'

'Yes.'

'You know her pretty well don't you. She likes you eh?'

I felt a flush mounting up the back of my neck at this intrusion into my private dream. But the Captain took my embarrassed silence for consent and rolled on.

'Now this is what I want you to do. Tonight's the fancy dress ball. You see this little dingus?' He pulled out from his breast pocket a bangle on which was perched a small artificial canary. 'Now you just take that over to Miss Mills and tell her Captain Wright thought she'd like to have this—you know—she could come jazzing in with it on her wrist at the grand parade. Eh sonny, you'll do that for me?'

'Yes sir,' I said and took the ludicrous object in my hand.

'Well cut along then,' he said sinking back in his chair, 'and let me know what she says.'

I moved towards my Guinevere-Circe on leaden feet, for a strong vein of boyish intuition told me that my demi-goddess would refuse the Captain's importunate and asinine request. Seldom can Hermes have sped on a message to a goddess with less winged sandals. Finally I stood before the beauty, who raised an enquiring eyebrow at the 'dingus' on my wrist and said very naturally,

'What on earth's that?'

I replied sulkily and as if by rote 'Captain Wright told me to give you this so that you could come jazzing in . . .' and felt uncommonly foolish as I repeated the litany.

My goddess predictably, though kindly, replied:

'You tell Captain Wright to come himself; I don't take gifts from messengers.' She leaned forward and patted my arm reassuringly. From that instant I hated her. I retraced my steps across the deck with my cheeks burning and held out the mascot to Captain Wright who feigned great surprise.

'What? Wouldn't she take it?'

'She said you were to come yourself.'

The Captain roared with laughter and slapped his thigh. 'She did eh? Ha Ha! Mission accomplished! Here.' He fished in his pocket and handed me a shilling. 'Go and get yourself a lemon squash in the bar.' I took the shilling but my heart was broken far beyond the power of any lemon squash to mend. Indeed it was broken almost until lunchtime.

The next day we were in Australian waters and stood for long minutes at the rail, straining to see the strange new land. But we came upon it during the night and landfall was the mysterious half forgotten earth smell that came in at the porthole with the morning sun.

Chapter Three

VAN DIEMEN'S LAND

Y OU'D have thought that after travelling the best part of twelve thousand miles the Thirkell-McInnes family, having reached Melbourne, would have stayed put. Not a bit of it. After two days in the Oriental Hotel on Collins Street we were off again. As Mother said brightly: Off by the morning train to cross the raging main; off to my love with a boxing glove ten thousand miles away. The Quiet Arrival had a lot to do with it. Everyone on board the *Friedrichsruh* had been expecting further uproar from the Diggers when they hit Port Melbourne; and a number of passengers had hinted darkly at the complaints they were going to make to the authorities, the letters they would write to the Prime Minister, the Premier, and the Lord Mayor about the dire events on board the *Friedrichsruh*. But in the end nothing happened. The Diggers walked off the ship like lambs, singing *Pack up yer Troubles in yer Old Kit Bag*, *Carry me back to Blighty* and *Australia will be There*. The armed guard went away and the people with complaints were so glad to be back in dear old Aussie that they forgot their troubles in no time at all. This freed my stepfather from emergency duty and after two days of sightseeing in Melbourne, we were off to Tasmania to meet our new step-grandparents.

The Bass Strait is at best a stormy sea and the entrance into it from Port Phillip Bay is exacerbated by treacherous cross-currents known collectively as 'The Rip'. The nonchalance with which my brother and I survived this harrowing voyage was a source of wonder to our fellow passengers. All about us they were vomiting into 'strawberry boxes' while we raced up and down deck in the twilight or sang part songs softly in our bunks. Even Maybie was immune and apart from claiming that she had a 'brilliant headache' appeared quite cheerful.

Our ship was the *Loongana* of some two thousand tons. Mother and Dad had a cabin to themselves, but we two boys and Maybie

The Road to Gundagai

had bunks in an enormous semi-circular 'ward' amidships which Mother said looked like Florence Nightingale's hospital in Scutari. We slept blissfully throughout a tossing night and awoke to low blueish mountains with a lighthouse winking in the slate coloured dawn. By the time we were up on deck the ship was sailing down a broad estuary between rolling tree-clad hills. Little wooden houses with red and green tin roofs sat blinking in the morning sunlight among apple orchards. In the distance rocky mountains crouched like lions. We could hardly be torn away from an Australian breakfast of porridge, two chops with an egg poured over them, toast and butter and jam, before we were back on deck again savouring the alien landscape. The boat twisted and turned down the narrowing estuary and, approaching one great sweep, passed the *Rotomahana* on its way to Melbourne. Then ahead lay mudflats and the smudge of smoke. Launceston, and we were bundled down to the cabin to get our coats and trunks.

There followed a train ride which seemed to take all day. The distance from Launceston to Hobart is only about one hundred and thirty miles, but it was night when we arrived tired and bleary. A blur of unknown faces; a forest of legs and skirts. Lengthy conviviality at a large table with a white cloth and our first taste of banana custard during the course of guzzling which I was aware of the following conversation.

'Angela? Such a lovely name! George is so lucky.'
'Thank you. So am I.'
'And what will you call me dear? My name's Emma but my friends call me Nymmie.'
'I shall call you Mamà.'
'Mamà? Well, dear. . . .'
'No, Mamà.'

Bed in a tiny whitewashed room off a screened second floor back verandah and immediate oblivion.

* * *

We woke up the next morning in 405 Elizabeth Street, Hobart, Tasmania. The contrast between this dun-coloured weatherboard house with its tin roof and any other conceivable dwelling place was so enormous that to live in the house was an adventure in itself. What Mother thought of it I simply cannot imagine. Over the years the address, as I wrote dutifully to my new step-grandparents, became a litany which could be intoned in sonorous dactyls, thus:

'Fóur oh five Elízabeth Street

Van Diemen's Land

Hóbart Tas mánia'

On the grounds of its persistence alone 405 deserves a description.

Elizabeth Street was the main stem of Hobart and indeed the main road of the Island, crossing Tasmania from south to north. It began at the docks and after leaping the enclosed remnants of the Hobart Rivulet, started to climb steeply. The city was built on the lower slopes of Mount Wellington which rose direct from the magnificent harbour, formed by the estuary of the Derwent, to a height of over four thousand feet. Elizabeth Street was therefore one long sinuous climb until it breached a low pass between Hobart and Newtown. It was threaded by narrow gauge tram lines on which ran double decker trams that bounced and rocked fearsomely as they galloped downhill or gave out a steady purposeful whine as they climbed the slope. Towards the top of the hill, where the street ran in a corniche, stood number 405, on the east side of the street. This was significant and denoted a lower position in the social scale. The houses on the west side of the street were perched up on the hillside, two storeys in front and one behind, with a fine view over the harbour and hills. But the houses on the east side faced the street with one storey and no view, while their two storeys were at the rear and looked into the backyards of neighbours. This difference in position was a source of sharp discontent for we wanted to see the mountain and the sea, and neither was visible.

The house itself, like so many Australian houses in that continent of gigantic space, was jammed between its next door neighbours with only room for a narrow tradesman's alley at one side and nothing at all on the other. It was set so close to the street that three steps down from the front porch took you to the little breast high paling gate which clanged to in a gamboge coloured paling fence. The upper half of the front door was of stained and pebbled glass and opened into a passage leading straight to the back of the house. This again was an Australian feature, as was the room plan: to the left the parlour, and the bedroom occupied by Mother and Dad; to the right the sitting room and Mamà's bedroom. Across the back of the house ran a screened balcony. Off one end of it was a bathroom with a chip heater (i.e. a small boiler beneath which could be lit a fire stoked with wooden chips and which in due course would produce enough hot water for a bath). Off the other end of the screened balcony was the tiny whitewashed cubicle which served as a bedroom for Colin and me. The effect of this arrangement was that the windows of the two 'best bedrooms' were at the sides of the house and looked across six feet of vacancy at the blank weatherboard wall of 'next door'.

Since the house was built on a steep slope the bottom floor at

The Road to Gundagai

the back was only half the size of the top. It was reached by very steep stairs from the top passage and contained two rooms. On the right was a kitchen of quite appallingly penumbral gloom with a gas cooker and an old fashioned shiningly 'blacked' wooden range. On the left was a dining room so crowded with massive late Victorian mahogany furniture that it was almost impossible to squeeze into one's seat at the table. The room gave the impression—which was correct—of having to accommodate furniture from a much larger house. Outside, an open porch duplicated the upstairs screened balcony. Off one end of this was the washhouse containing a 'copper' beneath which could be lit a wooden fire for boiling clothes. Off the other end was a mysterious little room inhabited by Mamà's husband, into which we were never allowed to penetrate. As it was exactly the same size as our own cubicle it could not have afforded him much room.

The porch gave onto a garden no longer than that behind a reasonably well-endowed central London house, that is to say, about twenty-five feet square. It was surrounded by a six-foot wooden fence of overlapping shingles. In the far corner, tastefully screened by a trellis of wistaria, was the lavatory, or the 'dunny' as Dad used to call it. I was astonished to observe, on first using it, that one's wants were provided for by a swatch of neatly cut squares from the Hobart *Mercury* stuck on a nail in the wall. I spoke of this to Mother who made two points. First, we were lucky to have arrived after the installation of 'the flush'; less than six months ago we should have enjoyed the services of the 'night man' and therefore I was not to complain. Secondly, she too had noticed the pieces of newspaper and was going to ask Mamà to have them replaced by a roll of toilet paper. In the meantime I was to use tissue paper from the chest of drawers because, she said, printer's ink contained antimony and frequent applications of antimony (especially from department store advertisements) were harmful to little boys' backsides.

The above arrangements struck me as squalid, but at the other end of the scale, to excite wonderment and awe, was the parlour. Like the dining room below it was so cluttered with furniture that one could hardly navigate, but the fittings were of some grandeur. There were two big sofas and six overstuffed armchairs; four or five occasional tables were covered with silver ornaments, chinaware and bric-à-brac. An upright piano held an assortment of silver-framed photographs so large that there was room for no other. The chimneypiece over the fire that was never lit, was similarly loaded, and the striped wallpaper was covered with Chinese willow pattern plates in wire holders, empty sconces which on the night of our arrival had been filled with flowers, and water colours of a large stone house with an air of reluctant nobility. This was *Bellevue*, the house that had once belonged to Mamà's people, but did so no more. The room fascinated me because it had two carpets on the floor, a 'wall-to-wall' covered by an Axminster. It also had two sets of spring roller blinds on the windows and two sets of floor length curtains. These were never drawn back nor the blinds raised, in case, I was told, the carpet should fade. Apart from the night of our grand arrival, the room was never used during the whole of our stay at 405 Elizabeth Street, which lasted six months. Indeed it was kept locked as the 'best room' and the family— Mamà, her husband, Mother and Dad, Maybie, we two boys and later my step-Uncle Winston and his bride Stella from New Zealand —all crowded cosily into the tiny little sitting room opposite.

If this description sounds absolutely hideous then that is exactly the impression which the house conveyed. It was hideous both inside and out and I can now see that it was no more and no less (apart from the outside lavatory) than the Australian equivalent of tens of thousands of lower middle class houses in the red brick terraces of Battersea and Wandsworth, or Hendon and Cricklewood, immortalized in Noel Coward's *This Happy Breed*. Yet because it was new to us, it was exciting. Furthermore the mean little house and a thousand like it in Hobart lay at the edge of a land of wild and magnificent grandeur and not a little terror; and it gained in stature thereby. Crowded with its neighbours on an inland plain the house would have been unbearable; but it stood on the shaggy flanks of Mount Wellington and ten minutes' walk brought to view an incomparable panorama of mountain and sea, inlet and island, harbour and crag. We lived, during my time in Tasmania, on the edge of a permanent adventure.

Dad used to read to us from the pages of a red paper-back called *The Adventures of Henry Thornby in Van Diemen's Land*. The stories were absolutely hair-raising and Dad emphasized, perhaps with pardonable exaggeration, that they had been commonplace when 'my Dad was a nipper'. This would have been about 1865 and since Van Diemen's Land became Tasmania only in 1853, Transportation for Life from England to the Antipodes having been abolished in 1852, it may be possible. But there is no doubt that the Island's brutal and brutalized past added a note of menace to the harsh and mysterious landscape, a note of beauty and of cruelty.

According to Henry Thornby, when he was homesteading in the Derwent Valley, there was a continuous, bloody and three-sided warfare between the mounted troopers of Governor Arthur,

The Road to Gundagai

the aborigines (the now defunct *Homo Tasmanianus*) and escaped convicts turned bushrangers. The aborigines dashed out the settlers' brains with 'waddies' in sneak attacks; troopers fired on aborigines and despatched maimed and writhing black men with a shot from a carbine. Ferocious escaped convicts, maddened by flogging with the cat, roamed the bush and occasionally sallied forth to raid isolated settlers' cabins where, if they encountered resistance, they hacked the men to pieces, raped the women and set fire to the homestead. The epic of Henry Thornby exuded an unrelieved miasma of terror, cruelty, treachery and sheer animalism, against an alien physical background, silent, resentful and aware. The whole chronicle was instinct with an overwhelming feeling of desolation and unrequited hope. Ovid never railed more plaintively against his exile on the shores of the Euxine than Henry Thornby did against the fate that had brought him some twelve thousand miles to the underworld of the earth with no hope of ever seeing again the land of his birth.

This overpowering sense of exile, this feeling of the hostility of a strange land, this insensate brutality of the early convict days lay like a cloak of Nessus over the Tasmania of my boyhood, and I reacted to it strongly. Later on, Tasmania became for me a gay and sunny place, but during these first months it was strange and awesome. Yet the fear inspired by the sombre tangled mountains, the slate grey seas and the mysterious 'bush' clinging like hair to the shoulders of Mount Wellington, had in it an element of excitement. In little suburban Hobart we lived on the borders of a world beyond.

For example, at the end of the Augusta Road tramline, which itself traversed a brace of lonely eucalypt-clad valleys, one could walk into the heart of the bush on a narrow dirt road which turned sharp into the flank of the mountain, and be lost in a primeval world. Above, the slopes of the mountain reared upward like petrified tree-clad combers, to froth against the base of the Organ Pipes, a great curtain of vertical striated rock which hung down from Wellington's summit. A thousand feet above the Organ Pipes a leonine head kept watch over the harbour. A swift turn brought the harbour into view: a maze of twisty sinewy interlocking intertwining arms, legs and necks of sea and land; a Laocoon of a landscape, sea and land writhing and twisting in perpetual conflict. Far away to the north the winter sun gleamed pewter on the Derwent where it narrowed and received the waters of the Jordan. To the south, hump on island hump crowded each other into a tangled oblivion through which could be caught glimpses of a distant steel-edged sea. Between us and Antarctica there was, in four thousand miles, not a speck of rock in this great waste of waters. Then round a turn in the bend, like an antipodean Delphi against the sombre eucalypts and harsh rock, stood a small doric temple in grey stone, dedicated to the memory of Sir John Franklin of Arctic fame, who had earlier served as Governor of Tasmania.

A favourite excursion was by tram to Cascades, often with a covey of our step-cousins, for a picnic on the lower slopes of the mountain at Gentle Annie Falls. Cascades, the location of a well known brewery, was so named because it was here that the Hobart Rivulet, emerging from deep eucalypt-clad slopes and enormous tree-ferns, fell in a slender silvery arc to its more mundane lower level where it received much filth and garbage before emptying into Sullivan's Cove. At this point we started the slow struggle up hill, lugging our picnic baskets, our way marked by the iron flume which sprang steeply down the mountainside carrying fresh water to Hobart from reservoirs higher up. Eventually we reached a small moss-covered dell overhung by giant tree-ferns, and spread out the picnic to the pleasant chatter of Gentle Annie Falls nearby. If the Franklin monument was Delphi, the falls were a niche for a new Campaspe. There were three stories about Gentle Annie. One was that an exiled Scotsman, enthralled by the view from the place with its prospect of rock, glen, mountain and, as it were, loch, had in a burst of filial piety named the falls after Annie Laurie. A second story was that the engineer who built the reservoir had named the falls after his wife. A third story was that the superintendent or lock keeper at the reservoir had had a little daughter called Annie. One day while gazing fascinated at the gurgling outflow from the reservoir, and mother's back being turned, she tumbled headlong into the stream, was swept downhill at incredible speed inside the flume and eventually finished up at the intake into the city ponding facilities five miles and two thousand feet below. There can be no doubt which of the stories appealed most to the young.

Another true delight, an unmixed joy, was a trip on a ferry boat. The Cornelian Bay Bridge was not yet built and the only method of communication between Hobart and the many little river communities both up and down stream was by ferry. The ferry slip at the foot of Elizabeth Street was as crowded as a bus depot. Little straight funnelled double ended ferry boats, painted green and white, dashed in to disgorge a shopping crowd from down river, or pulled out like busy waterbeetles to vanish round the edge of the dock in a frothing wake.

The shortest and favourite trip was to Bellerive immediately across the harbour. It was from here that the sketch was made for the famous twopenny Tasmanian purple stamp and it was exciting to

The Road to Gundagai

see the view gradually compose itself as the ferry steamed away from Hobart. About half way across the Harbour, Mount Wellington began to pull free from the town and its surrounding hills. As it did so it seemed to move forward and to overhang the entire harbour with a menacing grandeur. Then buildings, ships, docks and oil tanks sank to blurred insignificance and suddenly it was 'hard astern' and the crew were manning the ropes ready to sling them expertly over the bollards at the Bellerive dock.

The real fun of a ferry trip, whether it was up river to Lindisfarne, Claremont and New Norfolk, or down river to Kingston, South Arm and the Huon ports, was in the little boat itself. Each vessel was built around its engine and this was amidships, naked and unhidden, with all its pistons and flywheels and cranks and spinning governors and greasy oil caps clanking and nodding and pedalling like mad for any boy to see. It was tended by a shirt sleeved giant with a cigarette pasted to his lower lip and a great swag of cottonwaste in his hand. A fourteen year old boy in a peaked cap who helped him was the envy of us all.

Seats faced outward all around the ferry boats for use in good weather. If it was rough you went inside where, from a diminutive saloon, there was a view of the bridge with the ferry boat captain swinging his wheel with one hand and drinking a cup of cocoa with the other. We came to know the short cuts the ferrymen used in mooring and unmooring the little ships and were always disappointed if they didn't employ them. One trick on approaching a dock was to shove the pint sized gangplank three or four feet over the ship's side ready for instant sliding onto the wharf. Another was to sling the rope ahead onto the bollard as the ferry lost way. Yet a third, and requiring even more skill, was to give the rope a half hitch round the capstan while the engineer held the boat with his engine astern against the pull of the rope. The passengers had to look pretty slippy for at any moment, Ding! Ding! Cast off! and the little gangplank would be whisked on board and off to the next port of call. Many of these ferry runs were like water tram cars and a favoured Saturday afternoon caper, with my step-cousin Geoff Tabart, was to take the return trip to Claremont calling at Bellerive, Rosny, Lindisfarne and Montague Bay, zig-zagging from port to port like a cruising taxi picking up passengers in the rain.

In those days few of the ferry boats were built in Australian yards. Most of them were built on the Clyde and the Tyne, or in Belfast and some of them, though of no more than three hundred tons, made the twelve thousand mile journey under their own steam. Such a ship was the S.S. *Rosny* on the Bellerive run, which sailed from Greenock to Melbourne in twelve and a half weeks, via

Suez, Singapore and Perth. Geoff Tabart's elder brother Tom, whose father had an interest in the *Rosny*, sailed on her as supercargo for the journey from Melbourne to Hobart round the east coast of Tasmania. He told us it was like riding the Scenic Railway at Luna Park, but that he never at any time had a moment's anxiety. 'I'd rather shoot Niagara Falls in a barrel any day,' he said.

My step-grandmother was very fond of Tom. She often said that he was her favourite nephew. As we met more than a dozen nephews and nieces during our six months' stay in Tasmania, this was a significant admission. I pressed Mamà for the reason. By now we had affectionately and irritatingly transformed Mamà into Meoma and shortened it to Meo. She was kind enough to put up with it.

'Ah,' she said, 'Tom reminds me so much of Uncle Alfred.' Her voice began to sound soft and far away. 'And the wonderful days in *Bellevue*.' *Bellevue* was the home where Meo had been brought up, and she always spoke of it in soft, hopeless faraway tones as if recalling some lost heroic age when men and women were demigods and a golden sun washed the earth in its light. Listening to the endless stories of country balls, picnic parties, horseback riding, vast dinners with tables groaning under the spread, candlelight romance and, by implication, deferential servants always at a discreet distance, one could not but believe that Meo had come down in the world. This feeling was strongly reinforced by Dad's reference to his boyhood 'in the country near Richmond' and stories of riding to school on ponies. Where was all this now? Even to my innocent eye it seemed increasingly unlikely that we would ever see ponies at 405 Elizabeth Street. Though adventurous because they were strange, the suburban surroundings promised little in the way of the spacious country life. But when I pressed Meo,

'Ah dear, if only you'd seen me at *Bellevue*.'

'But can't we go to *Bellevue* now with you?'

A long drawn out, moist sucking in of the lips and then a sigh, 'No dear, it would hurt me too much. No one takes care of the place now. Besides it was a long time ago.'

This evasive action was accepted without undue reluctance because of the ever present and fascinating alternative of exploring Meo's bedroom. It was undoubtedly the most confused and untidy room I have ever seen in my life. She could rarely find anything and didn't often try. She lay alone in a great double bed patting the clothes vaguely and murmuring, 'Now I wonder wherever I put it? Be a good boy and see if it's on top of the chest of drawers, or perhaps on that table over there. Or I may have left it on the chair.'

'Which chair, Meo?'

The Road to Gundagai

'Oh, I don't know dear, any chair.'

'It' in this case was a comb, but it might be a book, a photograph, a nightgown, an apple, a brooch, a tram ticket or a hat. Impossible to find anything in the vast confusion. Drawers wouldn't shut properly because pieces of underwear and linen cascaded from the slits like the entrails of a slaughtered animal. The tops of tallboys, tables and chests were covered, like the piano and tables in the parlour, with innumerable family photographs on blue plush mounts in repoussé silver frames; with little leather boxes containing jewellery and old medals; and also with piles of clothing, both washed and unwashed, and here and there, dotted like islands in a sea of tumbled linen and pictures, saucers which might contain a peach stone, a banana skin, a half eaten biscuit or some chocolate creams. Like the dining room below, Meo's bedroom was crammed to overflowing with furniture, including two chaise longues. Here and there paths had been worn through the jungle; from the door to the bed, from the bed to the vanity, from the vanity to one of the chaises longues. The rest was impenetrable forest accessible only to children, which was one reason why we were so popular in her bedroom as retrievers and scavengers.

Meo really was fond of my brother and me, and the untidy bedroom which might to others have given an impression of sluttish disorder gave to us one of wayward and unexpected charm. Lying propped in her bed in the middle of the confusion Meo radiated an aura of sweetness and rather pathetic resignation. She had a beautiful soft skin and a big round forehead below which were deep-set eyes with light mauve shadows. She had a retroussé nose and a small sweet mouth and had in her youth been very pretty. Sepia photographs of her as a young woman hung on the wall and showed between the piled up hair and the low Empire *décolletage* a graceful neck and smooth round shoulders. Being highly susceptible I fell in love with the young Meo and was almost as disconcerted as she was to hear Colin exclaim one day, after a penetrating examination of an early photograph,

'Can that *really* be you, Meo?'

It must have been unsettling for her to have to accept, in her late fifties, a daughter-in-law with two ready-made sons who were not her grandchildren; but she was always vaguely affectionate to us both and when, later, she had a grandchild of her own, her kindness towards us remained undiminished. If she was embarrassed to greet her new daughter-in-law—with her precise English voice, her conversation studded with literary and classical allusions, and her uncomfortable way of putting people right with a sparkling epigram—in such unsuitable surroundings, she never said so. But there was resentment in her attitude towards her husband. We felt her quiet disapproval and even contempt, though she rarely spoke to him and, when she did so, addressed him as 'you'.

His name was Robert Anthony Claude, but he was known to his friends as Bob, or sometimes Poor Old Bob. To us he was known as Père—a sobriquet of really rather horrifying archness which Mother conferred upon him. Meo never actually blamed Père for the fact that she—or they—had come down in the world; but she did not need to, for it was blatantly evident in every detail of his dress and every set and gesture of his body. He was a stocky man of average height, with a knobbly bald head garnished by a tonsure of grey, and a Cyrano nose above an infrequently trimmed walrus moustache. In our eyes he bore a remarkable resemblance to Old Bill in the wartime cartoons of Bruce Bairnsfather. The illusion was heightened by the fact that he shuffled about the house in carpet slippers, held his trousers up with a pair of braces used as if they were a belt and, except on Sundays, never wore a collar. In fact, not to put too fine a point to it, Père was a bit of a deadbeat.

He lived in the house on sufferance, confined to his mysterious little room like a mangy old dog in a kennel. So far as we could see he never did any work, in fact never did anything at all except go out reluctantly on errands when requested, and read the paper in the kitchen. He had a shambling furtive air and it was clear that he was held responsible for the decline of the family fortunes. He did not drink and I'm inclined to think that 'the big farm near Richmond' where he and Meo started married life and where he lived for almost twenty years, was 'lost to the bailiffs' by sheer muddle and mismanagement; perhaps a combination of Meo's confused untidiness and Père's fecklessness.

There was something faintly degrading, even to a small boy's eyes, in seeing a grown-up person brought to such a state of squalor and what's more, having long given up caring about it. For Père had no shame. Even when he went down the street on an errand he would shuffle off in his slippers unless it were more than a couple of hundred yards. Nor did he bother about pretences.

'Just going out for a bit,' he would shout up the stairs when in fact he mightn't be back until nightfall.

'I wish you'd get the bread,' Meo would say to the wall.

'All right, Old. Give a fellow time,' he would grumble, sometimes with a broad wink in our direction.

To us boys Père was offhand and gruffly genial. He accepted our presence without demur; perhaps he recognized that he had abdicated the right to any say in what went on at 405 Elizabeth

The Road to Gundagai

Street. He was a great narrator of what he called 'wheezes' and would often come out with them while we were helping him to lay the table or to wash the dishes. Come to think of it, as these were the only chores he did around the house (though once to my embarrassment, but not to his, I discovered him sweeping off the front porch wearing a frilly apron) he must have welcomed even our inefficient assistance. We quickly learned the warning signal, 'Did I ever tell you?' and to reply, 'Oh do tell us Père.' His stories, though they now seem excruciatingly corny, were well angled to nursery appreciation and we thought them very witty. 'Did I ever tell you about the little girl? No? She was crying, see, and the Old Gentleman . . .'

'What old gentleman, Père?'

Testily, 'Never mind that, any old Gentleman. He says to her, "Are you in pain, my dear," he says? "Naow," she howls, "pains in me." '

Many other decrepit music hall gags were dredged up for our benefit. Our favourite was of the man who said he didn't believe in the equator. It happened on board ship and of course by this time we knew all about ships. 'Well,' says his friend, 'I'll lend you my binoculars and if you look through them you'll see the equator.' So the friend looks through the binoculars. 'See anything?' says the fellow. 'No,' says the friend. 'Keep looking,' says the fellow and quick as a flash he pulls a hair out of his head and stretches it in front of the binoculars. 'See anything now?' he says. 'Oh yes,' says the friend, 'now I can see the equator all right. It's a big line and there's a camel walking along it.' Ho, Ho, Ho.

Père also had a touchy temper and a sense of his own personal dignity that could unwittingly be affronted, as I early discovered. He came upon me standing on the hall seat looking at myself in the mirror and told me to get down. I replied to the general effect that I was King of the Castle. His brow darkened. 'I'll fix you, you young rip,' he said. He flashed a razor strop out of his pocket and began to belabour me sharply. I roared with mingled pain, fear and surprise, for though I was to be thrashed on many occasions in the future, this was the first time anyone had ever laid a hand on me. Pursued by Père I ran down the passage and burst into Meo's bedroom. He did not follow for he never entered that room save to bring Meo a cup of early morning tea, and I cowered in her shelter until the storm had abated. I dreaded meeting Père at lunchtime, but to my surprise he was all smiles and full of 'wheezes'. Since my own breast burned with resentment this struck me as the more astonishing. But later, during the course of many thrashings, I learned that grown-ups, whatever secret feelings of guilt they may harbour in their hearts, did have this amazing ability to let bygones be bygones—until the next time. Thereafter I treated Père with wary circumspection.

Of the multitudinous step-cousins whom we automatically inherited the only one to be treated with similar circumspection was Tom Tabart, the elder son of Meo's sister, Aunt Joe; and this was simply because he was a tall strapping fifteen and by far the most extrovert and censorious of the lot. He lacked the light touch, his favourite phrase being 'You're a dope.' If he disagreed with anything you said, which was practically every time I opened my mouth, his invariable comment was, 'That's a lot of balls.'

Tom's father was secretary to the Elwick Racecourse and took us there by ferry out of season to picnic and fish while he busied himself with track matters. The racecourse was beautifully sited, on a point overlooking a bay of the Derwent and set in a small amphitheatre of hills. From here too, Mount Wellington's posture had shifted. Instead of frowning beetle-browed over the little city, he lay couchant like an indolent lion who has had a full meal and doesn't wish to be disturbed. With the Tabart boys we fished on home-made rods of gum sapling, but all we caught was a gummy shark, a horrible diminutive facsimile of the real thing, about ten inches long with a sandpaper skin, a white under belly cut by the vicious gash of a spine-toothed mouth, a head like a hammer, and three triangular fins. We gazed at him with fascinated distaste and threw him back.

Nevertheless Tom had his tender side. One terrible day the Tabart's fox terrier worried to death before our eyes a kitten that had been presented by Meo to Colin and me. We screamed with rage and fear and afterwards wept with rage and sorrow. Tom took things in hand. A Tabart had committed a murder; a Tabart should arrange the obsequies. His sisters Edna and Pixie, at this time boisterous long-legged tomboys, made a coffin of a cardboard box lined with quilting. Tom stood over his young brother Geoff while he dug the grave in Meo's backyard, and he himself led the procession of six children to the graveside and read a brief funeral oration written in deathless prose by Colin and me.

Other new step-cousins were the Piesses who lived in a very lordly house down in Sandy Bay, which might be described as the S.W.1 of Hobart. Apart from the large old bluestone and sandstone mansions of the 'sixties and 'seventies which stood haughtily on the slopes of Davey Street, Sandy Bay was the place to live and Aunt Eva, and Uncle Les lived there with their only child, Wanda. Aunt Eva was Meo's youngest sister and her husband Leslie F. Piesse was a leader in the affairs of the Hobart Harbour Board and

The Road to Gundagai

a Prominent Citizen. Their house in Sandy Bay was full of bright lights and soft cushions and a general air of slightly flashy opulence. No doubt it was all modest enough, but it was impressive to have a player-piano, a large phonograph with a diamond disc and an early form of automatic record changing, and a hothouse. Soft drinks flowed freely and we looked forward eagerly to our rare visits where we would listen to funny records like 'Cohen on the Telephone' and 'Vas you dere, Sharlie?'

As for the golden haired Wanda with her sweet and friendly gaiety, she seemed to us then rather a 'poor little rich girl'. She was generous with her toys, extremely obliging in meeting any request for a drink, or a record, or 'a lend of your music box, Wanda' ('Don't say lend, Graham, say loan.' 'Sorry Maybie.'). But behind the easy smile and the bobbing golden head lurked, we thought, a trace of melancholy. No doubt she was spoiled and no doubt she moped a bit, but of this the only sign was the introduction by Aunt Eva as a companion of an older girl named Nancy. Nancy had a sardonic smile and was a past mistress of the acidulous aside. Meo used to observe to us darkly, 'She's certainly "fallen on her feet".'

Our favourite new cousin, and one who remained so through the years, was Terence Crisp. Terence was the youngest child of Meo's elder sister. ('I'm a little afterthought.') He was in his final year at the University of Tasmania, before taking up the law, a profession in which many generations of Crisps have distinguished themselves. Hobart society of forty odd years ago did not offer a great deal on which a young man could sharpen his wits, and Mother's arrival hit Terence like a thunderbolt. Her sprightly 'clever' conversation, highly allusive and bedecked with liberal quotations and literary analogies, as well as her total disregard for the conventions of what was then still basically a colonial society, excited Terence enormously. He was continually dropping over to 405 Elizabeth Street or inviting Mother and Dad to his house higher up the hill. We boys were the beneficiaries of Terence's infatuation, but we adored him because he was a comic fellow and could play jazz on the piano like a madman. When Terence sat at the keyboard to 'tickle the ivories', rip-roaring post-Armistice America with all its heady intoxication came vividly alive. It is epitomized forever by Terence's rendering of the masterpieces of Zez Confrey, *Dizzy Fingers* and *The Kitten on the Keys*, or by our full-throated soprano chorus, to his accompaniment, of such favourites as *How ya gonna keep 'em Down on the Farm* and *Everything is Peaches down in Georgia*. Who now remembers those far off ditties? They speak of an era still innocent after all

Van Diemen's Land

its blood-letting and today they sound heart-breakingly tinselly. But with Terence at the piano . . .

In the midst of this delightful tomfoolery we continued to hope against hope that, under Sergeant Corcoran, we had seen the last of our schooling. Mother had different ideas; so did Dad, who was anxious that we should attend his old school. Accordingly before they left for the West Coast and the Mount Lyell copper mine to visit the scene of Dad's early training as an engineer, it was arranged that we should be enrolled in Hutchin's School. Shortly after we entered Mother and Dad took off for Melbourne to find a job and a house and we were left in the care of Maybie and her 'revolever'.

Before she left Mother called me in and said that we would go to our new school under the name of Thirkell and not our own name (which she didn't mention). It would be simpler that way. Though Dad wasn't our actual father, he was becoming like a father to us and altogether, well, it would be easier. I nodded glumly, not really comprehending the magnitude of the issue at stake, but prepared to agree if I was told to. In some ways it seemed more natural to use the name Thirkell in these surroundings than my own name of McInnes, which was entirely unknown in Tasmania, and the pronunciation of which was so painful to Mother. I don't suppose that at the age of eight I could possibly have done other than acquiesce. Nevertheless the decision, made arbitrarily by Mother and without any legal sanction, opened up the way to all sorts of dubieties and uncertainties that were to haunt me through my school life and which were not resolved until in early manhood I sought out my own father in Canada.

Mother's action was characteristic and instinctive. She wanted to be quit of a distasteful episode in her life and naturally did not wish to have daily reminders of it. She also obviously did not want to go through the tiresome explanations that are required in such cases. 'How does it happen that your little boy's name is different from yours?' 'Well, you see I was married before.' (dolt, clot.) 'Oh really?' And if the interlocutor was curious. 'And who was he? Is he. . . ?' 'No, we were divorced.' 'How *interesting*.' And so on in an endless skein of gossiping enquiry. I can understand her natural desire to avoid all this and yet her action appears to me to have been heartless in the literal sense. It was based solely on her own convenience. Beyond that it was motivated by a streak of, as it were, solipsistic arrogance which said in effect: if a thing doesn't exist for me it doesn't exist. This was normally Mother's attitude towards anything that seemed to her unpleasant. It is the adult equivalent of the affronted adolescent walking out of the house and 'into the night'. She would sweep the dust under the

The Road to Gundagai

rug, shut the closed door on the rumpled confusion, scrape the mess off the plate and throw it outside where it would soon be covered by snow. But in due time the snow melts and the empty whisky bottles and old shoes and orange peel stand revealed in all their intractable permanence. And though I was a docile lad and accepted the arrangement without demur, nevertheless habit, the tie of blood, and perhaps an instinctive sense of propriety or possibly of basic irreducible human dignity, kept the deception—for so I regarded it—never very far below the surface.

One day in class we were asked to stand up in alphabetical order so that our names could be entered in a nominal roll. When M was called I unthinkingly stood up. The teached blinked and said testily:

'What's the matter with you, Thirkell, your name doesn't begin with M.'

'But my name's really McInnes, sir. At least . . . it used to be.'

'Well, sit down and we'll talk about it later.'

This incident was duly reported to Mother, who summoned me into her bedroom, shut the door and said in a voice deliberately deepened for dramatic effect.

'Don't ever say a thing like that again.'

It dawned on me that she must think there was something shameful, as well as inconvenient, about my name. But I was scared of her when she was angry and so I nodded my head. I kept the promise until I was fourteen, when I asked her where my father was (I hadn't yet found out that he was back in Canada). Her reply was 'I'm not going to talk about him.'

This and similar rebuffs naturally stirred our curiosity the more, but Mother remained adamant. And yet, so curiously complete was her sense of being a world to herself, her belief in 'If I say so, it is so', that she failed to take the most elementary precautions. She never had our name changed by deed-poll so that eventually all that was required of my brother and me was a simple announcement that we were reverting to it. And she kept her diaries and photograph albums in full view for any casual visitor to thumb through. In these albums were scores of photographs of my father in the early years of his brief marriage. In the diary at the time when my brother and I were born, her pretty, rounded Greek handwriting gave way for a few days to his passionate hurried scrawl. Thus, though banished from the house as unclean, James Campbell McInnes continued to lead a shadowy Plutonian existence.

Our step-father's attitude was simplicity itself, relaxed and uncommitted. He was not of course deeply involved; anything that Mother did about her first husband was all right with him. He

Van Diemen's Land

acquiesced in the arrangement; he never referred to my father at all, who for him just didn't exist. More than that, he lent his name with generosity and invariably introduced me as 'My boy Graham'. When he came to have a son of his own he treated us all exactly the same. If young Lance was a favourite it was because he was the baby, not because he was Dad's own son. Lance never had a favoured place and there was no discrimination against us older boys. Dad's genial off-handed goodnature flopped about impartially and his occasional rages never chilled us as much as Mother's, for they were unpremeditated. It was an absent-minded affection exercised by fits and starts, but what there was of it, all three boys shared alike.

Perhaps the greatest practical disadvantage was that of being known throughout my Australian boyhood by my stepfather's name, which I discarded as soon as I was twenty-one and able to find my own father in Canada. This had the effect of isolating my Australian experience under a false label. It meant for years afterwards, redrafted documents, lawyers' certifications, assurances to friends that I was the same old fellow, and of course endless, tedious explanations to them and to others of what had happened. In attempting to take away my own name, Mother succeeded in transferring from herself to me and my brother the burden of explanation and embarrassment which she herself was unwilling to assume.

* * *

Though I attended Hutchin's School only for a single term, it is graven on my memory with all the force of 'the first school'. In England I had attended the co-educational and vaguely progressive Froebel Educational Institute in West Kensington where Roger de Coverley and eurythmics mingled with stiff instruction in Latin, Arithmetic, conversational French and the geomorphology of the Pennine Chain. But Hutchin's was a *real* school. We stayed for lunch and the smell of Irish Stew still has the power, equalled only by that of Proust's *madeleine*, to induce almost total recall.

Hutchin's was not only the oldest school in Tasmania but one of the oldest in Australia, having been founded in 1846 when Tasmania was still Van Diemen's Land. Dad and his elder brother Winston had attended it in the early 1900's. Its Horation motto, V*ivit post funera virtus*, (which I construed, owing to the separation of the words on the school cap badge, as 'He stays at his post by virtue of the funeral') expressed to the full the zeal of the mid-nineteenth century middle class evangelical whereby one consecrated one's life to the purchase of a big tombstone to impress the

The Road to Gundagai

neighbours. The motto was forcibly brought home within the first few days at Hutchin's. As a new boy, and what's more a new boy with a 'Pommy' accent, I was put through the third degree about personality, tastes, antecedents and basic right to exist. At one point I was questioned on the voyage out from England. Where did I embark? 'Why, at Devonport.' There was a howl of derisive unbelief. He doesn't come from England at all! He's a fake! Grab his cap! A kind friend pointed out that there was a Devonport in Tasmania.

'My Devonport's older than yours.'

'It is not.'

'Yours was called after mine.'

'You're a liar.'

I swung at the tormentor with my left fist and followed it up with a smart right-cross with the school cap. The boy staggered backward and blood began to trickle down his cheek. In my fury I had forgotten the heavy enamel school badge held to the front of my cap with two safety pins. A low menacing growl came from the boys as they closed in. 'Coward! Hit a fellow with his cap badge.' 'Why don't you pick someone your own size, Pommy?' Hands grabbed at my grey sweater, someone kicked me in the shins and I was clearly headed for a good beating up when a master strode into the midst of the churning group.

'Now boys, what's all this? All right now, one at a time.'

When the case had been put to him by both protagonists he said to the other boy. 'Bramwell you're a fool. Go and spend ten minutes with the atlas,' and to me, 'Don't be so free with your fists or you'll end up in the detention room. Now both of you apologize and don't let's hear any more about it.' The apologies were subsequently cemented by a truce offering at the tuck shop, but neither Bramwell nor I ever really grew to like each other. *Vivit post funera virtus.*

The foundation was generally C. of E. and the Headmaster, the Rev. C. C. Thorold, was a sharp-nosed cleric with a blue chin and a dog collar. Form IIb was presided over by Mr. Muscamp, a jolly young man in his early twenties whom the class held in admiration because he could twiddle his ears. He used to say, with bland sincerity, that this was the way to keep warm. As it was the June term when the mercury in Hobart dropped to the twenties and we cracked the ice on the enamel pitcher in our little cubicle at 405 Elizabeth Street, this was obviously an accomplishment to be acquired without delay. On frosty mornings when we assembled in the bicycle shed before going to prayers, many was the sweater-clad boy, his hand pocketed against the numbing cold, his breath coming in frosty puffs, but on his face a look of intense concentration as he tried hard to twiddle his ears. The grounding received at Froebel, together with, I must assume, some native talent, quickly procured me a promotion and after that Mr. Muscamp became only a dim figure flitting across the playground, or heard from the school lavatory during break playing Sidney Baynes' waltz *Destiny* on a faintly off-key piano.

Under the new form master, the going was tougher. Mr. Tennent had a large tobacco-stained moustache and was a disciplinarian. He caned on the spot, and with extreme savagery, any boy who lightheartedly presumed to test the severe bounds which he imposed upon us. A boy who put calcium carbide in an ink-well was given a foot rule over his knuckles in the presence of us all. I can still hear the dreadful crackling in my mind's ear. Boys who could not manage the fourth declension were given a hundred lines, to be done after school, and woe indeed to the boy who endeavoured to shorten the task by the skilful wielding of three pens in one hand. He was held up to Mr. Tennent's ridicule, more fierce and rancorous even than his sumptuary punishments. 'Now here's a boy that's taken a short cut. You know what happens when you take a short cut? And you miss your way? Because you've been too clever by half? You get behind, boys. You come out from your short cut with brambles and burs sticking to your backside. And where are your companions that took the long way round? They're up ahead. And you're not.' Then turning with a fierce swish of his gown, 'And You're not either Davis.' Pause. 'Five hundred lines! You can stay after school two nights to do them.' Readers who crave an extension of similar memories are referred to the stories of Talbot Baines Reed which adorned the pages of the *Boys Own Paper* in the earlier years of this century. The pains and penalties meeted out in *The Fifth Form at St. Dominic's* and *My Friend Smith* had crossed the seas with inexorable finality, and faithfully reproduced themselves 'down under'.

We came clattering out of the grey stone building with the sky already getting dark and hurried along Macquarie Street to the G.P.O. to catch the tram up the hill to 405. One afternoon, much to my surprise, I found Meo waiting for me at the front gate with Colin in tow. 'I thought I'd give you a treat,' she said. 'We're all going to the pictures.' I had no idea what pictures these would be but joyfully accepted a break in the routine. We walked down Macquarie Street until we came to the brightly lit marquee of a theatre. Meo paid for the seats and I waited expectantly for something to happen behind the disappointingly drab curtains. After a little while the lights went off and a man in a celluloid collar, identified by a dim yellow bulb far in the pit, began to play the piano. It was tinkly

The Road to Gundagai

jazz, rather like the stuff that Terence played. I liked it but was still puzzled. The curtains parted revealing a white empty space. There was a feeling now of disappointment as well as puzzlement. Then suddenly, bang!

The space leaped to life, filled with enormous sepia-coloured people, while the piano surged and rippled in a series of magnificent chords and arpeggios. It was my first movie. It was called *The Third Kiss* and it featured, I think, Blanche Sweet and Richard Barthelmess, I was petrified in my seat, gripping both arms in ecstasy, my stomach churning, the image of total committal. But as the enthralling entertainment raced to its climax, interrupted by many portentous subtitles held on the screen far too long, I began to get alarmed. The bad man was after the girl; he had her cornered in a studio penthouse; the hero was desperately trying to reach her, by train, by car, even on foot; but he was going to be too late! The bad man approached the heroine with cat-like tread, to the time honoured piano theme of: Pom-pom-pom-pom TAAR, ra-ta-ta-ta, (vamp till ready). I stood up in my seat, 'Look out,' I cried. Meo pulled me down. 'Shush!' The villain threw aside his cigar the better to embrace and crush the heroine. But the cigar has rolled to the foot of the studio curtains! They ignite; flames spurt up the wall, billow from the windows and in an instant the whole place is a blazing inferno. I jumped up and down in my seat shouting 'Oh don't let it happen, don't let it happen!' Colin burst into tears and to scandalized cries of 'Hush', we were taken by Meo shrieking and bellowing from the theatre into the street outside. Meo was mildly annoyed at our performance. 'It's only pretend,' she kept on saying. 'You mustn't be afraid of pretend.'

But when Mother returned from Mount Lyell there was an almighty row. How could Mamà have been so insensitive as to take her two innocent bairns, who had never seen the inside of a cinema, to a film, *without asking her first*? Above all, to a film like this! Seduction in a studio setting, ending in a fire? Why, the very name *The Third Kiss*; what could conceivably be more unsuitable for those of tender years? The implication was that Meo was stupid rather than venal. But the full force of Mother's wrath was turned on Maybie. *Where had she been*? What was the use of the vast sums she was being paid to look after the children if, as soon as Mother's back was turned, *this* happened? She was worse than a fool, she was a criminal. Poor Maybie, whose regular afternoon off it had been and who had gone to have tea with a friend quite unaware of Meo's plans, turned bright pink and fled from the room. I found her later face downwards on her bed and tried to comfort her. Poor Maybie, never mind. You'll soon get well. But the film was nevertheless a real shock, and for weeks afterwards I had nightmares about it. Perhaps this only goes to show a sensitive or, if you like, neurotic disposition. On the other hand Mother can be blamed for not working us in gradually by way of educational movies. Or perhaps Meo *was* unthinking, if kindly. Or perhaps Maybie. . . . In any case the result was an absolute ban on our attending movies unless they were subjects approved of by Mother. The ban extended for over five years and during this whole period about the only film I was allowed to see (apart from such educational fare as Lowell Thomas' *With Lawrence in Arabia*, Colonel Pottinger's *British Everest Expedition of 1924*, and *Twenty Thousand Miles with the Prince of Wales*) was Cecil B. de Mille's *The Ten Commandments*. This latter film contained, to my mind, more gore and bloodshed, more holocaust and general mayhem than half a dozen sequels to *The Third Kiss*. But, said Mother, it was the Bible and therefore it was all right; which goes far to explain Cecil B. de Mille's great success in show business. The immediate effect of the ban was that we were the only boys in the class not allowed to go on a special school concession day to see the film of Shackleton's expedition to the South Pole. We bitterly resented this, but there was nothing to be done. Mother had by this time gone to Melbourne but such was the power of her fiat that in her absence neither Meo nor Maybie was prepared to run the risk of flouting it.

* * *

In the Spring the little city erupted in bunting and flags by day, and lights and fireworks by night. The school was summoned to the assembly hall where the Head announced that we were all to be given a full day's holiday (tremendous cheers) because of the visit of the Prince of Wales (less fervent cheers). We all knew what wonderful work this gifted young man was doing; strengthening the bonds of Empire; carrying a message of faith to the far flung British people . . . the courage of youth . . . bright new dawn . . . (our attention began to wander) . . . selfless dedication . . . solemn thought . . . people of Tasmania . . . the future . . . and so that you may watch him drive through the streets of Hobart, tomorrow will be a holiday (renewed and rapturous cheers). School dismissed.

We took up our position bright and early on grandstands in the park opposite to the G.P.O. The families of returned soldiers and sailors were given special treatment, and we were seated high above Macquarie Street up which I gazed expectantly and fixedly

The Road to Gundagai

until I had a crick in my neck. It seemed that the Prince would never come and the children relaxed in despondency, when suddenly a wave of cheers came cascading down the street with laughter hard on its heels. It was the outriders of the Tasmanian Police on their motorcycles. The initials T.P. waved on little flags from their mudguards and some wag shouted 'T.P.—Teddy Prince!' There was another cheer, a silence, and then a sudden ragged wave of uncertain cheering as if people had been taken by surprise. A little forest of Union Jacks and blue and red Australian Southern Crosses waved before our eyes. I looked down into the tonneau of an open car and saw two men in uniform. Three seconds and all was gone. Which was the Prince? Did you see him? Yes, he was the one in Khaki. Oh, but isn't he a sailor? Perhaps he was the one in blue then. I think he was the handsome one. Come along boys, people are starting to leave. And that was the Prince of Wales, that was. Or Edward P. as he was known to us from his signature on the letter giving us all a half holiday.

But later in the week his spirit reappeared in glory at the illuminated regatta. We went by train to Cornelian Bay, a little inlet of the Derwent estuary which lay at the foot of a lightly wooded hill known as The Domain. We arrived at dusk and an enormous picnic was spread on the shore under the friendly shelter of the gum trees. Out in mid-stream the warships lay like grey smudges against the hills; and low across the water came the sound of a banjo thrumming on the evening air. We waited in hushed expectancy and then, with a spitting crackle a quartet of rockets whooshed skyward ending in great parabolic starbursts, pink and greeny-silver and yellow against the night sky. The warships switched on their lights and the Derwent was transformed into a fairyland. The Prince's ship, H.M.S. *Renown* was outlined from stem to gudgeon, her upper works, her guns, the bridge, funnels, and strings of lights from bow to mast, mast to mast, and mast to stern. 'Ohs' and 'Ahs' of sheer ecstasy shuddered along the shores of Cornelian Bay. The smaller ships were almost as magnificent. There were two cruisers, and four destroyers of the R.A.N. and in the middle distance that battle scarred old dinosaur H.M.A.S. *Australia* which four years later sank to a watery grave outside Port Phillip Heads in accordance with the terms of the Washington Treaty. Up in the sky rockets burst and flared, and finally on the water there exploded a set piece of the German raider *Emden* burning after being beached by H.M.A.S. *Sydney* on the Cocos-Keeling Islands. As the fires sank to the water line and the last falling stars from the rockets sputtered and died away into the night, we packed our picnic in the faint light from the decorated warships

Van Diemen's Land

and went tired and happy to our beds. A week later we left for Melbourne.

The news was conveyed to us by Maybie who said that Dad had got a job with the Australian agents of Brown, Firth for whom he'd worked in Sheffield, and what was more important, he had found a house in a place called Malvern and we were to go to a new school. New boy again! Just after settling firmly into Hutchin's. But the prospect of travel bucked us no end. We learned from Maybie that we were to sail back to the mainland on the *Rotomahana*, known unfavourably to our school friends as the Rotten Banana. But we'd forgotten the ritual of the cathartic. 'I'm going to give you your castor oil,' said Maybie severely. We shuddered to the soles of our feet. It is possible, indeed I fervently hope it is certain that the present generation has not experienced the vile ordeal of castor oil: or that if they've had it under clinical conditions, it has at least been emulsified into total anonymity, though neither egg nor milk nor lemon juice, nor any mortal thing could ever disguise its disgusting and, in the literal sense, sickening taste. In vain I begged:

'But Maybie we've been to sea before, we're not going to be sick.'

'Don't be volegar,' said Maybie. 'Your Mother says you're to have it. I'll give you half a lemon in your hand to suck afterwards and I'll pop it in so quick you'll never notice it.'

She was dead wrong of course. I did notice it; it was the most noticeable taste ever devised by man and nature. The odious tablespoon (tablespoonful!) of castor oil approached. I held my nose, felt the odious fluid slide with lamentable laggard viscosity down my throat, rammed the half lemon into my mouth and sucked and bit furiously. Eventually the nausea and disgust died down, but so potent was the pestiferous fluid that it rose in the gorge at intervals for hours afterwards, each time shaking my body in a spasm as the Tabart's terrier had shaken our kitten.

And what was the object of this barbaric rite? To give us a good 'purge', a good 'cleaning out' so that we wouldn't be sick on the *Rotomahana*. But surely the very essence of treating seasickness, if one is prone to it, is to give the unfortunate patient something to be sick *on*? This solace was denied us, and we boarded the northbound train well and truly 'cleaned out', in fact exhausted. As a child I lived in the era when parents believed in purgatives; or else my particular parents believed in them, I cannot be sure. All I know is that from the time I was a small boy until I grew old enough to make an effective protest, I was the victim of a continual and varied series of these vile and violent concoctions. Castor oil,

The Road to Gundagai

epsom salts, calomel, magnesia, each and all of them have ripped my guts apart and caused me to writhe in discomfort and pain. It seems to me highly fitting that castor oil should at last have lost its place in the family pharmocopoeia through its loathsome use by Mussolini. I sometimes think it's a wonder I have any insides left.

Our little train pulled out of Hobart Town and for the first fifteen miles clattered along the estuary with refreshing views of interlocking land and sea; but at Bridgewater we crossed the river and began the long climb up into the central plateau. The rails were slippery after the morning frost and the wheels spun despite liberal use of the sander. We reached Launceston in mid-afternoon and boarded the *Rotomahana* with the nonchalance of world travellers. We went down to 'tea' and when we came up the ship was almost free of the Tamar. Leaning over the stern watching the wake I heard a stranger accost Maybie.

'Going to Melbourne, eh?'

'Yes.'

'Ah, it's a lovely city. A real big place compared to Hobart. Where will you be living?'

'Malvern.'

'A very nice place too, right next to Toorak. Know Toorak?'

'No.'

'Ah, it's a lovely place, the nicest part of Melbourne to live in. Would you care to let me have your address?'

'Come along boys, it's time to get down to your bunks.'

Night closed in; the lighthouse winked on Low Head, and Tasmania slowly dropped behind into the wastes of the Southern Ocean.

Chapter Four

THIS WILL BE THE PLACE FOR A VILLAGE

IN 1920 Australia had a total population of just over five million and Melbourne and its suburbs about seven hundred and fifty thousand. As we drove through the streets in a taxi from Victoria Docks on the Yarra River the city seemed to go on for miles and to be of incomparable majesty. I still think of it as one of the stately cities of the world. It is partly the light, which is Grecian, Melbourne being dryish, sunny and in the precise latitude of Athens. During the long hot summer days the sun casts wonderful raking shadows, sharp as the blade of an axe, down the façades of the tall buildings, and the great wide streets have an air of grandeur which even the razz-ma-tazz of neon cannot wholly mar.

Apart from the light it is the architecture, especially that of the best colonial period between 1850 and 1885 which Lady Casey and her friends so lovingly photographed and described.[1] Melbourne at its centre looks like a real capital, not a provincial town. The Australian states were independent colonies for many decades before they federated in 1901 and their capital cities reflect this. Melbourne, as the centre of the great Gold Rush of 1851 and for long the largest city in Australia, was built with added panache. The public buildings of the first period of growth and prosperity gleam with self-confidence and display a baroque Italianate brio which fits wonderfully with the Mediterranean sun and the clean white sky.

The city was planned in the grand manner. In 1834 Melbourne was, as John Batman its founder observed at the time "the place for a village". Fifty years later it had a population approaching half a million. Buenos Aires alone excepted it was the largest city in the southern hemisphere, with fifteen theatres and music halls, forty-two hotels, law courts, Houses of Parliament, a fine Tuscan palazzo set on a hill for its Government House and many stately mansions on

---

[1] *Early Melbourne Architecture* by Maie Casey, Daryl Lindsay, Dermot Casey. Oxford University Press, 1953.

The Road to Gundagai

the surrounding hills. But it could never have presented so grand (a Sydneysider might say so grandly smug) a face to the world if surveyor Robert Hoddle had not so planned it. Guessing at its future he laid the centre out in a grid of streets each ninety-nine feet wide framing magnificent vistas up the rounded hills north of the Yarra on which the city lies. Subsequent planners enhanced his noble vision. From the main axis, St. Kilda Road leads forth in boulevarded baroque magnificence, matched on a lesser scale by other tree-lined avenues with four-lane pavements and wide centre grass verges. There is a sense of spaciousness and of public occasion about the city, and the large buildings have an air as they flaunt their bold proportions in the bright sunlight; at its best a stately grandeur, at its worst assertive grandiloquence. In yellow sandstone, rugged bluestone, stucco and portland stone, they stand as monuments to self importance, but also to faith in the future. The self assurance of the Victorian age which in London produced the Albert Memorial or the wildly fretted skyline of St. Pancras Station became in Melbourne the superb self-confidence of the Customs House, the uncompromising rectilinear boldness of the Treasury Buildings and the grand sweep of the Houses of Parliament. Melbourne could never vie with Sydney's incomparable harbour whose inlets and arms create a constant flow of surprising and dramatic urban vistas. But Melbourne, built from nothing on low ridges rising from a river less than half the width of the Thames at Westminster Bridge, is a man-made triumph, in which unpromising raw materials have been moulded to the town planner's foresight and the architect's imagination into a coherent and highly individual whole: Turin in the antipodes with an Anglo-Saxon flavour.

But though Melbourne lacks Sydney's dramatic restless posture on the arms of a great harbour, it has a setting not without nobility, which redeems it from the terra-cotta. At a distance of from twenty to thirty miles it is encircled in a grand sweep by the outliers of the Great Dividing Range. Although these are of modest height, they provide a satisfying backdrop to the city itself which thus lies in a low amphitheatre. There are few places in Melbourne, where, either from the top of one of its many hills, or from the second storey of a larger house, one could not see this blue arc rimming the horizon. Clockwise one read from Mount Blackwood, rising above the Ballarat plateau; then the crouching tiger of Mount Macedon; then the long uneven escarpment, the watershed of the State of Victoria which rose abruptly to the purple massif of Mount Donna Buang topping four thousand feet. To the east and nearer at hand lay the camelback outline of the Dandenong Ranges whose scented gullies, together with the incomparable beaches of Port Phillip Bay, made up Mel-

This will be the Place for a Village

bourne's playground. South and west the mountains descended into a mysterious and slightly menacing plain studded with basalt rocks and outcrops of ancient lava. From this plain rose, about forty miles away, an enigmatic cluster of sharp volcanic peaks—the You Yangs.

Beyond the city proper, beyond Latrobe's original square mile and the broad arteries leading away from it, lies another city. It lacks the sharp edge of the poorer areas, the factory districts and slums to the north and east; and it lacks the coherence of the city itself; but it has a peculiar character of its own. Once past the botanical gardens and the big Toorak mansions standing almost in country estates, one encounters a blazing and monotonous expanse of red brick and terra-cotta roof that has flowed over the hills and valleys to the east like lava, and leaked slowly in an ever lengthening arc right round the eastern shore of Port Phillip Bay twenty-five miles to Frankston. This vast architectural anonymity is very far from being a slum. It is neither sordid nor squalid; it has no foul alleys, no evil smelling drains, no endless faceless barracks of apartment blocks, no filthy children playing in the streets, none of New York's cold-water flats, none of London's scabrous dead-ends with a communal watertap. On the contrary each little red-brick terra-cotta roofed house, or more modest weatherboard tin-roofed house, has its own paling or wire fence and neat hedge, and its own little garden with a few standard roses, its own circumambient space and air and light, the absence of which in most European suburbs might seem to make them poor indeed. But these immense deserts of brick and terra-cotta, or wood and galvanized iron induce a sense of overpowering dullness, a stupefying sameness, a worthy, plodding, pedestrian, middle-class, low church conformity. It was precisely in the middle of one of the largest of these endless aggregations of bricks, terra-cotta and gentility that Mother and Dad had found our new home.

* * *

We started off with our first Melbourne summer. It was like living at the open door of an oven, and its instrument was the hot north wind or 'brickfielder'. For four or five days the heat mounted inexorably. The blinds were drawn in the house, the tar bubbled in the streets and paint blistered on wooden paling fences. The sturdy springy buffalo grass on suburban lawns became parched and brown, and public warnings in banner headlines told of the hours when watering was permitted. Mirages shimmered on the roads, filling them with phantom pools and the ghostly masts of ships far away at Port Melbourne. The sun blazed down like a cyclops eye from a

The Road to Gundagai

blueish-white sky and day after day passed without a drop of rain.

The surging drone of cicadas, like twanging piano strings, broke somnolently on the still air from parched and listless hedges, mingling towards heavy evening with the shrill chirruping of crickets. This insistent monotonous chorus was the very voice of heat and at length it penetrated your head and crawled around inside your skull like a living insect. Bayside beaches became crowded with families seeking relief from the heat. St. Kilda beach, the nearest to town, was so crammed with prone bodies that there seemed to be more people than sand.

A heavy lidded pumpkin of a moon rose slowly over the oily waters and the more adventurous or fatigued, having missed the last tram home, might spend the night on the beach. Ice cream in cones oozed onto the ground in a drippy mess before it could slide down the gullet. At home we drank quarts of barley water. Steadily the mercury climbed, the evening paper noting in flare headings the always teasing difference between the temperature at the Weather Bureau up on Eastern Hill and on the roof of Gaunt's the jewellers in the centre of the city, where most people worked. One hundred, 102, 104, at the Bureau, 101, 103, 105.5 at Gaunt's. In these January dog-days the whole city sweltered with its tongue hanging out as the great semi-arid continent at our backs let us know that she was awake and aware.

A gust of wind in the dark night ought to have brought relief, but it was hot; no caressing zephyr but a sharp swirling blast as from a hastily shut furnace door. We stirred in our sleep, naked under a thin cotton sheet on the back porch, or 'sleep-out'. By morning the wind was gusting at fifty miles an hour and the sun rose blood red over the Dandenongs in a pall of yellow dust. The brickfielder had arrived. It had been born in the north west corner of the State in the semi-desert region known as the Mallee, where pioneer dry farmers strove to grow wheat inside the ten inch isohyet. Beginning perhaps as a 'willy-willy' it had whirled Mallee dust and sand high into the air; then, thrust powerfully from behind by winds rushing to fill the space left by torrid air rising off the central deserts, it careered southward. It swept high over the Wimmera, sucking up more dust and leaving a trail of dried up waterholes and gasping sheep. The Great Dividing Range was not high enough to stop it and the brickfielder roared above the heavily timbered slopes igniting bush fires which raced for days through the oily, tindery scrub. Then it blasted down on Melbourne with its mingled freight of dust and smoke. The hot wind careered through the streets, rattled doors, swung street lamps on their

This will be the Place for a Village

wires and obscured the sun at noon. Offices closed early and men poured into the pubs and their families to the beaches where the wind whipped and flailed the sand into stinging smarting knives. From city vantages you could see the baleful torches of bushfires in the ranges like angry eyes in the hot, dark night. Then the wind unaccountably dropped to a low whisper and the sky clouded over with great ominous thunderheads.

'A break in sight' crowed the press; but no such luck. In the sudden lull, rain fell; but it was 'red rain', dustladen and viscous and we woke next morning to find everything splashed and disfigured with orange mud. The wind gusted with renewed fury; creeks dried up and even the Yarra sank fatigued in its bed. A shimmering haze lay on the city and the Bay and the hills, and sweat poured down into our eyes adding to the shimmer as we walked slowly to the beach. The papers recalled with growing anxiety the great bushfires of the 1890's.

And then—usually it would be mid-afternoon—the wind dropped and for a moment hung suspended with its dust above the parched city as if hesitant which way to move. Out in the Bay, a sudden flurry sent a rash of gooseflesh fanning out over the water. Sweat dried on the forehead. Someone cried, 'She's here!' and the next minute an unbelievably cool zephyr caressed one's face. Within an hour the zephyr grew to a fresh breeze, and then to a cool wind that carried all before it. Within two hours the mercury at the weather bureau fell from 104 to 78 and at Gaunt's from 106 to 76. The Southerly Buster had blown into town, whooshing up from the high latitudes near Antarctica and covering the suffocating city with a blanket of blessed cool. Haze and mirage vanished and the land showed clear and clean once again. On the heels of the Southerly came driving sheets of rain. The bushfires went out with a prolonged gigantic hissing and in small, threatened hill townships men embraced each other in the roadway. In the city, children paddled in the gutters and walked in the street with their heads up and their mouths open to catch the blessed rain. Yet within a day or two, so perverse is human nature, we were all longing for the hot weather to return. Return it did, but not in such fierce gusts or with such prolonged intensity for by now it was February.

By March we were back to normal and then came the brief reticent Australian autumn, when the bush remained still and silent and alive, and only the imported deciduous trees in the Botanical Gardens, and the plane trees along St. Kilda Road and Collins Street remembered their former homes in the northern hemisphere, and shed their leaves. Racing-boats split the Yarra and

The Road to Gundagai

on its banks could be heard the baying of the coach wobbling along on his bicycle as he shouted warnings and exhortations through his megaphone. Cricketers drew stumps for the last time and rolled up their pads. The football crowds surged into the big stadiums that ringed the city. Presently, in the unheated Australian houses it began to get cold, and in poky iron grates in a thousand suburban homes flames smouldered and skittered.

Winter was cool and rainy, but apt to be fairly short and, apart from an occasional morning mist lying along the river valley, free of the gloomy fogs which seemed to be always nuzzling the window panes at 6 Pembroke Gardens. But it could be crisp and cold when it wanted to. Occasionally we could see traces of snow on the distant ranges and though it never fell in Melbourne, there were frosty nights when the pan of water that we had hopefully placed in the back yard would be covered, to our delight, with a creaking shroud of ice. The houses, being unheated, were apt to share with their English cousins the dismal distinction of being colder than the world outside. This discomfort was dulled by exiguous electric space heaters, but we all suffered severely from chilblains, and since wearing gloves (except woollen ones) was regarded as 'cissie' we carried our blotched and itching hands naked to the world. But the air was clear, the sun shone bright, and we never went to bed as early as in an English winter. No Melbourne afternoon in May was ever as brief and gloomy as a November afternoon in London.

With the September rains, spring began to creep imperceptibly over the bush, reddening the tips of eucalyptus leaves. In the city with its plane trees, poplars, oaks and beeches the change was more noticeable, but the real drama of spring, which we awaited each year with unfeigned eagerness, was the coming of the wattle. We would see its fluffy golden puffballs begin to break on our own little leather-stemmed cootamundra; but we knew that just on the outskirts of the city it was in full bloom. Word passed along the schoolboy grapevine, 'The wattle's out', and the next free Saturday we'd be off on our bicycles into the nearest bush to cut branches and bring them home strapped to the parcel carrier over the rear mudguard, weaving and wobbling like a great yellow tail as we sped homeward. The bush at this time looked absolutely glorious, the trees hung with great swags and curtains of yellow blossom, the little gullies dusted with yellow powder and, close too, each twig displaying a cluster of yellow fluffy bobbles like groups of molecules in a chemical diagram. Adam Lindsay Gordon, an Australian poet whose constrainedly romantic verse is out of fashion now, summed up the magic of the Australian bush awakening from its sombre grey winter:

This will be the Place for a Village

In the spring when the wattle-gold trembles
Twixt shadow and shine;
When each dewladen air draught resembles
A long draught of wine;
When the skyline's blue-burnished resistance
Makes deeper the dreamiest distance
Some song in all hearts hath existence:
Such songs have been mine.

In the spring the Melbourne and Metropolitan Tramways Board offered a special excursion ticket entitled *Sixteen Miles for a Shilling* which took you by means of transfers on a circular tour of the city and the inner suburbs. The great joy of this excursion was the section where we rode the cable car. The majority of the main tramlines in Melbourne were then served by cable. It must have been, in its heyday, the most extensive system in the world; certainly larger than those of either San Francisco or Seattle, and of course it operated on the flat. The cars were in no sense funciculars; they were not permanently attached to the cable. The cable ran about a foot under the street, and contact was made with it through a narrow groove no more than an inch wide which ran like a third rail in the centre of the track. On Sunday mornings, when no trams ran in the Melbourne of my boyhood, you could cross to the centre of the deserted street and, by straddling the third rail, could look down the crack at the oily silvery serpent snaking by beneath. It emitted a low hum and on quiet Sunday mornings the street sounded as if it were gently snoring. The cables were powered by steam plants near the termini where the one-and-a-half-inch thick steel rope ran over an enormous drum.

Each cable car consisted of two parts: the dummy (a curious name for the part that did the real work) and the trailer. The trailer was, quite simply, a small enclosed tramcar, seating about thirty people, hitched on behind the dummy. No one ever wanted to ride in the trailer; it was no more exciting than sitting on a living room sofa, and with its wooden benches, curved to the dimensions of a human behind yet to be invented, much less comfortable. The dummy was the place; 'up front'! The dummy was essentially a hollow square of seats on wheels, in the centre of which stood the driver or 'gripman' with two levers at his disposal and a bell-pull over his head connected to a little gong in the white painted roof. One lever was a brake, the other, the working lever, ran down through the slot and ended in a mechanical claw which gripped the cable. When he received the signal to start from the conductor, the gripman went bong! bong! on his bell,

The Road to Gundagai

released the brake lever, and pulled back slowly on the grip. The passengers felt first a slight slithery shudder as the car nudged forward, rather as of an automobile with an imperfect clutch; next a sudden and exhilarating jerk as the claw clamped firmly onto the cable and the little equipage was drawn smoothly forward with no sound except the soft swish of the wheels. When the gripman wanted to stop he simply disengaged the grip at the strategic moment, coasted to the stopping place and braked. He also had to disengage the grip when rounding corners or at intersections, and coast where the cable was constrained by rollers or where one cable crossed another.

Conductors and gripmen varied in response to their differing functions. Gripmen tended to be taciturn and morose, and when asked whether the next stop was the Hospital or Domain Road were apt to point to an enamelled sign which read, 'Do Not Talk to the Gripman'. Occasionally, though, they would relax, perch themselves on the corner of their little box and chat with the conductor standing on the front platform of the trailer. Conductors were more cheerful and extrovert, perhaps because their work involved an element of daring and gave them an opportunity to show off to young ladies. In order to collect fares on the dummy they had first to straddle the abyss between it and the trailer and then proceed along the outward-facing seats, hanging onto upright stanchions with one arm as they dispensed tickets and change from a leather bag with the other. Thus poised perilously above the roadway rushing by beneath them at about fifteen miles an hour they swung themselves right round the dummy with extreme agility often whistling and calling 'Fez please, fez please' as they went.

Because of their sedate pace cable cars were often the victim of hit-and-run raids by intending passengers. When a car failed to stop on signal, athletic men would run after it and board the dummy from the side. If there were a spare seat all was well, but if not then the intending passenger had to stand clinging awkwardly to a stanchion while an angry argument went on between him and the gripman, which always ended in the passenger's defeat. He would let himself off, hitting the road at a run and soon be lost to sight. A favourite game among the 'larrikins' (delinquent teenagers they would now be called) was to grab a free ride on the dummy while the gripman's eye was elsewhere, and then, when they saw the conductor straddling the gap to collect fares, leap lightly off onto the roadway with a derisive shout. For me the preferred seats were those right in front of the dummy where, with the wind in my face, I had the sensation of being on a boat moving

This will be the Place for a Village

gently through calm seas. Next best was on the seats facing sideways: 'Passengers are warned not to project their limbs outside the dummy.' On Anzac day and certain other public holidays, the dummies carried crossed flags at the prow. The last cable car plied in Melbourne in 1940 and tears were shed as it slowly climbed the slope towards the Houses of Parliament, Eastern Hill and the boneyard. An era of calm, sedate and orderly progression had ended.

The Victorian State Railways had taken an early lead in electrification of track. When our family arrived at the end of 1920 certain key inner lines had already been converted, and during the Twenties the entire system was electrified. We spent many happy after-school hours watching the riggers and steel erectors put up the big overhead gantries and string the catenary. Nevertheless, and inevitably, it was steam that caught our fancy. We were all veteran engine spotters and explorers of abandoned railways. With these Melbourne was only too well supplied, relics of the extreme optimism of the Nineties and the subsequent collapse of the speculative land boom. A favourite excursion was along the deserted Outer Circle, which had been flung far to the east of the city in the spacious days at the close of the century, and to which the city did not really attain until the 1950's. Fortified by a picnic lunch in a knapsack we set out like young archaeologists bent on finding traces of a lost civilization in the tumuli of abandoned embankments, the caverns of brush-choked cuttings, or the grass-grown ruins of deserted wayside stations. At one point a high wooden trestle bridge, several hundred feet long had been thrown across a tributary of the Yarra. This monolith, derelict in the sun-filled empty silence, was to us an impressive Paestum or Temple of Poseidon.

In pre-diesel days there was a great variety of blackened monsters to vary the tedium of a long morning's train spotting at Flinders Street, Spencer Street or Prince's Bridge. The A2, noble workhorse that pulled the Gippsland Limited and sometimes worked in double harness with the Dd, a lithe leaner brother, to pull the train doubleheaded up the long climb to the east. The DDe and its smaller brother the E, both tank engines used on short suburban runs and into the hills. The C's that hauled the Adelaide and the Sydney freights, big 2-8-0's with an enormous head of power. The K that hauled trains in the mountains. We were all passionate defenders of the broad gauge of Victoria and highly conscious of the fact that Melbourne, which had once exceeded Sydney in population, now took second place, as indeed did Victoria to New South Wales. We thought it ridiculous for the boys from New South Wales to have chosen four-foot-eight-and-a-half inches and what's more to try and impose it on poor little Victoria by persuading the Federal

The Road to Gundagai

Government to build the Transcontinental from Port Augusta, S.A. to Kalgoorlie, W.A. as four-foot-eight-and-a-half.

Though most of us had never been out of our home state and a good many of us not more than fifty miles from Melbourne, we were well up in the railway geography of the six states, and were determined defenders of the five-foot-three. Didn't a broader gauge give you a more comfortable ride? Wasn't five-foot-three the only gauge shared by two adjoining states, Victoria and South Australia? So the New South Welshmen wanted a unified gauge from Sydney to Melbourne did they? Okay then, let it be ours, not theirs! What really infuriated us was when visitors from Sydney referred to the New South Wales system as 'Standard Gauge' as if ours was a freak, an eccentricity not to be tolerated.

* * *

The beaches were an endless pleasure in the hot weather. Stretching in a great arc thirty-five miles from Port Melbourne to Sorrento and Portsea, they fronted the calm waters of Port Phillip Bay with an almost continuous line of yellow sand. They naturally lacked the drama of Sydney's great surf beaches, but when visitors from Sydney bragged, as they almost always did, about the beauties of their incomparable Harbour, we replied that they couldn't enjoy their beaches because of the sharks. In point of fact, there *were* sharks in Port Phillip Bay and a shudder of horror greeted the news of the young man who had dived off the end of the Middle Brighton Pier ('practically in the city') straight into the mouth of a shark which bit off his leg neatly at mid-thigh. This danger was attested by the construction of the various Men's and Women's 'Baths' along the seafront, every one of which was protected by a shark-proof enclosure of piles and wire netting through which the sea vigorously slopped.

The Baths presented to the street (or the Esplanade as it was called by St. Kilda) much the same entrance as that to an English pier; an arch, flanked by ticket booths and a turnstile. Beyond this lay a wooden hall where you could buy 'lollies' or ice cream and also rent locker keys, towels and an exiguous male bikini known as a pair of Vees. Thus equipped you entered the baths proper, a wooden oblong with a runway and a series of cubicles at the shore end and down each side. Cubicles were shared by two or three boys and after climbing into your Vees and hanging your key round your neck on a piece of salt-toughened string, you entered steps at the shore end. The entire structure was weathered ash grey with a permanent scurf of salt. Of whatever wood the baths had

This will be the Place for a Village

originally been constructed—red gum or jarrah or imported Scandinavian pine known as 'deal'—the sun and the sea had washed it all to the same soft scuffed grey.

Where the bottom shelved into deeper water, ropes strung across assisted non-swimmers. As the protecting piles progressed seaward they became more thickly encrusted with a heavy growth of mussels, like fungus on an old tree, but gleaming jet black in the troughs between incoming waves. With sharks safely out of the way the only hazard came from jelly fish. These varied from small hunks of grey ice to full fledged blueish-white parasols trailing a hundred tentacles which stung very smartly and raised an unpleasant rash. The less noxious jelly fish were used as ammunition in fights between gangs, or slipped into a fellow's pants as he was preparing to dress after a swim.

The way home was routine: a stop at the ice cream stand for 'a cup or a cone' and then a long ride back in the tram, skin all sticky and tight from the dried salt and sand. But on Saturdays if we were very lucky there might be an extra treat. The Baths lay in that stretch of St. Kilda Beach devoted to innocent and garish popular amusements. On our way to the tram stop we first passed the Palais de Danse, a great barn of a place with a large circular galvanized iron roof like a nissen hut for giants, and two silly, pseudo-Moorish towers at one end. Next came the Palais Pictures, an even larger barn with a similar roof but no towers. Beyond that lay Luna Park. This was a really magical place, partly because we hardly ever had enough money to go there. Our pocket money, threepence a week at age eight, sixpence at age ten and a shilling at age twelve somehow never seemed to go far enough, even when augmented at Christmas and birthdays by beloved pink postal orders from grandparents and aunts and uncles in England. We had to be content with standing outside and watching people go in.

The entrance to Luna Park was in the form of an enormous grinning mouth with an impossibly large number of teeth. Above the mouth two huge eyes winked invitingly. Around the periphery of the Park looped the vertiginous dips and bends of the roller coaster Scenic Railway. Inside were all the paraphernalia of an earthly paradise: the hall of distorting mirrors; the House of Ghosts; the Funny House where streams of air blasted screaming ladies' skirts up over their heads, and where men found themselves lurching and skidding on rollers; the Tunnel of Love; the Water Chute; the slides both smooth and bumpy; and, towering over all, the Big Dipper from the top of which, as they faced the sickening descent, the screams and shrieks of girls—half fearful, half delighted

The Road to Gundagai

—could be heard in the night before being drowned in the roaring rattle of the downward plunging car.

On Saturday noons after a swim, Luna Park was closed and given over to the maintenance men and the cleaning women in preparation for the night's entertainment. But if a certain side door were open and if Mr. Mortimer was on duty, there'd be a wink and a beckoning finger and in we'd go.

'Feel like some polishing today, nipper? All right then, you go around to the slide and tell 'em I sent you.'

We walked through a maze of plasterboard and white-washed scantling, and peeped cautiously inside. We stood at the base of two enormous slides: one of them stretched as smooth as silk in an unbroken diagonal from the lofty roof to a canvas mat on the floor; the other, of equal height, had bumps and curves. At the foot of the two slides lay a pile of mats, coir on one side, canvas on the other. Beside the pile stood another friend known simply as Ginger. He was a lean cadaverous fellow with a sunken chest, thin scrawny arms and huge bony hands with very strong fingers. He was dressed in a pair of brown dungarees covered with paint and grease, and an old-fashioned singlet with sleeves, and buttons up to the neck. In front of him was a large pot of grease into which he was scraping off two big paddles like enormous butter pats. Beside him stood the giant's version of an O-Cedar mop.

'Hull-lo there, young feller-me-lad! Where'd you spring from?'

'Mr. Mortimer let us in.'

'He did eh? Must've known I needed a bloke to give me a hand with the polishing.'

He cocked a ginger eyebrow and his grotesquely freckled face sliced itself all up one cheek in a lopsided grin.

'Better get yourself a mat and get started. You know the drill. Don't want to see any of that grease left by the time you've finished. Now, imshee-allah!'

To get to the top of the slide was like climbing a four storey house and on the way up we could see the dull streaks where Ginger had applied the grease too thickly. We'd have to iron those out. Ginger's job was to grease up the slides on Saturday mornings ready for the big week-end crowd; but to hone that grease to a fine silky polish it needed more than his mop. It needed kids to come skidding down the slide until you could almost see your face in it. That way the Saturday night customers would be satisfied and Ginger's kudos with the management would be enhanced. We reached the top and Ginger called up from far below at the bottom of that immense descent.

'Okay! Let her go, Gallagher!' Feet first for an opener; head first could come later. We mounted the mats and eased gingerly forward.

This will be the Place for a Village

Wheeeeeeeee!! A rushing sliding swish, here and there a slight jolt as the mat hit a swatch of grease, then stomach in the mouth, wind in the face and, wallop! I landed on my back on the collision mat at the bottom. Ginger nodded sagely.

'Not bad. Now back you go again and see you get all those bumps out.'

And so for half an hour we slid backwards, sideways, forwards, head first, feet first, and even upside down, doing Ginger's job for him and dissolved in the nearest a boy can come to pure bliss. We could have gone on forever but Ginger said 'Time to knock off now and get some grub. I'll have to lock up. Next time bring some more pals with yer and yer can do the bumps as well.'

'Thanks Ginger, that was a bonzer go.'

'Any time, pal, any time.'

* * *

Port Phillip Bay was almost a salt water lake. It was forty miles from north to south and about the same distance at its greatest width, but its entrance was only a mile and a half wide between The Heads. The Bay was 'our' Harbour to set up against Sydney's super-duper challenge and we liked ours better, perhaps because you could get away from the city and bathe with the hills and 'the country' at your back. In Sydney you were never out of sight of a house, and besides—the sharks.

'What d'ya mean sharks? Why, we've shark proof nets at Bondi and Coogee.'

'Yeah, but people never use them.'

'What about it? We've the Life Savers and the Shark Patrol air spotter with a loud hailer!'

'And didn't a man have his leg nipped off right up the George River, beyond tidewater almost?'

'Aw, you're just windy! How can you enjoy the water if you're windy all the time?'

So the battle raged. 'Our 'Arbour, Our Bridge and Our Bradman' was the Melbourne jibe at Sydney.

'I spent a week in Melbourne.'

'When was that?'

'On a Sunday,' was the Sydneysider's counter jibe.

Chapter Five

FOUR GRACE STREET, MALVERN, S.E.4
TEL : U 1373

MOTHER had an invincible contempt for things Australian and made no bones about it. So far as she was concerned it was an entire continent peopled by the Lower Orders. Hence (Australians being the last people in the world to take this lying down) her relationship with shopkeepers, officials, neighbours and local tradesmen, was an unending guerilla warfare. Australia also had a way of springing up, just when Mother thought she had it firmly flattened, and hitting her on the head with a resounding 'Boing-g-g ! ! !' A good example of this was Four Grace Street, Malvern, our home for ten years, described in interminable and tedious wrangle with tradesmen and shopgirls.

'I'd like you to send this.'
'Where to?'
'Mrs. Thirkell. T-H-I-R . . .'
'Just a minute. T-H . . . *what?*'
'Don't be impertinent !' (Sullen female face gives up-from-underlook with baleful eye, and purses lips). 'T-H-I-R-K-E-double L.'
'Go on.'
'4 Grace Street.'
'Grey Street?'
'G-R-A-C-E. . . .'
'Oh *Grice*, you mean !'
'I do *not* mean ! I mean Grace.'
'Sign here.'
'Malvern. Sign where?'
'Here on this sheet.'
'I'll report you to the Manager.'
'See what good that does.'
And much more until we were all red with shame.

Four Grace Street, Malvern, S.E.4.

On a trip home to England Mother secured an embossing stamp which read:

>   4 Grace Street
> Malvern   Tel: U 1373

But while she'd been away, Melbourne had adopted Postal Districts. We drew this tactlessly to her attention. 'This gadget's no good Mother, you have to have S.E.4 on it.' She literally ground her teeth and for a long time after this, whenever she had to put S.E.4 in ink after using the embossing stamp we'd hear her mutter 'Sold again!' as if to say 'How dare this upstart vulgar continent further complicate my life.'

Well, what was it like, this 4 Grace Street? It is preferable to start, à la Dr. Pevsner, with the approaches to it. He is on one of his 'perambulations' through Malvern:

'The best way to approach Grace Street is from the S or Wattletree Road end; that way one avoids the impression of dreariness which prevails at the N or Stanhope Street end. The general area is one which Mr. Osbert Lancaster has wittily described as "By-Pass variegated" and except for the prevalence of red terra-cotta roofs one might imagine oneself to be in the streets off the Great West Road, in Surbiton, or perhaps Bromley S of the station. It dates almost entirely from the period immediately preceding the First World War (ca 1900-1912) though one or two houses may with confidence be dated 1915 (see ventilators and chimney pots) so that this description is not entirely accurate. Turning N off Wattletree Road one enters Coonil Crescent where a double S curve does something to break the monotony of the grid imposed on Melbourne's hills. To the L a large grey Victorian Mansion with slate roof, crocketed wooden gables and scroll work and a small Frenchified tower, all behind a tall closecut paling fence backed by a cedar hedge. This building is now St. Benedict's Hospital staffed by nuns. (Passing down the crescent, note innumerable short cuts across buffalo grass verges which, despite vigilance of local council, continue to be trodden out by residents and tradesmen as means of shortening distance between two points). At end of Coonil Crescent turn E into Canberra Grove, noting to the W two adjoining red brick terra-cotta roofed villas, each with a gaping "sleep-out" below a heavy gable and each entered through a Japanese "tori" or ceremonial wooden arch singularly out of place in this desiccated environment. Names of villas l to r, Linooc (clearly Coonil backwards) and Lanark (but with accent on first syllable). Fifty yards down Canberra Grove (plane trees; bulbous fire hydrants with inscription Shanks & Co. 1911) one turns N into Grace Street.

'This street differs from most of its neighbours in that a complete

The Road to Gundagai

vista is blocked by a kink which also divides the street into two widely differing portions both as to period and (for there is such a thing even in Australia) as to class. The end at which we now stand looking N is a series of modest single storey and one-and-a-half storey red brick with red terra-cotta roofs. To the L. Corner House (entrance actually on Canberra Grove) has slate roof with terra-cotta ridge pole. No. 1 has gaping "sleep-out" similar to "Linooc" (see above). No. 3 has curiously high steep-pitched terra-cotta roof and gable fronted with chocolate barge-boarding (known in Australia as weatherboard) suggesting that the builder contemplated but later decided against an attic storey. No. 5 single storey with centre door; pitto sporum hedge. No. 7 (on the kink) with asbestos shingle dormer facing diagonally. To the R No. 2 with square slate roof and small raised wooden verandah. No. 4 (see below); No. 6 two storeys throughout and somewhat too high for the general set or feel of the street; also being built too close to No. 4 and to its N obscures the sunlight (saltash hedge). No. 8 (on the kink) back to single storey but with gravel driveway at side. Names of houses L, S to N and R, S to N: *The Almonds, Ben Cairn, Hiawatha, Staleybridge, Duncansby, Ti-Tree Lodge, Ripon*, No. 4 (the only house in this portion of the street that is without a name) *Doonside, Mon Repos.*

'Below the kink the street degenerates rapidly, via semi-detached bay window and side-door addorsed cottages of the nineties to a group of weatherboard houses with "tin" (galvanized iron) roofs set meanly in minute lots close to the pavement and intersected by service lanes with the exception of No. 13 (where Parkside Street enters on the L from the municipal sand and gravel dump). These houses continue to the end of the street. Here, where it debouches into the late Victorian Stanhope Street, are set on the L a white stucco villa with gay cast iron tracery and fluted pillars and on the R a low spreading bungalow reflecting the timid style of the inter-war years.

'To return to No. 4 and taking our stance opposite it we note that the house (in contrast to its neighbours which are fenced with wire "cyclone" ring lock) lies behind a gamboge paling fence some five feet high with two chocolate gates; and that a strip of buffalo grass with a single twisted white gum, separates the pavement from the street. The house itself is set back from the road and is of red brick with yellow roughcast above and with the usual terra-cotta roof. The gable to the L, which leads forward, and that to the R sited laterally, are both marked by machined fretwork in creamy wood and are connected by a diagonal wooden arch of the same material, covering a red tiled porch off which are the front door, centred, and a window in the shape of a porthole with local stained glass. . . .'

So much, and a great deal more, might Dr. Pevsner's gimlet eye

Four Grace Street, Malvern, S.E.4.

have seen. Names such as *Mon Repos* are supposed to distil the essence of tree-lined suburbia, but he might have preferred the great string of names which adorned seven consecutive detached yellow brick houses on Stanhope Street. They had double bay windows and Gothick battlements and they faced the great Catholic Brigidine Novitiate, with its reinforced concrete statue of the Virgin in a cave surmounted by a cast iron halo set with electric light bulbs. Their names ring sonorously down the years; *Clare House, Castle Eden, Darjeeling, Inverleith, Coimboon, Branksea* and finally, in incised golden capitals, *Roma*. But as Dr. Pevsner never had to live in Grace Street he may be spared a more detailed description. Instead we shall follow the footsteps of one who was for ten years an inmate.

When Mother and my step-father came over from Tasmania to Melbourne—from the provinces (population at that time 220,000) to the Big City (pop. 750,000)—they were looking for a house with a 'study' for Dad, near a tramline and costing not more than five hundred pounds. What they secured, partly by means of a loan made by Stanley Baldwin to my mother at the time of her divorce from my father, and partly through a mortgage from the Star Bowkett Building Society financed through Dad's demobilization gratuity, was an eight room bungalow set on a lot 5 ft. by 150 ft. in a part of Malvern— itself a solid suburb—that was neither affluent nor disreputable, but very middle-middle class and excessively suburban.*

Four Grace Street was flanked, at a distance of about twelve feet over a vertical board fence, by its neighbours. The front garden, when we moved in, had two enormous and ugly cotton palms which it was one of our first chores to uproot. The paling fence and two gates, 'the front gate' and the 'tradesmen's entrance' originally gamboge and chocolate, were painted white and green under Mother's direction. She had a horror of muddy colours and was right, I think, to be appalled and depressed at the miles and miles of Melbourne residential streets which, in the 1920's, alternated gamboge and burnt umber with chocolate, and what Terence accurately described as 'pale vomit and baby stool'. She painted the house, fence and gates bright green and white and she even persuaded the municipal council to turn the bandstand in Malvern Park and the kiosk in Malvern Gardens from the familiar muddy brown to white and green.

The 'front gate' led by a short slightly curving asphalt path to the front door which, as Dr. Pevsner has already related, was set katy-corners to the lie of the land and the plan of the house. The 'tradesmen's entrance', or 'side alley' as it was more often called, opened

* Looking back it reminds me of Humoresque Street, Moonee Ponds, featured in Barrie Humphries' wonderfully funny L.P. records of Australian wild life in Suburbia.

The Road to Gundagai

onto a narrow asphalt path which ran down between the house and the high wooden fence dividing us from the Trists (who lived in the two storey house next door). The path could barely squeeze itself into this narrow crack and it ended at a trellis gate. This gave onto an asphalt area at the back of the house, a glimpse of the back garden or 'back yard' and a small group of wooden sheds. These, which Mother also had painted green, consisted of (a) the washhouse, with a wood burning 'copper', twin slate tubs and a galvanized iron scrubbing board; (b) the 'workshop', really a small toolshed for garden implements and later, in the days before service stations, the storage of petrol (forbidden by local bye-law) for Dad's motor bike; (c) the woodshed for the logs to be split into chips for the copper and for the 'chip-heater' in the bathroom (d) the coalshed, filled usually with mallee roots and damp peaty brown coal from Yallourn, never the hard, shiny (and more expensive) black coal from Wonthaggi; finally (e) the outside (and only) lavatory, known locally as the dyke, furnished, since it had no electricity, with a brass candlestick and screened from the world's eyes, if not its ears, by a trellis covered with yellow jasmine.

During the night time the brass candlestick, placed on a small red painted three-cornered shelf, filled the little closet with a ghostly light. During the day a pleasant ten minutes could be passed by observing activities in the washhouse through a convenient knot hole. You held up before the knot hole a piece of toilet paper and upon it there appeared miraculously in full technicolour Todd-A.O., though upside down, a little view of the world outside which could be expanded or contracted by moving the paper away from the hole. Where others beguile our necessary tedium by supplying a five foot shelf of paperbacks, we supplied the camera obscura.

The outhouses gave onto the back garden, a modest oblong of mixed buffalo grass, couch grass and 'English lawn' broken here and there by Dad's enthusiastically planted (but desultorily tended) orange, lemon and tangerine trees, the latter known in Australia as mandarins. It was one of the delights of life in Melbourne that, despite brief raw winters, you really could go out into your own back yard and pick oranges and lemons right off the tree. Even as a boy it gave me, perhaps because of my early English upbringing, a curious sense of illicit and evanescent pleasure. Down one side of the garden was a large vegetable bed containing very tough rhubarb and some brambly untended loganberry canes. At the base of the garden, three equal sized red brick houses, facing away from us, raised timid terra-cotta pinnacles to the sky. Here was 'the boys'' vegetable bed. It was usually empty save when we attempted to outline jokes in mustard-and-cress or planted the 'Canadian Wonder'

Four Grace Street, Malvern, S.E.4.

whose heart shaped leaves, after bursting magically from the dried-up purple bean, fell an easy prey to slugs and snails. These were a real pest and we used to go on wonderful snail hunts (the underside of rhubarb and dock; in the crotches of iris and the armpits of arum lilies) filling a petrol can with a sizzling mixture of tobacco juice, water and oozing snails.

The far bottom corner held the open-work brick garbage incinerator surrounded by a wild untended grove of Jerusalem artichoke. Pulled from the ground, and their tuberous thumbs and fingers scraped and scrubbed, they made good bubble-and-squeak or soup. The living plants were useful for training the kitten. Lobbed gently into the air, he would come down with claws spread-eagled, grab the top of an artichoke stem and sway gently to earth. At the top of the garden an alley of abandoned ground led up between the house and the fence towards the front lawn, and was filled with scrawny lilac and more artichokes which grew like weeds in the sandy soil. Beneath the sand was a thick layer of yellow clay, wonderfully malleable and ductile to young hands, but hardening brick-like when brought to the open air. In this clay we constructed a series of large and semi-permanent caves into which we retreated with a candle, salted walnuts and copies of the forbidden *Gem* and *Magnet*. In these damp and smokefilled holes, crouched squatting over the candle, our sweaters smeared with clay, we used to read aloud to each other the immortal exploits of Tom Merry and Billy Bunter, shaking with laughter to the unforgettable line 'Ha-ha!' roared the Fifth Form.'

Best to taste these forbidden fruits (borrowed from Norman Birt across the road) in the cave, for if Mother found them they would be confiscated and used to light the copper for the Monday morning wash. Later the clay formed a basis for the permanent moorings of my younger brother's model railway. While prolonged immersion in the sand and damp clay rusted the rails and corroded the rolling stock, it made possible a Norman Bel Geddes world of soaring ramps, viaducts, tunnels and cuttings, which delighted him—and me.

This alley way of scraggly ground later became the site of a swing and a trapeze slung from stout posts of red jarrah from Western Australia. From this vantage point one could look directly into the bathroom window, either to shout insults at a brother or to hurl a paper bag filled with cold water on top of Dad, having his weekly warm bath on a Sunday morning. It was also a point from which one could climb onto the roof. Once over the eaves and up the shallow slope to the ridgepole you were in among the peaks and troughs of a terra-cotta sea, extending over our own roof and the roofs of many neighbours and blocked only by the towering massif

The Road to Gundagai

of No. 6 next door. From the eyrie of the main ridge you could see the Malvern Town Hall, look down onto the sedate white-hatted figures trundling bowls on the shaven green across the street, or take in with one sweep of the eye the whole circle of blueish-purple hills that ringed Melbourne to the north and east.

With a little agility you could clamber up the chimney stacks and peer down the sooty oblong or drop paper bombs into the depths. These apertures became like periscopes in reverse, or rather eariscopes, enabling one to listen surreptitiously to what went on in the various rooms below, or to interrupt a conversation by shouting down the chimney such witticisms as 'Balls' or 'What the hell do you mean?'

But eavesdroppers seldom hear good of themselves and I once descended from the roof with burning ears after hearing one of our innumerable 'lady helps' describe me as a 'bumptious brat'.

On other nights I would take a blanket up onto the roof and lie uncomfortably in one of the zinc lined sloping gutters to gaze at the stars, some of which I hadn't seen since Sergeant Corcoran aboard the *Friedrichsruh*. had shown them to us those far off days a year or so ago.

It is time now to take the lid off this Family Antipodean Peyton Place and see what it was like inside. We enter the house from the back since this is invariably the route chosen by the boys and their friends whenever they come in for a drink of cocoa after Wolf Cubs, sneak in late at night through the casement window into their bedroom, or rush banging in after school. First then, round the corner of the feeble lawn which is forever being trampled down because it lies across the short cut from the house to the outside lavatory, and as constantly rebuilt and refenced by Mother's tenacity. At the centre of the house is the back porch or 'sleep-out' where I've spent many a cold winter's night, first with a teddy bear and later with Smut, our cat—if I could get him from my brother—crammed down below my buttocks. The 'sleep-out' is asphalt floored and lying in bed I can see above the rafters from the underside of the terra-cotta tiles that they were made in Marseille.

Up one step, bang the screen door and you're in the dining room, surely the most inconvenient ever designed with no less than five doors leading off it. It has one window giving onto the rear 'sleep-out' with a view of my bed covered with Dad's old military ground-sheet, a couple of clotheslines with skinned stringy-bark props, and the yellow jasmine trellis outside the toolshed. In one corner of the room is the linen press, effectively clamorous and eccentric with its sheet of William Morris wallpaper pasted over one end. The walls are surrounded by low bookcases crammed with boys' books, perhaps

Four Grace Street, Malvern, S.E.4.

six to seven hundred: R. M. Ballantyne, Jules Verne, Captain Marryat, Hugh Lofting of Dr. *Doolittle* fame, John Masefield (the totally unreadable *Sard Harker*), cheap sets of Dickens and Scott, *The Parents' Book: Answers to Children's Questions*, Judge Parry's *Butterscotia*, the fairy tales of Mrs. de Morgan and a few school prizes and family albums. In these latter are photographs of my father, dark, rascally, and moustachioed, which embarrass me horribly but don't seem to affect Mother at all. Against the vacant wall is the 'dumb waiter' or 'traymobile' on which food and crockery come in from the kitchen next door; behind it the damp creeps splotchily up the white plaster wall each successive winter. Wonderful patterns here, forestalling non-objective art of the 50's and 60's. The five doors lead to the back garden, the kitchen, the boys' bedroom, the bathroom, and (up another single inconvenient step) the passage off which lie the other rooms. In the middle of this strange sunken area (hardly a room) stands a round table of stained and well worn mahogany-veneer at which we have eaten some thousands of meals beneath the single overhead light hanging from its inverted china saucer.

Mother presided and carved; Dad, who was rarely in on time, ate and talked. Once he brought an office friend home to dinner late and without notification. Mother was in a grim mood and hardly civil as she wielded the knife at the 'head' of the table, while the poor fellow found the evening hanging pretty soggy on his hands. In walked the Lady Help with the all too familiar spotted-dog, and laid it steaming darkly before my Mum.

'Would you care for some suet pudding?' she asked in icy tones, flourishing the knife.

'Well, I don't mind if I do,' said the well-meaning but luckless guest.

'In that case,' said Mother, 'you don't mind if you don't.'

The quiet that followed was so awful that I rose without permission in order to draw on my head the inevitable reproof that would at least break the paralyzing silence.

Another crisis occurred on one of the many occasions on which Mother valiantly strove to impart an air of Oxbridge distinction to suburbia by arranging, single-handed, a scholarly black-tie dinner for eight to which my brother and I were necessary adjuncts in the form of serving boys. Dressed in carefully brushed blue serge and school ties we served the food and cleared away the empty plates into the kitchen where we were allowed to eat the scraps with the Lady Help—banished below the salt for this high powered occasion and resenting it visibly. No doubt our innocent faces, well scrubbed under maternal supervision, were designed, along with our amateur

The Road to Gundagai

but patently eager performance, as a 'talking point' on which to hang what was inevitably an off-beat evening for the guests, redeemed by Mother's relentless, crackling literary conversation.

It was the era of aigrettes, black sequins and velvet bandeaux and we asked if we could 'see the guests'. Mother, harassed beyond endurance as she endeavoured to cope with a dinner for eight on a gas stove with two burners, snappishly refused, ripped off her apron, wiped her steaming visage and rushed off to 'put on her face'. When our fury was added to that of the despised Lady Help, a plot was soon brewing to make their meal memorable.

Solemnly, carefully—and liberally—we spat on all the half cantaloups, mixed in the sugar and sprinkled lightly with ginger. Then with angelic faces we bore in the lethal loads and set them gently before each guest to the accompaniment of beaming smiles. We retired into the kitchen and observed proceedings through the keyhole.

'They're eating them! Professor Scott has taken a huge bite! Now Dr. Busing! Oh, Mrs. Streeton has an enormous mouthful. . . .'

The bell rang. We walked blandly in, removed the empty rinds and began to serve the next course. No matter what the guests might think the evening was now a triumph for the servants.

Among the many cronies of the A.I.F. whom Dad used to bring home few intrigued us more than Captain Donovan ('Donie') Joynt V.C. To have a V.C. in the house was itself a tremendous honour; but it was important to find out how he'd won it. We hadn't learned the unwritten law which forbids those whose military exploits are publicly recognized from talking about them. So when Captain Joynt sat down to dinner (shepherd's pie and steamed roll with treacle),

'Sir, how did you win your V.C.?'

'Eh, what's that?'

I repeated the question. Captain Joynt, who was swart and chunky, scraped his chin with his thumbnail.

'You really want to know?'

'Oh yes!'

'Well, I was sitting in my dugout one day when along came a ration party. "Hey," they said, "we've got a load of V.C's here, in this dixie, and we're handing them out. Now who wants one?" So I put up my hand and, well, there you are!'

There was a chorus of disbelief.

'No, but sir, tell us truly, how did you get it?'

'Like I said.'

'No, but honestly.'

'Well, we were eating supper one evening in the dugout when

Four Grace Street, Malvern, S.E.4.

along came an orderly with a tin of stew, lovely it was in the midst of the mud and slime of the trenches. He ladled me out a great jugful on my tin plate, and lo and behold, right in the middle of it, all amongst the potatoes and the onions and the bits of catmeat— there was a V.C. so. . . .'

'Oh, oh, oh! Captain Joynt, sir. You're kidding us.'

'No, honest I'm not.'

'Oh come on, tell us really.'

'Well all right if you *really* want to know . . .' he cocked a quirky eyebrow.

'Yes, yes, we do.'

'I was walking along one day and I met a German and I pushed him out of the way and then I met another German and I pushed him out of the way, and then I got a V.C.'

We looked very dubious at this, but Captain Joynt had finished his steamed roll, and now bent on us a replete and friendly eye.

'Sir, are you in the Dictionary of National Biography?'

'I doubt it,' said Captain Joynt.

'Dad is!' I said proudly perhaps with dreadful memories of the incident on the *Friedrichsruh* over the 'Common Digger'.

Dad said, 'Let's get the dictionary and find out.' I wrenched it from the shelf and started reading.

'There's no Thirkell,' I said, 'but Thorkill a Danish Thegn.'

'That's me,' said Dad.

'And Thorkell, he's a Scandinavian bard.'

'That's me,' said Dad.

'And THURTELL?'

'That's me too,' said Dad.

'Then let me read you this. THURTELL, William. Murderer! How do you like that?'

'Donie,' Joynt said. 'Well you know, that's what war is after all. Legalized murder.' This from a V.C. was undoubtedly impressive.

* * *

Of the five doors, the first led obviously into the kitchen, a gloomy room overshadowed by the huge two-storey bulk of the Trist home next door, and with one meagre casement window giving onto the side alley. It contained a square deal table, a deal dresser and, set back in two enormous caverns, a gas stove and an old fashioned woodburner. The latter, which was never used, was thus the more mysterious, and upon returning one Christmas from a scout camp we begged to be allowed to light it and cook flapjacks.

The Road to Gundagai

Permission was reluctantly granted, but we filled the little kitchen with sulphurous greenish smoke, and had to fall back on the gas stove. This was notable for two brass nozzles projecting outward into the kitchen. One could turn these up, light them and obtain a rare jet of hissing flame about six inches long. Though it was strictly forbidden we often turned up these jets and once, with vague memories of the physics lab, attached rubber tubing to the nozzle and then very foolishly lit the other end. It burned all right; so did the rubber tubing with an abominable stench and a frightening crackle. Thereafter Mother had the jets sealed. Later a Lady Help blew the oven door right off its hinges by premature and reckless lighting technique. This, I was able to point out, was just as irresponsible as lighting gas jets and rubber tubing. So, I added, was my little brother's habit of crawling round behind the stove and eating plaster off the wall (though maybe that was calcium deficiency, for rare indeed were the vitamins eaten at 4 Grace Street and we all had appalling teeth. 'Show me a vitamin and I'll believe in one,' was Mother's oft-repeated and sibylline locution.)

Off the kitchen was the larder on the door of which was pinned a calendar with the following jolly jingle beneath the months:

> Three cheers for the red, white and blue,
> Three cheers for the old kangaroo
> When he came with his gun
> The Huns started to run
> What else could the poor b.....s do?

The larder window, by another of the queer anomalies of 4 Grace Street, gave onto the 'slep-out' and onto my bed, and often at night I would see Mother's outline behind the wire screen. Usually I lay still, but sometimes after a wait I would say in a low voice: 'Mother, what do you want?' She never answered, but the pale blotch behind the wire screen would move silently away in the darkness.

The larder was notable for two very un-Australian and ludicrously inadequate gadgets. The first was the butter cooler. It was an earthenware double-walled beehive filled with water; beneath it was an earthenware dish in which the buter sat. This in turn was kept in a 'cellarette', known to Mother as The Hole. It was simply a hinged lid which, when raised, revealed a small oblong cave about two feet deep and lined with zinc. When I think of the summer temperatures in Melbourne in the high nineties and often well over a hundred for several days on end, I am amazed at this primitive arrangement. This was our 'refrigerator' and it meant that the butter was always soft and that we never had any ice-cream, except in a cup or cone

Four Grace Street, Malvern, S.E.4.

from the corner store. No doubt refrigerators, even ice boxes, were a rarity in urban Australia in the 1920's, and of course once outside the range of electricity the common country refrigerator was the famous Coolgardie Safe. This was a regular issue 'meat safe' (i.e. a square tin box with wire mesh sides) with a galvanized iron tray full of water on top and beneath. The two trays were connected by strips of towelling down the sides of the safe and these, soaked by capillary attraction, cooled rapidly in any wind; in fact, the hotter the wind the cooler the Coolgardie Safe. The same principle is at work in the canvas water bag, and the 'desert cooler' used in India. But for a solid suburban house with the normal utilities our 'butter cooler' and Hole seemed eccentric.

The other gadget was the Fireless Cooker into which it was my job to put the saucepan of porridge the night before. It was a wooden box filled with straw and an old blanket and provided a cosy and frugal nest for stews and other simple dishes. Next to it—perhaps the most dramatic object of the whole larder—was an earthenware demijohn of whisky in a wicker basket. Dad used to buy it this way because he said it was cheaper than buying by the bottle. H'mm.

Next to the larder was the scullery which looked across the asphalt yard to the woodshed and in which we did several thousand washings up. We graduated from boiling a kettle to a crude precursor of the 'Ascot' gas heater—known to various Lady Helps as the geezer, the gayzer or the guyzer. Plates were air-dried in an immense wooden rack which always looked as if it were about to tear loose from the wall. The draining board was of that permanently wetted and soaped wood which turns to scruf under the knife and oozes a grey scum at the corners. From the window, the tedium of the endless stream of sticky pots and dirty pans could be relieved by rear-end views of the washer woman, Mrs. Robotham—known to us as Mrs. Robust Bottom—going about her chores.

Outside the scullery two empty kerosene tins, nailed to the fence between us and the Trists, were receptacles for bread and milk. The independent Aussie tradesman, having come all the way down the side alley, would condescend to leave nothing, nor even to make his presence known, unless the order had been placed out the night before or unless someone were there permanently to receive him. We had two school slates on which to write 'One large' or 'One loaf' or 'Two pints please'. The milkman delivered the milk by dipper from a large can, ladling it into a white enamel 'billy' which we kept in the empty kerosene tin. The milk often looked blueish and one of our Lady Helps told of a witty reply given to an importunate milkman. He had conversationally observed, scanning the sky, 'Looks

The Road to Gundagai

like rain today' to which she made the merry riposte: 'Yes, but it *does* bear a faint resemblance to milk.' All this, when bottled milk and pasturization were not uncommon. No wonder our school friends thought us a bit odd.

Our bathroom, also reached directly off the dining room, was regarded as more conventional, with its short bath, corrugated iron shower screen, chip heater and corner basin, all linked by an invisible chain of command to the place of meditation behind the yellow jasmine trellis. The fact that the bathroom had no running hot water went unremarked; but Mother's loofah—an exotic instrument unknown in Melbourne suburbia—generated many a giggle. Hung not quite over the basin was Dad's triple shaving mirror. To open the window it had to be lifted off the wall and then rehung. To close the window required the same procedure.

Finally, also off the dining room, was the bedroom which my brother and I shared for six years. It was small, square, white plastered, with a bed against each wall, a cupboard and a dresser against the other wall, and opposite it a casement window through which, by lightly cocking a leg, one could land on the battered flower bed between the cootamundra and the peach tree and hence, day or night, shin up onto the roof. It was from this room that my brother and I attempted on three occasions to run away. The first time we did this was the result of a beating administered for our failure to carry out in detail the provisions of a document devised and typed out by Mother and bearing the title:

'Programme of work and play for Graham and Colin during the holidays.'

The holidays in question were the annual Christmas or summer vacation which lasted from mid-December to mid-February. Mother was expecting our little brother at the time (though we did not know it) and this prospect, together with the inevitable burden of discomfort in the Australian heat, must have made her feel, perhaps rightly, that to have idle youngsters hanging around the home for two months was more than she could bear. To head off this possibility she composed the famous document (in black type for work and in red type for play) and thumbtacked it to the back of our bedroom door at a height suitable for a nine year old eye. If the following is not an exact rendering it is nevertheless true to its spirit:

7.30	Get up
7.30- 8.00	Prepare breakfast
8.00- 8.30	Eat breakfast
8.30- 9.30	Wash up breakfast things, make beds, sweep and dust own room

Four Grace Street, Malvern, S.E.4.

9.30-10.00	Play
10.00-11.00	Do any shopping errands that may be required and bring goods home
11.00-12.00	Study
12.00-12.30	Play (or help Dad in garden)
12.30- 1.15	Lunch
1.15- 1.45	Wash up lunch things
1.45- 3.00	Rest QUIETLY
3.00- 4.00	Hose down back yard and side alley. Sweep woodshed or washhouse (alternate days)
4.00- 4.30	Chop chips for chipheater
4.30- 5.00	Tea
5.00- 6.00	Play (or help Dad in the garden)
6.00- 7.00	Dinner
7.00- 8.00	Play QUIETLY during grown-ups' dinner
8.00- 8.30	Reading aloud
8.30- 9.00	Prepare for bed. Bath on bath nights
9.00	Bed

This monstrous document filled us with a strong sense of injustice. It was our first long holiday and we'd looked forward to pleasant outings and fooling around in the garden (but not helping Dad in it). We decided nevertheless to abide by the procrustean schedule as far as we could; but neither we nor Mother made allowance for the heat and for the many distractions which kids can find even in a suburban house and garden. We fell behind with our tasks and some of them were not performed. Mother said nothing but on a Saturday morning the storm broke with devastating fury. We were finishing our beds when Mother's face appeared at the window.

'Graham, Colin. Come here, I want you.'

We went to the window still half dressed. Mother was standing on the flower bed outside with a piece of paper in her hand; some distance off stood Dad with his army swaggerstick. We were mystified but not alarmed. The following 'statement' then issued from Mother's lips.

'You have both neglected your tasks. Because of this Dad is going to give you a beating.'

We were speechless with indignation, but in a gesture of brave defiance my brother lashed at Mother with his shorts which—having been surprised half dressed—he still held in his hand. She ducked but one of the buttons caught in her hair and untwisted the bun. The hair lurched and cascaded to her waist and we screamed with laughter and relief. This was a mistake because it made her angry.

The Road to Gundagai

'Come here at *once*, and be beaten!'

We knew better than to demur and scrambled out of the window into the Saturday morning garden. The painful ritual began, in the best manner, it seemed, of 'For the Term of his Natural Life'. Mother called out the charge sheet while Dad administered the whacks.

'*That's* for doing the washing up badly! And *that's* for leaving the woodshed dirty. . . !'

Parent and step-parent at last moved majestically away leaving us burning with a rich destructive hatred. Our rage was not directed against Dad for we divined in him a mere instrument. We kept subdued during the rest of the day but at night we began to plot. First we thought we would kill Mother; but then, if we did that, what about Dad? We didn't want to kill him; it wasn't really his fault. And after all if we killed Mother, it might make him unhappy. Besides we might be found out; and while the court was bound to take a lenient view because we had acted under extreme provocation, still, we might be sent to Pentridge gaol. After a good deal of discussion we agreed that it would be simpler to run away. We decided to wait until the grown-ups were asleep and then leave the house by stealth. We waited and waited . . . and suddenly it was daylight and time to get up and do our 'Programme of work and play for Graham and Colin in the holidays'.

But the next night we secreted a tin of sardines and some gingernuts under the pillow and at half past two sneaked out by the side alley and were soon merrily on our way. As we strode through the darkened streets we regaled ourselves with dramatizing the consternation that would greet the discovery of our departure. We tramped on through the night past Glen Iris, which was the end of the carline, over the bridge at Gardiner's Creek. Dawn found us near the Ashburton billabong in among the sheoaks and the straggly ironbark. We'd come about five miles and had eaten all our provisions. We were tired and hungry and neither of us wanted to be the first to say it. While we hesitated the sun came up and the birds began to sing. The Grimm's fairy tale atmosphere of ogresses and trolls and norns rolled backward with the night, and sunny Australia reasserted itself.

'I'm going back.'

'Okay, so'm I.'

We were dead beat when we straggled back to 4 Grace Street about eight o'clock on Sunday morning. The house was strangely quiet as we slunk down the side alley in stockinged feet. They've gone to look for us, we exulted, and falling to in the kitchen we ate ravenously of what we would have had for breakfast: Cereal ('Yours for breakfast Willie Weeties') boiled eggs and lots of bread and

Four Grace Street, Malvern, S.E.4.

butter. In the middle of our feast Dad walked into the kitchen in his dressing gown.

'Well, what are you two up to?'

'We're just—having breakfast.'

'Hm!' he grunted, looked a bit odd and went out. It dawned on us that our absence had not been noticed. It was Sunday morning and they had slept in. We didn't know whether to laugh or cry. The chagrin of finding that our escapade had gathered no drama was matched by the blessed relief of being home. Yes, 4 Grace Street was home, in spite of programmes of work and play; in spite of beatings. But a moment later a distant but deep contralto chilled us to the marrow.

'George! Their beds haven't been slept in!' A moment later she burst into the kitchen like a whirlwind. 'Where have you been?'

'We tried to run away.'

'Very well! For that you're going to get another beating. George!'

Poor George hadn't the strength of will, and we hadn't the strength of body, to resist her. After the beating we lay, each in our own bed, with smarting buttocks, injured pride and streaming eyes, while outside in broad daylight children played and the neighbourhood was full of Sunday morning sounds.

Most boys of my vintage in Australia had their hides tanned, I'm sure. What it seemed to me, set our tannings aside from the normal run and invested them with the distasteful ferocity of Australia's own earlier convict days was the deliberation and the ritual: Mother's presence like a gaoler or wardress; our stepfather's hesitation followed by a teeth-grating frenzy as, despite himself, he warmed to his work and made up in physical fury what he lacked in backbone. He had no will, only brute strength; but, and we didn't really blame him, he'd do almost anything reasonable—and beating the daylights out of small boys who were someone else's children must have seemed reasonable—to keep in Mother's good books, to avoid the rough side of her tongue, and to head off her sullen rages.

Yet Mother was also quite prepared to read us *David Copperfield* aloud, lingering with dramatic colour over the episodes involving Mr. Murdstone, imitating with marvellous theatricality the voice of the dramatis personae. It may have occurred to her that little pitchers with big ears were comparing Mr. Murdstone with someone not a thousand miles from 4 Grace Street. If so, she never let on. The beatings were a regular accompaniment of the years from eight to thirteen, when they suddenly ceased. It may have been that we were getting a bit too big to thrash; or perhaps Dad sickened of the unwelcome task. At any rate one blessed day they stopped. I

The Road to Gundagai

looked around the room shared with my brother and decided that I needed a room of my own. I exchanged a table for a desk; a camp bed for a proper bed (i.e. a brass bedstead with iron slats instead of springs, and a kapok-filled mattress); the framed photograph of Longstaff's *The Great Bush Fire* for a framed photograph of *The Menin Gate*. I took with me my temperature, sunshine and rain charts and my small collection of 'British Empire' stamps and hung my own clothes at last behind curtains among the family trunks rather than in the stained green cupboard with my brother's.

Chapter Six

GOOD OLD SCOTCH, WE'LL EVER SING

MY brother and I came to be enrolled in Scotch College ('Oldest in Victoria; biggest in Australia; best in the world!!!') entirely by accident. When Mother arrived in Australia she professed to be appalled at the lower middle class, non-conformist atmosphere. Being highly establishment-minded, her first thought was to enrol us in Melbourne Grammar which was the pukka C of E school. The prep school was known as Grimwade House and Mother went along to interview the headmaster to see if he would accept us (and she him). Though the creeper-clad surroundings appealed to her she was so shattered by the Head's devastating Australian accent that she did not honestly feel she could let us be corrupted to that extent.

Remembering that her own father had been born and bred a Presbyterian in Scotland and was an alumnus of Ayr Academy, she bethought herself of Scots Dominies. So she went to visit the preparatory school of Scotch College, and there interviewed the Head, Arthur J. Waller, known to us as 'The Dog', on the cockney rhyming analogy of Waller-collar, dog-collar. The Dog's command of English, his expression and accent were sufficient for Mother to be convinced that Good Old Scotch was where we were to go. I wrote 'Home' to my grandmother in far-off England to tell her that I'd joined a school whose colours were red, yellow and blue. I was very proud of this and of my new school cap, but the class bully got hold of my letter and read it out to his fellows. I had committed an unforgivable sin, for the colours of the school, far from being red, yellow and blue were cardinal, gold and royal blue. 'We're fighting for the cardinal, gold and blue. We'll carve our way to glory!' was one of the many boastful songs that I learned to sing with gusto during the next decade.

As new boys we received notebooks in which to do our homework. On the cover was a label with name, school, number and form. We wrote in our borrowed names, and our numbers, mine was 1064,

The Road to Gundagai

Colin's 1065. Opposite the word 'form' I wrote 2B, but Colin who had misread 'form' as 'from' thought he was supposed to write his address. Spelling not being his strong point, he wrote: The 4 Gas Set, Melborn, Austriala, Sea, World, Sola Systim, Univers. The school's motto was *Deo Patriae Litteris*. This was generally construed by the Latin scholars as follows: (To the glory of) God: (For the good of one's) country: and (for the advancement of) learning. During my period at Scotch the student at the lamp of learning, hunched somewhat after the manner of Rodin's *Le Penseur* was replaced by the flag of Saint Andrew, the voyaging lymphad, the Southern Cross and the Burning Bush common to both Moses and the Presbyterian Church.

Scotch College Preparatory School had opened in 1919 and was the harbinger of the 'big school', still housed among the decayed and genteel terraces of East Melbourne, close to the centre of the city. The new site was just about incomparable: sixty acres of rolling farmland at the confluence of the Yarra and Gardiner's Creek, and dominated by a pine-clad hill rising steeply to a bluff crowned by one of those mid-Victorian Gothick palazzi so dear to the wealthy merchants of Melbourne in the 1870's and 1880's. In later years there was to be room for a complete school with chapel, science block, gymnasium, cricket pavilion, swimming pool, tennis courts, the lot: for twelve hundred boys. There would be three cricket or football fields, and there would still remain a large amount of wilderness land in which boys could roam at lunch-time enjoying the illusion of being in the country.

The prep school occupied the extreme north-east corner of this sixty acres along a mystically named Callantina Road, and consisted of a terra-cotta roofed block in red brick and white rough-cast with a cricket field behind. The Headmaster, Arthur J. Waller, B.A., Dip. Ed. ('The Dog') lived in the battlemented Gothick house and sometimes his housekeeper would give us a hunk of bread, without butter but with jam, for the morning break if we skulked long enough at the back door and asked politely. Munching ecstatically we then careered through the long grass on the top of the hill until we came to its brow and sat down beneath the pines which really did whisper. Here we could look across the valley of Gardiner's Creek and its flood plain, heavily embanked to contain behind levees the Kooyong Tennis Courts of Davis Cup fame. Beyond lay one of Melbourne's early efforts at electrification, the little single track railway that followed the valley of the creek until it disappeared into a deep rock cutting where the mansions of the mighty raised themselves on a high steep bluff overlooking the river. At this point one was in snobby Toorak, treated with a vast and derisive contempt

Good Old Scotch, We'll Ever Sing

by Scotch as being more properly the domain of Melbourne Grammar.

There were six 'Great Public Schools' as they were pompously called, in the State of Victoria. All the others were looked down upon by us, either because they were grammar schools or because they were State schools (i.e. free schools which the vast majority of all boys and girls attended). But the six 'Great Public Schools' commanded a loyalty, not only from their pupils and their parents but from the Melbourne public itself, which was both frantic and fanatical. The place and time to see this loyalty displayed was at the annual Head of the River which by tradition took place on the Yarra for two years and, since two of the six schools were located in Geelong, on the Barwon every third year. On these occasions enormous frenzied crowds lined the Yarra, surging with excitement and jumping up and down, pounding the banks into tacky mud and slush as they sang rival school songs and yells. It was the Melbourne equivalent of the Oxford and Cambridge boat race. Schoolboys, Old Boys, breathless Mums, young sweethearts, kid brothers, hangers-on, all lined the banks decked in enormous rosettes, with ribbons flying from lapels, parasols and hats. On the roof of the *Herald* building the colours of the winning crew were displayed fluttering in the autumn breeze for all to see.

One boatrace day we got out of school early and to save time decided to hop off the tram at the Punt Road footbridge, cross the river on foot and walk down the tow path among the rushes, to get a better sight of the oncoming eights. In taking a short cut we became aware of an unknown but appalling stench. Closer investigation revealed the clothed body of a man floating face downwards on the river. One of us gave him a slight nudge with the boot and the corpse turned over revealing something grey, doughy and unrecognizable that had once been a face. We were profoundly shocked; it was the first time we had ever seen a dead body. Our first thought was to have nothing to do with it, but then visions of our old friends the police, the Johns, arose: 'If we don't tell them they're bound to get us.' It was agreed that I should leave a friend with the corpse and go to the Richmond Police Station. Greatly to our surprise the cops received the news with relish, congratulated us on our enterprise, and subsequently handed us in the precincts of the Station, and with great solemnity, a reward of ten shillings for finding the body.

* * *

We at Scotch naturally considered ourselves not only biggest

The Road to Gundagai

of the six schools (which we were) but also the best. But we recognized uneasily that Melbourne Grammar and Geelong Grammar had the edge on us in terms of social status. Not of course that any Scotch boy in his senses would ever have been interested in Society; Heavens no! We were far too democratic for that. But just the same you couldn't help noticing that the Grammar boys came from the wealthiest homes, were C of E and Establishment and blessed by the Anglican Bishop and had ivy-covered walls and generally behaved as if they owned the place. They were known to us as *tonks*, which is an onomatopoetic description of what they were. When we saw them in their blue serge suits and blue caps with the white bishop's mitre on the peak, walking superciliously down St. Kilda Road we used to yell at them: 'Who-ah? We-ah! Melbahn Grammah!' At the Boat Race such feeble exercises in mutual rivalry went unremarked, but in the football season 'disgraceful' scenes took place. At half-time it was customary, in playing Australian football, to change ends; instructions from the headmasters of both schools were that the boys should rotate anticlockwise. But invariably there would be a hard core of perhaps a hundred Scotch or Grammar boys who would disregard the order, and a mêlée of unexampled ferocity would ensue at the narrow barred gate through which we had to fight and claw our way.

'Deplorable,' said the *Argus*, 'that the sons of our privileged citizens should so behave.' Not that we took all that notice of the *Argus*; it was hard to take seriously a newspaper whose masthead motto read: 'I am in the place whereof it is demanded of me that I speak the truth, and therefore the truth I speak, impugn it whoso list.' But there's no doubt that Melbourne Grammar was our real rival and when we beat them at games, which was sometimes, or in exams, which was more often, we were very pleased indeed. Their headmaster, an extremely tall man nicknamed 'Lofty' Franklin, was popular with us because he was once seen publicly to congratulate the Scotch racing eight when it won the heat against Grammar at the Head of the River. This was considered very sporting and later when word seeped around that the Governor General, at prize giving at Melbourne Grammar, had expressed to the boys the hope that their ambitions 'would be lofty', this gained as much of a laugh at Scotch as at Grammar.

Nearer to us in spirit, though not in the same wonderful love-hate relationship, was Wesley College. This was a Methodist foundation and the boys, who wore purple caps, were jeered at by us in the streets and followed by the refrain: 'Wesley wowsers wet their trousers.' This feeble sally had its origins in the belief that if you must be Low Church it's better to be Scots and Presbyterian

Good Old Scotch, We'll Ever Sing

and different entirely, than to be, as we used to say, 'one of the Methody boys'. This stricture did not, of course, apply to that distinguished Old Boy, R. G. Menzies, K.C., when he came to adjudicate inter-school debates.

The fourth of the 'Great Public Schools' in Melbourne was Xavier College. Being Roman Catholic it was to us extremely mysterious. The school was run by the Jesuit Fathers and the headmaster had the recondite initials S.J. after his name. We yelled after them, and I'm sorry to have to relate it: 'Catholic dogs jump like frogs!' But they remained aloof; not supercilious like the Grammar boys, but remote members of an arcane cult which we did not understand and which vaguely frightened us. Their black caps carried a red mitre and beneath, the words *Sursum Corda*—lift up your hearts. We wondered in our Presbyterian innocence why it was that Roman Catholics should feel constrained to lift up *their* hearts. What good would it do *them*? Weren't they already condemned to hellfire and damnation?

The other two schools were not in Melbourne at all but in Geelong, the second city of the State about fifty miles away. Geelong College, being a Presbyterian foundation, was supposed to be our sister school and we did our best to like it, but we had little in common. They were very small, we were very big. Our Head was a bearded layman; theirs was a cleric with a large adam's apple. We met once a year and that was that. Nearby, situated on a bay about five miles outside Geelong was what all of us recognized as *the* public school of Victoria, a quite different institution from ours and one that you really didn't compare yourself with at all, because it was not a question of rival excellences but of a difference in category. Geelong Grammar was of course C of E but it drew the bulk of its pupils from the sons of wealthy squatters and sheep station owners of the Western District. There must have been more money per square inch of pale blue Geelong Grammar school cap than in that of any other colour. The great pastoral names of Victoria, the Fairbairns, the Manifolds, the Baillieus, the Staughtons, the Russells, attended Geelong Grammar. To us it was less a school than an institution, a belief, a state of mind (or if you like, of grace), into which you were born and to which you could not and perhaps did not wish to aspire.

Of course when we joined 'Dog' Waller's emporium in 1920 all this was in the future and the life of the little prep school was highly circumscribed. The summers seemed to be extremely long and hot and in the two weeks before prize giving we used to sit, without benefit of cushions, on the red cement assembly hall floor open to the winds and sing *en masse* the songs with which we

The Road to Gundagai

were later to adorn the prize giving ceremonies held in the local town hall. As usual, Kipling's Gods of the copy-book stand out, among them Mr. Cock who, it was rumoured prior to his arrival at the school, had only one leg; later that he had no legs at all; finally that we could expect to see him carried in by the 'Dog' in a basket. When he arrived and proved to have two legs, two arms and a petulant temper we were greatly disappointed.

The younger boys had women teachers, or mistresses as they were known. The tradition of the Scots Dominies was well foreshadowed by Miss Grace MacMillan. She had a burr that you could split with a hammer and chisel, and she ruled by a draconian system of rewards and punishments. Bad work: three raps across the knuckles, not the flat of the hand, with her ruler. Good work: a 'sugar medal'; that is to say a disgustingly glutinous home-made sweet which she fished from the inside of her purse. She taught us absolutes and perhaps for the very young these are what should be taught. If there was a doubt in her mind about anything, we never knew it. Things were so. God was above; Satan below. The shortest distance between two points was a straight line and this we must cleave to at all costs.

Yet outside, making a mockery of Duty, dancing around in his sleeveless singlet taped with blue and his neat little pot jumping up and down, was Sergeant Cartwright, drillmaster and humorous thug who set big boys boxing against weedy ones so that we could all enjoy the vicarious thrill of a bloody nose or a broken tooth. There was one enormous fellow called 'Jumbo' McCabe who must have had some glandular disorder for he towered a good head over us all and was built like a scrum-half. He gloried in his heftiness which he hurled about with roars of frightening irresponsible laughter. Nothing delighted Cartwright more than to set McCabe at chopping up some smaller fellow, stopping the bout just this side of outright massacre. With boyish perversity we wished to leave the safe haven of Miss MacMillan for the sadistic world of Cartwright. Most boys are born with lethal desires, but for myself, being one of the ignoble cowards. Cartwright's lectures on anatomy interested me more.

'Now this 'ere's the tibia and across from that this 'ere's the fibia and if I bang you on the knee cap, so, you leg'll bounce. That shows you got a nerve. Now Merton, say that again after me, which is the tibia?'

'Here sir.'

'No you fool, that's not the tibia, that's the fibia.'

At this time I was suffering from incipient mirror vision and had a tendency to try to write with my left hand. This was rigorously suppressed in the fashion of the day, by Mr. Edmonds, the writing master, who tied my left hand behind my back. Edmonds had a grey, highly waxed moustache which he twirled with his fingers, and an Imperial which he greased with powerful unguents. He pranced about the dais like a dancing master brandishing a wonderful piece of apparatus which enabled him to draw simultaneously six exquisitely parallel chalk lines. He taught the scrolly baroque commercial copper plate, but not to me. I was unteachable. I didn't suffer unduly from the hand tied behind my back, though who is to say, since the suppression of a natural urge to do something with the left hand often sets up the most curious nerve blocks. Outside the classroom this showed itself in a total inability to obey commands in the drill and P.T. classes of Sergeant Cartwright. If he said left-turn I would turn right and in the game 'Do what I do but not what I say' I was always the dunderhead. He finally hit upon the effective but humiliating device of singling me out by name, thus: 'The class *and* Thirkell left turn! The class *and* Thirkell right turn!'

The real sadist at the school was not Cartwright but a big shambling hulk of a man named Armitage, with a loose cruel mouth. It was habitual then as now in public schools for masters to use the ruler, to throw bits of chalk and even blackboard dusters at boys when they were asleep or inattentive, but Armitage was the only man I ever knew who actually beat boys. I don't just mean that he boxed their ears, I mean that he hit them with such force that they flew from the seat. We determined to be revenged upon him. It was a chemistry class and we were seated upon high stools, seventeen of us in a row. It was arranged that the boy on the extreme left was to commit an egregious error of the type that would make Armitage lose his temper. This he successfully did. Armitage dealt him a resounding cuff on the ear upon which all seventeen of us toppled over, one after the other, like a pack of dominoes. But we were not revenged on Armitage, it was he who was revenged on us; for the result of our merry jape was an hour's detention after school.

Even more unnerving, because totally unpredictable, was Cyril B. Hayes. He was an old thin-faced fellow with high cheek-bones and lean lips who danced rather than walked and who played favourites amongst the boys. Hayes taught geography, and his field excursions in the May holidays were the wonderfully enjoyable outdoor complement of the classroom. He took us on day outings to Sherbrooke Forest in the Dandenongs, to the gorge of the Werribee River and on the narrow-gauge railway line through the ranges of Western Gippsland. Although these were on a Saturday, deny-

The Road to Gundagai

ing us the exquisite pleasure of a day off from school, they provided in my case a day off from Dad's 'Works' or from weeding the rose beds, and so were more than ordinarily glamorous.

With a cut lunch in a haversack thirty odd boys would board the breathlessly early morning train for Fern Tree Gully where we transferred under Hayes' supervision from the broad gauge of the Victorian Railways to the little two-foot-six-inch train which puffed its way slowly up through the foothills. The engine burned wood and the coaches were mere cattle boxes with benches back to back down the centre. The speed was barely twenty miles an hour but once the foothills were climbed and the distant city hidden from view, we emerged onto rolling heavily timbered country with enormous vistas of high blue sky, scarred with our echoing clatter through damp mossy gullies where giant tree-ferns brushed the windowless cars as we chugged slowly up the hill. Hayes was everywhere, lean lithe and high cheek-boned, with a blonde quiff of hair and a curious half mechanical smile. He would swing himself along the outside of the cattle boxes enquiring after the welfare of each boy. When we picnicked on a slope too close to a tree infested with bull-ants he was the one who produced the cologne for the injured backside. With the same air of sprightliness he could hit a boy on the head with a chalk at twenty feet, or drop a piece of sodium into a pneumatic jar and skip lightly aside to avoid the subsequent hissing explosion.

At a place called Cockatoo he was something more than sprightly; he was a hero. A bush fire, burning the very sleepers to which our rails were tied, blocked the panting train. Great roaring gusts of wind sent fire-balls of incandescent leaves high over our heads starting new fires all around us. It was Hayes who got water from a nearby creek and splashed the sides of the cattle car while the train backed slowly. It was Hayes who provided us with masks of torn up dampened strips of *The Herald* for us to gag ourselves as the train leaped forward and galloped through the fiery barrier like an old horse. At the gorge of the Werribee he was a hero too. The river surged down from the high plateau onto the bright green irrigated flat lands around Bacchus Marsh, and it was Hayes who scaled the fearsome sides of the eight hundred foot deep gorge. When a rolling stone hit a boy in the back and he collapsed carrying a slither of screes with him, it was Hayes who halted the boy's fall and carried him on his back all the way to the railway station.

No wonder we worshipped him; he was so unlike a schoolmaster. And since he was so wonderful, what was wrong if he showed partiality to a particular boy? It all seems very easy looking back; but who could have known, particularly by the euphemisms and circumlocutions with which other masters and our own parents shrouded his failing? But those who went on a three week visit with him to Tasmania found out, and he left the school 'under a cloud' never to return. My memory of Hayes is of a friendly, disconcerting faun in a lounge suit, a rangy figure cracking dry schoolmasterish jokes with a sort of amused asperity, leading us onward with his steady lope at a pace just a little too fast for us to keep up with. And then, the brilliant dazzle of the smile, followed, almost with a click, by shuttered lids. There if anywhere was the mystery: the gap between the perceived and the inferred.

Our form spent a weekend with Hayes on the upper waters of the Yarra near the foot of Mount Donna Buang, at over 4,000 feet by far the highest mountain near Melbourne. Up the steep woolly sides of its huge shoulder crawled a timber-track down which great logs were skidded, but up which Hayes forced us at a killing pace. The angle of incline was so steep that the sleepers became steps, but we begged in vain for a rest period or hoped emptily that the steel cable down the middle of the track would miraculously start to turn and a little téléférique would appear to carry us all up high in the clouds. But Hayes never took anything easily and we weren't allowed to stop until we'd left behind us the wooden rails, scuffed and bruised by the passage of hardwood logs, and were clambering up a dirt road towards the top of the mountain. It was worth it. Bursting on our sight as we rounded the last curve were traces, albeit grey or sugary, of genuine snow. This was such a rarity that we soon forgot our fatigue in playing timeless merry little snow games; forgot to watch for Hayes who disappeared into the bushes.

Hayes was wonderful at getting the best from a schoolboy. His geography classes filled us with a vivid and permanent image of the State. In the junior classes they dinned into us the litany of the Victorian rivers. Our State was bounded on the north by the Murray River and on the south by Bass Strait. The Great Dividing Range ran down the middle of the State from east to west and the rivers which had their sources in it flowed north and south so that the map of the State looked like the bones of a herring. We had to recite them reading anti-clockwise round the State from the extreme east and they had a faintly poetic ring:

    Mítta-Mitta, Óvens, Góulburn, Campáspe
    Lódden, Avóca, Wímmera.
    Glenélg, Hópkins, Bárwon, Yárra
    Latróbe, Mítchell, Támbo, Snówy

But neither wavy lines on a blackboard nor poetic jingles in the memory provide the clue to reality or to geography. It was Hayes who made the rivers real, by taking us to see them and by giving them a personality which related them to the land and the people through which they flowed. With Hayes bounding lightly before us we inspected the upper waters of the Yarra. With Hayes we camped on the high bridge overlooking the Latrobe as it flowed mysteriously from Victoria's woolly backbone towards the brownish sea. With Hayes we saw the Goulburn cut its slow path through the ranges and spread out onto the flat Australia that extends two thousand miles north and west to Darwin. When he left we were heartbroken. We could not believe the enormity of his crime, nor indeed that his crime, since it was but vaguely hinted at, could have been enormous. But we noticed that when his name came up lips tightened, eyes averted and conversation tended to dry up. And so in due course Hayes was mysteriously transferred in our mass memory into one of the band of eccentric explorers who have loped purposefully into Australia's enigmatic interior: one with Eyre, parched with thirst at the Head of the Bight; one with Leichhardt tramping gaily but doggedly onward into oblivion beside rivers which shrank as they moved further from their source; one with Burke and Wills driven onward by an ambition compounded of nobility and madness; one with Sturt, bouncing down the Murray in his battered wideawake hat or shielding his eyes with his hand against the blistering desert sun.

* * *

At last, loaded with Certificates of Merit and prizes bound in hand-tooled red leather with gold along the spine (*The Boyhood of Nelson*, Woolley's *The Sumerians*) it was time to say good-bye to the 'prep' and go down the hill to the Big School, now building with such elephantine slowness on the flats below. The Big School or the 'New School' as it was known to the eight hundred boys who moved there from East Melbourne and who were as strange to us as Tartars or men from Venus, was built in a vehement shade of red brick, surmounted by grey roughcast and the inevitable red terra-cotta roof of Melbourne. It was in the form of a quadrangle, connected by a covered archway to a science block. Jutting forward from the quadrangle was the school hall or chapel. For some time it fulfilled both functions, until the day—long after mine—when a true chapel could be paid for. It was a building notable for its extreme Presbyterian bareness, its harsh angularity and the ludicrous smallness of its tiny finial. (Spires would have been out of character since we were Scottish and Low Church, and indeed a meeting

Good Old Scotch, We'll Ever Sing

house atmosphere would have been preferred to that of the opulent ivy-covered towers of Melbourne Grammar. The transfer, holus bolus, to Australia, of England's ancient prejudices, was far above our heads.)

In order to help to pay for this enormous exam factory where Scots Dominies ruled over the academic advancement of some twelve hundred boys, a fête was held on the grounds at which it was hoped to raise five thousand pounds. Although every boy was required to work as a volunteer as well as to purchase rides for himself, his parents and his friends, on the ferris wheel and the merry-go-round, the fête raised not much over two thousand pounds and the school started under a heavy capital debt. With schoolboy superstition we believed that the reason for this was because the fête opened in the week that Colin Ross was hanged.

The murder of Alma Tirtschke by Colin Ross, his subsequent conviction and execution, was a sex crime which gripped Melbourne for weeks. The case—its sadistic aspects unknown to us—almost submerged the popular press. We were not supposed to read about it and Mother was careful to confiscate the *Herald* which Dad brought home in the evening. But needless to say it circulated rapidly and surreptitiously at school. Around the case grew up an extraordinary amount of schoolboy folklore. It was assumed by us all that Ross was guilty because the murder had taken place in Gun Alley. If you did wrong in a place called Gun Alley that meant you were going to 'get the gun'. Another belief was that the Russell Street Police had drawn a sketch-map of the area and placed a cross where the murder took place. Obviously if you wrote down the word 'cross' on a piece of paper what could it be but C. Ross? In fact my brother underwent an uncomfortable if transient notoriety in school; boys stared at him simply because his name was Colin. But none of us ever believed that Ross would hang. It was not that the boys at Scotch were any less blood-thirsty or had any more advanced views on capital punishment than the boys of other schools; but Ross' conviction had been based mainly on his own alleged confession. Later, in connection with another crime, there were big public demonstrations against the hanging of another criminal Angus Murray who, quite flagrantly and in full view of a number of witnesses, shot dead a bank manager named Berriman at Glenferrie railway station. But because he was believed to have been framed by an accomplice, Murray he was the object of much sympathy and there was a strong movement against his hanging including the circulation of a petition with a thousand signatures —all to no avail.

A legend grew up around the Berriman killing. Australia has a tradition of sympathy for the underdog, stronger even than that which exists in Britain; it is in fact a championing of the underdog. The tradition arises no doubt from the convict days and perhaps more importantly from the exodus of workmen and small yeomen farmers following the Chartist rising of 1848 and the migration to the Australian gold fields round Ballarat in 1851. Men and women came roaring into the empty land with a passionate sense of the individual's rights and the Irishman's wrongs, and a grim cantankerous determination that here in a new world the old class distinctions, the old prejudices and the old injustices of England should have no place. As a comic essayist of the day put it: 'Our ancestors came out to Australia because they couldn't get a fair go in Britain. And if *you* don't want a fair go they'll bloody well *make* you have a fair go!' The exemplar of this attitude is the great Australian underdog hero, that sardonic Robin Hood figure, Ned Kelly. The phrase 'He's game as Ned Kelly' was the highest praise you could bestow.

The two other men involved in the Berriman murder were 'Squizzy' Taylor and Richard Buckley. Buckley disappeared and despite an extensive police search could not at first be found. 'Squizzy' Taylor proved too slippery for the police. He was one of those petty gangland Caesars who specialize in the manufacture of alibis and whose network of interests is so wide that they cannot be categorically linked with any one particular crime. 'Squizzy' was tried for complicity in the murder but acquitted and lived as a gambler long enough to be bumped off in 1927 by one of his own gang. Meanwhile Buckley became a sort of poor man's hero as he lay low and dodged the police. It was a stroke of luck for him that he had the same name as the castaway sailor of early Australian history who had lived with aborigines and had eventually, against all probability, been rescued and returned to civilization. From his exploit came the phrase 'Buckley's chance' and it was felt that this latter-day Buckley was in some way proving the truth of a great Australian myth. He was the object of much surreptitious admiration, some of which found its way into the following ditty, to the tune of *Yes, We Have no Bananas*:

> 'Yes! they have not got Buckley
> They have not got Buckley today.'[1]

---

[1] Finally in 1930 the elusive Buckley, by now in his late sixties with hair dyed and a beard, was arrested at Ascot Vale. He was tried and condemned to death but the sentence was commuted to imprisonment for life.
In 1946 he was released as it was thought he was about to die, but he lived on 'in retirement' until he died of old age in 1953, at the age of 89.

Good Old Scotch, We'll Ever Sing

We didn't think, in our innocence, that either Murray or Colin Ross would be hanged. Yet lo and behold, here we were and Ross ready to be 'topped' as the vernacular had it. On the last evening of the fête the boys who were supposed to be collecting money at the ferris-wheel, the round-a-bout, the coconut shy and the Aunt Sally, were busy reading by flashlight the details of the Ross execution in the rear of the various tents. No wonder the fête was a failure.

* * *

After the fête came the floods. Because of its porous soil the area around Melbourne was subject, as much of Australia still is, to the alternate ravages of fire and water. When the Yarra and Gardiner's Creek were both in spate then came the annual spring flood. In the year of the fête it was unprecedented. The New School lay right in the triangle formed by the Yarra and Gardiner's Creek and almost all of this was under from six to eight feet of water. It was a wonderfully exciting time. Brown rivers of muddy water swirled treacherously where once asphalt paving had so firmly stood. Great matted bird's nests and fuzzy-wuzzy heads came rolling down in the flood and wedged tight in the crotches of trees, to remain, after the flood had subsided, as objects of astonished unbelief. With the flood came the helpless tide of animals and reptiles: bloated cows with feet sticking in the air, sheep a mass of grey faceless sodden wool, rabbits by the hundred, scurrying for cover on the upper reaches and easily caught by schoolboys in their flight, necks wrung and taken home for supper; snakes and lizards; goannas, poisonous and non-poisonous, twisting and writhing or floating, white bellies upwards, in a loose sausage as they moved downstream.

School was closed; the new foundations were flooded and the workmen sat under their tarpaulins on the high ground and looked morosely out through the driving rain while they smoked sullen pipes. As the flood began to recede thousands of frogs emerged, and when it was known that Johnnie Agar, whose father was Professor of Zoology at the University, was prepared to pay a penny for every frog captured alive, then indeed the squelching, muddy, bog-like slopes were filled with a horde of boys up to their knees in muck, with an empty jam-jar, all groping for the fabulous reward. Agar himself remained seated haughtily beneath a pine tree in dry contentment, occasionally handing out a few pence to some mud-spattered lad with a couple of frogs in a jar. But all too soon the flood subsided, the stench of death and decaying vegeta-

The Road to Gundagai

tion was drawn upward by the strengthening spring sun, and we all went back to our classrooms, most of us to the new ones in the Big School.

* * *

As innumerable school ditties mournfully attest, the great figures of our schooldays hold Jovian proportions in the recollections of middle age. This was no less true of the masters at Scotch. But what still comes over larger than life is not their great stature, their bellowing roar, their none too subtle sarcasm; nor on our side the refined cruelty whereby an unpopular master was mercilessly lynched, tarred and feathered. What comes echoing down the years is the grating, granitic yet sympathetic and authoritative Scottish burr. As its name implies the school was founded by the Presbyterian Church and the senior staff were Dominies who had left Caledonia stern and wild with a degree from one of the four Scottish universities and whose accent stuck to them for life. Unlike our English masters whose crisp upper middle class voices soon became overlaid by the open sunny Australian accent, the Dominies' voices remained locked in craggy glottal fastnesses for the whole of their lives.

The Principal, Dr. W. S. Littlejohn stalked the corridors in mortarboard, curly white hair and crisp full white beard, an object of fear, veneration and affection to us all. The Vice Principal was Dr. W. F. Ingram, also with a beard (dark brown) and a waistcoat liberally bespattered with generations of food and dribble. His voice was even more unreconstructed than the headmaster's. Beneath them both, spread a pyramid in which Australians predominated but which was sprinkled with Englishmen and Scotsmen. The resulting amalgam showed characteristics of all three nations. Scots was the religious tone, the moral fervour, the insistence upon examinations and above all exam results as the eye through which even the most bulky camel could enter the Kingdom of Heaven. English was the emphasis on innumerable societies—debating clubs, dramatic societies, camera clubs, science clubs, stamp collecting clubs, the orchestra—with their passionate amateurism. English too was the emphasis on games; but the overwhelming importance attached to them and the prowess attained in them were both indubitably Australian. Moreover, though the school itself was located in a city of almost one million inhabitants, it could not escape from its hinterland; and the grey brooding bush, the deep sunny skies and the enigmatic wariness of the Australian landscape gurgled and flowed around the school buildings and permeated us all.

Good Old Scotch, We'll Ever Sing

Dr. Littlejohn—'Old Bill'—was an administrative dynamo driven by evangelical Scots fervour. The day began with the chapel doors clanging shut very precisely at nine-ten, all stragglers ruthlessly cut off to await the prefect on duty with his detention pad. Then the masters, in flowing though tattered gowns, led by Old Bill carrying his mortar-board, swept up the aisles of silent boys towards the dais. Bill himself clambered up into the pulpit above which was a large sounding board of Queensland maple. There he took prayers and made the daily announcements, so that the pulpit was a mixture of the clerical and the lay. No written dialect can possibly hope to produce the precise gritty burr of Old Bill's voice: but that he believed in hell-fire and damnation rather than in the possibility of salvation, and was determined to make us believe in them too, was evident from his delivery. His eyes tightly shut, rebuking those of us who had kept our own surreptitiously open; his pudgy hands clenched or wrung in ecstasy on the pulpit's edge; his whole body convulsed with moral fervour; he importuned God directly to intercede with Scotch College and its sinful pupils. I am sure that Old Bill had direct communication with God, and that He was equally bearded; a Jupiter-Jehovah sitting up in the sky and wagging a stern finger at us all. Blake's concept of God as 'old Nobodaddy' would have seemed blasphemous to Old Bill. Five days a week, forty weeks in the year he stood in the pulpit wringing his hands, shouting to God (and at us) and calling on Him to help us all to be better schoolboys, which for him meant, and he told us so, working harder for the examinations, playing harder to beat Grammar in the football match, studying harder to be better men. I used to wish as I stood erect during prayers at chapel that I too could be in communication with Old Bill's God, but this was never vouchsafed. Though shamed by Old Bill's simplicities, I remained stubbornly self centered.

Suddenly the prayer finished. Old Bill put on his mortar-board and became the streamlined academic administrator. Boys had been discovered smoking in the basement of the science block. Not only would they be visited with hell-fire and damnation; they would be caned. Any boy who brought live frogs into chapel would be detained for an hour after school. The sports master had reported to him that the racing eights and fours were not being properly stowed in the boatshed after practice. This must not be. Mr. Orton, the singular enthusiast who combined mathematics teaching with training the school choir, would like us to stay behind for half an hour. Then with a brisk swish of his crisp gown Old Bill stalked down the aisle towards the rear of the chapel with an occasional 'Come to my office, boy', which, even if it meant only a fearful-

The Road to Gundagai

friendly analysis of his latest report, smote terror in the breast of the most complacent.

Ingram, known as 'Bumpy' (he was so brainy that the bumps of knowledge stuck out all over his skull), was much less frightening. As Vice Principal it sometimes fell to him to deliver sermons and to make announcements, but chiefly he was the administrative head of the great assembly line. His accent was grittier than Old Bill's but, disconcertingly, though he was a person who could be fooled with, his ground-rules were so elastic that the boy who carried foolery too far would unexpectedly find himself on the receiving end of a blast of Caledonian invective. Normally Bumpy was the kindliest of men. He lived many miles from the school and was often to be seen padding benignly to work in a curious grey Billy-cock hat, carrying a small attache case. His habit of dribbling through the fungus, which accounted for the state of his waistcoat, endeared him to us all. When cricket matches were in progress he allowed a boy to stand at the window and repeat the score at one minute intervals.

During classroom tests Bumpy was invariably the victim of cheating. Boys opened their cribs under the desk while he walked solemnly up and down gazing ruminatively from time to time at the cricket field and announcing the score himself. But should he leave the room placing one of us in charge, the cribs would immediately vanish. It was all right to cheat when Bumpy was there but not when he was absent. His benign laxity bred inevitable skylarking and at a certain point, which none of us ever quite knew, Bumpy would suddenly turn from the dear old tweedy Scottish ghillie into a slightly less formidable version of Old Bill himself. We would be treated to a sermon: we were unworthy to be sent to such a great school; we were unworthy of him; we were unworthy of our parents, of God. In the ensuing silence the class crawled back to work.

The layer of hard-headed flexible discipline which these two men and their staff imposed upon us bore fruit both in the examination room and in public life though perhaps not quite so often on the playing field. For though we sang *Forty Years On* and made it our own (as we thought), and though we translated the *Eton Boating Song* for the benefit of boat races which took place in the autumn and with a southerly instead of a hay harvest breeze, we remained essentially Scots and Presbyterian in outlook. That is, we were, and realized that we were, puritans: the flesh pots of Melbourne Grammar were not for us. Because of this sense of dedication, the interminable round of drudgery to which we were subjected was very cheerfully borne by all concerned.

Good Old Scotch, We'll Ever Sing

Within a month of the beginning of each term came an examination known as the First Minor. This was followed a month later by the Second Minor and at the end of the term by the Terminal. Since each year had three terms this meant nine thorough-going exams for each boy in the school each year. On top of this Old Bill would 'spring a test' on us if he thought that the school was lax or behind-hand in any particular aspect of the work. Sitting quietly at our desks we would suddenly be told that we were going to have a test on spelling, or on the 'arrow method' of simple proportion, or on theorem twenty-nine. These tests were conducted with frenzied fanaticism, often spurred on by the presence of Old Bill himself who would descend on a classroom and stand in a corner, thus injecting a strongly competitive air into the proceedings. Yet few complained of there being too many exams or that we were always working, and I think the reason for this was that the puritanical attitude of rewards and punishments was so deeply ingrained in us that it was felt to be a really shameful thing for a boy to loaf or to fail to do his best. There were dunderheads and dumb bells, this was understood; but for the loafer there was no place at Scotch.

* * *

Workhorse teacher and jack of all trades was V. R. Hill. He was that most generalized of a much harassed profession, the form master who is everything by turns and nothing long. Yet after school he blossomed in the most unexpected way, for he was ex-officio president of the Dramatic Society and the producer each year of The School Play. I first encountered Hill in this guise at a reading for parts in Ian Hay's *Tilly of Bloomsbury*, a hoary, class-conscious, Barrie-esque excursion into kind hearts and coronets, simple faith and Norman blood, which didn't then seem quite as silly as it does now. Because my voice had not yet broken and my accent was thought to be vaguely snooty, I secured the part of Lady Marian Mainwaring, the heroine's mother. I was very proud that my 'side' was the third longest, though in school plays the grandeur of the parts conflicted sharply with the exigencies of school life. I was thirteen and my 'husband' the Hon. Abel Mainwaring was in real life a prematurely elderly footballer of nineteen. In Mother's cast-off clothes and with a pair of lorgnettes, my face covered in Number Five grease paint and my arms with Chinese white, I was supposed to terrify this craven fellow on stage with a freezing hauteur. 'That will do Abel' and 'Come Abel' were the most frequent expressions Lady Mainwaring used. But off stage

The Road to Gundagai

I was just a cheeky fourth former and my 'husband' often used to kick my rump in the wings, much to the annoyance of Hill who, though he recognized that our effort was amateur, did not want it to become amateurish by the projection of off-stage noises into the pit.

The comic lead was taken by the vice-captain of the school, the scion of a big Sydney wool firm. His part, that of a comic butler named Stillbottle was, God knows, hammy enough, but Carson managed to ham it up a good deal further. He was furious if, often through sheer stupidity or inattention, I upstaged him or masked him from the audience, particularly when he was inserting into the body of the play one of his many bits of 'business' unauthorized by Hill. I was the one who got my ears boxed then, but fortunately my 'daughter' was of roughly my own vintage and came to my rescue by tripping up Stillbottle as he emerged from the stage when the curtain fell.

The September tour was the high spot of the Dramatic Society's year and many boys used to try to get into the cast of the school play simply to go on the tour. During term time rehearsals necessarily took place after school and there was considerable annoyance among masters at the extent to which 'being in the play' interfered with normal work. In the September holidays all this was cast to the winds. With Hill in charge, accompanied for the occasion by Mrs. Hill, a good natured blonde who helped with the make-up and costumes back stage, we would pick up, provided they were willing to pay their own fares, a couple of extra senior boys to act as property and business managers, and off we went in a special coach of the Victorian Railways.

With *Tilly* we travelled through the Western District going first to Warrnambool and then on to Portland, and returning by the health resort of Daylesford and the gold mining city of Bendigo. The skylarking of the train journeys in which we sometimes spent a whole day trundling gently across the melodious countryside was followed by a late arrival in the town where we were to play. We were billeted among the local townsfolk, usually two boys to a home through the courtesy of the local Presbyterian Church, to whose charity Hill had already promised the box office receipts. Together with a pass on the railways this meant a free holiday for Mr. and Mrs. Hill and the cast. On entering the small town we would first inspect the theatre. This was usually a parish hall or an abandoned silent movie house. Being by now sophisticates of the Melbourne theatre we were able to smile with good natured tolerance at the primitive arrangements made for our reception. We would smirk deprecatingly as we accommodated ourselves to

Good Old Scotch, We'll Ever Sing

a too shallow apron or found that the 'flats' that we had brought with us were too high to go under the top lights. But these difficulties were soon forgotten in the excitement of the play itself and the kindliness of the townsfolk who clutched the little metropolitan darlings to their varied bosoms.

En route we stayed overnight in a hotel in Ballarat, the fabulous centre of the great 1851 gold rush. None of us had ever stayed in a hotel before and were deeply impressed by this provincial caravanserai with its battered verandahs, its sagging corridors, its rancid brown linoleum and its mangy green plush curtains in bedrooms with four boys to a room. Edna Thomas, the American singer of Negro 'spirituals', was touring Victoria at the time and was spending the night in our Ballarat hotel. She asked some of us into her suite and gave us Kola beer and sandwiches while we listened to her sing *Swing Low Sweet Chariot*, *Nobody Knows but Jesus*, and *Was You There When They Crucified My Lord?* The pulsing throb of her deep contralto suggested disturbing worlds far beyond our own, and after Edna Thomas, the Daylesford spa was something of a let-down, particularly as its waters far from cleansing our stomachs and aiding our digestion, tended to make us sickly. We roared on to Bendigo by the only double track railroad in the State and gave two tremendous performances 'to packed houses' in a goldmining town where headframes still lifted their shoulders among the gravel-tailings on the city's edge.

After such a tour and the ebullition and fussing which it produced, we were much above ourselves when it was time to return to school. Boys in 'The Play' always needed to be cut down to size when they returned from tour, or 'rendered down' as one master put it. We were the object of finger-wagging lectures on buckling down to the stern tasks of life: exams were ahead, we should remember; much was expected of us etc. But there were just as many boys anxious to go along with Hill when next year's play came around. It was a lugubrious American farce called *A Pair of Sixes* based on a poker game in which two partners in an advertising agency agree that one shall become the other's servant for a month according to the draw of the cards. The dialogue, even in the Twenties and even to those of us who had to utter it, was appallingly vapid, and the play depended for its punch on being able to deliver the clinch lines in a rich American accent. Hill's notion of an American accent was of the 'Waal, I kinda sorta guess and calkerlate' variety. The audience being as ignorant as ourselves, the farce was a great success and off we went on another tour.

This time a tremendous treat; across the border into New South Wales. Albury, the border city, is technically in New South Wales

The Road to Gundagai

but the Riverina was always regarded as *terra irridenta* by Victorians. We visited the Hume Weir, then in course of construction, and descended into Ned Kelly country, playing Wangaratta. We saw the site of the famous Glenrowan hotel in which the Kelly gang sheltered and which was eventually burned over their heads while Ned and Dan walked away in their suits of armour made from plough shares. We played Beechworth where the Kellys languished briefly in gaol. There was a surprise performance at the Mount Buffalo Chalet. This was a ski lodge run by the Victorian Railways above the five thousand foot level, which for Australia is pretty high. We were transported in stage-coaches from the Ovens Valley up steep gullies into clefts in the great escarpment and then—snow! Not a few dirty sugary granules but acres and acres of it, and the road snaking between tall markers to indicate its whereabouts in a blizzard. A log shelter with roaring fires, a performance of *A Pair of Sixes* in the lounge using as our stage the bandstand where normally Joe Rivers and his Hot Five gave out, followed by bed in dormitories and next morning snowballing with the girls from *Fintona*.

This was an unexpected bonus. We used to engage the girls from *Fintona* in staid debate once a year, usually on some hoary subject such as 'Resolved: that this house views the current American experiment of prohibition with disfavour' (as if *that* isn't a loaded question). I was inhibited in this scampering with the *Fintona* ladies at Mount Buffalo because although my voice was starting to break I was still playing a woman's part. I was in fact Nellie Nettleton, wife of George B. Nettleton, one of the partners in this unlikely firm (the other was T. Boggs Johns) but was delighted and abashed when one of the girls complimented me on my eyebrows—both as a male and as a female. The rest of the tour was an anti-climax, ending again in Bendigo which, as we had played it the year before, we treated with a blasé indifference and therefore put on a lousy performance. However, the local Presbyterian Church cleared £70 and all was well.

As a result of being in the play I failed my year. With much regret Dad forbade me to enter any of the readings for next year's play. Stage struck, I mooned around as a supernumerary back-stage, hoping that a flat would fall on some member of the cast and that I'd be asked at the last minute to take his place. However the enforced abstinence enabled the time of the breaking voice to be filled with work, and the following year I was able to take a male part.

At this time came the discovery by 'Froggy' Orton, the music master, that my newly dropped voice was of great power. A

Good Old Scotch, We'll Ever Sing

colleague and I were therefore asked to sing, in unison but in duet, the part of Sir Joseph Porter, K.C.B., at the annual Foundation Day concert. Even as Hill came into his own through the School Play, so Froggy Orton dominated the weeks leading up to the Foundation Day concert. This took place in the large auditorium in the Melbourne Town Hall and was designed to commemorate the anniversary of the foundation of Scotch College in October 1851. Normally Froggy would be seen only by his own class or at morning chapel when he played the piano for the School Hymn. His slapdash attack on the 'vamp till ready' which precedes the singing of a hymn shocked us a good deal. It seemed that in banging a series of common chords in C Major up the whole length of the piano before giving us 'the note' Froggy was just never able to hit it right. But, put a baton in his hand and give him a chorus of eight hundred boys singing in unison, and he was a different man.

His selection of songs was a curious pot-pourri of pre-war music-hall items and genteel songs of the Edwardian era, of the kind either sung by young ladies at Church socials or more often played by half hearted trios in the tea room at the end of Brighton pier. His programme leaned heavily on the works of Alfred Ketelby and Easthope Martin. We rehearsed at length and bellowed out in full throated brazen zeal such nondescript items as *The Sword of Ferrara*, *Comrades in Arms* and *Heigh-Ho Come to the Fair* as well as the usual school songs. Of these undoubtedly the most lugubrious, was the School Anthem *Hail Thou Best of Schools and Dearest*, which managed to combine the melancholy of evangelical hymnology with the lack of distinction which normally attends amateur composition. We sang it as a duty and never felt we could put our hearts into it as we could into the boat race song, to the tune of *On the Mississippi*, rip-roaring ragtime of the best early Twenties which had us bellowing at the tops of our voices.

The best of all songs was not ours at all, but one which we borrowed unashamedly and with full acknowledgement, from Harrow: *Forty Years On*. It is one of the great communal songs: part hymn, part battle cry, part poetic dedication. It has the magic ability to make a boy, as he sings it, believe implicitly that he *will* be 'shorter in wind as in memory long, twenty and thirty and forty years on'; and with the passing years the song manages to appeal specifically to each particular decade. Certainly I have found it as pleasant, as stirring, as nostalgic a song to sing in my fifties as in my forties, thirties, twenties or teens. Dressed in our best blue serge-suits with our cardinal-gold-and-blue ties knotted as well as may be, we stood eight hundred strong on the platform at the

The Road to Gundagai

Melbourne Town Hall, with the great organ pipes rising like a brassy forest behind us and roared our hearts out to two-thousand parents and friends gathered adoringly in the concourse below.

Froggy Orton was also responsible for the choice of hymns at chapel. He accompanied them in his usual slapdash manner giving the impression that his hands were hinged at the wrist: but he was not responsible for the content of the hymns themselves. These came from the Australian Presbyterian School Hymnal and they were a powerful battery of mid-nineteenth century evangelical fervour and stomping christianity. Though we occasionally borrowed a hymn from the C of E Hymns Ancient and Modern (for example, *Oh Worship the King* and *Angel Voices Ever Singing*) this was rarely necessary because Anglican hymns of the revivalist period and the Evangelical Movement were themselves included in the Presbyterian Hymnal, and the names of John Henry Newman, Henry Francis Lyte and Montague Augustus Toplady were well known to us all. There were two types of evangelical hymns, the first that of muscle-flexing derring-do as exemplified by *Onward Christian Soldiers, Fight the Good Fight,* and *Stand Up, Stand Up for Jesus*. The second type was the salvation-through-self-abasement exemplified by *What a Friend we Have in Jesus, Lead Kindly Light,* and *Abide With Me*. But all shared a common belief that God was somehow at the head of an army and that if one could only see Him, He would beckon one forward to an arduous but rewarding future.

The presence of Old Bill's Jupiter-Jehovah and the sense of puritanical guilt which hung over us, nevertheless had its limits. A wowser diet for boys with sunny dispositions and scampering feet had to coincide with the more pleasing reality. Thus, when the hell-fire breathing Rev. A. R. Uren came to address the school on 'The Modern Babylon' we considered his language excessive, though his cadences remain with me still.

'None other than a pathological optimist,' said Rev. A. R. Uren, 'can contemplate with equanimity the inebriated rhythms of the jazz orchestra. They are an index of the aesthetic degredation and spiritual poverty to which the age has sunk . . . luxurious courtesans and licentious libertines. . . . Milton received five pounds for "Paradise Lost" from a grateful world which pays George Robey, a London comedian, five hundred pounds a week. . . .' In the true old fashioned Wee Free hot-gospelling tradition, he ladled out the brimstone while the boys seated below lapped up the drama. Rev. A. R. Uren's sermon was subsequently reprinted in the school magazine, where its polysyllabic anger was read anew, and for many weeks boys could be heard yelling at each other, 'You luxurious courtesan!' 'You licentious libertine!'

What a relief it was to escape from chapel and Rev. A. R. Uren to the gymnasium and Petty Officer Tierney. He put us over the horse and through the ropes and endeared himself to us by a discipline which was as lax outside P.T. hours as it was formidable when we were on the bars. He used to whack boys' bottoms as they sailed over the horse or urge them up the rope with a little skilful goosing, but after P.T. they were allowed to use the gymnasium for roller skating, for improvised jazz combos and even for playing darts, until the noise became too uproarious, at which point Tierney would emerge from his little room in his P.T. shirt and, shaking his head sorrowfully, deliver himself of the following invariable rubric:

'I let you boys into the gymernasium and what do you do? You abooze the privilege. Same old think, yer know, familaarity breeds contemp'.'

The contrast between Tierney at work and Tierney coming to work was always piquant. He lived far on the other side of town and no one would have recognized the man in the blue serge suit with the tall celluloid collar and the crushed brown fedora neatly perched on the crown of his head as the ogre of the gymnasium with his harsh Petty Officer's comments punctuated by the blast of a whistle. On sports days Tierney was a guest and sat with the masters. Not exactly an honoured guest; he was somewhat below the salt. It was conceded by the masters that he ranked above Mr. Wood, the gardener, with Bob Horne, the groundsman, but below benevolent uncles.

My particular benevolent uncle was George L. Dickson, a well-to-do squatter who had a station near Mount Gambier across the border in South Australia and who for unknown reasons befriended my brother and myself when he was in his sixties and we were not yet in our teens. I was told with melancholy certitude by a man whose age lay midway between Mr. Dickson's and mine that as soon as my voice began to change he would desert me. I disbelieved this passionately, but in the end that was exactly what happened. George Dickson's favoured boys were those between eight and twelve and for them he created a perpetual fairyland in which he and we were contemporaries embarked on devilish Jekyll-and-Hyde escapades. He had a mansion in Toorak with a garden of several acres where one could imagine oneself lost in deep country. The house, lurking behind a high impenetrable board fence, was named *The Moorings* in recognition of the Dicksons' determination to stay put after they had travelled twice round the

The Road to Gundagai

world immediately prior to World War I. 'Dicky', as his wife called him, who would greet us in his sixty-fifth year by sliding down the banisters from the top floor and then suggest that we should go out in the car and visit Luna Park, knew exactly what boys of that age want, which is to do what is forbidden in an innocently circumscribed field of activities. He drove us down to Geelong for boat race day in his open Overland and Scotch was Head of the River on the Barwon. He took us to cricket matches and on one occasion to The Wattle Cafe where we all ate ice cream until our heads ached. His interest in me dropped abruptly as I moved into the teens and I have a later vision of George Dickson as I offered my arm to help him across the Sydney Road near the University where I was to entertain him to tea in my digs, and he testily shook his arm free and grumbled, 'I can cross myself.' Crabbed age and youth may not usually be able to live together, but if they are far enough apart they sometimes can. Part of the secret in this case was that Dickson was a Scotch Old Boy. Good old Scotch we'll ever sing!

Chapter Seven

THE EMIGRANT VESSEL

Port Melbourne saw the big ocean liners, but the real hive of activity lay in the heart of the city around the docks artificially created by widening and deepening the Yarra as it swung in a curve towards The Bay. Here about five miles from the river's mouth, at the head of the Coode Canal, bristled a great jumble of coasters, freighters, dredgers, sailboats and tugs, and a dockside heavy with the roar of straining trucks and the clatter of iron rimmed drays over the cobbles.

We used to visit the docks after school. This was strictly forbidden as it meant passing through the centre of the city on a bicycle. But traffic at four in the afternoon was not heavy and in those still largely horse-drawn days sufficiently sedate for safe manoeuvre by a schoolboy and his wheel. Along Flinders Street the forest of masts and funnels pricked at the sky ahead and over the drone of traffic came the hoarse bray of a siren. It had been raining and Flinders Street was splotched with rainbow petrol puddles and steaming piles of wet horse manure. Beside the long curving viaduct that carried the railway from Flinders Street (City and Suburban) to Spencer Street (Country Lines) and beneath which nestled the shops of brokers and ship chandlers, the roadman plied his brush and pan. His humble but essential job was to clean up the droppings from the big drays and waggons that rumbled to and from the docks. He and his kind were known, with apposite Australian wit, as 'sparrer starvers'. Beyond him rose two conical lead-roofed towers with weather vanes; at this point a wide brick arch led to the dock area proper. Here was Melbourne's aorta, the great pump that fed in the goods from overseas and to which clung one end of the umbilical love-hate lifeline that tied Melbourne to The Mother Country. Here were the big mortgage and stock-and-station houses where wool was finally baled and cleaned for export; Dalgety, Elder Smith and Goldsbrough, Mort. They showed long solid bluestone façades to the docks, broken by severe windows arched in brick.

The Road to Gundagai

The docks themselves were a wonderful litter of bales and crates among which the 'wharfies' moved with lazy loose-limbed nonchalance like bronzed giants in the sun: blue dungarees, grey flannel singlets edged with navy cotton tape and big wideawake hats, bashed-in, stained and noble. The papers said they were always striking, or on the point of striking, and they certainly moved in their own good time. But there were no electrically driven fork lifts in those days and to our admiring eyes the sinewy giants earned every penny they made. From the derricks of blackened freighters great hooks came hurtling earthward.

'Outa the way, Snowy!'

We leaped nimbly backward and deft sinewy hands looped four rope nooses over the dangling hook. The foreman spread his arms wide and whistled through his teeth. The man at the donkey engine on the freighter's deck engaged his lever with a jerk, the engine rolled and the great load of wool—scoured, pressed, baled, wrapped and bound in springy steel tape—soared majestically aloft, missed the ship's side by a hairsbreadth, paused, poised above our heads, swung inboard and dropped like a stone into the hold below.

We wandered bemused among the wealth of Ormuz and of Ind, among all the goods and goodies that spoke of the outside world: sacks of bagged wheat from the Mallee and the Wimmera manhandled to the derrick cradle by muscly wharfies; mutton and lamb carcases tightly shrouded in cheesecloth ready for the chilling chambers of the big freighters; crates of peaches and boxes of apricots from the Goulburn Valley; tottering skyscrapers of canned fruit bound for Britain; Massey-Harris tractors and binders to compete with our own McKay's from Sunshine (thirty years later they amalgamated); crated automobiles from Britain and single cars, pasted over with stripping tape, cradled down at the end of a boom and a hawser to land smack on the dock; bales of newsprint from Canada and Scandinavia, looking like giant rolls of towel paper. The customs man in shirt sleeves and peaked cap moved slowly around checking inventories; and the shipper's agent, armed with his stencil, slapped it on the side of crates and bales and punched out mysterious hieroglyphs with his stubby black brush.

Further down the docks the small inter-state vessels bound for Tasmania or for Adelaide and Perth were taking on passengers, and already a shroud of paper streamers stretched from deck to dock, gripped in the cheerful or tearful hands of departing friends and those who would be left behind. As the ship cast off and slowly backed away from the dock the streamers tautened, tightened and finally snapped, the remnants curling disconsolately away to fall into the widening river of bilgey water between the ship and the

The Emigrant Vessel

dock. A few bold or frantic passengers would hurl fresh streamers towards the shore in a last attempt at contact. Some landed in the water to the disappointed ohs and ahs of the crowd. Others, better aimed, hit the dock, to be grasped by eager hands which paid them rippling out until they too snapped at their utmost extremity and fell into the water.

The sight never failed to move me, and it still does. Is there anywhere else, apart from Australia and New Zealand, where this strangely haunting rite takes place? In Melbourne, no matter where a ship was bound (unless it was just going 'down the Bay' to Queenscliff, Portarlington or Geelong) this ceremony was invariably performed. It might be a great P & O or Orient liner bound for Britain or it might be the *Rotomahana* on a night's crossing to Tasmania; but wherever it was bound, friends and relatives and sympathetic idlers and onlookers lined the docks. The streamer boys passed through the crowd selling their circular packets of nostalgia and heartache at threepence a time. Those on the dock hurled their little rockets of love up to eager fingers at the rail, and those at the rail threw down little coloured bombs of affection to grasping hands on shore. Pretty soon there would be a solid awning of coloured streamers stretching from deck to dock, and then the slow agonising parting, the literal parting of linking strands while the band *Aloha* or *Now is the Time* or *Australia Will Be There*. It was terribly sad but very exciting and we often used to bicycle down to the docks, or even to Port Melbourne, just to see a ship sail, and hope to grab somebody's abandoned streamer. Unconsciously I was becoming Australian in the sense that I hoped, when a big ship was sailing, that one day I too would take A Trip Home.

The description of England (it never seemed to be Scotland or Ireland) as Home was not an affectation then, though it was on the way to becoming one. Despite its massive contribution to the Allied war effort in blood and treasure and its seat at the Versailles peace negotiations as a sovereign power, Australia at the end of the First World War was still at heart very much a colonial society; in fact many people would have been affronted by the suggestion that it was anything else. In a country 98.4 per cent British, as the speech makers were always telling us (and to which we replied in ribald chorus, 'Lux! 98 and 44 one hundredths per cent pure and IT FLOATS!') it was natural to think of England as the Mother Country. And in 1920 nearly a quarter of all Australians had been born in The Old Country. Though convict days had been left far, far behind, the era of the Emigrant Ship was still with us. The talk of Home and the ritual of the streamers were both part of its legend. One has perhaps to remember that until the coming of

The Road to Gundagai

steam in the 1850's and, still more, the opening of the Suez Canal in 1869, the voyage by sail to Australia took from three to five months. It was as near to certain as anything could be that those who bade farewell to their loved ones at Gravesend or Plymouth would never see England again. The mixture of quiet desperation and enforced hopefulness has been portrayed forever in Ford Madox Brown's painting 'The Last of England'. Though convictism had been finally abolished in 1852, the Emigrant Ship still meant Transportation for Life. The enormous difference was that it was voluntary; no longer was it a case of

> 'True patriots we for be it understood
> We left our country for our country's good.'

Those who filled the Emigrant Ships did so to escape from the intolerable conditions of the working class in Dickensian England, and to make a new and more spacious life for themselves in the Antipodes. But though they tackled the often grim challenge of their new home with courage and optimism and grew to love it even in its stern or heartbreaking moods, they still longed passionately for the unknown might-have-been Back Home. The ambition of most of my contemporaries was to 'get away' to 'go on a trip' and even if they didn't think of England as Home, or at least didn't speak of it as such, it was always implied that this was what they had in mind. The whole mystique of the life-line to Britain was designed to perpetuate such hopes and to titillate such fancies and expectations.

A tremendous amount of space was given in the press to ships and shipping, and to both shipping and shipboard personalities; and the devotion of this space was justified by an avid readership. If there were a change in sailing schedules, a shortening of the length of the run from Melbourne to Tilbury, the launching of a new ship in far off Barrow-in-Furness or Tynemouth intended for 'the run', it was reported in exhaustive detail. Lists of arrivals and departures and of ships in port were not confined to 'commercial intelligence' but slopped over onto the news pages. The arrival of any ship from overseas was treated as an event, with reporters and photographers at the dockside and a lengthy write-up in the press. The arrival of a new ship on her maiden voyage was a gala occasion with speeches of welcome by the Port Authority and the Lord Mayor, flag-decked approaches to the piers, and crowds of sightseers. When the P & O put their first large ships, in excess of twenty thousand tons, on the Australian run in 1924 we all went down on our bicycles to see them arrive. They were the *Maloja* and the *Mooltan*, long since gone to the knacker's yard, but to us they were adventure and

The Emigrant Vessel

technical wonder rolled up in one. We never got near them in the end, because thousands of others had had the same idea.

The amount of publicity accorded to new arrivals from these ships was quite astounding. Their photographs appeared in the papers with their biographies and itineraries and their views on world problems and of course their opinions of Australia. Needless to say these were invariably uniform and highly laudatory. Those visiting for the first time were always greatly impressed with 'my first views of your magnificent country'; those who made regular visits were always 'delighted to return to this magnificent country and to see the tremendous progress since my last visit'. Returning Australians were invariably 'delighted to be back in Australia' even though they might have scrimped and saved for years to take The Trip. The mere fact that someone, if he was of even marginal importance, had been abroad, or was visiting Australia for the first time, was enough to make his views worth ascertaining and listening to with attention, if not respect.

These perpetual panegyrics reached their gushiest in the social columns of the daily papers and in the pages of the glossy weeklies: the *Bulletin* from Sydney and *Table Talk* from Melbourne. I was enthralled by these inane and ludicrously snobbish jottings, and devoured them eagerly in doctors' and dentists' waiting rooms for, of course, we did not subscribe to them at home, Mother having taken the view that, broadly speaking, nothing worth while ever happened in Melbourne anyway. They were in fact about the only thing that made a visit to the dentist even moderately bearable. Yet the social gossip had a genuine basis in the social structure and, perhaps more important, the social aspirations of the city at that time. We were reminded by politicians and editors, and of course at school, ad nauseam, that Australia 'lives off the sheep's back'. The sheep station owning landed hierarchy—the 'squattocracy' as they were called—were in some ways as true Australians as you could find anywhere: shrewd, outspoken, honourable, coarse-grained, extrovert, great puncturers of humbug and rooters out of cant, with a stylish approach to life and yet a democratic relationship with those whom they employed on their enormous semi-feudal estates. It was they, together with the bankers and a few professional and big business men (mostly importers and those engaged in commerce rather than industry) who set the tone of Melbourne society. Many of the squatters had houses in Melbourne as well as their huge stations, and to these they repaired for Cup Week, to attend the Test Matches between England and Australia and to observe similar rites dear to their class.

Because their links with England, through blood ties, frequent

The Road to Gundagai

visits, and the marketing of their wool were so strong and deep, and because, though Australian to the core, their standards of excellence in the things they valued most—good horses and horsemanship, good equipment and clothing, stylish education for their sons, dresses and manners for their daughters—*were* English, they gave an additional weighty cachet to English mores, English ideas and English trends. Society in general followed suit. What people like the Manifolds or the Fairbairns thought about things was important; because although they would see them through squatters' eyes, their immense substance gave their views both a weight and a laconic detachment. Thus the shipping lanes and the shipping lines were invested with an additional glamour, and the strands of parting streamers were identified with the whole community. It was a rite in which the people as a whole took part and in which they found deep, if unacknowledged, satisfaction.

* * *

Our periodic visits to the docks were varied by two awesome naval occasions, the cruise of H.M.S. *Hood* and H.M.S. *Repulse* and the goodwill visit of the American Fleet. *Hood* was the largest ship we had ever seen and overwhelmed us by her grey majesty. She towered over the Port Melbourne pier like an iron cliff, and made even *Repulse*, sister ship to *Renown* and not much more than half *Hood's* size, look modest in comparison. The school received a half holiday to visit these two battleships (more properly battle cruiser in the case of *Hood*) and polite bluejackets escorted us over *Hood* and answered our endless and pointless questions with goodnatured patience. The most dramatic part of the tour was a visit to one of the forward turrets and a demonstration of the loading (with blank ammunition) aiming and firing of the fifteen inch guns. The shell carrier burst up from the belly of the ship like a surfacing submarine with a brazen clang of metal on metal. A giant rod appeared from beneath our feet and rammed the shell home; the huge breech locked tight with a clattering metal-fingered finality, and all the time the enormous turret (with us inside it!) pivoted slowly with smooth and oily precision on its axis, while the triple tier of big guns probed at the sky as if sniffing for their prey, and quiet crisp voices gave monotonous unhurried commands. When *Hood* was tragically destroyed seventeen years later while hunting *Bismarck* it was the inside of that great turret that focussed sharply in memory.

If the visit of *Hood* and *Repulse* struck us as noble and majestic and filled us all full of Empire sentiment, the goodwill visit of the

The Emigrant Vessel

American Fleet was more lighthearted and in some ways more enjoyable. These were foreigners; foreigners with a difference of course, but we didn't feel the same awe and the necessity to be on good behaviour (arms at the sides, thumb along the trouser seam) as we had felt with the British. This was no doubt due to the carefree, friendly attitude of the Americans themselves who seemed to gangle and sprawl nonchalantly over their ships with the lithe grace of panthers on the prowl. The British had seemed more like the bulldogs they are supposed to be.

The flagship of the Fleet was U.S.S. *Seattle*, an object of puzzled and slightly contemptuous wonder because of her twin lattice masts. The virtues of this ungainly erection were hotly debated at school. 'It's a soda of a target. The enemy couldn't miss.' 'Yeah, but if a British mast was shot away the ship couldn't function; with these masts, even a big hit would still leave part of the mast.' *Seattle* was under the command of Admiral Coontz whose name was at once punned and malformed into a variety of ribald limericks and pithy apophthegms by the ingenious Australians. Mother had an introduction to Rear Admiral Magruder so we were all bidden to tea with him in his cabin in U.S.S. *Richmond* and afterwards shown over the ship, a ten thousand ton cruiser. The splendour and opulence of the Admiral's stateroom were awesome compared with the more spartan quarters of the British: soft landlubber armchairs and sofas, a big leather-topped desk, a thick wine carpet on the floor and to cap it all, tea served from a silver tea tray and teaset by a deferential negro orderly in a white mess jacket. I began to make snobbish comparisons in my mind between Persian voluptuaries and disciplined Greek athletes. But at this moment came a new sensation —hot buttered cinnamon toast—and the enraptured thralldom of taste buds produced in a flash a violent affection for America and the American way of life.

Afterwards a seaman was detailed to take us over the ship. The armament, the engines and even the bridge did not strike with overwhelming force; indeed how could they, after visiting *Hood*? But undoubtedly impressive was the way doors opened and seamen stood aside each time our guide intoned, 'Admiral's guest.' Only once did this open sesame fail. We paused at the top of a vertical iron ladder and began to descend into a lower deck where groups of sailors lay about taking their ease in the afternoon sun. Many of them had only their pants on; someone was playing a ukelele and a crap game was in progress. As we descended a voice called out.

'Hey, Cottrell, what's the big idea comin' down here?'

'Admiral's guest,' replied the guide imperturbably.

The Road to Gundagai

But the sailor below was rightly affronted at the prospect of a twelve-year-old boy invading his privacy.

'Well he can't come down here.'

'I told ya, he's the Admiral's guest,' repeated the guide.

'I don't give a goddam about the Admiral's guest,' cried the exasperated sailor. 'He ain't comin' down here.'

Our guide accepted the rebuff philosophically. 'Guess we'd better get round another way, buddy.' I was so enthralled at the whole performance that I quite forgot to be affronted—on behalf of the Admiral, of course.

The free-wheeling behaviour of the gobs in Melbourne streets as well as the inevitable pubside kerb arguments as to 'who won the war' degenerated at one point into a series of brawls which threatened momentarily to defeat the object of the visit. Beer-happy ex-diggers chanted, in parody of George M. Cohan's *Over There*:

> 'The Yanks are running, the Yanks are running
> And they won't get there till it's over, Over There.'

And of course there were the usual scraps over girls. The exploits of the visiting gobs—to be repeated on an even more Homeric scale seventeen years later after Bataan and Corregidor—became the subject of a Tin Pan Alley hit, of which the following poignant lines remain in memory:

> 'She was just a sailor's sweetheart,
>   he was just a sailor lad
> But he left her broke in Aussie;
>   he was all she ever had.'

But P.R.O.'s were active even in those far-off days, and emollient statements soon oozed from the highest official sources on both the Australian and American sides. The *Herald* (read by 186,713 people daily) was able to headline triumphantly, FLEET CANARD SCOTCHED.

'Mother, what's a canard?'

'French for duck.'

'Yes, but what's a Fleet Canard?'

'You mean Cunard, the Cunard Fleet? You must have misread it.'

'No Mother it's Fleet Canard.'

'Well I don't know, a fast duck, I suppose. Show me. Oh that! Well it means a rumour.'

'It means, the rumour's wrong?'

'That's right.'

Chapter Eight

POLICEMEN AND LEPERS

After the Fleet's departure, complete with coloured streamers and shrieking girls, came a passion for speleology. My companion on these expeditions was a tough resourceful fellow called Tiger Webb, later a first class oarsman.

Gardiner's Creek was a sluggish, muddy tributary which flowed into the Yarra at the boundary of our school. If you followed Gardiner's Creek about a mile upstream you came to an immense maroon-painted gasholder and immediately opposite this the creek bank was broken by the outfall of three large storm drains. These openings were circular in form, lined with brick and on the afternoon when we first saw them, had only a small trickle of water showing. We sniffed gingerly at the entrance. They smelled clean and Tiger suggested we should explore them. One of them, which was particularly large, could be explored on a bicycle. As this would take planning we agreed to postpone the exploration until the next day. I filled and tested the carbide lamp, and my satchel of books next day included a candle and a couple of boxes of matches and, remembering Theseus and the Minotaur, a ball of string and a five hundred foot fishing line.

We decided to tackle the large drain first and with Tiger on the bar we pushed off into the circular gloom. The bike proved a mistake; we were crouched too low to get a good purchase and about a hundred and fifty feet in we came to a ledge two feet high and an underground waterfall. We decided to abandon the bike and go forward on foot. Our progress was slow because we had to straddle the small stream of water as we walked; but our lamp sent a bright white light on the brick tunnel ahead. Sometimes its walls glistened with slime but mostly we were glad to notice that they were dry. We seemed to be climbing. We ascended perhaps a dozen ledges and from time to time underground tributaries joined us from smaller tunnels. The air seemed to get hotter and stuffy. I began to think we'd gone far enough when there came a faint rumble. We

The Road to Gundagai

crouched tense in the ill-lit pit as the rumble mounted to a low roar.

'It's the water,' I cried.

'Jesus!' said Tiger.

The roar mounted. We were petrified, expecting at any moment to see a wall of sewage rushing towards us. We would be engulfed. Sorrowing parents. RIP. The roar changed pitch and began to sound like a distant train. Gradually, while we stood rigid, expecting instant annihilation, it died away. Tiger slapped the tunnel brickwork with the flat of his hand. It reverberated uncertainly.

'Got it!' he said. 'A tram.'

We trudged onward for another five minutes and then the tunnel unexpectedly widened and we were at a broad underground junction with vertical cement walls up which ran iron handholds. Another tram went by with a tremendous roar; it sounded as if it were coming right down the tunnel after us. We looked up and saw light far above.

'Tiger, we're under a manhole!'

I clambered upward for about twelve feet and found myself peering through a grille at street level, like Orson Welles in *The Third Man*. It took me a while to get my bearings; then I saw a tram-stop and a grocery store and it dawned on me that we were underneath one of the main intersections in the suburb of Malvern. I had a foreshortened view of a man walking slowly by. On an impulse, deepening my voice as much as I could, I shouted: 'Hey, what's the big idea?' The man stopped abruptly and looked mystified. 'Yes you!' I shouted again. 'Jay walking.' The man walked perplexedly on. I broke the joyful news to Tiger who swiftly joined me at our ringside seat. There, clinging with crooked elbows to the iron stanchion, our faces three inches below the street, we amused ourselves for some time shouting imbecilities at the puzzled public, fancying ourselves to be undetected.

Eventually the sport palled. Our sides aching with laughter, we descended to the junction and began the long underground walk back to Gardiner's Creek. We were disturbed to find that it was almost supper time. We hurried on but it seemed to take much longer than on the road in. Eventually we reached the final ledge and waterfall.

'Where's the grid?'

'My bike!'

'Yeah, the old mangle; isn't this where we left it?'

My heart sank. 'Maybe there's another ledge,' I said. Tiger shook his head gloomily. 'It's gone.' He was right, for within a few moments we turned the last curve and saw the round O of fading daylight ahead. We came out onto the muddy banks of Gardiner's Creek. Tiger said morosely, 'Well, I wonder who did that.'

'I wonder,' said a sharp voice. We jumped. A police constable stared at us from his vantage point on a table of rock. Behind him leaning against a gorse bush was my bicycle.

'You the lads making a nuisance of yourselves up at the High Street corner this arvo? Come on, don't look innocent. You were down the manhole.'

We agreed; we felt pretty windy. The constable took out his wallet.

'Jakeloo! Let's have the names then, *and* the addresses.' We gave them sullenly and almost inarticulately. 'Come on, son, speak up.'

When he'd written them down he said, 'I could give you boys in charge.'

'It was just for a bit of fun, sir.'

'Don't "sir" me,' said the cop irritably. 'It may be fun to you but what's fun for you can be bloody annoying to other people. What were you doing there in the first place?'

We told him. 'Exploring eh? You know one good rainstorm would've washed you, and your bike all the way down to Port Melbourne?'

'We thought it would be kind of an adventure.'

'Adventure!' said the cop with withering contempt. It's just plain dense! Now take your bike. Go on! Take it! I'm not giving you lads in charge this time. I'm just giving each of you a good roost in the tail to teach you some sense.' He did so with a well placed boot. We stood rubbing our bottoms. 'But the next time . . .' He wagged a warning finger. 'Now cut along home and hope yer Mum don't bawl you out for being late for tea.'

We were off like the wind and the constable, who had earned himself the title of 'The Friendly John Hop' for life went back to the station. We decided we were going to give up drains anyway, because Tiger wanted me to help him finance and build a canoe. He planned to construct it in his father's garage from a pioneer do-it-yourself instruction kit in *Pals*, the boys' weekly newspaper to which we both subscribed. I weighed in with the contents of my money box—3/11½d—and we started work with a will. This could be real he-man adventure stuff; no more childish business of walking down drains.

We set up a workbench in the Webb garage and for about two weeks progress was brisk. We bought three square yards of canvas, waterproofed it, painted it grey and cut out the 'pattern' according to instructions, for the bow section. We procured a willow sapling for the keel and left it, nicely oiled and polished to 'mature' in the

The Road to Gundagai

garage. We also bought about a third of the red gum slats for the ribs, planning to screw them into the keel with copper screws and later bend them to fit slots in the two gunwales. We started in the middle because, according to the plan, the bending would be simpler and more gradual. At this point the money ran out. Tiger appealed to his father who donated ten shillings; I borrowed half a crown from my brother. But this didn't get us very far. The nights were beginning to close in, there was less time to work after school, and Tiger had been selected for the House football team. But what really brought our work to a complete standstill was the discovery that in order to bend the ribs, especially those further away from the centre of the canoe, we would require a rather more elaborate and costly apparatus than our finances would permit; to be precise, a steam box. We tried to construct one of packing cases, an old soap-making can, and a tube of galvanised iron downpipe which we disconnected from the eavestrough at the rear of the Webb's roof. We erected this Heath Robinson apparatus over a brick incinerator in the back garden and soon it was steaming gaily away. But when we tried to bend the ribs the first two broke and the next bent the down-pipe out of shape. Under Dr. Webb's wrathful supervision we straightened it out and reconnected it to the eavestrough.

'It's no use,' said Tiger. 'We need proper apparatus. If we don't get it we may as well give up.'

I had a brilliant idea. 'How much would it cost?'

'According to this article in *Pals* you could build a really good one for about five quid. But where do we get five quid?'

I tapped him on the shoulder and looked mysterious.

'What's up with you?' he said sourly.

'Give me a week,' I said, 'and I'll get you two.'

'Go on!'

'Could you manage the rest?'

'Where are you going to get the money?'

'Never mind,' I said, 'I'll get it.'

Tiger laughed scornfully. 'Okay,' he said, 'we'll make it a week.' I took Tiger's laughter in good part because of course he didn't know about Doctor Uniapon and the little Leper Box.

* * *

'Boys, I want to introduce you to a great man. Doctor Uniapon is head of the Leper Mission at Yurrabunga in the Northern Territory. He is also one of the First Australians. We who have built a great democracy in this young land of ours are apt to forget that

Policemen and Lepers

his people were here twenty thousand years before we came. . . .'

The Headmaster's introduction droned on, but nobody listened. We were watching Doctor Uniapon with wide-eyed eagerness. He was a dusky Australian Aboriginal perhaps fifty years old, but to us he seemed a patriarch. He stood on the dais beside the Head with his long arms hanging down before him and his sinewy black hands loosely clasped. Six feet high, he towered over the Head and though his form was skeletal, his chest was a solid fortress of bone and gristle across which his coat and shirt stretched tight as parchment. Above the dog collar rose his black face, crowned with a massive aureole of white hair. The squat nose with its gaping septums, the dusted mulberry lips, the coal-black eyes darting in their white saucers: all kept us spellbound.

'Boys, Doctor Uniapon!'

A great wave of applause went on for so long that the Head had to clap his hands for order. Through it all, Doctor Uniapon smiled a grave secret smile and bowed ever so slightly. As the applause died down it blended with a few suppressed giggles which drew from the Head a severe frown. The school wag had surreptitiously circulated a scrap of paper on which was written the witty jingle:

> 'You can't rely upon
> Doctor Uniapon.'

Because of this the speech was punctuated with flurries of unseemly laughter. But those of us who had not been corrupted by the wag's jingle felt the magic of the story. It was a simple tale of grotesque suffering endured by the lepers in his mission, of foul shapes assumed by the disease, and of how the lepers, in the steamy heat of tropical Australia, longed for contact, however tenuous, with the world outside. The dry school assembly hall seemed to deliquesce in monsoon rainclouds. The brick walls dissolved into jungle trees trailing giant creepers, tall pandanus palms fringing sluggish sinister streams, and polygonum swamps over which the long legged jabiroo flew creaking on its way.

The Head thanked Doctor Uniapon who again gave us his secret smile and his slight bow. The applause was not as enthusiastic as at the start, for we detected in the Head's intonation the prospect of an appeal to our pockets. Doctor Uniapon stepped forward, and this time he held in his hands a small wooden box.

'Boys of Scotch College, I can tell by your applause that your generous hearts have been touched by the story of the lepers. It is my humble hope that some of you may be able to show your appreciation in tangible form.'

The Road to Gundagai

('What did I tell you?')

'In my hand I have a small box with a slit in one side of it. If any boy cares to take one of these boxes home, he can fill it with pennies, and I will come to his home to collect it. Believe me, your gift—no matter how small—will help to make the festive season one of joy rather than privation.'

He paused with the box held up in his hand. There was an uncomfortable silence.

'I'm sure there must be some boy who wants to help the lepers.'

But we were thinking of the Easter holidays and of the money saved for our own presents. The Head cleared his throat.

'Come, boys, we're not going to send Doctor Uniapon away empty-handed!'

'Please, sir!'

A surge of heads turned to the speaker. The Head beamed. I was aghast; it was my brother.

'Ah, Thirkell II. Come forward boy! I'm delighted to see that at least one boy is prepared to uphold the honour of the school. And what about you Thirkell I?'

'Please, sir, I . . .'

'Ah well, we must not expect too much from one family. Is anyone else going to follow Thirkell II's example? Ah, Johnson! Well done! Jacobs! McPherson! This is much better! Come forward boys!'

Doctor Uniapon disposed of sixty-four boxes. The Head dismissed us in high fettle, and we poured out into the breathless afternoon.

'What are you going to do with the leper box?' I asked Colin.

'Doctor Uniapon gave me a religious feeling,' he said primly.

He looked at me with great earnestness, and I felt Doctor Uniapon's spell.

'If you give me a shilling I'll cut your share of the lawn on Saturday.'

'You're crazy!'

'If you don't want to help the lepers, you can at least get out of doing some work.'

During the next few weeks the virtues of Doctor Uniapon were extolled so frequently that mention of his name was banned by Mother at meal times. So was mention of leprosy. Colin sent me to the Presbyterian Bookshop and I obtained free copies of Doctor Uniapon's speeches and lectures. In the evening, when we were supposed to be doing our homework, Colin read these aloud to himself, and often invited my opinion as to the truth of the Doctors' statements or the excellence of his prose. He drew pictures of the Doctor in his exercise book; tending the lepers; reading prayers;

ANGELA MCINNES, LONDON 1915
From a charcoal portrait by John S. Sargent

THE EASTERN RANGES &
THE WESTERN DISTRICT

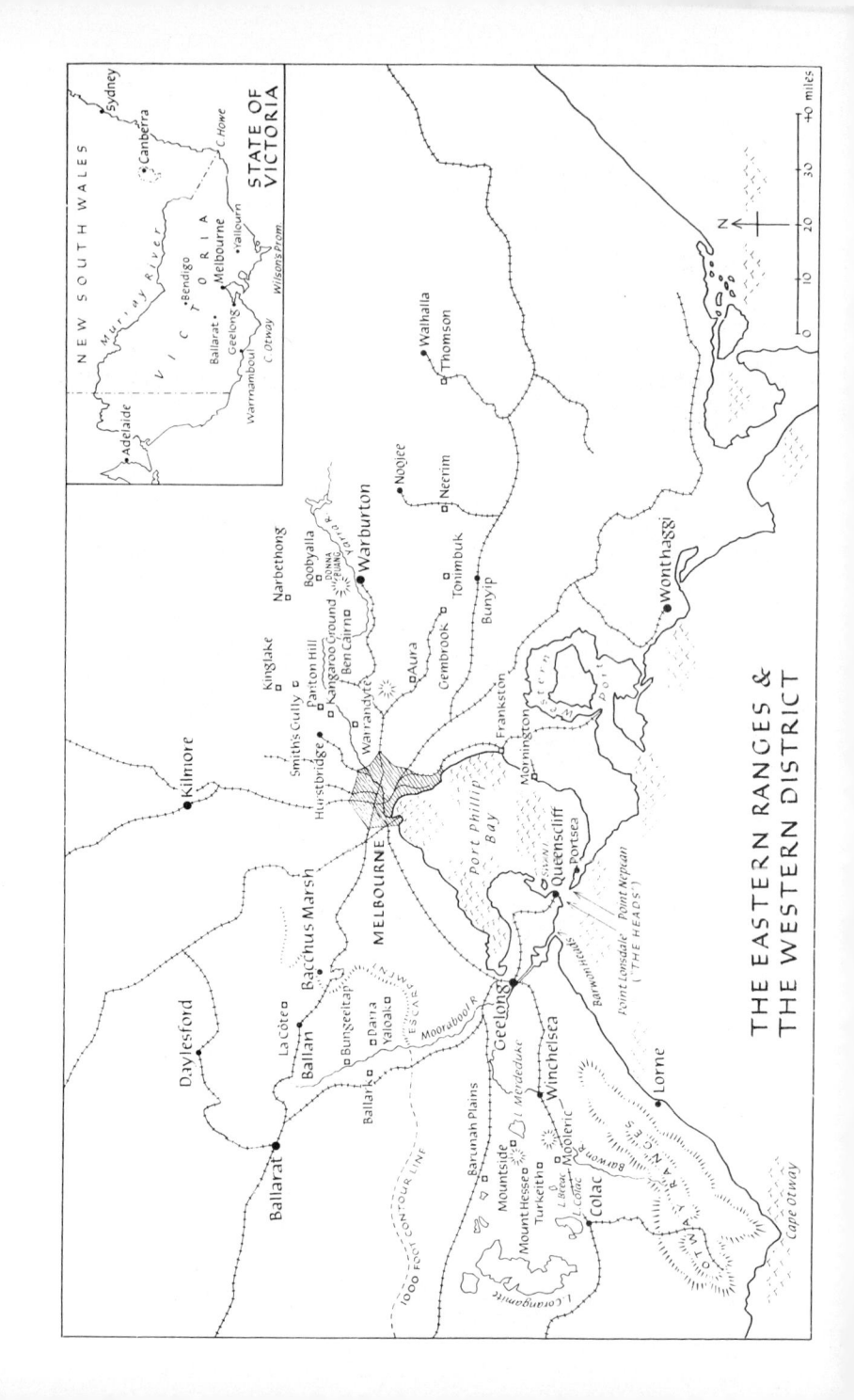

JAMES CAMPBELL MCINNES WITH HIS WIFE AND SONS,
BOURNEMOUTH 1915

THE AUTHOR WITH HIS MATERNAL UNCLE,
DENIS MACKAIL, LONDON 1913

MARGARET MACKAIL (BURNE JONES) WITH HER GRANDSONS,
GRAHAM AND COLIN MCINNES, LONDON 1918

GEORGE THIRKELL WITH GRAHAM AND COLIN MCINNES, SHEFFIELD 1919

FAMILY GROUP, 4 GRACE STREET, 1925

ANGELA THIRKELL, MELBOURNE 1925
From the drawing by Thea Proctor

killing crocodiles in the jungle; sitting outside a tent at dusk and being thanked by God who leaned down from the sky with a rod of fire.

Each evening he weighed the box in his hands and rattled it. On the wall at the head of his bed he kept a tally. Ten days before Easter the box contained one pound five and seven-pence half-penny. I'd even put in sixpence myself, for I'd begun to harbour designs on the box. Tiger and the canoe! I brought the conversation skilfully round to the leper box.

'Would you like a canoe?' I asked Colin.

'I haven't any money.'

'Yes you have.'

'Where?'

'In the leper box.'

Colin's lips tightened and his green eyes looked at me from the depths of a dell of freckles.

'You're very wicked even to think of that. What would Doctor Uniapon say?'

'Suppose we get a few pennies out with a knife, he'd never know.'

'God would.'

'Not if we tell Him about the canoe.'

Colin shook his head. 'I tell you it belongs to Doctor Uniapon!'

'If you let me have a few pennies from the leper box I'll pay you back at Easter.'

'I don't believe you.'

'Cross my heart!'

Colin said reluctantly, 'If you write down that you promise to pay me back . . . I'll think about it.'

That evening after supper I wrote on a piece of paper, to Colin's dictation.

'I hereby promise to pay my brother Colin twopence for every penny which he kindly permits me to have from his leper box.'

Colin examined the document carefully and put it in the top drawer of the bureau in one of his clean shirt pockets. Then he took down the leper box and shook it. It was so full that it hardly rattled. I dashed out to the kitchen and got a knife, but Colin snatched it from me.

'I'll do it, not you!'

He inserted the knife in the slit and played it skilfully. I watched him with eager anxiety; but after struggling for a few minutes he gave up.

'Let's ease off the bottom with the tommy-axe,' I said. 'We could nail it on again and no one would notice.'

'Well, all right, but we must be very careful.'

The Road to Gundagai

I picked up the axe, but Colin stopped me.

'It's my box, I'll do it!'

He put the little leper box on its edge, squinted at the join along the bottom, took careful aim and struck. A shattering split revealed the golden hoard inside and wrecked the box. We looked at each other in dismay. Colin seized the axe, swung it over his head and brought it down with a crash. The leper box smashed into pieces and scores of pennies poured out onto the floor and rolled away under the bureau. Colin threw the tommy-axe into a corner.

'There,' he said, 'that's fixed it!' He started to gather up stray pennies.

'What are you going to do?'

'Spend it.'

'All of it?'

'Yes, all of it.' His face was very red.

The next day we divided the leper loot and went off to school, our pockets heavy with coins. During the morning break Colin paraded to the tuckshop in a hollow square of dancing clamorous boys. His popularity was unbounded for ten minutes, at the end of which time another Maecenas took his place. My share was held in my school kitbag for subsequent handing over to Tiger. That night fears for the future smote my heart.

'What about Doctor Uniapon?' I whispered to Colin.

'No need to worry,' he said calmly. 'I've written him a letter and when he comes to get the box, he'll understand.'

'Did you tell him everything? I mean, the canoe and how we spent the money?'

'Yes, I did. I told him about the other boys too.'

'What other boys?'

'Well some of the other chaps opened their boxes too. But no one's was as full as ours! We really did better than anyone else!'

* * *

We were playing in the garden when Mother called us.

'The man from the leper mission is here.'

'It's Doctor Uniapon!' shouted Colin.

He ran round the corner of the house. I followed to find him staring in unbelief at a white man in a brown suit, an open shirt and a pair of two-toned shoes with very sharp points.

'Well, young fella-me-lad, you'll know me next time. Yurrabunga Leper Mission. Here's my card—Alf Sharp. Now, about that little box of yours.'

'Did Doctor Uniapon send you?'

128

Policemen and Lepers

'We all work for the Mission.'

'Did he get my letter?'

'I'm sure I couldn't tell you sonny. He's up in the Northern Territory. But if you sent him a letter, he'd get it all right. The G.P.O. never let anyone down yet. Now suppose you give the box to me, and I'll see that the Doctor gets it.'

'I haven't got the box.'

'Haven't got it? Well, well, you're not the first. Boys will be boys. I suppose you lost it, eh?'

'Yes, we lost it,' I said. 'At least—a boy took it off us at school.'

'A boy? Which boy?' asked Mother, appearing at the front door.

'I forget. Just—a boy. It had quite a lot in it.'

'About how much?' asked the man quizzically.

'One pound fifteen and threepence halfpenny.'

Mother said, 'It's very careless of them.'

'Bless you, lady, it often happens. This here Doctor Uniapon, you see, he's quite a salesman. The boys get filled with good intentions and it's hard to live up to them. We don't count on getting back more than half the boxes. They get lost, or mislaid; or the money finds its way into—other places, eh?'

We stared at him dully.

'Well,' said Mother, 'we'll have to make it up to you. I'll give you ten shillings, and it can come out of their pocket money.'

The man smirked. 'Thank you, lady. Here's my card; Alf Sharp. Yurrabunga Mission: always glad to be of assistance.'

I found Colin alone in the woodshed. His eyes were red.

'I'm glad I smashed the leper box,' he said bitterly. 'And Doctor Uniapon; I hope he gets leprosy too!'

* * *

All this had taken much more than the week Tiger had allowed me in which to raise the money, but now that I had it I rushed over to his house the very next day. I parked my bike in the side alley as usual and went round the back of the house to the garage. The door was shut and the place seemed singularly quiet. I called out, there was no answer; I opened the garage door.

In the gloom, supported on two trestles, lay a monstrous shape. It was a canoe of sorts, but it was swelled and distorted into the form of a gibbous moon: part row-boat, part coracle, part canoe with a bunion on its left side. I stared at it in stupefaction, but soon with rising anger. So Tiger hadn't waited; he'd gone ahead on his own without me and never a word about it! Footsteps sounded on the asphalt driveway and Tiger peered in.

The Road to Gundagai

'What you doing in the garage?' he said belligerently.

'Why didn't you *tell* me!' my voice was quavering.

Tiger shrugged. 'No point,' he said laconically. 'You didn't get the money, so . . .'

'Well I may've taken a bit longer than I said, but now I've got it.'

'It's a bit late,' said Tiger.

'It certainly is,' I blazed, 'now you've gone and made a balls of the canoe—our canoe.'

'Tut, tut, the language.'

'Well I'm darned if I'll put my money into—into that!' I said pointing at the monstrous shape.

'Don't want your dough,' said Tiger. 'Most of the dough was mine anyway.'

'That's a lie!'

'Say that again!'

'That again!'

'Think you're very clever.'

'Well, I don't make balls of canoes.'

He flew at me and in a moment we were writhing on the grass locked in each other's arms in a catch-as-catch-can wrestle. I was furious with indignation and thus reduced my chances to zero. Pretty soon Tiger was on top of me.

'Both shoulder blades on the ground,' he yelled.

'They are not,' I cried squirming violently and trying to keep one shoulder up. With a violent twist I managed to wrench myself free and rolled off the grass onto the asphalt. As I did so the golden hoard fell from my pockets and pennies and sixpences rolled all over the driveway. Tiger helped me to pick them up and handed them to me in silence. I mounted my bike and rode off without a word, my heart as heavy as my pocket. After all the trouble with Dr. Uniapon, now what good was the money?

But my friendship with Tiger was made of durable stuff and a couple of weeks later he came up to me after school. A curious light shone in his freckled eyes.

'How about coming over to my place this arvo for a wrestle?'

'Catch-as-catch-can or Graeco-Roman?'

Much would depend on Tiger's answer to *that* one. He knew I was better at Graeco-Roman with its stylized clutches, and this was a way of saving face. He paused.

'Graeco-Roman,' he said at length and off we went.

But we only had one round of wrestling when Tiger, with an elaborate show of nonchalance strolled over to the garage. 'Like to show you something.'

He pulled open the doors and there to my stupefaction was a

Policemen and Lepers

canoe; smooth, slick, grey painted, two paddles lashed to the thwarts, ready to take the water. Gone were the bulbous deformities.

'But, but—it can't—it can't . . .'

Tiger grinned. 'No, I scrapped the old one. It was really no good. Dad gave me this, as a reward for trying.'

'Gave *you*?' I was thinking of the money I had put into the first venture.

Tiger scratched his nose. 'I know you contributed but I worked it out. It was only about two pounds altogether. This canoe cost Dad eleven, so if I give you two back then we're square and it's my canoe? Eh?'

I must have looked downcast for he added quickly.

'Course you can always ride in it, and use it when I don't need it.'

I looked longingly at the smooth lines of the canoe and then I thought, well that's almost as good as *owning* one and anyway if Tiger gives me back two pounds I can repay my share of the Leper Box.

'Okay,' I said, 'shake.'

We shook solemnly and I looked forward to long bold afternoons paddling up unknown creeks to mysterious islands. The actual outcome was a good deal more prosaic. Dr. Webb had decided that the canoe was under no circumstances to be paddled alone by a thirteen year old boy on the Yarra and its tributaries. The sea was too rough, so this left only Albert Park Lake, a sheet of fresh water in South Melbourne with a maximum depth of about six feet. This seemed a terrible let down, but in fact Albert Park Lake provided the only memorable incident in the life of this canoe, which from now on I regarded as being entirely Tiger's. It concerned a friend named Marcus notable for the prodigious size of his feet.

* * *

We planned to invite this man-mountain on a trip across the Albert Park Lake and maroon him on a small island. We calculated that he would easily wade to safety and that if he held his boots upside down under his armpits they would act as capacious reservoirs of air and he would probably float quite easily the fifty yards to shore. We approached the big-footed Marcus with what we thought was deep-seated guile and he agreed to come with us in the canoe the following Saturday morning. We had considerable difficulty in embarking because none of us was familiar with the correct method of steadying a canoe. We were also disconcerted by Marcus' immense weight. Although only fourteen years old he weighed more than 170 pounds and as he stepped carefully into the canoe ('For Christ's sake

The Road to Gundagai

put your bloody feet on the centreboard, Marko!')—it sank to the gunwales. When we paddled gingerly out into the turbid waters of Albert Park Lake we had a freeboard of less than two inches.

The result of our stratagem may easily be imagined. We paddled slowly to the island and suggested blandly to Marcus that he be the first to disembark. Instead Marcus gave a convulsive jerk and the next moment all three of us were in the lake and the canoe waterlogged. We splashed and struggled and swallowed a great deal of dirty brown water that smelled of tainted pondweed and oily mud. Then, perforce composing our differences, we struggled ashore pulling the waterlogged canoe behind us. We dragged it up on a bank of tired brown grass and began to search for damage. Tiger was so worried about the canoe that he'd forgotten our treacherous design on Marcus. *He* hadn't though. While we were stripping off our dripping sweaters he lunged toward the beached canoe and with a cry of '*That's* for trying to desert me!' launched a terrific kick at it. Tiger's canoe was not proof against Marcus' size twelve boots and he stove it in. We sprang on him with snarls of rage but at this moment the well known and hateful voice of authority was heard above the fracas.

'All right now, ace it up. Ace it up! What's going on here?'

The Law in the person of a plainclothes cop in a brown suit and black snap-brimmed fedora surveyed us sourly. The cops always turned up when we were having a bit of fun. How we hated and feared them. Following the unspoken rule that ranks close when the john-hops are around, we remained silent, declined to answer questions, pretended dumbness and generated for the cop's benefit a great deal of spurious backslapping bonhommie. Marcus positively beamed at us and we grinned back. The cop retired with an admonition that unless we had the bashed-in canoe out of the park by closing time he'd take us 'along to the station'. We three shouldered the canoe and chanting 'Sons of the Sea, All British Born' at the tops of our voices, made off for the boatsheds.

Marcus repented of the damage he had done, and offered two shillings in recompense. Tiger spurned this offer; but by now we'd become interested in bicycle excursions, so much more romantic than canoeing—something really worth while. Marcus and the canoe faded slowly into oblivion, the canoe in the boatshed and Marcus in his enormous boots ('When're ya laying the keels for the next pair, Marko?') We put aside the river as childish.

Chapter Nine

UP THE COUNTRY

At the western end of Swanston Street the National Gallery and Library of the State of Victoria presented a Corinthian façade, based on that of the British Museum. Up the shallow bluestone steps went the visitors, between the statues of St. George and the Dragon and Joan of Arc. One Sunday afternoon Mother, having secured an introduction through the Mackail-Burne Jones old boy net, took us to tea with the Director, L. Bernard Hall. We reached his spacious office through long corridors covered with pictures so heavily glassed that all you could see was your own reflection tramping hopefully by. The only painting to arrest us was John Longstaff's 'The Return to the Depot', showing Bourke, Wills and King, 'three haggard men grouped around the fatal tree', in Alan Moorehead's words. The afternoon was literary-artistic and we were bored, but two people emerged as engaging and exciting. They were Basil Hall, the Director's son, and his wife Nell; they lived on an orchard in the country. The country! How wonderful a vision arose against the drabness of 4 Grace Street. 'You must come and see our orchard,' said Nell Hall; tall, angular, big grey eyes, a face of patient kindliness.

'Next school holidays,' said her husband. His tanned face glowed with the red flush of country and health. He wore, very dashingly, a blue cotton shirt and a paisley bow tie. His black hair was cut en brosse and he had a hook nose, a pipe, a square mouth and shrewd brown eyes. With dim memories of England I imagined a high wall of plum-coloured brick with perhaps some peaches or pears espaliered along it. The reality when it came opened a dramatic door through which we walked out of 4 Grace Street and into Australia.

The great day came and at once the adventure began, for the train plunged into two tunnels—the only ones in greater Melbourne—under the Eastern Hill and then ran on a vertiginous embankment until it crossed the slashing gully of Merri Creek on a high viaduct. It was clearly an ideal railway with every adornment that an

The Road to Gundagai

enthusiast could require. Now we're burrowing through the London clay, then up, up climbing the Selkirks and the Rockies and emerging from the Galera Tunnel, sick with *soroche*, to plunge breathlessly down hill into Lima. Up again, straining on the rack-and-pinion of the Rigi; higher still to the nightmareish top of Pilatuskulm, then whoosh! through the Simplon and the St. Gotthard, and we're laying track on the Prairies at the incredible rate of five miles a day! Going to make a packet out of our sub-contract, but look out! here come the buffalo, the Indians, the Mounties; we've just time to escape by the long bridges over the Godavari and the Ganges to reach Clapham Junction in safety.

The total distance to Hurstbridge was no more than 24 miles but each rattling rock-cut, each looping embankment and low trestle bridge carried us further into an unbelievable land where boys could do as they wished. At Diamond Creek the last passengers left our compartment and we danced up and down on the straw-filled seat cushions and thousands of gay motes danced in the swinging sunbeams as the train pulled on the curves. Hurstbridge station was a low gravel platform with a small rabbit hutch of a booking office painted in the country gamboge favoured by the Victorian Railways. Beyond lay a dusty yellow road with grey weatherboard houses on stilts, false-fronted to show the signboards of the butcher, the blacksmith, and the feed-and-grain merchant. There was hot, bright, heavy sunshine with the tang of eucalyptus and stringy bark in the air and dust in our noses.

'Hello boys!'

Out shot a brown sinewy arm covered with black hair and ending in a rolled blue shirt sleeve. The hair en brosse was covered by a battered wideawake hat with a frayed band. Our host toted our kit-bags into a two wheeled sulky with patient Betty standing in the shafts. We got up beside him, squashed together between the driver and the splash board. Basil Hall took a plaited leather whip from a shiny brass whip-holder, laid it gently over Betty's rump and off we went. The sulky, well sprung and with high thin rubber-tyred wheels, furrowed the yellow road; the little grey township disappeared into the dust while the trit-trot, trit-trot, slowed to take the first hill.

From Hurstbridge to Panton Hill, where the Halls lived, was about three miles and the road rose all the way. The unattainable mountains glimpsed in the distance from the roof of 4 Grace Street suddenly loomed as enormous new neighbours. The immediate countryside was undulating park-like bush with the trees widely spaced, or else rolled aside by the fastidious patterns of orchard. As we bowled along merrily on the downhill stretches the neatly planted rows of peaches, apples, nectarines and pears went by like wheel

Up the Country

spokes and made a neat line from every angle. Between the orchards were vineyards with great heavy swags of purple grapes hanging from fencing wire that sagged and strained. In front of each field of fruit trees or vines was a little square wooden house with a galvanized iron corrugated roof, dazzling in the hot sunshine. When we stopped to walk up hills our own dust driven by us was full of the dry oily eucalyptus smell, and the cicadas shrilled and screamed all around us making the heat seem solid noise. Then we were on a narrow dust and gravel track with a single telephone wire strung from convenient trees and up ahead on a rise was a weatherboard house with a twin gabled tin roof, a verandah and a couple of big round water tanks on stilts.

'That's "Fairview"; that's where we live.'

We swung up a short curving rise and opened a cast-iron gate between two tall pine trees, and there was Nell Hall in a plaited straw hat smiling at us and a great vista in every direction of apple trees, vines, park-like paddocks with cows grazing and beyond that the bush, the hills and the magenta mountains now shimmering less as the sun drew down. Supper of milk, still warm from the cow, boiled eggs, innumerable scones and cakes, rich local honey, and as the early dusk fell we walked from the house across a small yard with a peppercorn tree under which white Leghorns, black Orpingtons and Rhode Island Reds rooted and scratched in the twilight dirt. The outhouses loomed ahead; stables for the horses and the sulky and the dray; workshops and a cellar for apples and a small platform leading to the loft. The fifty feet or so from the house to bed in the loft was beset with innumerable perils. The kerosene hurricane lamp, casting enormous shadows of boys' legs amid the encircling gloom, could scarcely keep at bay Dr. Fu Manchu, or the evil old woman who shot her husband at his own request in Sax Rohmer's *Batwing*; or, for that matter, Carl Petersen and Henry Lakington, the arch fiends who kidnapped Phyllis and aroused the fury of Bulldog Drummond.

'But the bath means death, death in agony!' shrieked Lakington.

'Then that will be the worse for whichever of us goes into it,' replied the soldier.

The veins on Drummond's forehead stood out . . .

The following morning, before setting out to explore this earthly paradise, we borrowed the brush used to mark the apple boxes for shipment, and stencilled over the door 'The Loft: Rest Home.'

* * *

The generosity of the Halls is something of which it is hard to write without sentimentality. My brother and I thenceforth spent

The Road to Gundagai

all our school holidays at their country home. Throughout our boyhood we could always count on getting away from 4 Grace Street to Panton Hill every Christmas, every May holidays, every September holidays and sometimes Easter as well. When the Halls later moved from Panton Hill to Greendale, much further away near Ballarat, we went with them. During a period of ten years I spent a total of eighteen months as their guest. At the time I accepted this unquestioningly, but later I used to think that there must surely have been some arrangement whereby Mother had the Halls take us as paying guests, or that she helped them out in some way for their never-ending kindness. When I asked Mother this she replied quite candidly that she had never offered the Halls a penny. I was therefore forced—since I couldn't believe that they wanted me for myself—to fall back on the assumption that my brother and I must have been useful to them because of the small farm chores which we undertook with such unquenchable enthusiasm. To us it was a never-failing source of delight to chop wood, round up the cows in time for milking, fill and trim the kerosene lamps, churn the butter, pump water by hand up into the storage tanks, feed the chickens, gather the eggs and play games with and amuse the Hall children who began by being one and ended by being four.

But I'm convinced now that this explanation is wide of the mark. The relationship was one of those wonderful accidents which sometimes seem to be only predictable features of life. In this case it was sheer kindness on the part of the older people, and simple enthusiasm and prankishness on the part of two boys, with perhaps the added spice of an articulate humour which, to be fair, was largely a reflection of Mother's mordant wit. Whatever the reason, the friendship was the making of my boyhood and brought me into direct contact with the open, empty Australia which loomed in the background of life in crowded suburbia. The Halls gave me their Australia and turned me from an intolerant, suspicious little 'pommy' into at least a reasonable facsimile of a dinkum Aussie—despite a Canadian father and an English Mother.

There was of course the element of hero worship and I'm sure that this was as pleasant to Basil Hall as it was to us. In the usual Anglo-Saxon fashion they soon became Uncle Basil and Aunt Nell and I think that what overjoyed me most, both then and in retrospect, was the way in which they answered all our asinine questions soberly and helped us to understand and even to be expert in the ways of running a small homestead in the Australian bush. I was given responsible jobs to do, slightly beyond my capacity, so that the challenge was always there against a background of otherwise carefree boyhood holidays, far removed from the 4 Gas Set.

Up the Country

So strong became my passion for 'Fairview', and corresponding hatred of Melbourne, school, home and all the unpleasantness that one associates with those names that sometimes, when I was out rabbit shooting or fishing for yabbies in a billabong, or simply on top of the high empty hill at nearby Kangaroo Ground with the wind blowing through me, I would lay a curse on the city of my adoption. The War Memorial on top of the Kangaroo Ground Hill afforded a distant prospect of Melbourne lying in its smoke on the plains twenty odd miles away and I sometimes ran panting up the steps to the Memorial, bellowing at the top of my voice, with only the rabbits and the apple trees and the onion fields to listen, how lucky I was to be here and not there.

* * *

The first job Uncle Basil gave me was to ride to the village of Panton Hill, a mile away through the bush to get the bread and the mail. This meant saddling and bridling Betty the pony which in turn pre-supposed being able to ride. This was painfully learned on a sheepskin saddle, the great mark of the new chum, and a series of nerve-wracking canters up and down the rough track leading to the cow bail. Uncle Basil's method was simple. After showing me how to strap on the sheepskin saddle he would urge me to mount. The pony, with her round tight belly cunningly distended against the girth, was docile enough, but a formidable mountain of flesh upon which to scrabble and clamber. Her favourite trick was to breathe out just when I had a firm grasp of the sheepskin. This made the saddle slip round until it was under her belly instead of on her back, dumping me on the ground. Uncle Basil then showed me how to give the pony a sharp jab with the fist when tightening the girth. This at first alarming trick was swiftly learned.

Pretty soon I could ride on the sheepskin without stirrups and with only a rope halter for bridle; and from this it was an easy step to a leather saddle with proper stirrups, and a bridle and bit. But Betty had first to be caught. I learned how to do this with an apple or with a couple of lumps of sugar, holding my hand at first rigidly flat, in fact, almost arced backwards to make sure the fingers weren't bitten off. Bridle and saddle having been rubbed with dubbin and given a spurious sheen with boot polish I took down the canvas mail bag from the hook, slung it across my shoulder and ambled gently down the drive toward the ringlock gate. By continuous practice I was eventually able to manoeuvre balky Betty into a position where she would stay quiet so that I could lean down from her and unlock the gate. The trick then, having sidled through, was to be sure it didn't swing wildly back in the opposite direction. If this happened I must dismount, tether Betty by her bridle to the barbed wire fence and shut the gate by hand, thereby losing much face. But if the gate swung gently, as with skill one could ensure that it did, all that was needed was to nuzzle the pony uphill against the gate until it clanged to. At this point I would often discover, through a combination of sniffles and yowls, that Venus had been left behind.

Venus was an enormously ugly, broad-chested, heavy-footed, gallumphing bulldog bitch. To this slavering, wheezing animal the Halls and their two children, Barry and Joan, were greatly attached. Her prognathous lower jaw stuck so far out that she could not breath properly and suffered from asthma, sniffles and 'dog dreams' when lying full length beneath the dining room table. From these dreams she would jerk to awareness in a most tremendous bout of sneezing and snuffling until someone gave her a swift kick in the ribs. She was a liability on the run to the post office and I always tried to leave her behind. Her gallumphing rolling-sailor gait could barely keep up with the horse at a trot, let alone at a canter. I had to wait until she caught up, tongue lolling out and an expression of comic anxiety in her two piggy eyes. This time though, nothing for it but to dismount, open the gate and let her through. Digging my heels into Betty's belly we started off down the hill at a brisk trot.

First on the left came the Cracknells, a stolid weather-board house with centre door, wooden ginger bread on the verandah eaves and a tin roof gleaming in the sun. On the right came the Cartwrights. They had just returned from their Trip Home, the envy and admiration of the neighbourhood for having achieved the Australian's wild and cherished dream. Their son Tom had brought with him a Hornby model railway. With Tom and his sister Isobel we used to go mushrooming in the May holidays; not the small tight little pink buttons beloved by gourmets, but great flabby, floppy black umbrellas and pink parasols which, fried to a delectable mess, gave off the aroma of true ambrosia.

Next on the right was the road to Watson's Creek where Mr. MacPherson Robertson, known to us all as 'Mac Robertson The Chocolate King' had a summer home. We never actually saw him, but his face, with its thatch of white hair and benign white cavalry moustache was well known to us from a book which he had autographed and sent to my grandfather when he was on his lecture tour of Australia. This was one of the more poignant episodes of Grace Street life. When we learned that our grandfather had declined to visit MacRobertson's chocolate factory in Fitzroy and had therefor missed forever the chance of being showered with free samples of

Up the Country

Old Gold, Dolly Varden and *Beau Brummell* chocolate, our incredulity knew no bounds. Small consolation was the signed copy of *A Young Man and a Nail Can*, the autobiography of Mr. later Sir MacPherson Robertson. We'd far rather have had the chocolate.

I suppose the Chocolate King, in his commercial innocence, must have thought that MacRobertson and Mackail, being fellow Scots in the alien Antipodes, should stand together; and that the academic afflatus conferred on the chocolate factory by my grandfather's visit would be more than counter-balanced by the injection of a few rich commercial corpuscles into our pale Burne-Jonesian fluid. Anyway it was not to be, and the road to Watson's Creek became known principally as the road to the summer cottage of 'Old Boy'. Old Boy was R. W. E. ('Bung') Wilmot who wrote masterfully on cricket for the *Argus* and the *Australasian* and with whose son Chester, the famous war correspondent, I grew up. Though Chester went to Grammar and I went to Scotch, among the miraculous hills and enigmatic gullies such differences were soon forgotten.

Next on the left lived the Shannons, not to be confused with the Shanhuns. Whereas the Shanhuns (Mick and Bertha) were a tough Irish family who lived down at the bottom of the gully and eked a living from felling timber and shooting rabbits, the Misses Shannon were maiden ladies of marked civic virtue, tweedy weather-beaten good looks and libraries full of bound volumes of *Punch* going back to the 1860's. They were always glad to see me and I drank innumerable glasses of stone ginger beer going to and from the post office up the dusty road past their house. Around the next corner, edged by papery eucalyptus drooping in the fierce sun, the road forked down the hill to Hurstbridge and along the level to Panton Hill, Smith's Gully and Kinglake. The Anglican Church and vicarage, blackened weatherboard without a spire or tower, lay somnolently among flowering gum trees. Opposite it was the parish hall where one memorable evening we were taken to see a travelling troupe, 'The Musical Gardiners'.

Theirs was a wonderful mixture of war songs, conjuring tricks, humorous monologues and acrobatics. In the saccharine finale the five Musical Gardiners, Mum, Dad, Thelma and the two boys, sang with heart-rending emotion, to the accompaniment of a piano accordion, the immemorial ballad *Call Me Back, Pal O' Mine*. Dimly discernible through it all is the English music hall tradition and one can follow the thin wavering line whereby, diluted and strangely transformed, it poured out to an audience of one hundred sitting on backless wooden benches in the parish hall at Panton Hill one breathless summer evening.

Beyond the parish hall was the village itself: Mrs. Adams' general

The Road to Gundagai

store and post office, a butcher, the Presbyterian Church and a hotel which had no rooms but was quite simply a place to drink heady draught Australian beer. The other side of the village was largely unknown territory though we did occasionally penetrate it to visit the first farm house. This belonged to Captain and Mrs. Biggs and the name on the gate—*Grodno*—was viewed with suspicion by the locals who searched it vainly for significant anagrams. In point of fact it was the place where Biggs, with the British expeditionary force after the Russian Revolution, had met Mrs. Biggs, then a V.A.D., and they had plighted their troth. They ended up in Panton Hill growing peaches, apples and berries. Once, being desperately short of pocket money, I asked if I could pick fruit for Mrs. Biggs and she gave me a day in the raspberry patches for five bob. As a form of employment I've never tired of not recommending it.

Once we went further afield to Smith's Gully for a picnic, all of us in a brake, that half-forgotten vehicle looking rather like Constable's *Hay Wain* with a high freeboard, four huge squeaking iron-tyred wooden wheels, and wooden brake shoes, applied by gross manpower on a lever beside the driver's box as he strained, along with his two enormous grey percherons, against the steep hill. To the north, the serrated blue line of the Kinglake Ranges was a constant invitation to lands of dreamy mystery, and Uncle Basil was always promising that one day we would go on 'a picnic to Kinglake'. He finally hired a 1924 Essex with genuine isinglass curtains and a canvas roof, and we chugged off up into the ranges where we picnicked in the middle of a great burn. A forest fire ten years before had cleared away the timber, leaving sweeping slopes of bracken with here and there charred sentinels lifting against the sky as a reminder of the former forest. Everywhere second growth was coming up, the kind of wonderfully springy saplings up which you could shinny until they began to bend slowly under your own weight, finally depositing you in a graceful arc in the soft bracken below. We boiled tea in a billy can and cooked chops in a grill over a wood fire.

I asked for and received the special and coveted task of 'swirling the billy' to make the tea settle. When the billy was on the boil, hung by its handle from a pole supported over the fire on two forked sticks, I would throw tea by the handful into the bubbling water, then quickly, before it started to stew, unthread the billy, grab the handle firmly and swirl it around in a vertical circular motion among admiring friends who were amazed, so they said, that when the billy was upside down above my head its contents did not drench me with boiling tea. 'Aha,' I replied wisely, 'it's the centrifugal force keeps it in, you see.' Replete with food and lazing under the tang of eucalyptus, our eyes swept far over the great plateau leading to Ballarat and the gold fields, and in the extreme south-west the humps and hummocks of the You Yangs.

* * *

We returned from this picnic so full of beans that the amiable hired girl, Myrtle Tosch, simply had to be tied to the stake once again and, in the sweet apple-smelling cellar below the loft, re-act the martyrdom of Joan of Arc. Myrtle was sixteen with a peasant's stocky figure, plump red cheeks and dimply blue eyes disappearing behind an enormously bulgy forehead. She gladly consented to be our butt, and out of sheer good nature allowed us at least once a week to enact this drama provided we untied her when she told us that the cords were beginning to bite. She never supposed, nor for that matter did we or Tom Cartwright or the McLachlan kids from across the gully, that there was anything sadistic in the red-Indian war dance which we whooped around her when she was on her 'pyre'.

'Joan, do you swear that you will forever recant the blasphemous heresies which you have learned at the courts of the English?'

'Yes Graham, I promise.'

'Please try and remember that I am *not* Graham. I am the Archbishop of Rheims.'

'Yes, My Lord Archbishop.'

'And please remember,' added Colin, 'to call him your Eminent Grace.'

'Yes, Your Eminent Grace.'

'Add fuel to the flames!' cried Tom and the McLachlan kids giggled, not sure whether it was about time to take all this seriously. But the martyrdom always ended at this point, less because we were worried about the bonds biting poor Myrtle's pudgy flesh, than because Uncle Basil had warned us that anyone starting a fire in the cellar would be sent home by the next train. There was enough danger of fire already, according to him, from the incubator and the brooder which disgorged Aunt Nell's chickens at regular intervals.

Myrtle, who was Aunt Nell's only help, walked to and from work every day two miles directly through the bush. She lived on the Tosch farm opposite the McLachlans on the Watson's Creek road and having tramped through the gully myself to play with the McLachlan kids I stood in some awe of Myrtle's performance. Every evening she had first to struggle slantwise across forty acres of peach trees and stagger over furrows and concrete-hard clods of summer ploughing. Then she negotiated a barbed wire fence and tramped on through open parklike fields with the blackened stumps of trees long

The Road to Gundagai

ago ravaged by fire, or occasionally the gaunt, grey skeletons of trees which had been ring-barked and left to die slowly. The great sport among the ring-barked trees was the tarantula hunt. Between the decaying bark and the smooth ash-grey bole of the dead tree lurked large colonies of tarantulas, some of them quite enormous with bodies the size of a thumb nail and furry legs two inches long. There was a mystique about tarantulas as there was about snakes. We believed that their sting was mortal. Another school held the view that if you put a tarantula in someone's bed they would get such a fright from seeing it that they would die of shock and wouldn't need to be stung. Neither story was true, but like snakes and indeed all reptilian or insect forms in the bush, tarantulas existed to be destroyed. The technique was to tiptoe quietly up to the dead tree, rip the bark quickly off and lay about among the scurrying tarantulas with a tomahawk.

Beyond the tarantula country lay a deep gully where the trees and ferns met above the pathway and the sunlight filtered down with a mysterious greenish hue. Pausing for breath you could hear the 'thwack' of a whip bird, the hazy heat-wave drumming of cicadas, and sometimes the uproarious cackle of a kookaburra, and beyond it the heavy thud of the Shanhuns chopping wood in the hollow. The Shanhuns lived in a humpy of ironbark slabs tilted diagonally against each other to form a gable over a ridge pole. Across the opening hung gunny-sacking and at the far end was a crude chimney made of four sheets of corrugated galvanised iron. Uncle Basil said the Shanhuns were 'up to no good' and we always gave their house a wide berth. Beyond their humpy the trees thinned again and presently came open pasture full of McLachlan Jerseys and Anguses, and down the hill came running McLachlan kids ready to go fishing for yabbies.

These small fresh water crayfish, which inhabited every muddy pool in the bush, were the easiest things to catch in the world. All you needed was an empty jam tin and a piece of string with a bit of rancid meat knotted into the end of it. Lower the string into the muddy water and as soon as you felt a nip give a sharp tug and whip the jam jar underneath; and there in the bottom lay the yabbie with its claws waving feebly in the air. At the end of a morning's yabbie fishing with the McLachlan kids we would have an empty kerosene tin three or four inches deep in a seething mass of claws, legs, miniature armadillo segmented shells and eyes on stalks. That was the end of the fun, for yabbies, even to us, were inedible; and the final act was to give the can a great heave-ho and send all the yabbies cascading through the air in a tangle of claws and eye-stalks back into the muddy pool.

Up the Country

At the back of the McLachlan's lay mystery country; the Christmas Hills. Above their bushy tops we could see the great purple horst of the mountains, but what lay between was hidden—until the arrival of old Henry Shuter. Henry Shuter was our host's maternal uncle and he surprised and delighted us by turning up unexpectedly one afternoon in a calf-length white motoring coat, a cloth cap, a pair of goggles and a neat Van Dyck beard. His wife was suitably garbed in a floppy straw hat held under her chin with several windings of a pink crêpe-de-chine scarf, the ends stuffed into a motoring coat like an outsize burberry. They were driving a 1922 De Dion Bouton with brass fittings and spare tyres mounted on the running board on either side of the front seat. Frantic with delight we accepted an invitation to go for a drive to the Christmas Hills. We mounted in what was still known as the tonneau and jolted off behind Uncle Henry's upright bearded figure at a sedate twenty miles an hour over the bumpy yellow gravel roads. The journey was uneventful until we reached the Christmas Hills post office, a single storey frame building with a hitching post outside; but at that point we emerged on to the top of a precipice.

The Christmas Hills were hills only from our side; from the other and unknown side they were the edge of a steep scarp. We found ourselves looking down from an enormous height across the flood plain of the Yarra, winding lazily through the middle distance among water meadows fat with sheep and cattle. Tall tops of Lombardy poplars surrounded the farmhouses and far off the plains petered out against the bastion of the Donna Buang Ranges and the shrunken extinct volcano of Mount Riddell clothed from top to toe in dense eucalyptus like shaggy fur. This was Australia Felix, the scene that inspired Streeton and the Heidelberg Group of painters.

* * *

Next spring the Halls took on a jackaroo. He was a plump young Englishman in his middle twenties with a pink face, an irascible disposition and the style of hair known admiringly to us as 'the brushback'. His name was Ford and he slept in a large bedroom off the stables which, though he did not know it, made him highly vulnerable. For behind his head was a knot hole leading into the stables and we soon discovered that, since we rose earlier than he did, it was wonderfully rewarding to poke pieces of straw through the knot hole from the stable side and 'tickle Ford awake'. By this and similar petty annoyances we harassed his life and made it increasingly tedious. He bided his time.

The Road to Gundagai

We normally bathed in the 'little' dam where the water, a turbid yellow and like warm soup in the summer heat, was about four feet deep. Diving was precarious as the cast iron outlet pipe had to be avoided and the bottom was tacky gamboge ooze. The 'big' dam was much older, deeper and further down hill. Into it one could dive with safety. It was romantically ringed with reeds and sedge, witness to its thirty years' existence, whereas the 'little' dam was a raw yellow scar in the middle of the orchard; in fact Uncle Basil had dug it only the year before. He had at this time one four-acre field in alfalfa but the deep purple flowers drooped listlessly in the heat and as the long days of summer drought continued he decided to dig a new dam. He did it single handed with a scoop pulled by Bunny and Belinda, the two brown Percherons, and very soon it filled with muddy water. Both dams, like all those in the Panton Hill area, showed bright yellow in the sunlight, for beneath the light grey loam in which the fruit trees were planted—Five Crown and Jonathan apples, Alameda peaches and tight shiny nectarines—lay an overburden of clay and gravel. But with irrigation and a little artificial manure the loam produced a wonderful crop, aided of course by Uncle Basil's brow sweat.

On the wall of the little 'office' off the verandah at *Fairview*, next to the big round water tank, hung a photograph of himself taken for the Chilean Nitrate of Soda Company, in a before-and-after pose. He stands between two tilted displays of apple crates. His wideawake hat with its roller coaster brim and bashed crown is rakishly settled over his hair en brosse; below it the brown weatherbeaten face smiles out through a row of strong white teeth gripping a long pipe as he leans ever so slightly towards the larger assembly of crates. On his left is the sign 'Before using Chilean Nitrate of Soda' and on the right 'After'. Next to this photograph hung a calendar with a picture of a plump man eating Purina Crispies and beneath it the legend: Uncle Henry fat and jolly, says to worry it is folly.

After a long day of fiercely enjoyed and enormously unproductive boyhood play we went down to the big dam accompanied by Uncle Basil without whom we were not allowed to swim. Ford was with us and his air of nonchalance was sufficient to put me off my guard; but when I surfaced after a dive he was there all right. He plunged my head beneath the water and gave me a severe ducking. Choking and breathless I flailed my way to the bank whence I hurled abuse and small stones at Ford's red roaring visage. Later in the evening when we trod barefoot hippety-hop over the great clods of earth among the trees Ford tripped me from behind and I crashed to the ground amidst renewed laughter. Colin thought

Up the Country

Ford had gone far enough and a large clod of earth burst in the middle of his back. Ford gave chase but Colin was far too spry to be caught. Another clod sailed through the air, a signal to Uncle Basil to tell us all to 'stow it'.

We were revenged in a curious way for Ford got himself a second-hand motor bike, a twin cylinder Harley Davidson. This enormous monster reared up at the slightest provocation and with Ford clinging on grimly, roared down the road to Panton Hill amid ripping staccato barks and great flashes of blue flame. The final excursion found Ford, having described a neat parabolic curve, huddled in a ditch with a broken leg. The bike went on gaily down the hill and ended up at the bottom of a rocky gully. Old scores were at once mutually forgotten, and we were tender to Ford for the remainder of the vacation. In order not to disturb him we even did some of his chores. We made the rounds of the hens twice a day, kicking them off their nests and collecting the eggs in a white colander. We dipped deep into great bins of pollard and bran, added the requisite amount of Karswood Poultry Spice and gave it to the silly broody creatures as they sat on their captive nests. The rest of them came careering hopefully to the wire gate at the banging of a dipper with a spoon, their short waddly legs flying up behind them like old women running to catch a bus. They would then wait expectantly, heads cocked on one side with a sort of dumb-Dora inquisitive chuckle until the feed appeared in a shower of wheaten shrapnel from the air.

The mad scurry of chickens and feathers often ended with the horrible task of killing 'one for the pot'. The victim seemed to know, as you approached her, that she was doomed, and the elderly broody hens which most often found their way to the pot could run faster than the pullets. The simple method, once a hen was caught, was to swirl it around in the air by the legs until dazed, and then wring its neck. I could never bring myself to look at this operation, preferring to clutch the doomed hen behind me, while I looked steadfastly in the opposite direction waiting for the unnerving crunch. Colin was better at this and when he had the chook mesmerized he would chop its head off neatly with a tommy-axe after which it did indeed run around like a chicken without a head. All this and more we did for Ford, striving to cleanse ourselves of the guilty clods flying through the air.

During the final period of Ford's convalescence came the hay making. Uncle Basil had built an open-ended, open-sided barn with a corrugated tin roof and it had been crammed with hay and straw by the Shanhuns. There appeared from nowhere a large stationary engine with a high smoke stack and an enormous flywheel with the

The Road to Gundagai

inscription 'Ronaldson and Tippett, Ballarat'. This was connected by a leather belt to a mechanical chaff cutter and it was my job to wield a hay fork with lethally sharp tines, high up among the straw, sending the bales down towards the little escalator which fed them into the machine. During the few weeks that had elapsed between the arrival of the hay and its cutting myriad colonies of mice had established themselves. They were of every description, from hoary grey old men with beards to little litters of new born pink baby sausages. Soon the mouse hunt took precedence over heaving down the stooks of hay onto the machine. Starved of fuel, it began to run hot. The monster from Ronaldson and Tippet had to be stopped and allowed to cool off, and I got a thick ear.

* * *

After a week's work had filled an enormous zinc-lined bin, big as a house, with chaff for the horses and cows, came the magic words: 'Would you like to go rabbit shooting?' This exciting invitation we never refused. The bewitched hour was sunset when rabbits could be detected sitting outside their warrens with ears cocked, a perfect mark, though Uncle Basil with his twelve bore shotgun, moved by some distant folk memory in a land where rabbits were game rather than vermin, would never pot a sitter. The ritual was unvarying except if we were going shooting beyond Kangaroo Ground over at the Bourchier's place. They had by far the most fruitful rabbit warrens—a sad commentary on the ability of their land to hold sheep or water—and they lived five miles away so that we had to start early. While Uncle Basil was milking the cows we harnessed Betty and got her into the shafts of the sulky, adjusting now with nimble sophisticated fingers the crupper under the tail, the breeching behind the rump and onto the shafts, the big collar pushed up underneath the pony's patient neck, the bridle, and finally the reins trailing backwards through the little lyre-like silvery metal bridge to the driver's hands. Up into the sulky came not only the driver but the two game bags opening bottom and top, and stained with the ancient dried blood of many previous outings. Then off we set for the Bourchier's.

Old man Bourchier was a cousin of the famous *Times* correspondent who had been in Bulgaria at the time of the First Balkan War. But he himself was as Aussie and as dinkum as they come, and kept for us an uproarious back-slapping heartiness because, of course, he was Scotch Old Boy. He had a son and two daughters and the one we liked best was Jean who was dark and vivacious and about ten years older than we were and a lot of fun and had a collection of stamps issued by the Government of Bulgaria in commemoration

Up the Country

of the services of the *Times* correspondent. Orchards were not favoured on this slope of the Kangaroo Ground hills and Bourchier had a sheep run—it was too modest to be called a station—of about three hundred acres and perhaps sixty head of cattle down in the bottom lands which fronted on the upper reaches of the Yarra, here clear, shallow and silvery. His land was absolutely riddled with rabbits. It was the most wonderful area for sport that could be imagined, but you were always tripping over burrows or having the ground cave in underneath you as you ran; and the steep hillsides were a network of gully erosion caused by the rabbits. It was for this reason that old man Bourchier favoured the ferret rather than the gun, though we boys frowned on the method because of its uncertainty.

The plan was to head for a well known warren with the ferret stinking abominably in a small box out of which his ferocious mean little face and red beady eyes glared through the bars, as you slung the box on your shoulder. Having surveyed the warren the procedure was to net every opening *except one*, and then send the ferret down. What happened next was dramatic in the extreme. There was first a prolonged silence and then, suddenly and unexpectedly, a quite tremendous underground thundering as of distant hooves and, if you were lucky, out into the nets like acrobats fired from a circus cannon came rabbits from every hole, frightened to death by the smell of the ferret. If you were not so lucky what happened was that the rabbits would come hurtling, like rush hour passengers out of the London tube, from the one hole you'd forgotten to net or had failed to find. Unless at this point someone with a gun was standing by, the whole evening's work was ruined. Worse, though, would be when the rabbits came into the nets and, the nets having been removed there would be no sign of the ferret. He'd probably decided to devour a baby rabbit somewhere in the depths and you could either wait till he was finished or calculate the hazard of sending down a second ferret who might stay with him to share the meal.

It was because of these hazards that we much preferred shooting and it also had an element of companionship lacking with the taciturn inhuman ferret. Uncle Basil would let us beat the bush about fifty feet on either side of him but 'behind' his gun and it was our task to flush the rabbits from the tussocks where they were crouching and give him a chance at them. To see a rabbit in full career, to watch Uncle Basil, who was an excellent shot, raise his gun to his shoulder and fire, to see the rabbit hurtling over and over like a ball of fur instead of running, gave a sharp pleasure which it would be dishonest not to recognize as sadistic, but which

The Road to Gundagai

is common to boys—and perhaps to older boys. While Uncle Basil 'broke' his gun, ejected the smoking cartridge and blew through the barrel it was our job to rush up to the fallen rabbit, and if it were dead, hold it aloft in triumph. If it were not dead then we brained it quickly against a nearby stone. The job of skinning and gutting also fell to us and we learned to be expert at these two essentially inglorious operations. Having nicked the hind feet and got the fur off laboriously over the tail it was wonderful to be able to skin a rabbit tail to head in one single sure thrusting pull. Nothing was so smooth and pink as a freshly skinned rabbit's flesh; nothing so soft and white and mucid as the underneath of its freshly pulled skin. Knotted together by fore and hind feet, the skins, stretched on a piece of bent fencing wire, were put out in the sun to dry. Our pocket money came from their sale at one and threepence a dozen to the itinerant skin merchants: not a very quick way to make money.

On this particular evening as we were emerging from a copse of stringy bark and sheoak along the edge of the river Uncle Basil flushed a bronzewing pigeon and couldn't resist a shot. It plummeted to earth and I later boasted of this exploit on his behalf to the Bourchiers, only to draw down on Uncle Basil, much to my embarrassment, the rebuke that bronzewings were protected and didn't he know better than to be setting a bad example to the boys? Seldom have I been so mortified. However there can have been no permanent ill feelings for it was old man Bourchier who that night suggested that Uncle Basil should stand for election as councillor for the Shire of Eltham and thus launched him on a brief but vivid political career which reached its climax at *Proclamation Hurstbridge Township Week*.

Uncle Basil was easily elected, defeating an elderly buffer long past his prime, and he became Cr. B. Y. Hall (misinterpreted as 'coroner' by Colin). He let us accompany him on his parish rounds where he touched his hat to local Mums with shapeless unbrassiered bosoms and harassed faces, with their hair in their eyes over the washtub; kissed snotty little babies; handed sugar lollies and peppermint sticks to older children; and discussed the weather and the fruit crop with the farmers. Although he was obviously a gent, he was not a 'tonk' or a 'nana', and the hard-faced orchardists leaning over a five-barred gate in a grey flannel singlet, their terrible ill-fitting Australian store teeth shifting unevenly behind their thin calculating lips, would nod grudgingly: he was all right. We knew he had their confidence and therefore when he was made the principal figure at a ceremony proclaiming the little village of Hurstbridge to be a township, we were not at all surprised.

Up the Country

It was a memorable day. The rough football field between the creek and the railway track had been hung with bunting for the occasion and a police band from Eltham was playing gems from *Little Nellie Kelly*. ('The Boys are all mad about Nellie, the daughter of Officer Kelly.') There was a marquee and lots of free ice-cream and the local M.P., resplendent in a Prince Albert and gold chain came up from Melbourne to make a speech. But the climax of the afternoon's proceedings was an oration by Councillor B. Y. (for Yaldwin) Hall which was to end with breaking out the Australian flag at the head of a freshly erected forty foot pole, cut in the hills by the Shanhuns the day before and erected in the football ground last night. The flag, neatly furled at the top of the pole, hung as expectantly as we did while the Councillor's peroration rose to its height.

'And so, we in the township of Hurstbridge and in the Shire of Eltham can nevertheless count ourselves one with the vast reaches, the myriad peoples of the British Empire, spread out across the world like our spreading Australian flag!'

He turned to the special constable whose duty it was to jerk the cord that would free the Southern Cross and send it floating out over the little country town deep in the bushy hills. Jerk as he would the flag remained unbroken. Uncle Basil did a quick gear-change and reversed his simile.

'. . . members of an Empire who remain, despite our many differences, bound to each other with human and material ties as firm as those which bind that flag of ours into its little bundle at the head of that mast!'

Thunderous applause.

* * *

Thus Elysium continued for five beatific years: mushrooming in the crisp May holidays when the sun set early, tingeing the stringy barks with red; or one awoke in the morning to see—could it be? Yes it was—snow on distant Donna Buang; the September holidays full of golden wattle spread in a misty cloud through the olive grey bush, and in the distance a cow bell drilling a neat melancholy tunnel of sound through the spring silence; the long, hot droopy summer days with the haze of bush fires turning the sun to a silver disc. Down at Hurstbridge and even further along the line to Melbourne, life flowed on. The track was electrified from Heidelberg all the way to Hurstbridge. The panting little DDe locomotive disappeared and a two-coach electric suburban train replaced it, with rhomboid pantograph striking sparks from the overhead wires,

The Road to Gundagai

but with the illusion of the countryside preserved by gum tree poles instead of a steel catenary. Relentlessly Melbourne crept nearer, the ever widening stain marked by the insertion of new stations. Dennis (named for whom?) sprang up next to Fairfield Park; Darebin and Eaglemont, raw yellow gravel glinting in the sun, arose between Alphington and Heidelberg. Beyond Greensborough a marriage between the Victorian Railways and a smart real estate speculator produced a ludicrous progeny named Montmorency. From the top of the Kangaroo Ground Hill you could see junior skyscrapers rising in a thicket of distant matchsticks.

There was an eclipse of the sun and those of us who didn't watch it through carefully sooted glass shone little shards in the sun and dazzled our friends. Barry became a sturdy six and refused to call me 'Your Eminent Grace'. Joan was able to ride on horseback. To excite both kids we rigged up an aerial ropeway from the barn to a tall blue-gum and slid them on a pulley by this primitive téléférique from the barn's height towards the ground. (The rack railway up Mount Pilatus had nothing on this.) Myrtle Tosch married; the McLachlans left the village and went to school in Melbourne; old Miss Shannon died; Mrs. Tripp stopped taking in boarders. We abandoned the sulky for a Ford half-ton truck; the wonderful Model T which nuzzled you gently from its parking place as if it wished to slide slowly and effortlessly into gear. In the back of that half-ton truck Colin and I and John Grant Bruce bumped over the now familiar road to Christmas Hills while up front rode Mary Grant Bruce, beloved author of endless stories of Australian childhood, and her ramrod-stiff husband. But the long days which would never cease, with the rabbits bowling over like catherine wheels in the twilight, the magpies gurgling in the dawn, the tarantulas scurrying for shelter, the cooling splash in the yellow dam and the kookaburra cackling from the ring-barked tree, suddenly did come to an end.

One breathlessly hot, still day I woke to see Uncle Basil framed in the oblong of light at the entrance to the loft where we slept.

'Sorry to wake you boys, but I have to go over to Box Hill and thought you'd like to come. I'm going to sell the sulky,' he added.

'Why, oh why?' we questioned in wild surmise.

'Tell you later,' he said. 'Maybe Tom Cartwright would like to come too. Nip down the paddock and get him. Quick now, we have to have an early breakfast.'

I dashed across the paddock and found Tom even at this early hour shooting at empty kola beer bottles with his pea rifle. He said he'd be over right after breakfast. Would it take all day? Yes, I said, it would.

Up the Country

We went into the cavernous kitchen and I noticed by the alarm clock, an old five shilling Westclox which shook and shuddered like a marine engine, that it was only half past six. Why were we bound away so early and why to Box Hill? I pestered Uncle Basil. 'There's an auction on,' he said briefly and that was all we could get out of him, though I noticed that Aunt Nell seemed unusually preoccupied. The kids were not yet up.

Once we got outside it soon became clear why three boys were needed. Under the pepper tree stood the Ford half-ton truck and lashed on to it was Uncle Basil's little charcoal forge that he used for shoeing Betty. At the sight of it the rancid, frightening glue-factory smell of burning hooves rose in my nostrils with memories of the unbelievable stoicism of horses. The rest of the half-ton truck was taken up with household goods: a tin bath, a wooden mangle, a dismembered bedstead and some iron skillets. I had a dreadful premonition. 'Are you selling Fairview?'

Uncle Basil laughed. 'It's not as bad as that,' he said. 'Come on, give me a hand with the sulky.'

Standing horse-like in the shafts I pulled the sulky laboriously across the yard and Uncle Basil lashed it firmly to the rear of the Ford.

'Now,' he said when he had us all gathered around, 'one of you boys had better ride with me up in the cab. I want a second boy to sit in the back of the truck and keep an eye on the sulky. And the third boy,' he grinned sardonically 'he's going to have to sit *in* the sulky to weigh it down, otherwise it's going to bounce all over the place. The fellow that does that is going to have a pretty dusty ride so you'd better draw lots for it.'

We decided to take it by turns every half hour. The first turn was mine and this was lucky because swaying and jolting behind the half-ton truck, even at twenty miles an hour, was pretty rough, but the road was damp from recent rain. Colin, who took the second turn, was sometimes hidden from view in boiling clouds of dust and emerged a baked yellow mummy at the end of his half hour. We took the high land over to Kangaroo Ground and then worked slowly down hill towards the Yarra valley which we crossed by a ford near Warrandyte and had a picnic of beef sandwiches and lemonade, under the column of heat thrust down by an enormous white gum.

Box Hill was then the end of electrification for the line to Healesville and Warburton and when we reached the little town, covered with dirt and sweat, we headed straight up the unpaved main street and into a rough square surrounded by pepper trees where an open air auction was in progress. The auctioneer was a great

The Road to Gundagai

fat fellow in striped shirt sleeves, no collar but a pseudo gold stud winking at his throat. He reminded me of Mr. Foss the jobbing carpenter whose belly was so fat that when he clambered over joists and roofs he lost sight, beneath his sagging folds, of the leather pouch in which he kept his nails. The auctioneer spoke in an interminable monotone and the bidders were mostly leather-cheeked farmers in battered fedoras and blue dungarees, with here and there a sharp looking fellow in a collar and tie on the outskirts of the crowd. The auction was endlessly tedious and the auctioneer droned on through the heat, occasionally refreshing himself with swigs from a jar of stone ginger beer beside him. He stood on a little dais with an empty packing case before him as a desk, and over his head was a sheet of corrugated iron to shield him from the pelting heat which was now making everything white-hot. The ground and the people and the things which were to be sold—forges and carts and bedsteads and even horses and cows—seemed to mix and shimmer in the heat, and we longed parchingly for a drink, especially when we saw the farmers shamble off to slake their own thirst at a severe square wooden pub with the romantic name of *Rose Garland*. But Uncle Basil wanted to get everything sold in one fell swoop, and so we had to hold on while the auctioneer droned interminably on through the dry oppressive heat.

At last the forge was disposed of, excitingly, for seven pounds. The bedstead, the bath, the mangle and the iron skillets brought eight pounds and the sulky itself seventeen pounds. Uncle Basil, we felt sure, must be well satisfied with the day's work. So at any rate he appeared. He came towards us with his big broad brimmed hat casting his handsome, hawk-nosed leathery face into shadow and his powerful forearms shooting forward out of the dark blue open necked shirt as he ground Havelock shag tobacco between his hands and filled up his pipe.

'Well boys, I expect you'd like a swim?'

'Good-oh!'

'Let's go to the Surrey Dive then.'

This we'd never heard of, but ten minutes' drive in the jolting, jouncing heat brought us to the lip of an enormous abandoned quarry filled almost to the rim with translucent greenish water. It looked unbelievably inviting at the end of that hot droning day.

'There you are, boys,' said Uncle Basil. 'Strip and enjoy yourselves.'

At this moment Authority appeared in the form of a wizened man with a tattered cap. 'That'll be sixpence each,' he said.

'Fine,' said Uncle Basil fishing two bob from his pocket.

The wizened fellow pocketed the two bob and observed us undressing down to the buff. He waited a bit and then said sententiously, 'You can't swim here without bathing togs.'

Our hearts sank. Uncle Basil interceded. 'They've come all the way from Hurstbridge, officer, and their tongues are hanging out from heat. Can't you make an exception, just this once?'

The wizened fellow shook his head. 'Couldn't do it. Never hear the last of it from the council. Might lose me job.'

It was evident he was not in the mood. Uncle Basil demanded with dignity and was handed back with ill grace, his two bob, and we all scrambled back into our hot, dirty, sweaty clothes and into the half-ton truck, unwashed and unslaked.

Uncle Basil was unusually silent on the long drive home and when we finally reached *Fairview* in the hot dark of the night he dismissed us with less than his usual pleasantness and we went to bed, but not before the following exchange had taken place.

'Oh Basil, is that all you got?'

'It's not bad considering it's the wrong season of the year. Anyway sulkies are going out and cars are coming in. We need to sell all we can, before we leave.'

So that was it! They *were* leaving *Fairview*! I kept the secret to myself until we were in the train going home, and then, while Colin did his best to keep the little tabby-and-white kitten that we had been given as a farewell present from scrambling out of his kit bag, I told him the sad news.

Chapter Ten

WE ARE SCOUTS OF TOORAK

Passing the massive gold and black wrought iron gates of our Government House, *Stonnington*, I saw through the bars some green-capped boys marching. It all looked woefully unattainable and I gazed hopelessly, holding young Lance's go-cart handle so that he wouldn't hurtle at gathering speed down Glenferrie Road. The green-capped boys tramped on round the corner and into the playing field, their black kerchiefs dangling neatly, their polished boots scrunching on the gravel.

'Graham!'

'I was watching the boys, Mother. I want to be with them.'

'Very *well* then. We'll see.'

Never one to take half measures Mother did an abrupt tack to leeward and strode masterfully through the big gate. Almost at once a policeman was upon us. I saw the prospect of a crunch with officialdom.

'Yerss?' said the unfriendly man in uniform, clearly lacking in respect for the upper middle classes and equally clearly an Aussie. But Mother took him smartly aback.

'To whom have I the pleasure of speaking?'

'Eh? Well, er, I'm on guard duty here.'

'I should like to know what those boys are doing,' said Mother in much the same tone as she might ask the way to Malvern Town Hall.

'It's a boy scout rally,' said the bobbie.

'I should like to speak to whoever's in charge.'

The bobbie scratched the back of his neck. 'In charge?' Well that's not easy. It's some kind of a charity for the Governor, see? But the fellow in the tent over there might help you.'

'I'm greatly obliged to you,' said Mother, pressing a coin into the astonished John Hop's hand. She swept on, calling to me over her shoulder.

It happened that on duty in the recruiting tent was the representative of the First Toorak Troop. His mimeographed voucher bade

We are Scouts of Toorak

me report the following Friday night at Troop Headquarters in Fairbairn Road.

* * *

To a Melburnian the names Toorak and Fairbairn have an aristocratic ring. Toorak is the Belgravia of Melbourne, and the Fairbairns an old pastoral family. But names can be misleading. The First Toorak Troop drew the bulk of its boys from the poorer area down near the railroad tracks and from adjacent industrial Prahran. The great mansions perched among flowering gumtrees and curving streets on the heights above the Yarra sent no boys to the First Toorak Troop. But the shopkeepers' sons from Toorak 'Village', the sons of railwaymen from Hawksburn and the South Yarra electric yards, the sons of fitters and carpenters and automobile service station owners from Prahran and St. Kilda: these boys composed a little democracy in the heart of snobdom. As for Fairbairn Road it was a dreary cul-de-sac ending at the railroad track, and open at the top to the grounds of a co-educational State school fringed with desiccated cotton palms. In the middle was the First Toorak Troop. Separated from the street by a neat paling fence and from a winding back alley by high scantling, circular gravel paths led to a spanking new weatherboard single storey house. In front stood a large flagpole with the Southern Cross fluttering from the halyard. This was Troop Headquarters or T.H.Q. the site of many triumphs and disasters during the next four years.

One winter Friday—a crisp June night with just a touch of fog hovering over the green and amber signal lights of the railway—I arrived timidly at T.H.Q. in a blue sweater and my cardinal school cap. Steps led up to a great barn door, big enough to accommodate a hand-hauled wagon; a flood of light spilled out and a pandemonium of noise from the tramping of forty or fifty boys on a wooden floor. Someone spotted me and pulled me in; but it was not at all like being a new boy. As soon as they saw the mimeographed enrolment sheet in my hand they hustled me over to one corner of the large oblong noise-filled room. A very tall young man with soft fuzz on his chin stood with one foot on a pine stump seat, before which was a wooden bench.

'Another one, C.M.,' boys shouted.

'Hey C.M. a new cub for the pack.'

C.M. was Cubmaster. This military, or as we might now call it United Nations, shorthand was much in vogue at T.H.Q. C.M. was Keith Ring, about nineteen, but seeming to me to have the serenity, strength and wisdom of an octogenarian. He shot out a huge arm covered with blonde fuzz.

The Road to Gundagai

'Sit down with the rest of the cubs. Your six will be the Grays.'

I could hardly believe it. I was accepted; it was as simple as that.

'You'd better just watch us for a bit, till you get the hang of things.'

'O.K. C.M.,' I said happily.

But he bent a stern brow. 'That's one thing we don't say in the cubs,' he said. 'We say "Yes".'

'Yes. C.M.'

Slightly, but not much, abashed I watched bewildering and simultaneous activities. The wooden hall was full of busy noisy boys, but all working as the small teams into which they were divided. In one corner a 'six' was demonstrating the basic scout knots: reef-knot, sheepshank, clove hitch, sheet bend, bowline and thumbknot. The concentration was intense and when the 'sixer' in charge produced a bowline-on-a-bight they hoarsely cheered his versatility. In another corner a six was learning the basic first-aid bandages on their black cub scarves. These, removed, turned out to be triangular in shape. They were reduced by simple pleating first to 'broadfold', then to 'narrowfold', and finally to a sling for an arm injury realistically faked up with red ink and boot polish. Down the middle of the hall three teams were competing at medicine ball: leader bowl it backwards through the legs of his 'six'; rear man pick it up; run to the head of the line and bowl it backwards. The noise, as the knotters and bandagers cheered the medicine ballers, was terrific; and dust motes boiled in the 100 watt naked bulbs that hung trembling from the rafters below the high pitched roof.

A shrill whistle blew. The cubs scattered to their corners and the bedlam sank to a murmur. We all stood to attention while the dust settled along the lemon bars of light. Someone whispered what sounded like, 'Here comes the boss!' A side door, hitherto unnoticed, opened slowly and the C.M., tall and lanky crossed the room to the large open brick fireplace. He was followed by one of the strangest men I have ever seen.

He was about five foot three and not significantly taller than the cubs standing at attention. He had a large skull and an enormously broad high-domed forehead which shone and glistened in the cruel light from the ceiling. Beyond the forehead was fine blackish hair culminating in a bald spot. His nose was thin and bony and an old fashioned pince-nez on a gold chain made it look even thinner. The pince-nez had pebble lenses and his eyes looked enormous through them, deep sunk behind haggard cheekbones. He was

We are Scouts of Toorak

dressed in regulation scout uniform: black scarf and short-sleeved khaki shirt from which protruded lean bony arms, one hand weighed groundward by an enormous wrist-and-stop-watch combined; grey twill shorts from beneath which thin and knobby knees bunched like pollarded trees; thick wool socks and green garter tabs over meagre legs; brown brogues with crepe rubber soles. Although he was so small he walked with a heavy stoop and beneath his shirt showed what, had he been a woman, would have been a dowager's hump. To make up for the stoop and the smallness he walked with a long limping lope.

He stood before the fireplace and eyed us with a kindly but gaunt face. Here was a man possessed, eaten up by a mysterious fire. He seemed to swell and dominate the room as he stood silently regarding us, aware of the skull beneath the skin. He frightened just a little. This was The Boss, or 'The Baas' as he liked to be called; otherwise Scoutmaster of the First Toorak Troop of Boy Scouts and Wolf Cub Pack. He began to speak.

His voice made me jump for it was startlingly, theatrically, broodingly deep. It was an extraordinary speech: an amazing hodgepodge of half developed social theories, religious-cum-sexual mumbo-jumbo and patriotic scoundrelisms. But it made a tremendous impression. I felt that I could follow him anywhere. We all felt the same and of course what this queer bony little man had was the power of leadership. He spoke with a terrible compulsive earnestness that tautened his own neck strings and pulled his head forward as he projected the deep voice through a hall that was silent as the desert at night.

He started off by welcoming the new cubs (there were two others beside myself). He told us of the Wolf Cub Law: the cub gives in to the old wolf; the cub does not give in to himself. He reminded us that the C.M. was the Old Wolf and that we should listen carefully to what he said and carry out his orders. C.M. looked solemn and immensely tall as he towered by the Baas. His hairy knees came almost to the Baas' midriff; the Baas' huge head came not quite to C.M.'s shoulder. We should remember, said the Baas, that cubs went on to become scouts and great things would be expected of us. We could in the fullness of time become Rovers. It was a life of hard work and dedication but it was also a life of fun. It was not work all the time. He spoke of the Scout's code:

> Trusty, loyal and helpful
> Brotherly, courteous and kind
> Obedient, smiling and thrifty
> Pure as the whistling wind

The Road to Gundagai

Purity, cleanliness; those were the things. And GUTS—what the British called pluck or grit; what the Americans called sand (I never heard an American call it sand in my life). Sticking to the job; staying at one's post. We should remember the boy who took the Message to Garcia; and the Thin Red Line; and the Holiness of Women; and the Honour of the Troop and Pack. Of course we all knew that girls existed, that would come later; but there were other things, bigger things, loyalty to the King and to the Flag. No foul language. Naturally a fellow could hit his thumb with a hammer and say, Darn it! But . . . well, a mug of cold water poured down the shirt sleeve was a good remedy for that. Remember to keep your uniform smart and tidy, be a credit not only to the Pack but to your parents and even to the Unseen: be like the Rhineland carpenter who carved the *underneath* of the chair seat so exquisitely and who rebuked a ribald doubter with the words, 'God sees it.'

All this and much more, from the strange earnest man with the resonant voice, and the 100 watt bulbs streaming down on his high domed forehead. We took it all with the utmost seriousness. As the twig is bent . . . Then, suddenly, a great crooked smile, the impulsive stretching out of both hands in a big dismissive gesture, and it was over. He stumped quickly from the room and C.M. shouted, 'New cubs, come and get their uniforms in stores after the parade. Paaaack! Diiiisss-MISS!!' I fought my way over to the stores and breasted the counter. A black headed Irish fellow named Quayle, with a grin like a scimitar and a face covered with moles, blotches and freckles said:

'O.K. cub. Here's your issue.' I received a cap, but no badge ('Not till you pass yer tenderpad test.'), a scarf, First Toorak shoulder tabs in Cash's woven names and a copy of *Scouting for Boys*, a heavy paper-covered tome by our founder Lt. Gen. Sir Robert Baden Powell, as he then was. There was potent magic between its covers, I discovered later; but I'd had enough magic for one night. I was dizzy with magic and wanted to go home. At the door C.M. said:

'The Baas would like to see you before you go.'

I followed him into a small office off the main hall and there, sitting behind the desk was a little man in an unobtrusive grey suit and a subfusc tie, looking like a clerk in an insurance company. But the big domed head remained, bobbing pumpkin-like above the lean nose and the glittering pince-nez. He shot out his hand.

'Good luck,' he said with vibrant earnestness. I shot out my hand with manly vigour. The two hands, thirty inches apart, grasped air. I felt myself crimson. Scouts—and cubs—shake with the left hand. I corrected hurriedly.

We are Scouts of Toorak

'Sorry sir.'
'Call me Baas.'
'Baas.'
'We expect great things of you. See that you don't disappoint us.'

'I won't,' I cried fervently. I hadn't yet become bored and resentful at being told that 'great things' were expected of me. That came later, along with Kipling and Baldwin and Burne-Jones and J. W. Mackail, when it was discovered that they were my distant relatives. He nodded me out and I went forth on air into the cold fog-reek of the June night, clutching the new uniform to my chest. Inside it was wrapped the scorned school cap. On my head I wore a green cap with yellow piping. I was a cub.

* * *

Although cubs were not exposed to the full blast of The Baas' apocalyptic vision, no one so intense could fail to penetrate a boy's defences. While C.M.—good old phlegmatic, reliable, hairy armed C.M.—remained our combined sergeant, wet-nurse, games-master, schoolteacher and doctor, it was the Baas who held the flaming torch aloft. He was a product of the generation which grew to manhood between 1900 and 1910 and for whom the Romance of the Boer War was a living, indeed a quivering experience. Rider Haggard and John Buchan set the guide-lines for imagination and for heroism, as Baden Powell did for morality and Milner for political acumen. To them was perhaps mercifully denied the vision of fifty years later; the Peace of Vereeniging was to them what Locarno was to their sons. Generous co-operation of Briton and Boer; victor and vanquished shaking hands in a romantic landscape of neks and kopjes and drifts. Baden Powell a hero, but no less Botha and de Wet and, of course, Smuts above all. No Caudine Forks here but a generous and genuine confrontation of friend and foe; the end of Britain's (and Australia's) long period of isolation, and the simple hearty pleasures of *Jock of the Bushveld* and of women who had 'a youth's eager grace.' The Baas was steeped in it; and he steeped us in it. He was *the Baas* and he went on *treks* with a trek cart which we *inspanned* and *outspanned*. We knew about *sjamboks* and *spoors* and *laagers* and it was all about as Australian as a gnu.

But Aussie, good old dinkum Aussie, kept breaking through in the person of Bill Jackson: the Assistant Scoutmaster, top sergeant and devoted R.S.M. Bill Jackson was dark, swart and chunky, of medium height, great physical strength and unassailable moral

The Road to Gundagai

purity. He was about twenty-five and wore his black hair en brosse. When the Baas was walking ahead of the Troop on a hike (or trek) his eyes shiny with a vision, it was Bill who whistled up the stragglers, shouted the necessary commands and supervised all the administrative arrangements. He worshipped The Baas because he was 'an officer and a gentleman' and the Baas leaned heavily on him for the mundane business of running the Troop and the Pack. Bill was the disciplinarian who spotted barley-sugar socks, unkempt scarves and roller-coaster hats; he handled the indent for the canteen and was i/c Q.M. Stores for tentage, ropes, dixies, frying pans and other camp equipment; he saw that grounds at T.H.Q. were kept in order; he planned all the transport and logistics for the annual Christmas Camp; he replaced electric light bulbs, handled the rental and building account, ran the inter-patrol sports and swimming competitions; he personally issued rations from the stores tent at Camp, saw that loads were properly distributed not only in the trek but between big youths and little boys, strong scouts and not so strong tenderfeet; he supervised advance parties, cleared campsites and pitched tents: he repaired bicycles and sports equipment and torn uniforms and bloody noses. He was loud, irascible, lovable, strong and as utterly dedicated to boys as the Baas was to ideas. If the Baas were ill or away the Troop ran forward, a smoothly oiled machine with the momentum of Bill's drive and energy. The only thing he couldn't do was inspire us. The Baas, weedy, bald and visionary, did that. They were a perfect team.

After the Baas and Bill came 'Chief', a young man named Tilley; small, neatly built and with a sense of humour which the Baas lacked. He was a former Troop Leader and he took over at the time of the great Scout Jamboree at the Empire Exhibition in Wembley when both The Baas and Bill were away for six months. Like The Baas, he could command or make his presence felt without raising his voice and he was an expert in the quiet kidding and gentle deadpan sarcasm which gets under a boy's skin. One of his chores was to read us the weekly 'Budget', written by The Baas in far-off Wembley and carrying, six to eight weeks later (for this was long before the days of airmail) news of improbable deeds and unbelievable ceremonies in a faraway land.

'Standing on the chimney you could see right through to Wembley, if it wasn't for the houses in between,' said Mother cryptically when I told her breathless third-hand tales of King George V, Sir Alfred Pickford, the Deputy Chief Scout, and even B.P. himself.

Because of my height—which C.M. erroneously assumed would carry with it a corresponding air of authority—I was promoted

We are Scouts of Toorak

within two weeks to be Second of the newly formed White Six; and by the time preparations were on foot for the annual scout camp, to which a small group of cubs would be attached, I was promoted to be Sixer of the Whites. My colleague and opponent, the Sixer of the Tawnies, was a wily fellow named Giles. He had been a cub for a long time before my arrival—perhaps a year. I think he rightly resented my being jumped up so rapidly, particularly as all I had was height and a certain amount of book learning which was quite useless when it came to broadfold and narrowfold bandages, sheepshanks and sheetbends, or lighting a fire in the rain with only two matches. But inordinately puffed up by my advancement and very proud of the two yellow rings on my blue sweater, I was blithely unaware of pits being dug for me.

Though the Baas did not care as a rule for troops drawn exclusively from public schools, he made an exception in the case of Wesley. Mostly he preferred a troop to be drawn from several suburbs so that the boys would be sons of butchers and blacksmiths and even night-men, as well as of lawyers and doctors. One of his objections was that I brought too many Scotch College friends into the troop. However, a school troop unashamedly so branded, which operated as an offshoot of Wesley College was tolerated. The Baas was Low Church and if Scotch was Presbyterian, Wesley was Methodist and scoutmaster Kennedy was all right. But although the scoutmasters hobnobbed, somehow the two Troops never got on well together. We were too cliquy, too inward looking in our own particular claques and gangs, and when one weekend a joint camp was held at Templestowe on the upper Yarra it was much of a failure. We slept in separate tents; there was an attempt to make us mess together but they didn't like our Johnny Cakes and we didn't care for their flapjacks. The camp fire songs were not a success because they didn't know ours, nor we theirs. Kennedy however hit our funny-bones because he was a man who used long words with an extremely sober face and he also sang us a stirring song, I suppose the music hall equivalent of an evangelical hymn, which created a deep impression on all who heard it. The scene opened, in the verse, after the 'vamp till ready', with a tall young man lying in a hammock. He is 'dreaming his chances away'. Up to the hammock comes an older man who wags a finger at him and addresses him in these terms:

> 'It's pluck not luck that wins
> In the race of life you'll find, my lad;
> You'll go drifting if you dream
> So buck up and hustle against life's stream.'

The Road to Gundagai

At this point there was a long rallentando while Kennedy gathered breath for the punch line:

> 'But if you've plenty of bull-dog grit
> And your heart is staunch and true,
> And with brain and muscle you are willing to tussle
> Then the world wants Men Like You.'

This was just the sort of simple ditty, reducing life to its inessential and never-to-be-encountered blacks and whites that would appeal to boys of twelve. Although we were never told so, we imagined the tall young man leaping smartly out of his hammock and, as Stephen Leacock has put it, 'dashing off madly in all directions.'

* * *

The Christmas Camp was held near a hamlet called Tonimbuk in the foothills of the Baw-Baw Ranges about sixty miles east of Melbourne. We were to disembark from the Gippsland Express at a railway station named Bunyip. This seemingly innocuous name carried fearsome overtones and filled us with a delightful dread. For the Bunyip sat, stood or crawled—one wasn't quite sure which—at the very apex of the antipodean Grimm's Fairy Tales with which the aborigines used to beguile their children's long evenings. To Australian ears it had a sound not unlike that of Kraken, Vampire or Werewolf to Europeans. There were disputes as to what the Bunyip really was. Some said it was an enormous white kangaroo that bounded noiselessly through the bush with immense leaps. Others said it was a nameless monster that dwelt in swamps or billabongs and emerged only on the nights of full moon to claim its victims, who were usually disobedient boys. Accordingly we shuddered with pleasurable dread at the thought of visiting a place called Bunyip and even the prosaic camping list, handed out a week before we were to set off, failed to dampen our feelings. The final item, Snake-bite outfit (to be worn round neck), was the subject of a special lecture delivered by Bill on snakes and their habits.

The Australian bush, he said, was full of snakes and we should remember that nearly all of them (except the Queensland Carpet Snake which we were unlikely to encounter as we were camping in Victoria some thousand miles south of Queensland) were—POISONOUS. The commonest types in the bush in Victoria in order of viciousness are the Copperhead, the Tiger snake, the Brown snake and the Black snake. As you know, the idea they had in

We are Scouts of Toorak

olden times that snakes had forked tongues is all my eye. You can see from this diagram here on the board that the snake has two large fangs or teeth on the front of its mouth and these are connected by ducts to poison glands secreted in the snake's cheeks. When the snake strikes it punctures your skin with these hollow teeth and the poison rushes in through the hole. The tongue does dart and it may be forked, but it's the teeth not the tongue that do the harm. And that poison is DEADLY. In five minutes, less than five minutes if you're bitten on the trunk (though of course that's very rare; usually you get bitten on the arm or the leg), in five minutes the poison has reached the heart and paralysis *and death* result! Now, normally you wouldn't see a snake anywhere near a Scout Camp or even when you were hiking because, don't forget, for one thing, snakes are more afraid of you than you are of them.

'Who's he talkin' about? Not me!'

'Quiet!'

But of course if you were to tread on a snake by accident when it was lying asleep in the sun, or to irritate it in some way such as shoving a stick down a snake hole ('What dope would ever do *that*?'), or above all, if you come between a snake and its nest, then, it may attack you.

'But Bill, how do you know you're between the snake and its nest, when you don't know where the nest is?'

'I'll come to that later.'

So the thing to do is to be on guard against snakes and for this purpose we do the following:

One, we wear puttees up to our knees so that the snake can't strike at our flesh.

Two, we never jump over a fallen log or stone in case a snake might be basking on the far side and you might jump on him.

Three, we never start fishing around with our bare hands in deep grass or scrub; trample it first.

Four, in addition to what you've already learned in first-aid, you carry this little snake-bite outfit round your neck on a piece of thread or string *at all times*. Bill held up a small wooden tube about two inches long and half an inch in diameter.

This is your snake-bite outfit. It unscrews in the middle and, as you can see, the top half contains a small sharp metal lancet about half an inch long; the remainder of the outfit contains this purple powder—about as much as will cover a halfpenny—known as permanganate of potash or Condy's Crystals. Now, all right Quayle, you come here. You're a tough fellow; we'll assume you've been bitten in the arm by a tiger snake.

The Road to Gundagai

('Bitten on the ass by a hornet.')

'Quiet there!'

Quayle came forward pantomiming extreme terror and sat down on a bench near Bill.

'Now here's what we do. Quayle's been bitten on the left wrist by a tiger snake. How do we know that?'

'Well you see,' said Quayle, 'I've got two little dark spots about half an inch apart right next to me funny bone.'

Bill scowled. 'We'll have a little co-operation, thank *you*. Now that's right. Look for those two little spots and the first thing you do—the very first—is rip off your scarf.' He ripped off his scarf with a dramatic gesture. 'And tie it tightly in what we call a tourniquet *between* the bite and the heart—that is above the bite. That way you stop the flow of blood. Want it tighter Quayle? Okay. Give me a knife someone, thanks.'

Bill thrust the handle through the knotted scarf and twisted it several times. Quayle's arm looked empurpled and swollen and he cried,

'Hey, ace it up Bill, that hurts.'

Bill grinned and loosened the tourniquet slightly.

'That's just to give you the general idea. Now comes the outfit. First you take the lancet and make a couple of fine scratches joining the holes and drawing blood. There!'

'Hey, that's my blood you're using!'

'Won't be long. Then you apply the mouth to the wound, first making dead sure your lips aren't cracked or your gums in bad shape. Then you suck the blood AND the poison and spit it out. Like this. Holy smoke, Quayley, when did you last have a bath?'

'Friday night is Rexona soap night,' said Quayle.

'Okay. You do that three or four times, spitting out each time. Then you take the Condy's Crystals and rub them well into the wound, and then repeat the sucking and spitting. I've had enough Quayley; when we're finished have a wash.'

'Phe-ew, what a pong,' said someone.

Bill continued, 'Then, because by now the fellow's getting drowsy from what little of the poison may have reached him, you walk him up and down, up and down, while you send someone for the doctor.'

'S'posin' you're alone?'

'Then you walk him to the doctor.'

'What if there's no doctor?'

'Well then you walk him to the Camp First-Aid Post. And then you get him a cup of hot tea or coffee and wrap him up in blankets till the doctor comes. Oh, and don't forget. Loosen the tourniquet from time to time, or else the fellow's circulation is going to stop and he may get gangrene. All right Quayle, you can go back to your seat. Any questions?'

'Bill, supposing you're not bit on a limb but on the trunk?'

'Well, it's very unlikely of course, unless you were doing something stupid like lying down in the bush for a snooze. You'd just have to hack at the poisoned part and hope for the best. Prevention is better than cure and the proper answer to that question is don't get in a position where a snake can bite you in the trunk.'

'But Bill, what about if you're in the tent at night and a snake creeps into your groundsheet or your blanket?'

'Snakes don't come out at night. Any more questions?'

'Bill what do you do if a snake bites you on the head?'

'The head! Well, it wouldn't make much difference to your head, Morris. Any more silly questions? O.K. Trooooop Di-i-i-s-miss!'

That night each of us bore away our little snake-bite outfit and an overwhelming load of nightmarish stories about snakes: brown snakes, black snakes, tiger snakes and copperheads; Queensland carpet snakes, pythons and anacondas; snakes that got in under the flaps of tents; snakes that crawled up the pants' leg of a sleeping scout, round his crotch (a favourite, that one) and down the other leg and away into the bush; snakes that chased boys through the bush, hissing as they went; snakes that brave scouts picked up by the tail and cracked over their heads like a stockwhip so that the reptile's back was broken; snakes that remained unharmed and alive when cars ran over them until the driver reversed and braked and skidded his back wheel right *on* the snake; snakes that put their own tails into their mouths and pursued boy scouts like rolling hoops; snakes carried skyward in the beaks of Kookaburras and dropped to the ground where, broken backed, they made a tasty meal . . . it was a relief to board the train for Bunyip.

* * *

We awoke at six to a transfigured morning. The sun shone powerfully, the sky was a bright watery blue and the bush steamed itself dry in the bold light. The birds were deafening: the heavenly gurgle of the magpie, the high metallic cackle of the Kookaburra, the screech of the grey pink-combed galah and the rattle of the wattle-bird. Breakfastless except for a cup of tea (we'd eaten all our rations the previous night) and prickling all over from hay and straw, we marched off in the morning light. The bush sparkled with watery spangles, and the yellow mud road led straight to the

The Road to Gundagai

clear blue line of the mountains. Within an hour we reached the edge of a small gully and looked down onto a fern-matted stream making a wide meander. This was Cannibal Creek. Tonimbuk. In the middle of the meander a tent was already pitched and a voice shouted: 'Coo-ee!'

All that day we worked at pitching camp. The scouts did most of the heavy work but the cubs were assigned appropriate chores. My job was to carry forks and ridgepoles for the tents, after they'd been cut down in the bush, and then hold them in position while they were rammed home. The tents were eight feet by twelve with front flaps and a fly, and the method of erection was simple. Having selected flat ground you dug two holes into which you put a forked branch six feet high and tamped the earth down solid. The ridgepole was then threaded through the tent on the ground and carried on the shoulders of two scouts to the upright forks. The trick was to get uprights and a ridgepole that were straight and not too knobbly; scouts cut off the knobbles with tomahawks and the more enterprising de-barked the saplings so that for a wonderful few hours, before they began to turn brown, they shone in the sun with the smooth gelatinous glow of a fresh chicken bone.

Another trick was to get the tent straight and taut by guying it. Lazy scouts whose poles were too crooked or whose holes were too shallow endeavoured to correct this by taut guying, but C.M.'s sharp eye soon spotted these short cuts and the culprits were made to start all over again. After the tent was ship-shape the fly went on over a second ridge-pole sufficiently elevated so that the guyed fly would not touch the actual tent roof and permit leaks in a rainstorm. Once the tent was up it was the cub's duty to peg down the drop fly round the back and sides and then to scrape the floor with a mattock, and a besom of gumleaves, to make it smooth, soft and aromatic. By lunch time each patrol and each six had a neat white canvas home $8 \times 12 \times 6$ in which eight boys were supposed to sleep; and with the erection of the special tent for the Baas and the stores tent, the little scout village had began to take shape along the margin of Cannibal Creek.

I was never much good at sleeping in a scout tent on the ground. I didn't have a sleeping bag, and my two blankets and one rubber groundsheet got mixed up during the night. Invariably I awoke in the small hours either naked and shivering, or clammy from contact with the ground sheet, or sweating in a ball of tangled blankets. I tried digging a hip-hole but either lost it or couldn't get my hip to fit it properly. I tried sewing back numbers of the Melbourne *Age* and *Argus* into doubled blankets for warmth; but

We are Scouts of Toorak

they split and tore and I ended up with a giant newspaper sausage at one end of the blanket. I tried sleeping with 'more under you than over you' but this wasn't a success either.

These periods of wakefulness did help to show the wonder of the bush in deep night. I would ease myself stealthily out of my sleeping kit and, at first with fear of snakes, step outside the tent away from the fug of sleeping boys and into the stars and the silent grey ghosts of the gumtrees. Such nights were wondrous because the bush was then very mysterious and aware. A low moon shone like a cold unwinking eye and cast a cool barred light through the tall eucalyptus. A tremendous dusting of stars glowed in a pale congregation above the tree tops. Cannibal Creek gurgled softly in the background but there were other songs and sounds: the sad two-tone cadence of the mopoke or Australian owl; the whirr and faint grey shadow as a flying fox sailed from one high tree-top to another; the furtive scratching of a wombat. At such times came the awesome knowledge that trees, animals and birds had all squeaked and rustled in just this way for untold ages before we had come; that they were indeed the face of time. The bush was cryptic, ageless and self-contained: it was we who were totally irrelevant. A faint glow remained at the heart of the campfire's dying embers. A burned-out log fell, sending a small shower of sparks up into the night. Flames flickered from the resultant crash and amorphous shadows ebbed and flowed across the roof of the tent. Then a mysterious rustle, coming from far off as though the pre-cambrian forest were speaking, ended in the gust of a first-light breeze. The flame guttered out; the long strips of dry bark thrummed against the smooth bole of a tall white-gum, and I crept back to bed.

* * *

The most important place in camp was the Stores Tent supervised by Bill and we cubs watched its erection and the unloading of its contents with great interest. Tilley acted as indent agent and allowed us to help in stacking bags of flour, rice, dried apricots, potatoes and onions, tins of jam and sugar, processed cereals and oatmeal. Though our eyes popped at this display I must say that on looking back the food seems to have been both monotonous and inadequate, and certainly lacking in the basic balanced nutriment dear to dietitians. We were all abominable cooks; we burned flapjacks; boiled rice into a soggy glue; made tea strong enough to 'trot a mouse' and scorched the porridge. Here is a typical menu for the First Toorak Troop on the banks of Cannibal Creek, Tonimbuk:

The Road to Gundagai

Breakfast:	Porridge
	Prunes
	Bread and jam
	Tea with condensed milk
Dinner:	Bread and cheese
(i.e. lunch)	Bread and jam
	Flapjacks or Johnny Cakes
	Tea with condensed milk
Tea:	Potato and onion stew
(i.e. dinner)	Boiled rice and dried apricots
	Bread and jam
	Tea with condensed milk

Flapjacks and/or Johnny Cakes were made of flour, water and salt fried in lard, and our menu included no meat or fish, no butter, no eggs, no fresh vegetables or milk. At the end of two weeks, there was a mild outbreak of scurvy, and a ration party was sent two miles away through thick bush to a deserted farm where it stripped two gnarled trees clean of cherry-plums, and staggered back with four dixies full of good vitamin C and ascorbic acid.

After food, the disposal of waste; and to this too Bill bent his strength and ingenuity, and enlisted not-quite-so-eager-as-usual scouts and cubs. First apparatus to be constructed was the KYBO (Keep Your Bowels Open) sometimes known, even less euphonically, as The Rear. This was accomplished by digging a long trench, deep and narrow. At each end rose forked uprights, as if for the erection of a dwarf tent; we then placed on the forks carefully smoothed cross bars which provided a convenient if not very dignified straddle for communal use of The Rear. The trench was then surrounded by a neat fence of brushwood and gum saplings, stitched together at top and base with bracken stalks. Sooner or later this fence turned a sickly brown, giving as it were, a foretaste of the functions performed behind it. At the far end of the KYBO was the urinal. This was just a hole in the ground, though if the architect were of a decorative turn of mind he could line it with the stones and granite chips excavated while digging the KYBO. This particular amenity was for show rather than for use, as most boys just walked off into the bush and let go, despite daring speculations as to what a really ingenious snake might do—such as running up a stream of downward pouring water.

A less disagreeable chore was that of levelling and clearing the combined campfire circle and parade ground. This was done by stripping off the grass and scrub with entrenching tools, sweeping

We are Scouts of Toorak

the area with gumleaf besoms and then manhandling dead logs into a rough circle. We dug a four-foot posthole and a field party went into the bush to secure a tall straight sapling—the best were white gum. They cut it down: first a large notch facing the direction of desired fall, then a smaller notch directly opposite and a little above, then the magic cry, 'Timber!' The top of the tree shivered as in a storm, then dipped gracefully to the accompaniment of a sharp and prolonged Cr-r-a-a-a-ck; and finally with a leafy crash tore down small timber and leaped from its moorings to the forest floor, leaving a smooth yellow stump split by a toothbrush of splintered wood. The tree was stripped and a pulley wheel notched into its top. Halyards were run through and eager scouts elevated the pole as the Easter Islanders elevated their colossal statues: a sloping trench and all hands to the pumps. The Southern Cross, neatly balled, sailed up the halyard of the newly erected post, and at the top, after two or three frenzied jerks, it broke out and flew bravely over the new campsite of the First Toorak Troop: five stars and the great seven pointed star in the fly, and in one corner the small Union Jack with:

'The broad white diagonal stripe
Nearest the pole at the top.'

The final task, and by far the most popular, was the construction of the swimming hole by throwing a weir of stones and gravel across the local creek—whether it was the Cannibal, the Mystery or the Tarago—somewhat below the watering place. It usually produced a pool about four feet deep and perhaps twenty feet long. No room for diving but room for forty boys to splash and flounder in the heat of the afternoon, every one of them stark naked.

A typical day in the camp at Tonimbuk or Gembrook or Neerim —though it was always known as C.H.Q. I.T.K. T.P. (i.e. Camp Headquarters First Toorak Troop)—began with reveille at seven blown on a bugle by the duty patrol-leader. Patrols then prepared breakfast in the almost invariably chill dawn and spent half an hour cleaning up the tent and their personal kit, the cooking area and the patrol limits, of Eagles, Curlews, or Wolves. (I am assuming that all who read these lines are devotees of Baden Powell's *Scouting for Boys* and therefore *know* that every Troop is organized into patrols of eight boys under a patrol leader, and that they are named after animals, birds and even the more lordly reptiles: who can forget the great BP's instructions for the Call of the Rattlesnake Patrol, 'Rattle a small pebble in an empty potted meat tin.')

This activity preceded inspection, carried out by the Baas, accompanied by Bill and the Troop Leader and, if they happened to be in the Camp, the C.M. and Chief. This inspection was pretty rigorous and could be exacting for the Patrol Leader or Sixer. While the Baas contented himself with examining uniforms, watching for uneven hats or barley sugar socks, Bill would nose vigorously around the tent, shaking it to see if it were well pitched; the cooking area, peering into every pot and pan; and even the local KYBO, if you happened to have constructed one. After a final piercing nod from the Baas and a curt 'Good work, Curlews' or 'Must smarten up that galley a bit, Wolves', we trooped over to the parade ground and standing in a circle listened to a brief pep talk from the Baas and the orders of the day from Bill.

We then broke off and spent the morning in a variety of useful tasks designed either to keep the camp in better condition or to teach us the rudiments of scouting. You might be ordered with a companion to fell a tree so that its topmost branches hit the ground within a given circle. You might be told to take a compass and a sheath knife and fetch a circle through the bush back to Camp. Some boys would be detailed for a ration party to go into the nearest township for extra stores; others might be bidden to a colloquy with the Baas, seated on stumps and upended logs on 'What Every Scout Should Know'. One group would practise semaphore signalling with two flags; another would construct a watch tower against fire, using only saplings and lashing-rope.

This was a necessary and sensible precaution. The eastern ranges in which we camped were ravaged by bushfires almost every year and though our camps were never actually threatened we often smelled and saw the glow of distant fires and occasionally had to make our way through them. In 1925 we were at the tail-end of the great Noojee disaster in which many people lost their lives and families were saved by crouching all night in a creek bed covered with water-soaked sugarbags. On this occasion a trestle bridge that we crossed collapsed two hours later.

Of course there were always the fatigue jobs to be done, but even they were fun in the smiling sun and the shimmering bush: peeling potatoes; drawing rations for the Patrol or Six; cutting or gathering firewood; writing up the daily camp log. Then came lunch and after it a compulsory rest period of one hour followed by further useful or elevating chores and ending with a swim. This brought the camp to the preparation and consumption of the evening meal after which came the best time of the day when from six to seven in the gloaming of the scented friendly bush it was DAYP (Do as You Please).

This hallowed hour was a wonderful and relaxing time. You

We are Scouts of Toorak

could spend it any way you liked except, as Bill said, 'using foul language or lighting fires in the bush'. You could wander with a chosen companion, or by yourself, or with a group of pals. You could sit in the tent and read, or whittle a stick, or write home, or make a little kerosene moat to repel ants, or help with preparations for the evening camp fire. You could lounge from tent to tent visiting friends and rivals, or learn to throw a boomerang, or play football or cricket on the rude camp field, or sit on the banks of the creek and watch the waterflies skimming over its surface in the evening light. Some of our camps were pitched near timber tracks. These were crude railway lines made of roughened two-by-fours down which logs were skidded from the forest to the sawmill and which assaulted hill and dale at a fearsome sixty degree angle. These could be explored in DAYP. Or you could try and have a serious talk with the Baas about scouting, life, girls, work, the Universe, the War, or why some fellows have pimples. But whatever you were doing at seven o'clock the bush darkened, the cry would go up 'Campfire!' and you would approach a rapidly filling circle of boys facing inward to a noble pyramid of wood inside which the young fire already glowed and crackled. With a blanket draped over your shoulders and your tin mug ready for late coffee, you sat down on or below a log seat and prepared in the gathering darkness, and the boldness it conferred, for the most wonderful part of the day.

Sombre draped figures—the Baas, Bill, Chief—made their way to seats of honour. Though the Camp Fire Circle was supposed to be like the Round Table, nevertheless wherever the Baas decided to sit automatically became its head and there was some shuffling among the boot-lickers ('straws' we used to call them because they were 'sucking up' to the Baas) as they eased themselves nearer the seats of the mighty. The fire blazed up and in doing so seemed to pull the cooling starlit night down on top of it so that we became a snug, ruddily lit company at the bottom of a well. Master of Ceremonies was Bill who announced by the aid of a flashlight the items that would follow. The campfire sing-song was divided into choruses sung in unison (with a few wild spirits, frowned on in the dark, singing harmony) and individual items which were usually solo songs, but could be recitations. Much arm twisting had gone on during the day to dragoon individual scouts into promising solo numbers. Under cover of darkness quite a number normally agreed and generally kept their promise, though there was always the odd scout who, when his turn came, remained tongue tied under friendly entreaty until excused by the Baas. Once a young second with a piercingly beautiful choirboy soprano forgot the words in mid-song and dashed into the bush, blanket flying and racked with sobs.

The Road to Gundagai

I had a good clear voice and thanks to endless and compulsory Sunday evenings over the *Scottish Students Song Book* with Mother at the piano, a fairly large repertoire of pieces such as *The Mulligan Guards; Wrap Me Up in My Tarpaulin Jacket*, or *A Famous Scotch Professor Was Walking by The Nile*. Better received though, were English music-hall numbers which the ever-considerate Terence Crisp had sung and played for us on those same Sunday evenings, after the limp salad and the cold meat. Some of these were real favourites—no credit to me but to the author—and I was often given an encore ('Ongcore apple core, Kick 'im out the back door') for such numbers as *The Body in the Bag; When Flossie Found Her First Grey Hair; I do Like an Egg for my Tea; In the Jolly Old Winter Time* and *The Body's Upstairs*. The strains of such rollicking Edwardian numbers, wafted out into the silent antediluvian bush and the deep antipodean sky, struck me even then as having a faintly sinister incongruity.

The songs died down and the campfire sank to a ruddy glow. You had to hold up your hand or a blanket against the heat, and into the silence came drifting the smell of brewing coffee. This was the time, while the fatigue party was passing silently round the circle of boys serving steaming coffee into tin mugs, for the Baas to speak to the Troop. Shrouded in the darkness that flowed in at the edges of the circle, and blurred and bemused by the shadows of flickering flames, group intimacies and indeed the communion that is necessary between the leader and the led was established with superb and insinuating ease. The Baas started speaking in a strong low voice and we listened, drowsed by the fire and the hot coffee, varied by a yipe from those who had been unwise enough to bring aluminium cups. The talk was always the same and it was basically about man's relation to the universe (i.e. God) and his fellow man. The Baas was unaffected. He did not talk down; he did not hesitate to use big—or polysyllabic—words; but he did not talk up either. The exhortation to the practice of the golden rule and the carrying out of the scout law were quiet, and while intense, entirely lacking in either evangelism or mealy-mouthedness.

When it was over we staggered sleepily to our tents feeling better people than we were, feeling removed from the hurly-burly of daily personal relations with all their rough edges and sharp elbows; feeling—on coffee and a pep-talk—elated. Perhaps the magic of the bush helped out. For as we lurched tentward, some of us stopped to 'water the grass' and as we stood voiding in the eucalypt-scented darkness, we were lost in contemplation of the silent, Bunyip-haunted bush, over which the stars, minus the late-rising moon, looked down in chilly disapproval; and we felt at once very small yet filled with a

We are Scouts of Toorak

strange nobility, soon to be lost in foetid snores as sleep descended on the silent camp.

* * *

By the end of a couple of camps we could do an incredible number of useless and useful things. We could build a bridge across a dry ravine, suck venom out of a snake bite, put an arm in a sling, fry flapjacks and even toss them deftly so that the right side came down *up*, pitch a tent, light a fire with two matches and a bit of luck, and maybe a bit of cheating. But upon our return to town, stinking liberally after three weeks without a hot bath, the problem was to keep our interest at a high pitch in the drab surroundings of T.H.Q. by the edge of the railway track, the mean terrace houses and the grimy old lofts.

If our *taedium vitae* became too unbearable Bill Jackson had an unfailing remedy. We would bicycle out beyond the end of the car line to Ashburton. Here the houses thinned and the landscape was one of open paddocks dotted with bluegum, sheoak, and cootamundra. These paddocks were rented out to the local dairyman and they were rich in cow droppings. We would form up in two sides and Bill would organize what was known as a 'turd fight'. The rules were simple, you picked up a hard round cake of cow manure from the ground and hurled it at your opponent. Battle being joined, victory went to that side which forced its opponents back over an invisible line between two pre-selected trees. These lusty jousts were a wonderful way of letting off steam and we looked forward eagerly to them. There was only one rule: no soft turds. Anyone who broke this rule (and there was always at least one comic character) was convicted of 'ringing in a softie', and banished to the sidelines.

To mute the unbearable contrast between town and camp the Baas also started us off on frenzied extra-mural activities. One of these was to collect empty medicine bottles for the local hospital. This was a thankless business of door-to-door canvassing and at the end of the week all we had to show was fifty bottles. The Baas said that this, from a combined Troop and Pack of sixty boys, was just not good enough. We must try again. Never mind if the door is slammed in your face! Sift through dustbins or incinerators! A scout doesn't care if he gets his hands dirty! Go out and get those bottles!

As I cycled home after the meeting a brilliant thought struck me and I propped my bike up against the fence of our local G.P. and approached the surgery door.

The Road to Gundagai

'Good evening Dr. Gutteridge.' I stood at the 'alert' and gave the correct three-fingered salute.

Dr. Gutteridge was a tall rangy man with dark wavy hair. He was draped into a desk chair with his long legs stretched out and his stethoscope still hung round his neck.

'Well, what's this? A good deed or an apple a day?'

'Dr. Gutteridge,' I said lowering my voice, 'Have you got any empty bottles?'

'A few. Dead Marines. I take 'em to the pub every Friday.'

'I mean medicine bottles.'

'Oh, medicine bottles. Well, yes I must have, I don't know how many.'

'Can I have them?'

'What for? Oh I see. Well of course you can, but they're all out in the toolshed and they're pretty filthy. Some of them've been there for years.'

'That doesn't matter sir!' My eyes kindled with fanatical light. 'Can I come around with a trek cart?'

'You can, but you may not,' he teased in schoolmasterish waggery. When I laughed he said, 'Tomorrow's Saturday. Come any time.'

'Oh thank you sir!' I saluted and was off like the wind. My patrol leader got hold of the trek cart and next day three of us loaded it to the top with bottles, some of them opaque with dirt and cobwebbed with shrouds from which scuttled spiders and woodlice. Our arrival at T.H.Q. and the unloading of the bottles was a sensation. We quickly emptied the trek cart, and taking our stance at the 'gully trap' behind T.H.Q. we began the long process of sorting and washing. At the end of the afternoon we had three hundred and forty-seven bottles of every conceivable shape and size. Our patrol paraded in front of them and had its photograph taken. Quayle of the Eagles was torn between incredulity and admiration. His patrol had collected fifty-four bottles which was thirteen more than his nearest competitor, and he'd hoped to be the winner. The Baas strode by and gave us a knowing look.

'Larry,' he said to my patrol leader. 'You and Quayley come to my den will you.'

We chattered excitedly. What would our prize be? A new stave on which to carve the Kangaroo, our emblem? A trip to the beach? A resounding public commendation? Larry reappeared and we crowded round him.

'Well you blokes,' he said uncomfortably. 'The Baas thinks we ought to stand down. He says we've done very well but, it was kind of a fluke and he says, well, for the honour of the patrol, we ought to let Quayley and his boys have it.'

We are Scouts of Toorak

We were struck dumb at The Baas' perfidy. Everyone looked at me and I felt my eyes starting to smart. Larry said, 'Well, Turkey, it's up to you.' Everyone looked sympathetic and angry. I shook my head and out of a choking throat came a voice which must have been mine.

'Let's do what The Baas wants. As long as the hospital gets the bottles.' He put his arm on my shoulder. 'Never mind. It was a great effort.'

Everyone in the patrol shook my hand and fighting back tears I helped to arrange the bottles for the final display. After tea we crowded round the noticeboard. A typed sheet of paper thumb-tacked to the green baize, read:

Bottle Bee

Eagles	54
Curlews	41
Bears	27
Owls	18
Emus	9
Total	149
Kangaroos	347
Grand Total	496

The Baas never spoke openly about the result but he let it be known that the way to do good in the world was by hard work and not by trickery. I thought about this a lot because it seemed to me that the main thing was for the hospital to get as many bottles as possible, and I noticed in the local paper that the Troop was praised by the Mayor for having collected almost five hundred bottles in less than a week. 'A highly creditable performance.' Finally I became resigned. I convinced myself that I had somehow been too puffed up with pride and deserved to be brought low. The ever-present Presbyterian sense of guilt which hag-rode the boys at Scotch College played its part. Yet a secret intelligence told me then, and tells me now, that the Baas had a muddled set of values. After all if Quayley had protested . . . But you see, he didn't. No, we must do everything by the book, the hard way. The end does *not* justify the means!

My prestige was restored by an unexpected display of involuntary

The Road to Gundagai

heroism. One of the Troop's periodic fund-raising 'Picture Nights' was coming up. We rented a local movie house, charged five shillings for tickets and pocketed the difference between that figure and the two bob which the theatre manager charged us. Every boy in the Troop was called on to sell tickets, and the door-to-door canvas which ensued was no more popular (except among born Fuller-Brush men) than the collection of empty bottles. I duly received my quota and began the dreary business. Because I found it embarrassing to peddle my wares I made a poor salesman; but mindful of the stroke of genius which had brought the Kangaroos their immense total of bottles (and the honour denied them) I pondered on some similar stroke which could net me a blanket sale of tickets without the tedium of door-to-door canvas. Ha Ha! Dr. Crapp.

Dr. Crapp was a prominent dentist whose son Ian, a school friend of mine, had been grubstaked to Wembley *hors concours*, as it were. He was therefore obviously well heeled. On my way to T.H.Q. one evening I opened the wire-mesh gate to the Crapp residence and, bent on a quick sale, approached the front door up the asphalt path with a fiver's worth of tickets clutched in my hand. There was a rustle in the bushes, a terrifying growl and a huge airedale was worrying at my leg. I yelled and shouted and in the struggle scattered tickets to the four winds. Lights came on at the front porch and Dr. Crapp and Ian bounded across the lawn and called off the growling dog. I was carried into the surgery where it was found that my left sock was torn to shreds and I was bleeding profusely from two large bites in the calf.

I was more in shock than in pain; Dr. Crapp gave me a sedative, cleaned and bandaged my wound and offered to drive me home. But when I explained the purpose of my visit he agreed to buy a pound's worth of tickets. Though this was somewhat less than I had hoped for (especially when his dog had just bitten a chunk out of my leg) I was nevertheless elated and said it was best to take the good news and the cash down to T.H.Q.

My arrival caused a sensation. I was of course late owing to the mishap and though in a high state of euphoria, limping dramatically, and also very ashen in the face. Bill and The Baas rushed forward. When I came to I was lying in a chair with my bandaged leg up on a stool. It was now throbbing heavily and I was in some pain. I told Bill what had happened. He looked sober and the crinkly lines round his bushy browed eyes were thoughtful.

'Did he give you anti-tetanus?'
I shook my head.
'Then we're taking you round to see Doc Powell right away.'
'Thanks Bill.'

We are Scouts of Toorak

As I was carried out to the trek cart on the linked hands of two other scouts, with my arms round their shoulders, The Baas called 'Three cheers for Old Turkey Cock'. They lifted the roof. I think it was the proudest moment of my Scout life.

By now my place as efficient Second of the Kangaroos was secure and hints were dropped about my First-Class Scout test. I might get ahead. Great things were expected. . . . But before this could happen came the tragedy of the Warrandyte Camp. One evening I arrived at T.H.Q. without my 'tea', that is the usual paper bag containing a tin of kipper-snacks, an apple and a couple of peach-jam sandwiches. As was the custom, a hat was passed around the room into which morsels of food were generously chucked, and I ended up with more than anyone else. The most succulent and unusual item was a chocolate eclair. I was amazed and sought the donor. It turned out to be Lauchlan, Patrol Leader of the Emus. He grinned.

'Thought a skinny runt like you needed some grub.' He was a very tough, tall, sandy haired fellow, with a band of freckles across his upper face, and I fell for him like a ton of bricks. Later that evening I learned to my delight that Locky would be leading the two patrols in charge of the trek cart for the night hike to Warrandyte. This promised to be a real adventure. As The Baas put it, one foot up on a pine log seat, his calf-flattering khaki socks and his brogues with the fringed tongue, as usual the envy of us all:

'Fellow scouts; this is to be a real test. We leave T.H.Q. at nine p.m. with the trek cart. We expect to reach the site about six a.m. The advance party will have camp pitched and plenty of tucker ready. The trek cart will be fully loaded; it will be a long pull. But,' his eyes shone, 'there'll be cocoa on the way! Now go to it, and good luck!'

We assembled at T.H.Q. at eight o'clock next night. Willing hands had already loaded the trek cart. This was a two wheeled vehicle with a long boom projecting forward ending in a handle. Two scouts breasted the handle but theirs was a balancing act. The main motive power was provided by a thonged rope surcingled to the hub of each wheel. Each rope was manned by six scouts who pulled bravely up the hills and acted as a brake from the rear on the downward slope. Ahead walked six scouts and the Baas as an advance guard; behind walked six scouts and A.S.M. Bill, swinging a kerosene hurricane lamp from his belt. We were a bizarre if stirring sight as we swung along Burke Road; passing revellers in The Last Tram gave us a cheery halloo.

Then the street lights went out and we plodded onward in darkness until, after interminable tramping, and squeaking of the iron tire of the trek cart we heard the cry 'Smoke-oh!' and sank down

The Road to Gundagai

gratefully on the rough grass beside the dusty road. In the pitch dark, matches spurted and soon came merry flames and an aroma of cocoa. Everyone complained of blisters and a fellow whose watch had a luminous dial said it was one thirty a.m. The Baas and Locky strode up and down the line of bone-tired scouts 'putting grit' into us, (or as the Americans call it, 'sand'). But the hot cocoa, milk-and-sugarless, from tin cups, bucked us up a good deal more.

'Can you keep a secret?' Larry Tom-oh suddenly asked me in the dark.

'My oath, I can!'

'Locky's got a rifle with him.'

'Go on!'

'Honest! I felt it when I was loading his kit. They're forbidden. We'll have to split on him.'

'It's for the Good of the Troop.'

The chilly breeze raced ahead of the sun, making the long strips of bark on the bluegums drone like speedboats.

'Okay! Limber up!' It was Lauchlan calling the trek cart teams to their work; striding belligerently through the dark with his chest thrown out.

In the hour before first light we fell silent. After the cocoa we had beguiled the night with sing-songs including the inevitable 'Australia will be there-hair-hair' with its adjuration to 'Keep your eye on Ger-man-ee'. But in this weirdest of lights, in the treacherous time when two dimensions struggle to become three, we were quietened by silent phantoms, forming and reforming in a grey landscape without base or ceiling. Cathedral naves limned and dislimned into stationary locomotives, into long avenues bordered with chateaux and Rhenish towers, into dragons and bunyips. The swirling pre-dawn mist lay wrapped about the feet of every illusion and we were enclosed in a long tunnel constructed of familiar sounds: the scrape of boots, heavy breathing, muttered colloquy and the eternal creak of the trek cart wheel.

First light brought us back into the world and we saw each other as fellow scouts with sore hands, dirty faces and circles under the eyes. The eastern sky was stained brick red and the sun brought the scent of bluegum and sassafras and the gorgeous golden music of magpies. A long spear of light rushed slanting up the valley. A kookaburra, perched on the dead limb of a ringbarked gum, greeted the dawn with a raucous cackle. Lauchlan threw a stone at it saying, 'Hey you old jackass, don't you laugh at me!' The Baas turned sharply; his rimless glasses gleamed in the slanting sun and his knobbly knees were gooseflesh.

'Scouts! That'll do! No horseplay! Come on Locky, strike up

We are Scouts of Toorak

the Troop Chorus and let's get some spirit into the march. Only two more miles to go, Scouts!'

We raised a cheer, saw behind us a Brocken-spectre of skinny legs on the Yarra Valley mist, and in a final dash across an open paddock, with trek cart traces flying, we ran towards the curling smoke of a campfire among the trees by the river. Someone ripped fruit from an overhanging branch and handed one to me. I bit for the first time into the sharp memorable flesh of a quince.

Our camp at Warrandyte was on a peat-and-sand isthmus between the Yarra and its billabong. We stayed there less than a week but it was a time of overwhelming desolation because of Lauchlan, and the platypus. At the start of the drama the Baas was sitting on a kitbag in his tent, behind a table of soap boxes draped with the Australian flag. The flag had a tear in the middle of the big seven pointed star and he had covered it with his shaving mug. Tom-oh came to the alert and saluted with three fingers.

'Please Baas, I've something to report.'

'Well?'

'Locky has a rifle and a box of .22 longs in his kitbag.'

The Baas' eyes glinted behind his glasses, but he said coldly, 'Scouts don't sneak.'

'Yes Baas.' We saluted and made off.

* * *

The platypus appeared while the Troop was swimming in the river during the DAYP. In a few seconds a score of us gathered, half naked, in the lee of a fallen willow while the animal waddled methodically down the muddy bank towards the water, belly hairs leaving a trail in the ooze. It took no notice of us or our whoops and shrieks, almost as if it knew that it was protected by law. It flopped into the water and started to swim slowly down river, close to the shore. There was a shout from across the stream.

'Hey, what's all this?' It was Lauchlan in the camp canoe, paddling towards us.

'A platypus, Locky.'

Lauchlan paddled closer.

'Hey, look!' someone shouted. 'He's going into his hole.'

Lauchlan's canoe was within twenty feet of the bank.

'Out of my way!' he shouted. 'I'll get him before he goes in. Always wanted a platypus. Here, puss, puss, platty-puss!'

He raised the rifle and fired. The platypus stopped swimming and the water stained with blood. There was a horrified silence. Lauchlan

The Road to Gundagai

paddled expertly to the floating animal and picked it out of the water.

'Dead as a doornail,' he announced. He held it up for us to see, but no one spoke. Lauchlan laughed into the silence.

'Ever see a platypus-puss-puss?' he mocked. He beached the canoe and got out, holding the platypus in one hand. The Baas confronted him, his face pale with anger.

'You bloody murdering fool!' he hissed through clenched teeth. 'Now you've done it!'

We all gaped, and some of the younger ones huddled together. Such language was an enormity even more shocking than shooting a platypus. Lauchlan's freckles stood out from a whiter skin. The Baas snarled at him:

'Don't you know they're protected?' His rimless pince-nez trembled on his thin nose. 'What's this going to do to you, to all of us, to the Honour of the Troop? Answer me that! It means a fine—or jail, if it's found out.'

'Take it easy, Baas,' said Lauchlan slowly, looking at us frightened boys, 'who's to find out? I couldn't get you a rabbit today, so . . .' He held out the platypus but The Baas recoiled.

'I wouldn't touch it with a forty foot pole!' he gulped and raised his hand. 'Now listen to me, all of you. From now on Parker is patrol leader of the Emus.' Parker looked uncomfortable; Lauchlan shrugged his shoulders.

'Understand, Lauchlan?'

'Yes, Baas.'

'All right, carry on, Parker. Now, Lauchlan, throw that animal in the river.' Lauchlan ambled over to the bank and nonchalantly dropped the dead platypus into the water. We watched it bobbing up and down in the current—a grey-brown mass of wet fur—till it passed out of sight round a bend.

'Now, Lauchlan, the gun!' The Baas held out his hand; he was still trembling. I saw Parker half clench his big fists at his side. Lauchlan gave the rifle to The Baas, who strode back to his tent. Parker cleared his throat.

'Trrooooop, al-ert!' We sprang to attention in our swimsuits; but Lauchlan stood with his back against a tree. Parker reddened.

'Are you gonna fall in?' he asked slowly. Lauchlan, with maddening deliberation, inched into line.

* * *

The Baas was the first to see the waterlogged canoe floating lazily down-river opposite the camp-site. He was seated on a flour

We are Scouts of Toorak

sack in the middle of a circle of us younger boys giving us a talk on 'The Dangers of V.D.' We had all noticed Lauchlan's absence, and assumed that he was sulking in his tent, but when we saw the canoe, our stomachs turned to ice.

'Where's Lauchlan?' cried the Baas, and we knew the answer as he spoke.

'What'll we do?' wailed a cub. It was his first camp, and already it was assuming a monstrous shape in his mind. Instinctively we turned to The Baas who stared fascinated at the slowly drifting canoe, then he barked, 'Where's Parker?'

'Up at the farm getting eggs,' someone shouted.

The Baas took off his pince-nez and put them carefully in his shirt pocket.

'Come on, Tom-oh, Turkey!' he shouted and we rushed off through the underbrush.

Without his glasses The Baas was as blind as a bat. He stumbled over roots and stones and knocked against overhanging branches. While we, more sure-footed, raced ahead, brambles tore at his uniform and his breath began to come in wheezy gusts. We came out into the meadow just as Parker rushed breathless down hill. Parker was shocked by The Baas with his white face, dilated nostrils and uniform in disarray. He opened his mouth to speak, but The Baas cut him short.

'Locky's canoe stove in . . . empty. Can you swim . . . have a look?'

Without a word Parker started to strip. The Baas pulled a sheath knife from his belt and slashed Parker's bootlaces from ankle to toe on both feet. It was a dramatic gesture, and our open-mouthed awe did him good. This was action.

It didn't take long to find Locky. He was wedged in among the roots of a willow. His body was under water, but the current played with his sandy hair, trailing it downstream among the sedge. Parker shouted, 'Coo-ee!' and applied his wrestler's torso to extricating Lauchlan from the clutches of the root.

Floundering through the thicket, we heard Parker's cry. 'Gone, Baas.'

With dry sobs we crashed on towards the river.

* * *

The Troop stood in a circle on the worn floor at T.H.Q. Our shorts made a ragged line above a row of knobbly knees, dusty knees, hairy knees, knees bulging over wrinkled socks. The three fly-spotted 100 watt bulbs threw shadows from scout hats over

The Road to Gundagai

our serious faces. Above the fireplace, the Union Jack and the Southern Cross flanked a shining brass plaque around which the plaster was still damp. On the plaque was an inscription and beneath it a circle with a dot inside. 'Gone Home': the scout-craft symbol of a hundred paper chases, treasure hunts, hikes and treks now doing duty as an epitaph. Parker stood erect and massive with his Red Indian face set in a stolid stare straight ahead. The whole sad episode seemed barely to have grazed his mahogany presence. The Baas began to speak.

'Scouts of the First Toorak Troop. . . .' His eyes misted behind his rimless pince-nez and he strove to keep his voice steady. 'We all admired Robert John Lauchlan, Locky, as he was better known to us . . . sterling qualities . . . strength on the trek . . . protection of the younger scouts . . . love of the Great Outdoors. . . .'

He droned on almost automatically. We began to feel uplifted. We saw an endless vista of smoking campfires and neatly pitched tents in the bush. Beloved images rose before our senses: the pungent scent of dry eucalypt at breathless noon in the forest; the wattle blossom with its divine scent, floating in the springtime trees like puffs of golden mist; a great shower of sparks as someone threw a faggot of redgum on the campfire; the moon staring from behind the platypus torso of a ringbarked tree. Scouts singing. The anguish of mortality flowed away from us and we felt extraordinarily happy.

* * *

In a perverse but perhaps understandable way this melancholy episode set me seriously about facing the final hurdle on my way to becoming a First-Class Scout. This was an Easter hike through the outer ramparts of the Great Dividing Range. The planners of the hike had bitten off more than they could chew and by the time we reached the 4000 foot saddle between Donna Buang and Boobyalla we'd missed our way. When disconcerted, light a fire is a good Scout motto. But we were forced to dig for water and it was so peaty that it had to be rationed; the cook chose this moment to upset half a pound of salt into the chipped potatoes. We went to sleep with a raging thirst. Fortunately it rained in the night and although this made us wet and miserable it filled the billies.

Morning came streaming in on a grey day and no fire. Fortified by cold porridge, cold tea and bread-and-jam we lurched forward into the bush. After two hours' march it became clear that we were well and truly lost and Bill went ahead with instructions to get down into the nearest valley and follow a creek—if there was one—until he came to a road—if he did. The rest of us squelched glumly on.

We are Scouts of Toorak

We ate bread and cheese on the march and towards mid-afternoon we'd lost Bill completely and were in no mood to comply with the eighth Scout Law enjoining cheerfulness. It was at this moment, peering up from under a streaming hat brim, that I glimpsed, unbelievably, a tin roof through the dripping trees. I turned aside from the Indian file of squelching scouts and broke through the drenched undergrowth to emerge in a rough clearing in the middle of which was an abandoned sawmill. I blew S.O.S. in morse on my whistle. Within a few moments I heard, from deep and far away, an answering, 'Coo-ee!' I kept blowing until scouts appeared at the edge of the clearing. They were lyrical.

'Gee whiz boy. Are we in luck!'
'This is bonzer, Turkey.'
'Well, go and rustle up the rest of them.'

Soon the entire Troop except for Bill and his companion, stood in the dripping clearing. A tremendous cheer went up from the bedraggled scouts and they rushed towards the sawmill. Half an hour later we were all disposed in our patrols, on a warm, dry, earthen floor. The rain drummed monotonously on the tin roof but a roaring camp fire—sent swiftly on its way by half sawn logs and old shavings—shot flame and sparks up to the rafters. We cooked and ate our first hot meal in thirty hours and sat down for a camp fire sing-song before we turned in. Pretty soon the strains of those two dreadfully wonderfully Australian jazz lyrics, *Gundagai* and *Croajingalong* were floating out into the rain, while Bill, who had at last arrived, having found a slippery road leading out to Narbethong and thence to Marysville, wolfed his late night snack.

> 'No longer will I roam
> From my own Australian home
> I'll hump my bluey and I'll shout a "Coo-ee"
> Back to Croa-jinga-linga-linga-long'

The voices echoed against the rain and the Baas said solemnly, 'We're all very proud of old Turkey Cock. He showed initiative and that's a virtue highly prized in Scouting. Well, time to turn in. Lights out.' As I crept into my blankets and groundsheet beside the dying fire, it was a high moment; but within three months my scouting days were over and I had left the Troop in disgrace.

* * *

Easter that year was notable for the visit of Uncle Winston and Aunt Stella. Uncle Winston was Dad's elder brother, a bigger

The Road to Gundagai

chunkier version with a moustache and the most enormous crater blown out of his right shoulder blade on the Somme, which we peered at with horrified fascination whenever he was under the shower. Stella, his wife came from New Zealand and was known as 'Young' to her husband, a nickname we could never fathom since, like all grown-ups, she seemed about sixty-five. Their arrival was an occasion for rejoicing because an uncle in the house always meant forbidden pleasures. Winston was no exception. He took me to the Tivoli to see Wee Georgie Wood and to gaze enraptured at a beautiful chorine astride a paste-board globe chanting *I'm Sitting on Top of the World*. As we came out of the theatre Uncle Winston said, 'How would you like to come to Tasmania?'

I'd never travelled alone so far before and it was curious to see how the *Loongana* had shrunk in six years. The difference in the shape was as great as the difference between eight and fourteen. With immense pride I telephoned from 4 Grace Street for a Yellow Cab and rode down to the Victoria Docks. The steamer slowly inched out from the wharf and into the muddy reaches of the Coode Canal as the paper streamers snapped behind. The second-class cabin was shared with three men, one of whom was putting his false teeth in a glass to steep; but Mother had made a money-belt for me so that I felt no qualms. They served the evening meal just as we were entering The Rip. Dad said this was a favourite joke of Huddart Parker and the Union Steamship Company so that they could save money from the passengers who were too seasick to eat. However I managed this amazing Australian 'tea' of chops, steak, hard boiled eggs, salad, German sausage and tea, and went down to my bunk, fortunately the one by the porthole. With the money-belt around my middle I snuggled down onto the straw palliasse beneath the scrapey exiguous sheet that ship stewards always seem to fold too tight.

Meo greeted me with her wet affectionate kiss. What had happened during the interval? Well, the house had shrunk and the room used by Mother and Dad was now occupied by Winston and Stella. Mount Wellington was now climbable, as it had not been when I was eight. I bicycled slowly up the long steep shoulders of the shaggy mountain to the Springs Hotel. At this point a path led upward among stunted gum trees and finally low bushes, juniper shrubs and lichen-covered rocks until one reached The Pinnacle, marked by a rude stone cairn and a cross of wood. The Pinnacle was above the Organ Pipes, which hung down below in stupendous sheets of columnar basalt, a formation found in many parts of Tasmania where the fluted columns of Cape Raoul and Cape Pillar out-step the Giant's Causeway of the old world. Below, the many-fingered Derwent lay like some improbable watery animal whose myriad limbs

We are Scouts of Toorak

penetrated deeply into the land. To the north and west lay range upon range of tumbled hills and crags culminating in the great central massif and over all the yellow smeary light of an autumn afternoon.

With a group of business friends Winston had invested in a yacht and we cruised in the estuary of the Derwent. These amateurs—clerks, accountants and salesmen—were captained by an R.A.N. commander, who knew something of sailing. I got the job of cabin boy and spent most of my time below decks preparing meals and serving beer. As a reward, whenever we anchored in a cove to get out the 'niner' and booze between races, I could take the dinghy ashore and in a score of tiny bays up and down the shores of the salty Derwent, I encountered Crusoe, Man Friday, Long John Silver and his parrot, the Swiss Family Robinson (all of them, even the dull and earnest Franz) and of course, Jack, Ralph and Peterkin. We had wonderful times together until a bellow from the yacht recalled me to my duties; I pulled hard on the rowlocks and hitched the little dinghy by the painter to the yacht's stern. The season ended abruptly when our yacht was run down—it was nobody's fault—and we limped back to our moorings in Sandy Bay where the water lapped against the mussel-shrouded piles, minus a jib and forestay. Since drinking had been Homeric I had a real job sinking the 'dead marines'. One should never, said Winston, leave them bobbing about the bay the way careless 'yachties' did. I held them under water until they sank with bubbling groan. Altogether forty-seven bottles of Cascade and Foster's Lager went over the side. Troop Headquarters seemed a long way off.

* * *

Too soon the holiday was over and I boarded the train in dejection wishing for it to slow even beyond its customary crawl and for the gold braided inspector to come, courteous and grey down the corridor, and say with a barely perceptible lift of the eyebrow, 'A message for you.' I rip it open with frenzied fingers. My boat ticket has been mislaid! My baggage has been left behind in Hobart! Anything, any message to stop the inexorable forward march of the train towards the estuarine dock in Launceston that looked so dreary now among the tidal mudflats, and so exhilarating when we came in from the north on our arrival in the magic isle.

The boat pulled out among stale flat eddies of mud; the blistering wind from the Mainland came roaring across two hundred miles of heaving cobalt; and now it rushed down the convoluted estuary like a tidal wave, sheared the ship sideways and blotted out the beloved

The Road to Gundagai

contours of the Island in a swirl of greenish-brown haze. The folded hills became blurred; the dramatic snow-crowned tower of Legge Peak slipped backward into the mist. Down below the stale saloon air was thick with the smell of rancid linoleum, raspy cigar smoke, sickly sandwiches; the rattle of tea cups and the dull inevitabilities of ferry small talk. Better seek the tiny cabin, clutch memory to the bosom, hoping to still the dull ache. Down through the night; and the morrow was still mud and rusty iron: the Coode Canal cutting up through vacant lots, power pylons, the refuse from loading freighters, to the dusty yellow spires of Melbourne. Thus, inevitably, back to town and somehow the Yarra seemed muddy and flat after the drama of the Derwent, and the Bay smelled of stale fish and factory effluent, and the big green trams on their five-foot-three gauge looked squat and cumbersome against the spindly elegant three-foot-six of Tasmania, and in fact everything on the mainland began to seem a shade less attractive. Holiday sickness, the reverse of home-sickness, is sometimes worse.

* * *

At Troop Headquarters I encountered curious looks. Where had I been for the past month? The Baas was anxious to see me. There he was, behind his desk, with the broad domed forehead and the pince-nez and the eager vibrant voice, but this time there was an ugly note. I had absented myself for four consecutive meetings. It was in vain that I pleaded a visit to my relatives for the first time in six years. There was a flaming row and I was flung out of First Toorak Troop Headquarters and into the duller world.

Chapter Eleven

PRAHRAN DOCTORS AND THE SPIS ORPHEUS

WITH Saturdays now free, and at first unbearably empty, I turned once more to the city and began to feel proud of its bigness, to notice significant buildings, and the places where drama dwelt in brick and cement. We were immensely proud of Malvern and its Town Hall, and used to wait at the foot of the entrance steps after school to see the Mayor leave in his chauffeur driven car (a modest Morris-Cowley). Then we would climb the steps, leaving our bicycles chained to a lamp post (courtesy of the John Hops) and enter the great assembly hall with its square white-painted pillars and its gallery, to watch the charwomen stacking chairs, polishing the floor with O-Cedar mops and flicking with feather dusters at the dark oily portraits of former mayors. On Sundays the brass band of the P. and M.T.T. (Prahran and Malvern Tramways Trust) played in the bandstand in a small park behind the town hall. The romantic groan of the silver-plated euphonium and the bold precision of the golden trombones as they moved majestically through *The Blue Danube* filled us with delight. The bandmaster, who had competed successfully against the great brass bands of Northern England at Harrogate, signed my autograph book. He was an ex-sergeant and tram conductor with a small waxed moustache and a frogged coat with silver epaulettes. After this particular concert I retired to contemplation and private ecstasy in the lee of a tall cypress hedge and the enjoyment of smoking a tram ticket stuffed with pine needles.

Pursuit of the P. and M.T.T. hero took me down to the adjoining suburban city of Prahran, and to Chapel Street which was much more dramatic than our own local Glenferrie Road. You could see its five and six storey buildings with their turrets and towers sticking up on the western horizon long before you reached them, and when you finally arrived you found in the course of a single clangorous block, the excitement of a big city. To swing a bicycle down the pulsing canyon of Chapel Street was to discover the heady

The Road to Gundagai

delights of metropolitan glamour. It began with Maple's the furniture and piano dealers; four storeys of green and oxblood art nouveau tiling surmounted by a small turret. It ended with Chas Read's furniture and drapery store, five floors of biscuit coloured vitrified terazzo, huge windows with wire mesh incorporated in the lower levels, and a large round tower. On top of the tower was a beacon which beckoned across the river to the nearby Richmond store of Dimmey's which outshone Read's because it had a round ball like that on the Coliseum in London, which twitched and wobbled in a never-ending spin.

Halfway between Maple's and Read's was the Colosseum—a real colossus this, no genteel Coliseum. It was a sort of minor Selfridges with enormous corinthian columns supported, apparently, on plate glass windows, and crammed with all sorts of voluptuous goodies unknown in our simple home: satin bedspreads, brocade headboards, suede pouffes, standard lamps, hanging bookshelves. Into this half mile of commercial splendour were packed movie theatres, innumerable small stores, shoe-shine parlours, barber shops with gyrating peppermint twist poles and, in mid-career, the brawling caterwauling entrance to the open air Prahran Market. In Chapel Street the sidewalks were always crowded, the clanging trams moved swiftly and the great stores disgorged a constant stream of shoppers. I stood outside the Colosseum for minutes at a stretch trying to construe the mystic sign: TUO YAW, and wishing I'd enough money to go inside. This there never was, though in the watermelon season which coincided with my birthday, sixpence was all it needed to go into the market and spend an hour wandering around the stalls.

Some of the barrows were in the open, others under a great glass roof like a railway station. They came laden with oranges and lemons from Mildura, peaches, apricots and nectarines from the Goulburn valley, punnets of raspberries and red currants from Gippsland and great piles of rock melons and water melons. Gutted rabbits hung head down amid strings of saveloys and frankfurters, sides of bacon and hams. The mingled smells were heady with that of forbidden fruit and as I tied my lone water melon to the parcel carrier of my bike with a piece of inner tube, I envied the well fleshed citizens who could walk away with a couple of crayfish, a string of saveloys or a huge hunk of German Sausage—rare delicacies at home.

Mother maintained that Prahran was not of course a place where one *knew* anybody. Our friends were apt to live in genteel Malvern and frugal Hawthorn adjoining, or else in democratic Brighton down towards the beaches. But Prahran became wondrous through the

Prahran Doctors and The Spis Orpheus

presence of two remarkable doctors: Dr. Wilson and Dr. Leeper.

Dr. Wilson was, as the Americans say, a 'medical doctor'. He'd been in the A.I.F. on Salisbury Plain and had accompanied Thirk, as he then was, in his courting expeditions to Wilsford Manor. He was therefore *persona grata* in Mother's eye and while our local G.P. was called upon for running repairs and minor adjustments, any really mysterious or alarming symptoms were referred to Dr. Wilson. He was exactly as Australians are imagined by romantically-inclined Englishmen: somewhat above medium height, rangy, lean-faced and hook nosed with a bronzy out-of-doors air about him even when he sat in his surgery dressed in a black suit and a wing collar. He had what Mother called 'a divine Australian voice' by which she meant that it was quiet and firm, drawly without being lazy, slow but authoritative, gentle and reassuring and with a hint of iron in it that made you feel he was in the driver's seat, and a hint of sunshine far at the back of it that reminded you of distant horizons. When my brother slipped and fell on the bathroom tap and blood spurted from his behind it was Dr. Wilson who calmed him; and when recurring attacks of boils became unbearable both to the family and to me, it was Dr. Wilson who cured them.

His surgery was in the very heart of Prahran just below the intersection of High Street and Chapel Street and within sight of the green and oxblood art nouveau tiles of Maple's. The house, unusual for Melbourne, gave almost directly onto the street and over the gate was a red lamp through which his name shone ghostly white in the winter dusk. When I passed through that gate and mounted the three tiled steps that led to the surgery door I was, as far as a twelve-year-old can be, in a state of bleak hopelessness and dumb agony. I'd been undergoing a siege of boils which for sheer intensity, incessant pain and messy unpleasantness could have gained the unwilling sympathy of Job himself. To the family I'd become a curse and a burden and they shrank from me as if I were Thersites in the boat crossing the Aegean. I should have had a hood over my head and a bell to warn away the venturesome, except that I wouldn't have been able to get the hood on because I couldn't move my head, nor ring the bell because I couldn't swing my arms.

My schoolfriends had a well developed mystique about boils, as they did about warts. Some were in favour of squeezing, others of hot fomentations, bread poultices and antiphlogistine to 'draw the boil out'. A third school held that if you filled a beer bottle (preferably Foster's Lager) with boiling water, emptied the bottle and then clapped it steaming over the boil, the subsequent cooling would create a vacuum into which the boil would be inexorably

The Road to Gundagai

'drawn'. I tried all these miserable practices without avail; eventually the neck boils died down by themselves, only to reappear in more violent form in nostrils, armpits, and buttocks. At this point in my stink and misery I was denied the use of the family bathroom and sent to see Dr. Wilson.

It was a family story that my Aunt Clare had once said that if she couldn't go abroad in the summer, at least she could stay home and squeeze her blackheads. But this indulgence was not extended to boils. Mother would cheerfully, forcibly and frequently hold my head in one hand while with the other she squeezed out a blackhead with the hollow key to her jewel box. She would observe with interest my attempts to get rid of warts, including the use of a razor blade, acetic acid drops, milk from a severed dandelion, fungus from a cootamundra tree and water from a dead stump. She even withheld reproof when, attempting to stem these woody eruptions with nitric acid, I upset the bottle over my school uniform, a large portion of which literally vanished in a puff of smoke leaving a crisp bilious yellow crust behind. But boils were the end.

Accordingly, unable to sit down, turn my neck or bend my arms, I took a tramcar down to Prahran and stiffly and painfully entered Dr. Wilson's surgery. He was miraculously kind. He neither laughed at my discomfort nor took it too seriously. Instead he sat looking at me with his stethoscope hanging round his neck, his big capable hands outspread on his knees and his shrewd blue eyes probing on either side of his lean hooked nose. After a while he nodded slowly as if he'd reached a decision, rose silently and crossed with loping steps to a nickel and glass sterilizing cabinet that bubbled softly in a corner. From this cabinet he took a hypodermic syringe, a spatula and a wadge of cotton wool. My heart bumped as he approached for I have always been a coward in doctors' and dentists' surgeries. But he hadn't been an Anzac doctor for nothing and he knew men and boys, and knew that what frightens is what you don't know.

'You're in a nasty mess,' he said, 'but we're going to cure you with your own muck. Don't worry, it won't hurt a bit.' I've listened in my time to scores of doctors and dentists assuring me that 'it won't hurt a bit'. Liars, all of them; but somehow I believed Dr. Wilson. He started on the job while he was talking, took a smear from a particularly evil looking little volcano, and inserted it very gently—no nonchalant jabbing—into the upper left arm and covered it with gauze and bandage.

'Now,' he said, stepping back, 'you're going to get another boil there (Not another!), but you're not to worry because it'll start to fight those you already have, and I think,' he broke into a wonderful creased leathery smile, 'I think it's going to work.'

I went out into the clammy winter night full of disbelief, but the boils slowly began to ebb away. Thereafter Dr. Wilson was known in our house as The Healer of Prahran.

* * *

If Dr. Wilson cared for the ills of the flesh, it was Dr. Leeper who cared for those of the mind, especially if that mind were lazy. He was a born lasher and scarifier of sluggish brains, a dedicated intellectual gadfly, a professional needler of terrifying intensity and the most exacting standards. We stood in tremendous awe of him, and he also lived in Prahran.

Alexander Leeper had been sent out to Australia as a young man from his native Northern Ireland 'to die of consumption', as the phrase went. It was kill or cure, in the sunfilled spaces of the Empire, and Leeper was neither the first nor the last to be packed off in this way. Like others in similar dire straits he surprised the calamity-howlers by making a rapid recovery. Unlike most of them he embarked successfully on a long and distinguished academic career as a classical scholar and later as an academic administrator, and lasted on into his ninetieth year. Mother had an introduction to him from Professor Gilbert Murray who, as a fellow classicist and ex-fellow Australian, thought it would be highly suitable if Jack Mackail's daughter could be reassured that academic distinction flourished in the Antipodes and that the springs of Helicon watered Melbourne and Oxford with equal impartiality. At this time Leeper was living in retirement, having relinquished his post as the first Warden of Trinity College in the University of Melbourne some years earlier, and was cared for by a wife and two daughters in a rambling house on a tree-lined street off Malvern Road.

When we met, the Doctor was already in his eighties and so lean and flinty that he gave a totally misleading impression of extreme fragility; if one were to tap him lightly with a hammer he would smash into a thousand spiky shards. But from this bony carapace blazed watery eyes of intense concentration and from the depths of the gristly throat issued the Voice of Authority, all the more unnerving because it was threaded with a quaver. When we used to call at the Leepers for Sunday tea he was usually sitting in an armchair wrapped in a rug. From this place of vantage his voice crackled sharply across the conversation like static on a headset. Occasionally he made a point by stabbing the air with a stick. More often he would retreat silently behind a reading rest,

The Road to Gundagai

and we would forget all about him until a boy's voice, carelessly raised, brought a staccato rebuke. He was really a terrifying old gentleman. Rumour had it that when a student at Trinity was reading the lesson at Chapel and pronounced 'leper' as Leeper for a joke, the Warden grimly gated him for a month.

I didn't meet the full force of his authority until the celebration of the Bimillenary of Virgil. For this occasion my grandfather had, at Dr. Leeper's request, written an eclogue in which two shepherds, idling the time away in the Mantuan Hills, learn of the sad event from a companion and then enlarge, in rustic measures, on the poet's achievement. This eclogue, which was of course written in Latin and in Iambic pentameters, was to be given a single performance before the Classical Association and its friends. Dr. Leeper had persuaded two keen young classics masters at Geelong Grammar (former undergraduates of Trinity) to take on the production. The headmaster of the school was also an enthusiastic classicist and was considered rather daring and modern because he persuaded the boys to act out episodes from the *Odyssey* and the *Aeneid*. A paper-and-canvas Troy was burned on a headland and the boys rowed across Corio Bay in racing fours disguised as triremes. A prefect in the role of Odysseus resisted, from the prow of a racing pair, the wiles of a fourth-form Circe who sat on a rock surrounded by maidens from the Senior School, and sent forth honeyed words in an as yet unbroken schoolboy soprano. Because of these pioneer efforts it was decided that the eclogue should be produced as a true theatrical entertainment and that the shepherds should dress in sandals, cross garters and goat-skins, or the nearest equivalent that could be found among Melbourne's theatrical costumiers.

Of all this I was entirely unaware until the Latin master at school sent for me and gave me a long spiel about my prowess in Latin. I smelled a rat as soon as he said this for I had, with immense difficulty and aided by total visual recall of the set books, just managed to scrape through the Intermediate Certificate. I wondered what was coming next. Sure enough, my grandfather J. W. Mackail was a distinguished classics scholar and it would be wonderful for him to know that his grandson had taken part in the performance, *in Latin,* of an eclogue written by him for the Bimillenary of Virgil. Wonderful for the school, too. And wonderful for me, it was implied. I nodded reluctant agreement; with unseemly haste the master slipped out from beneath his gown a typescript bound in pink tape.

'You will report to Dr. Leeper on Tuesday evening at four o'clock after school. He will coach you in your accent and your quantities. His address is—'

'I know Dr. Leeper's address,' I said.

Prahran Doctors and The Spis Orpheus

'Of course,' he beamed. 'Dr. Mackail's grandson!'

I studied the typescript on my way home from school in the tramcar. Even a cursory glance was enough to show me that the cunning classics masters from Geelong Grammar had taken the two small parts and left me the enormous role of Glaucus who, as far as I could see, was a sort of garrulous elder statesman to whom fell the task of spouting the actual encomium on the Bard of Mantua. I was appalled at the thought of having to learn a 'side' of 123 lines of Iambic pentameters, though my natural vanity was aroused at the thought of making up to play the part of a dotard of fifty.

Dr. Leeper received me in his study with the blinds drawn. It was a cold May evening and he had a fire lit. He was sitting wrapped in a travelling rug in a large wicker chair and he waved me testily to a stool at his feet. Above and behind his head was a lamp which illuminated his snowy hair and his thin eagle's beak and cast the rest of his nut-cracker face in deep shadows. It was the only light in the room and I was expected to read by it.

'Well,' he said, 'this is a great honour that's befallen you.' Great Chore I thought, but I nodded. He rapped his cane lightly on the floor. 'Let me hear you.'

'I don't know it yet sir.'

'I don't expect you to know it, boy. I want you to read it!'

I read the first speech slowly and clearly, in a loud piping voice, doing my best with the scansion, eliding wherever it seemed proper to hit the beat. When I had finished he said:

'Who taught you your scansion?'

'Mr. Ingram sir,' said I referring to 'Bumpy' Ingram the Vice Principal and Classics master.

'And who taught you your elisions?'

'Mr. Ingram, sir.'

'And your pronunciation? Your vowel sounds? Mr. Ingram too?'

'Yes sir.'

He remained silent for some time; then he raised his thin old vulture's head and, looking abstractedly at the ceiling, began to speak half to himself, half to me.

'How much time is there before the performance? Two weeks you say. Well it's quite clear we can't undo the effects of five years —you've been doing Latin for five years?'

'Yes sir.'

'Yes. Undo the effects in two weeks. We shall have to accept Mr. Ingram's methods as they stand. And concentrate on your quantities; your quantities boy, and making yourself heard!'

'Yes sir.'

The Road to Gundagai

'Then let us hear you on Virgil himself. Here!' He handed me a copy of *The Georgics*, open at his bony thumb. I managed ten lines before he stopped me with a skeletal hand.

'I'm not one to insist on veenye vydye vyecye,' he said with a thin smile and a glint of his steel-rimmed spectacles, 'but neither do I accept bogus Italianate Vayni Veedi Veechi. It's effeminate. The Romans did *not* speak like that. Who taught you for example to say, Werry nowow instead of Very Novo? Now don't tell me it was Mr. Ingram?'

'It was sir.'

'Then don't say it. And don't make false elisions. You can feel the rhythm. As soon as you start to recite. Poetry was made to be read aloud, by bards, by songsters and by boys reading eclogues.' He smiled again, this time more cordially. 'But the rhythm, let's hear it.'

'Vere novo gelidus canis cum montibus
  Umor liquitur.'

'Hear it? There's no need to mouth it or be stilted. Try again.'

I read slowly through to the end and waited. But Dr. Leeper was asleep. I waited longer and said.

'Sir; sir excuse me.' But his head was nodding on his chest and I crept quietly out and told one of the faithful daughters. Six sessions with Dr. Leeper finally hammered me into shape. On the day before the dress rehearsal he favoured me with a thin grunt of approval and added:

'If you don't show up those fellows from Geelong I shall be very much mistaken.'

Dr. Leeper couldn't come 'on the night'. The journey into the Assembly Hall would have been too much for him but the Class Ass, as its members called it, told him all about it and he sent me a note in Greek, which I couldn't read. I showed it to Mr. Ingram who told me it was from Plato's dialogues and that it was to the effect that a man truly fulfilled himself in attempting something beyond his grasp. I thought this was rather a backhanded compliment, even from so distinguished an old gent as Alexander Leeper.

'The Night', as I remember it, was quite dreadful. It was midwinter and the Assembly Hall had been designed for lectures rather than performances. There were no dressing rooms and the two classics masters from Geelong and myself were crowded into the little anteroom where they made coffee. We were freezing cold in our sandals and cross garters (courtesy of the Boy Scouts' Association) and our goatskin cloaks (really rabbit fur, courtesy of the Myer Emporium Limited). We bumped backside to backside as we bent to lace ourselves in, and shared the single flyspotted mirror with the naked bulb for making up. As I was fourteen and supposed to look fifty, the wife of one of the classics masters, who had charge of the grease paint and chinese white, was convinced that I should have to make up at least as eighty. She whitened my eyebrows and pushed them the wrong way; she drenched my hair with flour, painted age lines round my eyes, nose and mouth, and my upper arms and legs she liberally smeared with calomine. As a result, instead of looking fifty, I looked like a boy of fourteen masquerading as an aged victim of the Spanish Inquisition. I shivered and shook on the exiguous little platform, partly from the cold and partly to convey, as I leaned on my stick, an impression of extreme decrepitude. But my voice, despite simulated croaks and quavers, remained that of a boy. This was particularly noticeable when I forgot my lines and had to be audibly prompted from the wings in the basso profundo of an over zealous Latin teacher who had taken on the job. Still, no doubt Virgil was pleased, and we certainly did our best.

* * *

The sad little performance by the Class Ass in the Ass Hall is far from giving a true picture of theatrical life in Melbourne in the Twenties. The city which had produced Nellie Melba and Oscar Asche, the fat hero of *Kismet*, was not likely to lag in this field; and a walk up Bourke Street with its brilliantly lit marquees was like a visit to fairyland. We were well placed to take advantage of this, for Mother's prohibition against the movies—the flicks, as we called them—still remained rigidly in force. My friends were all bound for an abandoned theatre turned movie house near Pascoe's drapery on Glenferrie Road. Inscribed on contorted stone shields on the façade were the words *Thespis* and *Orpheus* connected by swags of fruit. It was a place of mystery and wonder for the lettering had been imperfectly incised and it read *The Spis*, *Orpheus*. Who was the Spis? Alas, I would never know, for I was never allowed inside. It was a movie house! I returned to 4 Grace Street with a burning sense of persecution. I feared Mother's sharp-tongued cold temper but I kept at her until she snapped out,

'If you don't keep quiet I won't take you to see Allan Wilkie!'

This was a real threat, for on the south bank of the Yarra, miles from the bright lights, jammed in amongst the warehouses and dealers in automobile spare parts which infested the fringe of South Melbourne, and overhung by an enormous triangular electric sign which flickered A - S - P - R - O ASPRO, was another theatre, a tiny beloved little theatre where all the amateurs, and one spectacular band of professionals put on their shows at cut rate prices. It was a 499 seat theatre called *The Playhouse*. In that little theatre our

The Road to Gundagai

family saw no less than nineteen of the plays in the Shakespearean canon.

The actor-manager who directed this extraordinary company was Allan Wilkie. With his wife, billed as Miss F. (for Frediswyde) Hunter-Watts, he toured the capital cities of Australia for fifteen years. All he got out of it was a C.B.E.; we were furious and thought he should have received at least a K.B.E. and preferably a K.C.B. He certainly made little money, and a disastrous fire which destroyed much of the company's wardrobe, coupled with the onset and deepening of the Great Depression, finally forced him to wind up his affairs in the early thirties. He and his wife then toured Canada reading selections from Shakespeare and finally settled in England whence, as a young man, he had emigrated to Australia, in stock, thirty years before.

Wilkie had a commanding presence, a deep, resonant somewhat fruity voice, and was what would today be called a ham actor of the old Henry Irving-Beerbohm Tree school. He postured and pranced; he declaimed and pontificated with the result that all Shakespeare's plays seemed to be alike. Perhaps they all *are* alike, because our introduction was through Wilkie and in each play he took the lead. He was Hamlet, Othello, Macbeth and King Lear. He was the Melancholy Jaques, the cross-gartered Malvolio and the finger-wagging Prospero. He was Wolsey and Mark Antony and Henry V (though in *Henry IV* and *The Merry Wives of Windsor* he was of course Falstaff). He was Angelo in *Measure for Measure*, Shylock (of course!), Coriolanus, and Antony again with F. Hunter-Watts as Cleopatra. (Really a less unlikely combination can hardly have existed: he with his fruity baritone and portly waddle, she with her genteel eerie voice and blonde braids).

But though every lead was Wilkie, and he was always the star turn, you nevertheless longed passionately to see him because he attacked each part with much tremendous gusto. You actually wanted the principal character to *be* Wilkie so that you could see what he would make of it. Adulation and a personal following could go no further than that. He was the darling of all the English teachers and used sedulously to present the year's 'set' play which we were 'doing' in school. Reductions for school groups may not have brought in much money, but they always guaranteed a full house and there must be today many thousands of middle-aged men and women whose first and perhaps keenest vision of the bard's work was through the art of Allan Wilkie and Miss F. Hunter-Watts.

In appearance Wilkie was short and powerful with a large leonine head, heavy jowls, long sideboards and piercing thick lidded brown eyes. His voice, whether in rage or supplication, in joy or pain, whether he knew his lines or not (and how we used to relish his subtle sidle over towards the prompt side) was wonderfully plummy and Edwardian. Our favourite role was his performance in Shylock which he hammed most unashamedly, giving a villainous 'heh-heh-heh', tossing his eyes up to the flies and baring his breast when outwitted by Portia (Miss F. Hunter-Watts). We used to brandish rulers in the corridors at school crying 'Ay'll Huv Muh Bud!' (i.e. 'I'll have my bond'). His Hamlet—though somewhat weak in the middle aged joints—was almost as good.

If the besetting sins of actor-managers are supposed to be those of vanity and uxoriousness, then Wilkie qualified on both counts. Miss F. Hunter-Watts got all the really juicy female leads irrespective of age. She even played Juliet (though Wilkie shrank from playing Romeo and assigned the part to one of his supporting actors). She was, as we have seen, Cleopatra, Portia and Juliet; she was also Mistress Ford, Viola, Rosalind, Katharine, Princess Kate in Henry V, Calpurnia, Gertrude, Desdemona, Beatrice and Miranda. But above all she was Lady Macbeth. It was an old fashioned traditional rendering with no psychological overtones, no Freudian implications, and no tigerish strength. But though she muffed 'Infirm of purpose, give me the daggers', her 'Out damned spot!' and 'All the perfumes of Arabia will not sweeten this little hand' were thrillingly unforgettable. She glided across the stage like a greenish ghost, all blonde braids and trailing nightgown, clutched her bosom, pulled her voice down several notches and declaimed like a lost soul.

The rest of the company were as familiar and as comfortable as old slippers. The second female lead was Lorna Forbes, plump and darkly beautiful; the two male right and left bowers were Ellis Irving (no relation) and another whose name escapes me but who was known to us as 'The Rolly-Eyed Duke' (he played Orsino in *Twelfth Night*). Stage Manager was Miss Hunter-Watt's brother.

Almost as well known as the actors were the props: the familiar bench which served equally well as a hiding place for Sir Toby Belch, a seat for Caesar in the Forum, and a greenwood tree for The Duke in *As You Like It*; the 'ruin' of doric plasterboard which was Ninny's Tomb, Cleopatra's palace and Henry V's tent; the lances that bent at the critical moment of impact; the collapsible swords for running people through; the crowd noises off, which consisted of not less than three but no more than five extras growling 'rhubarb-rhubarb-rhubarb'; the armies of four soldiers in nondescript Gaulish-Roman-Frankish ersatz chainmail, which marched and counter-marched to a thunder of creaking boards; the shapeless whitish tabards-cum-ponchos which became Caesar's toga, Lear's robe or Lady Macbeth's

The Road to Gundagai

nightgown at the drop of a stitch. We loved them all and through them we saw Shakespeare, if not precisely as he is meant to be acted (and which of us knows *that*?) then at least we saw him off the printed page, away from the classroom and into the magic world of greasepaint and footlight and sweat, and the swish of the rising curtain.

But what about Australian plays? Where were *they*? Maybe, we argued fervidly in our English classes at school, there were no great —or perhaps even good—Australian dramatists? A fell thought. Perhaps, as a people, we were limited to music? Certainly the international welkin positively clanged with our great names: Nellie Melba, Florence Austral, John Brownlee, Elsa Stralia, Flotsam and Jetsam, Percy Grainger, Fritz Hart . . . what! will the line stretch out until the crack of doom? Fritz Hart was the only one that we knew, though through him we came within coo-ee of the great Melba herself. Fritz was Director of the Albert Street Conservatorium of Music which, in marked contrast to the Conservatorium run by the University of Melbourne, shone in the refulgent splendour of Melba's bounty and approbation. It was indeed something of a bear's hug. Melba who, at this time, had begun a long series of announcements of her impending retirement and an even longer series of 'farewell' appearances, had homed on Melbourne, where she had first seen the light as Nellie Mitchell some sixty odd years before. Being within easy reach of the city it was her habit to descend at short notice and with imperial splendour on the Albert Street Conservatorium. There she would listen to the young thrushes and keep Fritz, in some sense her protégé, from his work. Fritz used to visit our house and unburden his woes to Mother with comic resignation. He was a short wiry man with a white mane of hair which he kept tossing out of his eyes before our fascinated gaze, a beak of a nose, a twinkly eye and a voice like bees buzzing in a jam jar.

During one of her visits to the Albert Street Conservatorium, Fritz Hart spoke to Nellie Melba about Mother whose sharp wit and acrobatic literary allusiveness had already penetrated into the country where Melba lived at Coombe Cottage. Mother was summoned to the presence and received a signed portrait photograph which read, with the inimitable gush of the theatrical great on the strength of an afternoon's acquaintance 'To dearest Angela with love. Nellie Melba.' It sat on top of a bookcase near our little cottage piano and I can still see the generous swirling M. and N. starting far behind and above the letters, and rushing forward in a great sweep to engulf the down strokes, overwhelm the audience and slay the world. It was a wonderful conversation point, almost as good as my stepfather's mounted piston rings and camshafts. It was he who

Prahran Doctors and The Spis Orpheus

provided the real drama of the visit to Nellie Melba for while Mother went in luxury with friends in a heated and rugged limousine sent by the diva, Dad decided to go on his motor bike. Oilskinned from neck to ankle and with a leather helmet he set off into the rain-streaked gloom of a winter afternoon. In those days the road beyond Box Hill was unmetalled and near Ringwood he encountered a sea of mud and his journey came to a slithery end about five miles short of Coombe Cottage. Eventually he got a lift and arrived just in time to meet the departing guests.

Mother was sufficiently pepped up by her visit to Nellie Melba to have our piano lessons supplemented by classes in music appreciation. As in so many provincial societies the teaching of music was in the hands of young women of quality who arrived after tea, either by train or on a bicycle, and pounded away at an unwilling boy with the maddening iteration that only a music teacher can achieve. Miss Mitchell, sober commonsensical and grey-suited, was succeeded by Miss Thyrza Wettenhall, young, highly strung and hot tempered. I discovered I could quite easily reduce Miss Wettenhall to tears by repeatedly playing wrong chords with great deliberation, after endless demonstrations of the right way to play them. Thoroughly vexed, Miss Wettenhall would eventually take my hands and place her fingers and mine on the right notes which, leering up at her (I was twelve and she I suppose about twenty) I would again play wrong.

'You're a thoroughly disagreeable boy,' quivered Miss Wettenhall. Mother was severe in her strictures, but I said the trouble was, really, you see, Miss Wettenhall wasn't a very good teacher. God forgive me. No young woman could have taught me to play the piano. What it needed was a firm man with a sharp tongue.

Meanwhile, thanks to George Thirkell, Mother's fortress of film disapproval had been breached. Dad had come unscathed not only through Gallipoli but through the Somme and the Ancre as well, and he thought we ought to be allowed to see the great spate of silent war films of which *Mons* was the precursor. This was in the era when war was still glorified and the memories of muddy, sanguinary and futile battles were wrapped around with the Southern Cross and the Union Jack, and cheered by thousands. *Death of a Hero* and *All Quiet on the Western Front* were still years in the future, and a proper interest in gore and patriotism went hand in hand.

To us all these movies were the same. Because they were British or Australian semi-documentaries and lacked the majestic distribution machinery of the American features, they were all screened at —well, *The Playhouse*. The little theatre was decked out with flags

The Road to Gundagai

and bunting, and thronged by an audience of 'Returned Men' who had braved the long journey by tram or train from outlying suburbs, not for the bright lights, but for the fading memories to be roused in a 'fleapit' on the wrong side of the river. Each film was preceded by an address from a distinguished soldier of the A.I.F. who spoke from the little stage. Since it was the silent era, the soundtrack would normally have been provided by a piano. But as all the films—Mons, The Somme, The Marne—had in common much meaningless marching and counter marching of jerky silhouettes through mud and blasted trees, accompanied by continuous bursts of gunfire, it was necessary to supplement the pianist by two drummers. These fellows certainly earned their money. The man on the side drum supplied martial marching rhythms, rifle and machine-gun fire. The man with the bass drum and tympani was responsible for the heavy artillery. In the darkened *Playhouse* the screen shimmered and shook in silvery indecision while the rattle and banging of the drums rocked the little auditorium to its boots.

Religious films were now also permitted and we attended the 'Australian Premiere' of Cecil B. de Mille's *The Ten Commandments*, gloriously silent, with an 'atmospheric prologue' on the stage, and Mr. Weber at the Mighty Wurlitzer (known to us as the Wurtilizer). The film contained most of the ingenious and spectacular horrors and glories for which the Great Man was famous; but it was a religious film, and so that was all right. Lulled by the music of the Mighty Wurtilizer as it slowly sank from view I lay back in my seat and watched the concrete stalactites in the roof of the Capitol Theatre blend and merge from sultry purple to suffused red to pale watery green. Finally there was a slow dimming and with Weber shifting gear hurriedly on his organ, now hidden in the theatre crypt, the screen leaped to life.

War and religious films were now permitted; why not films on social problems? There slipped into our letter box one morning a leaflet advertising the opening of *False Shame*—at the *Playhouse*, of course. It was an educational film, said the leaflet, and dealt with the horrors of venereal disease and how to avoid them. I innocently suggested to Mother that a useful family evening might be spent at the *Playhouse*. To my discomfiture she burst into laughter, added that it would be most unsuitable 'for the young'. Accordingly I was driven to enlist the help of a cobber and we went to a Saturday matinee on our bicycles while we were supposed to be exploring down at the docks. As the film excluded children over six and under sixteen we had some difficulty in getting admitted, but I was tall for my age and my pal had a gruff voice so the man at the box office finally let us in but told us to sit at the back. The film turned out to be inhumanly clinical and for weeks afterwards the image of spirochaetes, larger than seals, wiggling their giant way into the screen-animated labyrinths of the urino-genital system, filled me with alarm and distaste. So Mother had been right after all.

Chapter Twelve

THE LADY HELP

Opposite my new room at 4 Grace Street was the spare reserved by tradition for the Lady Help. Being the only room not occupied by a member of the family it was arcane and mysterious, though the Lady Helps were far from being so. They might and did vary from bubbly to bleak, but all shared a paralysing gentility; indeed the name perhaps implies it. All without exception were mercilessly anatomized and exploited by my brother and me during the course of the never-ending family warfare.

Maybie, with her 'volegar' locutions, lasted for about two years and then shipped back to her native Swindon. Meanwhile she continued to suffer from her 'brilliant headaches' and to temporize with her 'It all *depends*' ('On what, Maybie?', 'Don't be volegar.') when called upon to adjudicate any weighty matter. She remained memorable for the Saturday litany on the tram to St. Kilda: 'One and two halves to the beach please'; and for the strangled silence which engulfed her whenever she broke a piece of Mother's green-dragon breakfast crockery, which was often enough. She had a bosom friend who lived in Kew, and she took us there once or twice, pausing on the way, in lugubrious and leisurely contemplation, at the great Kew cemetery. The tomb erected to his departed wife by a certain Dr. Springthorpe had a tremendous fascination for her, and she used to stand wrapped in unnamable thoughts before the great granite mausoleum. With my dog-Latin, I earned some slight favour in her eyes by being able to translate the inscription on the tomb as 'Farewell, half of my life'. Maybie thought this highly poetic, and would subsequently wander among the headstones, tottering in mildewed propinquity, with me trotting at her heels, and murmur over and over 'Farewell, half of my life'.

Maybie was succeeded, after a tiresome help-less interval, by a dark haired woman with the romantic and tongue-twisting name of Mrs. Francois-Xavier Laframboise. Her personality turned out to be not as romantic as her name. She was in fact a talkative shrewish

The Lady Help

gossip and she brought with her, as part of the terms of the contract, an odious little daughter called Nathalie who, it was supposed, might be a companion for my baby brother, but who in fact spent most of the time whining after her mother and clutching at her skirts. I used to make faces at her hoping to send her into convulsions but all *that* earned me was a hiding, in this case not unjustified. Mrs. Laframboise, though we soon learned that her maiden name was Robinson, liked to be called Madame; and Mother, driven to distraction for want of household help and anxious to preserve what little she had, became a party to this ludicrous pretence, and strongly counselled us to abide by it.

Boys have ways of getting around such obstacles. Mine took the form of coupling the salutation to what I fondly believed was an elaborate French bow. My brother hit more shrewdly by asking guileless questions as to the whereabouts of Monsieur Laframboise. He really infuriated Madame, and Mother put an abrupt stop to this particular game by telling us in confidence that Madame Laframboise had been 'left in the lurch'. We toyed awhile with an exhilarating possibility: 'Madame Laframboise?' 'Yes Graham?' 'Is it true that Monsieur Laframboise left you in the lurch?' But no, reluctantly we discarded this tactic and awaited calmly the downfall of the pompous Madame and her odious little girl.

It came from an unexpected quarter. One evening I returned from school to find Mother tight lipped and Madame Laframboise and the kid sitting with their suitcases on the porch with the front door closed behind them. In answer to my open-mouthed curiosity Madame assured me that she and Little Nathalie were leaving 'on the instant!' No one was going to speak to her like *that*; she jerked her head and her black straw hat towards the front door. Munching bread-and-dripping I sought enlightenment from Mother. Well, it turned out that little Nathalie and my baby brother, both aged about three, had wandered off, hand in hand as kids will, and had been lost for the best part of three hours. During the frantic search Madame Laframboise had not shown what Mother regarded as a proper concern and Mother had spoken to her sharply. The two truants were eventually found by the police at the Malvern railway station watching the trains go by. From this innocent pastime they were scooped up by Mother and conveyed home in disgrace in an improbable hansom cab. Madame and her daughter departed and 4 Grace Street, Malvern, S.E.4 shivered into silence.

The hansom cab, exciting relic of an era associated inevitably with Sherlock Holmes and Dr. Watson, plied from a cab rank outside Malvern railway station. The rest of the rank was filled with four-wheelers and one or two daring motor cabs; but old Mr. Sawston

The Road to Gundagai

with a checked cloth cap, a Prince Albert green with age at the cuffs and collar, and a frayed silk four-in-hand with a topaz stickpin the size of a cherry, was the proprietor of a hansom, the sole survivor of a vanished Melbourne of gas lights, electroliers and theatre parties with ladies in bustles and bare shoulders and men in curvy-brimmed top hats. Whenever we were going 'up the country' we always asked for the hansom to travel down to Malvern station.

There were three methods of summoning Mr. Sawston; you could write a letter requesting him for a particular day; you could, in an emergency, telephone the railway station and the booking clerk, if he had time and was in a good mood, would yell the order to Mr. Sawston across the railings. But the best way, one for which the competition was fierce between my brother and me, was to walk and run the mile down Coonil Crescent, Glendearg Grove and Claremont Avenue to the station, breathlessly summon Mr. Sawston from the pub and the horse from oat-eating somnolence and then ride back *alone in the hansom*! Mr. Sawston climbed puffing to his little crowsnest in the rear, slid back the Judas window in the roof to see if you were safe and sound, then with a swish and a click the curved doors folded shut. He whipped up the horse whose busy rump and flaring tail were now visible through the glass doors and behind the splashboard, and you were alone in a black padded leather circular cell jogging gently forward in intimate secrecy past familiar scenes. The hansom transformed the most mundane ride. Claremont Avenue became Baker Street; at the cobbled gutter at the foot of Glendearg Grove 'we rattled over Waterloo Bridge' on the midnight drive, Miss Morstan beside us, to Thaddeus Sholto's house in the howling wastes of South London. Mr. Sawston's hansom imparted a sense of urgency and secret delight to every excursion.

One shrivelling afternoon in early February I returned from a visit to the country. Sweating with a heavy kitbag I got out at Malvern station and toiled up the ramp to the outer world, yearning for Mr. Sawston's hansom. It wasn't in its usual place on the rank and I noticed that the familiar pile of horse manure was now sandy straw blowing away in the wind from the Mallee's oven. Apprehension stirred dimly. Behind the wheel of a Yellow Cab—those newly arrived robots from Chicago, with squat hoods, square roofs and black disc wheels—the driver was reading the paper and blowing smoke at the windshield.

'Excuse me sir, do you know where I can find Mr. Sawston's hansom?'

He pulled down the upper part of the *Herald* and looked at me with the disfavour with which one favours those who have interrupted a reverie.

The Lady Help

'Eh?' I repeated the question.

'Have to go a long way to find *him*,' he said laconically. 'He's kicked the bucket.'

I heard myself say 'But what happened to the hansom? To the horse?'

'I dunno. Sold I suppose.' He eyed my grip. 'You want a cab? How far you going sonny?'

'No thanks,' I said. Sadly and slowly I toted my grip all the way back to 4 Grace Street in the shimmering heat in a senseless but somehow meaningful penance for Sawston and his vanished hansom.

* * *

There followed a long help-less interval and then, just as Mother was beginning to wonder if we'd ever get another Lady Help, in burst Molly Mitchell. Molly was like her name: buxom, blonde, bubbly, and always ready for a lark with the kids. We were very fond of her and she stayed with us over three years. She was more of a friend and companion than a Lady Help and I don't think Mother really got much value out of her; but she was blazingly cheerful at all times and having been an active Girl Guide during her youth in England, had also a very practical nature, being able to fix leaky taps, replace fuses, unblock toilets, ease bicycle chains back onto sprockets and other useful accomplishments. It was a sad day for us when she was replaced by a dour humourless Irish girl; Molly's era in retrospect seems a golden romp. Partly this was because she was easily flummoxed and when flummoxed, easily blushed. Mother used to say 'You really are a very silly girl Molly' when she got entangled in flirtatious 'Oh-you-are-awful!' exchanges with the butcher, the baker and the candlestickmaker. But we loved her because she was human and fallible and therefore one of *us*, in whom we could confide. We serenaded her loud and often to the tune of a current hit:

> I love Molly
> M-oh-double-ell-y

Molly had come to us from India where, according to her, she had been an English Nanny ('No, *not* ayah') to a small boy on a big tea estate somewhere between Siliguri and Darjeeling. Molly always talked in superlatives but it seemed to me that India was worthy of them—her India at any rate; a vast concourse of faithful brown servants grovelling at the feet of the tea planter, chanting 'Burra

The Road to Gundagai

sahib, tu'm ichcha hai'; Kanchenjanga, austere and frosted beneath a cloudless sky and 'so near you felt you could put out your hand and touch it'; Molly writhing beneath a mosquito net in the throes of blackwater fever with its night of crisis ('And the next morning I woke in a lather of sweat, and I knew I was going to be all right'); cobras and pythons, elephants and monkeys, saddhus and fakirs. Oh how dull Australia was by comparison. 'But never mind boys, let's go and buy an ice cream cone. My shout!' Good old Molly.

When Colonel Pottinger arrived in Melbourne with his coloured slides of the 1924 British Everest Expedition up the Rongbuk Glacier, it was Molly who took us. I was gripped by the disappearance of Mallory and Irvine, made all the more memorable by Colonel Pottinger's British reticence and the primitive simplicity of his working tools. All he had was an enlarged magic-lantern screen in a small downtown silent movie house, a stick, a lectern and a dry matter-of-fact voice. But when he pointed at the snowy slope of Everest, liberally bespattered with monstrous fly specks, gargantuan bits of fluff and enormous quivering hairs like Manila hawsers and said, 'It was at this point, just above the tip of my pointer here,'—tap, tap—'that they were last seen,' I received intimations of mortality.

It was Molly who took us to hear Lowell Thomas deliver his famous lecture, also illustrated by lantern slides and silent movies, on Lawrence of Arabia. This fabulous character seemed to me to be both larger than life and simply not credible. Perhaps this was due to my confusing him with Lowell Thomas himself whose clipped black moustache and strong American accent coloured the whole story with an air of unreality. How could Lowell of Arabia (or was it Thomas Lawrence?) ever have done all the things he boasted about? But at the interval, in response to my request for chocolates, instead of Mother's tart, 'Those that ask shan't have: those that don't ask don't want', there was Molly's warm gullible 'Here's sixpence; don't lose it.'

Molly's generosity and her love of girlish conspiracy culminated in a really stupendous drama which was in some ways the high point of our years at 4 Grace Street. She used sometimes to walk a couple of blocks to meet me as I was coming home from school. On this particular evening we met at a large storm gutter grating at a nearby street corner, and as we stood waiting for my brother, I saw something glint at the bottom of the grating. In a moment I was on my hands and knees peering down into the muck three feet below. It looked like a ring. When Colin arrived we prised off the grating while Molly kept a look out ('kept yow', as we used to say); then he lowered himself head first into the hole while I held onto his legs. He came up brandishing a ring with a single large emerald. The

The Lady Help

three of us passed it round, gazing goggle-eyed at the treasure trove sparkling in our hands. We were rich. We could sell it for a thousand pounds. We could go on a trip down the Bay in the *Hygeia*: we could . . . Was it ours though? We stared at each other in consternation—not the least Molly.

'I tell you what we'll do,' she said at last. 'I'll 'phone the police and make a clean breast of it. We'll throw ourselves on their mercy. They'll tell us what to do.'

'But supposing they take away the ring?'

'Well, then we can claim the reward.'

'But what if there's no reward?'

Molly was stymied for a moment but recovered quickly. 'If there's no reward,' she said, chucking out her bosomy superstructure, 'they'll hear from me.' We believed her.

'Okay, but don't tell Mother.'

'Oh, no I won't. This is a secret between just we three.' She gave a jolly arch smirk and we trudged home with the loot.

The Malvern police told Molly that we should advertise for three consecutive days in either the *Argus* or the *Age*. If at the end of that time no claimant had appeared we were entitled to keep the ring. We were a bit crestfallen. In three days someone was bound to claim it, and what if there were no reward? But Molly took care of this by inserting at the end of the notice the cryptic question 'What offers?' We thought this was very clever and waited on tenterhooks for the three days to elapse. On a Friday morning Molly came into the boys' bedroom with shining eyes. 'Time's up,' she said. 'It's ours.' She sat down between us on one of the beds while we debated how to dispose of the treasure. I thought we should sell it to the highest bidder but Molly thought it would be easier to 'pawn it and lose the ticket'. If we tried to sell it people might 'ask questions'; and while of course the ring was indubitably ours, we might have to visit several jewellers before we could make a quiet sale. Pawning it we might not get so much; but it would be quicker and safer. I nodded sagely.

Molly met us by arrangement after school in Chapel Street, Prahran. It was agreed that we should pose as her children, if any questions were asked. Heaven knows why this deception was put in train. No pawnbroker would be interested in a couple of schoolboys and since I was twelve and Molly was about twenty-five, the proposal was on the face of it ridiculous. However it cloaked proceedings with an exciting conspiratorial air, and off we went.

The first pawnbroker glanced casually at the ring and offered Molly thirty shillings. To me—on sixpence a week pocket money—this seemed an immense sum, but Molly was indignant.

The Road to Gundagai

'Thirty shillings?' she cried. 'Why it's worth at least five pounds.'

'Thirty shillings,' said the impassive pawnbroker. We stormed out of his shop. The next man offered us a pound and again we stormed out. The third man wanted to know whether the ring was stolen.

'Let's go back to the thirty shilling man.'

'If it's not too late!'

We returned to the original pawnbroker much subdued. He couldn't have been less interested in whether we were exhilarated or crestfallen. All he said was 'Thirty shillings.'

Molly thrust the ring forward, the man handed us a ticket and in a trice we were out in Chapel Street again, all three of us capering quite ludicrously for joy. Molly was the first to stop, breathless and red-faced. She grabbed convulsively at our hands.

'Now boys, I'm sorry to have to say this but the advert cost me seven and six. That leaves us 22/6 to spend. What shall we do with it.' She leered owlishly. 'Put it in the bank?'

A chorus of protest.

'Right! Then let's have a spree!'

We mounted a tramcar, rode excitedly into town and getting off at Collins Street walked up the hill to the Georgian, where we ordered malted milk, ice cream, cream puffs and chocolate eclairs. A second round of eclairs left us cream from ear to ear and we staggered replete into a home bound car, with 16/- still to spend. At a book store near the Malvern Town Hall we bought four shillings worth of *The Gem, The Magnet, Nelson Lee, Comic Cuts,* the *Kinema Komic* and *Sexton Blake*.

Molly said: 'I really think you ought to put a little money in your Post Office Savings accounts—say five bob each?' Belching creamily we agreed; but that still left two bob. With this we bought aniseed balls and liquorice allsorts for the baby brother and as an afterthought, a pen wiper for Mother, and for Dad a sprig of heather tied with a ribbon on which was printed 'Weel ye no come back again?' We arrived home late and Mother was in a testy mood, not with us but with Molly who was beautifully contrite, managing to slip us a wink from time to time. It seemed to be smooth sailing, but unfortunately, coming in to bid us goodnight after dinner, Mother spied a *Magnet* sticking out from under Colin's pillow. A brief search and a bit of adroit cross-questioning soon revealed the hidden hoard.

'I can't think why you waste your pocket money on such disgusting things,' said Mother, in her indignation mercifully not hoisting in the fact that about six weeks' pocket money must have gone down the drain to purchase such a great swatch of comics.

The Lady Help

'What are you going to do with them?'

'Burn them.'

'Oh, Mother!'

'Can't we give them to Norman Birt?'

Norman was the boy across the street and if we gave them to him well, he was our friend . . .

Mother hesitated and then said rather crossly.

'If Norman wants to spend his time reading trash I suppose he can. Get them from me in the morning.' Bliss, and a dreamless sleep. Mother, we knew, thought Australia was a vulgar enough place without our reading comic papers. Dickens, Scott, Thackeray, Dumas, R.L.S., even *Pals* the wholesome boys' weekly; but not this junk. This was for Australian boys. What were we becoming?

* * *

Springtime brought headline news of the approach to Australia's shores of the Test Team from England. Though neither a good nor a devoted player of cricket, I followed the school, suburban and inter-state matches for the Sheffield Shield with intense, sustained and passionate enthusiasm. Bedded down at night on the 'sleep-out' I was able to intercept the paper boy as he tossed the *Argus* onto the dew-soaked lawn about 6.30 every morning. Grabbing Smut our cat for a footwarmer and ramming him well down the bed, I devoured the cricket news and gossip. The English team, it appeared, was a strong one. Though the captain, A. E. R. Gilligan, was unknown to me, the rest of the side fairly bristled with heroes: Hobbs and Sutcliffe the tremendous openers, Tate the fast bowler, Chapman and Woolley the stylists, Strudwick, prince of wicket keepers and Patsy Hendren, idol of the crowd. Still, our lads would give them a run for their money. Australia will be there-hair-hair! What about H. L. Collins who'd been Warwick Armstrong's doughty squire in the A.I.F. XI that swept all before it in Britain right after the war? It was an era of run-getters and although Bradman was still below the horizon, we had Ponsford and Woodfull and Hendry (all from Victoria too!), McCartney the stylist, Gregory the terrific fast bowler, Clarrie Grimmett the crafty slow bowler and our prince of wicket keepers W. A. Oldfield. Oh, we'd be out in front all right.

'You will not,' said Molly stoutly, sprouting Britannia's helmet as she spoke; the figure she already had.

'Down with England!'

'Then down with Australia!'

The passion that these encounters aroused! But in the end Molly squelched me with:

The Road to Gundagai

'Besides, I'm a friend of Woolley's.'

This, it turned out later was not strictly true, but at the time it staggered me. That anyone could *know* so lofty and remote a figure! I dashed from the breakfast table and returned with my autograph book. In it already were the names of the immortal A.I.F. team of 1919. I handed it to Molly in silence, but with a pleading look.

'Oh dear,' she said, 'now I've done it.' But she took the book.

The school was given half holidays for the Test in Melbourne, and Molly asked me to meet her after school at Flinders Street Station in the centre of the city. All she would say was that I would get a pleasant surprise. I took a lengthy tram ride to the great dome of Flinders Street where 'under the clocks' was the favourite trysting place of Melburnians. I waited for some time among expectant girls, impatient young men and exasperated mothers, but Molly was nowhere to be seen. I was beginning to be bored and didn't have an extra 1½d. for the evening *Herald* when all at once I saw, moving majestically towards me and looming over the head of the crowd like a Douglas fir among jackpine, a prematurely grey giant about nine feet tall. It was normal to have to look upward to adults, but to see this man I had to crane my neck. When at last I lowered it there was Molly's beaming face barely at his shoulder. One rarely recognizes heroes because their faces, when seen unexpectedly and close up, are both larger than life and detached from any credible resemblance to it. But Molly's face was real enough. She saw me and smiled, and as the group bore down she said,

'This is the boy I was telling you about, Frank.'

Frank? Was it, could it be. . . ?

'Say how-do-you-do to Mr. Woolley.'

A surge of mingled emotions rushed through me. First—and it made me feel guilty—disappointment that it wasn't Hobbs or Sutcliffe; then stupefaction at the larger than life face, all flesh and open pores and crinkly pink smile and utterly unlike any picture in a newspaper; and then a cataract of overwhelming pride at meeting a hero, which left me tongue-tied. Woolley grasped my hand and said.

'Glad to meet you Graham. This is Bert Strudwick and Jack Hearne.'

Two other God-faces materialized from the crowd and for a few brief moments I was the centre of a dazzling concentration of smiles from Olympus. The roar of the crowd and the traffic receded and I felt a buzzing in my ears out of which materialized, unbelievably.

'Well, Molly, you know the town. Where shall we go?'

Woolley was bending solicitously forward and behind the other

The Lady Help

giants two women came into view. They started talking and I was instantly forgotten. I stood rapt in a daze looking up at the heroes. They were discussing things like 'the flicks' and 'St. Kilda Beach' and 'Wattle Path' and these humdrum places became instantly hallowed. They turned to go.

'Goodbye Graham.'

'Goodbye Sir.'

'Oh, Frank, don't forget the book.'

'Thanks for reminding me, Molly.'

A huge capably tendoned hand passed over my autograph book and I clutched it convulsively. Molly's head was at my ear over the crowd roar.

'Tell your Mother we're going to the flicks and I'll be back about eleven. Better run along now.' Her eyes were shining, and it hit me with a powerful wallop that she was in Heaven too. I boarded the tram in a daze and opened the book. It was better than I could have ever dared to hope. They were all there, the English XI, every one of them, even the manager. I passed the journey in holy contemplation. Thereafter Molly could do no wrong and her prestige at 4 Grace Street (among those under 13) was enormous.

To Mother it was different. Molly was a 'silly girl', a 'man chaser' whose head had been turned. She intimated that my greed for autographs might have had something to do with it, and I sensed the seeds of displeasure. These burst into full flower when Molly unexpectedly asked if she could take her annual holiday the next week because she'd never been to Sydney and would like to see it. Dad, who was roguishly male and tolerant about the whole thing remarked, looking with studied detachment at the ceiling, on the curious coincidence that the English Test Team would be in Sydney at just that time. Molly turned a violent pink and said nothing. I nudged my brother under the table.

Of course when you have a single part-time piece of domestic help it's almost never convenient for it to go on vacation; but Mother eventually gave in and Molly went off in high spirits. Within a week she was front page news in every paper in Australia. She became a sort of camp follower or mascot of the English Team and began to be noticed. Her infatuation was not with Woolley or Strudwick or Hearne, but with the team itself and also with England, Home and Beauty. The adventure culminated at the Sydney cricket ground when, armed with the box Brownie and determined to snap her own unique record, she ducked under the barriers, ran onto the field and took several shots of the English team filing out of the Pavilion before the stewards hustled her off. She was interviewed at the Redfern police station and let off as a harmless female fan. The

The Road to Gundagai

incident exploded in our faces from the morning *Argus* and we were terribly proud of Molly. Even Mother laughed affectionately at the 'silly besotted girl' getting her picture in the papers. Molly returned two weeks later as calm and contained as her bubbly nature could ever be, but on her face the permanent secret smile of the cat who swallowed the cream. Shortly after this the wonderful Molly era came to an end. She went back to England and was succeeded by Eileen McBride and it was as if golden sunshine had been obscured by the sharp edge of a ragged pewter cloud.

* * *

Eileen McBride, though she came from the Six Counties and was a Protestant, fulfilled so exactly an Australian's notion of the comic Irish that Dad, much to her annoyance, at once nicknamed her Paddy. Beneath her severe brown bobbed hair was a face in which the snub nose and the excessively long upper lip were abetted by a grotesque smile, the result of a misplaced eyetooth, so that even when in joyful mood, she gave the illusion of a cornered wild beast. She had a fierce though transitory temper and was the only person whom I have ever seen 'flounce out of the room'. This happened often and was followed by a fit of the sulks from which she had to be coaxed by Mother to whom she was a sore trial. On the other hand she had a passion for hard work and her methods were as orderly as Molly's had been muddled. A state of armed truce varied by occasional forays from either side, soon marked our relations with Eileen. We hated her because we missed sunny and easy-going Molly; we exasperated her by imitating her accent and mode of expression, which was not hard to do. 'Faith Eileen, and I'll be after getting meself a cup of tea.' 'I'll "Faith" you!' She was in fact known to us as 'Faith'. Poor Eileen, she did try hard to get us to like her and her relations with me were complicated by the fact that I was by now a pre-adolescent, becoming sensitive for the first time about my appearance, and Eileen, conscious of our veiled hostility and Mother's sighs of exasperation at the tempers and tantrums, the silent bright-pink faces and the subsequent sulks, set out to create a fifth column in the citadel of 4 Grace Street.

A famous advertisement which appeared each day in all the Melbourne papers showed a picture of a young girl freshly cropped, holding in one hand a luxurious swatch of braided hair which curled round three sides of the advertisement. Another variant showed the rear view of a man's hand with a tonsure followed by a similar view of a richly dowered head of hair with the two captions: 'Bald for Ten Years: Not Bald. Use Shampuna'. I was in the process of con-

The Lady Help

vincing myself that my hairline was receding and happened to mention this to Eileen (for the armed truce did permit exchanges of small embassies and special missions). She had recently struck up a friendship with the daughter of the proprietor of Shampuna. Eileen offered to obtain for me—free—a sample bottle of the sovereign unguent. For a couple of nights I stank out the bathroom and was asked to move on. Eileen said I could use her room and she would even help me put the stuff on. I was touched by this act of generosity. For the next two nights, with the door ostentatiously open, though the motive for the ostentation escaped me at the time, she rubbed my head with the oily yet astringent compound. I could almost hear the hair growing under the firm deft fingers and by the end of the week we were on friendly terms.

The pact lasted for some weeks but was blasted apart by the arrival of Edna and Pixie Tabart from far-off half-forgotten Hobart. Their father had become an official of the Victorian Amateur Turf Club and the entire family had moved to Melbourne. The tomboys whom I'd known seven years before had become enormous, well developed, highly sophisticated 'bright young things' of the Roaring Twenties. Their knees visible below their short, tight skirts and the mounds of their bosoms swelling above the scooped out necklines threw me into a tumult of confusion. They lounged and gangled in the drawing-room chairs and I just *could* not keep my eyes off them. They started to tease and I scarcely knew which way to look. Eileen came to my rescue.

'Now girls, you leave him alone.'

This naturally brought roars of derision from the two young giantesses and perversely aroused me to a fury against Eileen. She had placed her hand protectively on my shoulder. I shook it off violently and cried, 'You leave *me* alone, Eileen.'

Eileen's face went white and her mouth opened to show the misplaced eye-tooth in a frightening grimace. Then it flashed deep red and she fetched me a terrific slap across the face. Without thinking I slapped her back, burst from the room and strode out 'into the night'. Behind me I could hear the blubbering of Eileen, the delighted squeals of the Tabart girls, and Dad calling out my name. I ran all the way to Glenferrie Road. There under the bright lights and the rattle of tramcars I stopped, heaving heavily, outside the Victory movie theatre. I couldn't go back, that was the only certainty that emerged from a whirlpool of conflicting emotions which included rage, shame, guilt, pride, fear and even retrospectively a growing delight at the dramatic exit. But certainly no sense of humour. I strode onward through the night and didn't stop until I found myself on the beach at St. Kilda.

The Road to Gundagai

I sat alone for a while on the sand watching the sea slop gently in the still summer night, watching the moon ride slowly through the web of white wooden girders supporting the scenic railway at nearby Luna Park. I heard St. Kilda Town Hall clock strike two. completely cooled off and drained dry I started to walk back home. I got to bed at five and fell asleep with clothes on in a silent house. I was awoken by a tap on the shoulder and saw Eileen standing over me with a cup of tea. We both started to tumble out apologies at the same instant and I buried my face in Eileen's lap and the tea slopped all over the bed. A week later Mother left on what turned out to be a visit of almost a year to England, taking with her young Lance, aged six, to be shown to his English grandparents and to Mother's friends. Left behind at 4 Grace Street, were Dad, Colin, me—and Eileen.

It seemed to me odd at the time that Mother should go away leaving in charge as housekeeper a single girl of twenty-six. I supposed then that she must think there was safety in numbers. It was a gesture either of supreme innocence or supreme indifference. Eileen kept to her 'place' with a fine sense of propriety, but I noticed that the drawing room seemed to be increasingly hers and that Dad was always bringing home friends from the Naval Military Club—men with matey military names like 'Oz' Caddy, 'Pip' Powell and 'Toc' Tait—because, as he put it to me, 'they find Paddy such fun'. We seemed to have an A.I.F. outpost, a local branch of the R.S.S.I.L.A., in permanent session in our drawing room. Poor Dad, he too was trying the safety in numbers gambit. And it was tougher for him than for Mother, because he was a man and he was here. To his 'Paddy', Eileen retorted with 'Speck' because Dad had speckled brown eyes. This seemed to me rather flighty.

Eileen did her best but I noticed that cigarette burns increased, and once when she thought it time for the men to be leaving she dumbfounded us all by emptying two freshly poured noggins of whisky into a bowl of daffodils. Half of me was still schoolboy and another quarter at least had got into the exam tread-mill and was fully and exhaustingly engaged. But the remaining quarter was perplexed and interested, worried and excited. I felt I ought to be 'taking charge' in some obscure way, but didn't know what I ought to do. Was it right for Eileen to assume the role of hostess? Was anything 'going on?' Not that I knew what I meant by 'going on'; it was just that I was conscious of the ground shifting disconcertingly beneath my feet, of an impairment of standards, of a slight air of good natured sleaziness. I don't think my apprehensions went any further than that, and I didn't do anything about them.

In the spring my cousin Hugh Poynter came down from Sydney

The Lady Help

to visit us. He was accompanied by two business associates and as Mother and Lance were both in England, Dad asked the three of them to stay for a few days. During this period Eileen worked like a slavey with breakfasts, meals and housekeeping for four men and two boys. But Dad made it like a picnic because he kept turning up at odd hours with loot from the Prahran market: strings of saveloys and frankfurters, pongy cheeses, crayfish, black puddings and huge Portuguese sardines. We dined al fresco night after night and the house seemed to be full of empty beer bottles. I enjoyed those few days but felt uneasy too. Suppose Mother should pop in? But Mother was 11,000 miles away. Not that we—any of us—were doing anything *wrong* . . . it was just that the house wasn't being run Mother's way. But could it be, if she wasn't there? Letters from her came plentifully, by every ship, for she was a most dutiful as well as an amusing correspondent; but as they were invariably from five to seven weeks late they had an air of unreality and seemed to have nothing to do with 4 Grace Street. Supposing I were to hint of my unease to Mother? It would be three months before I'd get a reply and by that time the situation might be totally different. In any case what was I uneasy about? I decided to confide in Cousin Hugh.

Sir Hugh Poynter, Bart, O. Medj was a jolly round-faced man of about fifty with a grey-white tonsure, a crisp grey semi-military moustache and very intense sparkling brown eyes, like black Greek olives. He was my maternal grandmother's first cousin, their mothers, Alice Poynter and Georgiana Burne-Jones, having been sisters. The Bart he had inherited when his elder brother Ambrose died unexpectedly young, and the original honour, conferred on Edward Poynter as President of the Royal Academy, had passed unexpectedly to Hugh. He was utterly unlike my idea of a Bart: friendly, garrulous, lacking entirely in pomposity and with a splendid streak of witty coarseness that delighted us all. He was perhaps much more like an O. Medj or Order of Medji which he had received from the Sultan of Turkey for work connected with the supervision of the Ottoman Debt before World War I. He was a bit of a Turk, the wily oriental rather than the young Pasha. Colin and I were supposed to shine the shoes of the distinguished guests each day and though we objected to the shoes of the two side-kicks, because they were in our view, too pointed ('nana' shoes, in fact) we competed actively for the honour of shining the Bart's shoes because their shape was noble (and also because we might get a tip).

I stood before Cousin Hugh's bed one morning after having handed him his freshly shined shoes and asked if I might speak with him privately.

'You're speaking privately with me now,' he said.
'Yes but this is *really* private.'
His bright brown eyes twinkled from the pillows (the parents' room, the parents' bed, and he was lying on *Mother's side*! I controlled my perturbation). He crossed his firm brown hands over the coverlet.
'Well of course. What is it?'
'It's difficult to explain, Cousin Hugh, but I'm a bit worried.'
'What about?'
'About—about—oh well the way the house is, well, going on, being run.'
'You mean Miss McBride isn't doing her job?'
'Oh, no, no. Not that. I think she's doing a very good job of course, but,'—I paused. I didn't know how to go on. Hugh cleared his throat.
'Let me see if I can help you,' he said cheerfully. 'If I'm right, you're a bit worried—aren't you? Correct me if I'm wrong—that Eileen and your Dad, as you call him, might be doing a little spooning on the sly?'
My cheeks burned and he looked at me quizzically.
'Well, aren't you?'
I nodded; he had cut short my carefully prepared elliptical preamble and pounced at once on what I'd been unable or afraid to define. How wonderful to be grown up! How even more wonderful to be both grown-up and worldy-wise. I gazed at Hugh with admiration. He shifted a bit in the bed and reached for a cigar. He lit it and the rich pungent aroma reached me. How wonderful to smoke a cigar! In bed. In the morning too. Of course he was director of the Australian branch of Baldwin Steel and was beyond the standards of ordinary mortals. Hugh cleared his throat again, looking as sharp and cheerful as a marmoset in a basket.
'I can tell you they're not. Absolutely not,' he said briskly and with an air of complete finality. I was overcome with remorse.
'Oh dear, Cousin Hugh, then do you think I . . . I mean I was wrong to. . . ?'
'No, not at all. You were perfectly right. Though I must confess that for a youngster you're pretty alert to these matters. But they're not and they're not going to; so you can go about your business with an easy mind and a light heart. And now, you'll have to vamoose, I must get up.'
'Oh thank you, Cousin Hugh! Thanks a thousand times,' I cried and tore out of the room and rushed off to school. An immense load was lifted from my mind and from that moment I never gave

The Lady Help

the matter a thought. The confessional had freed my conscience. I had dumped Christian's Burden on the broad insouciant shoulders of Cousin Hugh who left the next day for Sydney. The essential situation at 4 Grace Street remained, of course, entirely unchanged by this colloquy. It was just that I ceased to worry about it and hence to notice it.

That summer, when we were staying with friends up country a postcard came from Eileen. It was postmarked Sydney and it showed a view of Sublime Point near Bulli on the south coast of New South Wales. Romance breathed from the postmark and the view of unknown shores, but not from the text of the note.

'We are having a lovely time. We all three came over this pass yesterday. Driving back to Melbourne on Thursday. Love Eileen.'

Safety in numbers.

In January Mother returned. 'Speck' and 'Paddy' vanished instantly from the scene. Dignity, decorum and demure looks were the order of the day. The Grace Street ship shuddered, shook and altered course; it became more ship-shape; it became in fact less a happy ship than a tight ship. Within a month Eileen was gone.

Eileen was the last of our Lady Helps. Whether it was that we boys, even Lance, were now getting big enough to help around the house, or whether Mother had decided that living-in help was too hazardous a proposition, their days were over. The Lady Help's room was converted into a combination of Lance's room and storeroom, and a daily came on the scene in the shape of Nonie Cook. Nonie, whose real name was Iona, was a gabby willing girl with a cheerful disposition, not much sense, and a really shattering case of adenoids. She had, or affected to have, a horror of the slimy things in which boys delight, such as toads, snails, spiders and muck out of drains. Any mention of these used to send her into a shuddering ecstasy of horror. Colin was able, at will, to reduce her to a writhing jelly of delighted revulsion by bursting cheerily into the kitchen with a:

'Hey, Nonie, how would you like a glass of snot?'

'Aow! Ugh! You filthy beast.'

'Oh come on, Nonie, it's fresh.'

'Aow, get away frob be.'

Sometimes he was more guileful.

'Hey, Nonie, I've got a present for you.'

'A presed? What kide of presed?'

'A bowl of TONS backwards.'

'Tuds backwards. What's that?' Pause; slow double take. 'Aow, you filthy boy!'

The Road to Gundagai

Roars of laughter ensued until broken by Dad's voice bellowing down the corridor.

'Boys! Boys!'

'Shut up. He's waxy,' *sotto voce.* 'Yes Dad?'

'Be a good fellow and get me some whisky. Five eighths of an inch in the bottom of a glass.'

Chapter Thirteen

CENTRAL 434, PLEASE

FIVE eighths of an inch of whisky, usually in the middle of a wet Sunday afternoon when he was poring over his wonderful stamp collection, I shall take as the essence, psyche or anima of my stepfather, Thirk, Dad. There you have—in one nip, as it were—his engineering training, his happy-go-lucky geniality, and yet again (since it is not the kind of errand on which one might normally send a boy) his lethargy. With Mother everything was sharp and tight and on schedule. Bells rang, cannons boomed, gongs clanged, flags were run up and the form was more important than the substance. With Dad it was a world of laisser faire, sudden impulses, tuneless cheerful whistling, odd tasks begun and never finished. I think Mother gave him up fairly early, and in the end she left him: but the sons of the first marriage felt towards him a wary affection, and in small things he was always generous. Dad never paid a school bill of mine in his life and never kept an appointment on time; but if you wanted ten bob suddenly, or if you were in a jam with the cops, or if you simply *had* to have that striped tie, well . . . He was unkind only when forced by insistent browbeating to be Mother's instrument. Normally he was a lackadaisical believer in live-and-let-live except where his passions were concerned: stamp collecting, standard roses and The Works.

I spent so many uncounted hours in the dolorous tedium of The Works that they clamorously demand a place in this narrative. The full name was The Australian Metal Equipment Company known as TAMECO for short. Its products, displayed on the drawing room walls, startled dinner-jacketed guests to Mother's literary evenings. For there, mounted on neatly polished and stained squares of plywood, were pistons, bushes, hammers, valves, cold chisels, pinchbars and cylinders, all burnished till you could see your face in them. On top of a bookcase containing complete sets of the works of Dickens and Scott was the front bumper of an 'Essex', complete with hexagonal red badge (also produced by TAMECO). A highly

The Road to Gundagai

polished 'Overland' crankshaft stretched in tortured shining rigidity between two Dresden shepherdesses. An electro-plated crowbar gleamed like a silver spear beneath a copy of Burne-Jones' study of Merlin and Nimuë. Over the piano and beneath the Dürer print of *Tod als Freund* were two headlamps without glass, and a neat set of gudgeon pins, flanked by silver lustreware pitchers.

* * *

The Works were at the far end of Latrobe Street at the extreme southwest corner of Melbourne's planned quadrilateral laid out by Hoddle himself. The enormous hundred-foot-wide streets here looked bleak and empty, for most of the buildings were but one or at the most two storeys high and faced each other, behind dusty plane trees, over a void of bitumen across which they seemed to be straining anxiously to catch sight of friendly bricks and mortar. We stopped outside a blank two floor building faced in grey cement. It was clearly a pair of semi-detached houses knocked together; numbers 506 and 508. Across the front was written 'Haines Engineering Co.'; from within the building came a distant humming and whirring. I was terribly disappointed.

'Is this the place?'

'That's it,' said Dad proudly.

'But the name?'

'Oh we haven't had a chance to alter that yet. The deal only went through last week. Come in and meet Harry Haines.'

We walked in as one might into a private house except that all the interior walls had been stripped and the entire area, front to back, was filled with clanking machinery. Through a side door I could see that the adjoining room was a mirror-vision version of the one we were in. Men in overalls bent over turret lathes; whirling leather belts slapped ferociously against grilled safety guards; along the ceiling twirled the main shaft, whizzing within a few inches of stained and greasy relics of the plasterer's art: a floral centrepiece from which a lamp had once hung, foliated cornices and a deep opulent dado. The original paper was still on the walls and the men manning lathes nearest them had left great smears from their overalls on the vertically striped pattern. The clatter was deafening.

'Harry, this is my boy Graham.' Dad was shouting in my ear above the din and I looked up to see a worried looking middle-aged man in overalls, with curly grey-black oiled hair and, incongruously in the din and the dirt, a pair of fussy pince-nez. He held out his hand and muttered an inaudible greeting; then he turned to Dad and said something. Dad beckoned me on through the shop

Central 434, Please

with its nodding and slapping machinery. I realized that I was on display.

'My boy Graham, Bill. This is Mr. Hilliard.'

A rangy sour-visaged giant with curly red hair gave me a curt nod.

'My boy Graham, Don. This is Mr. McFadzean.'

A quizzical look from a sandy-haired fellow with a stubbly blonde beard, and a handshake that blacked me with grease and steel powder.

So the procession continued through both rooms and out into what must have been, in the colonial period, 'lean-to' back kitchens. I shook perhaps two dozen grimed hands and tried to stop wiping my own hand down the side of my pants. Then we climbed a pair of rickety stairs and were in the office: bare boards, a small battered square iron safe, a couple of green filing cabinets and two grimy desks behind one of which sat an elderly crone with frizzed grey hair and a hearing aid (what use it was to her in all that clatter I never knew). She had evidently been expecting us for on her desk was a brown teapot with a rubber spout, three stained cups without saucers and a half empty bottle of milk.

'Good morning Mr. Thirkell,' she said with a roguish leer. 'I made you some tea.'

'My boy Graham, Mrs. Green. Mrs. Green does the books,' he added. I drank the sweetish pre-sugared tea and looked out through the sooted windows at the plane trees in Latrobe Street. The noise, very slightly muted, beat up the rickety staircase from the machine shop below. Mr. Haines was restive. He kept walking up and down, drumming his fingers on the desk, taking off his pince-nez and squeezing his tired grey eyes. I decided that he was a fusspot.

'George,' he said, 'I've got to talk to you.' He looked across at me.

Dad said, 'Graham, how would you like to go on the roof for a bit.'

* * *

After a while we left the factory and drove down by the railway yards until we coasted to a stop opposite the great gaunt head office of the Victorian Railways, with its billboards advertising citrus fruits from Mildura:

> 'Children, yes and grown-ups too,
> Orange juice is good for you.'

We stopped outside a pub, strategically placed right on the corner: the *Sir Charles Hotham*. His medallion portrait hung out over the

The Road to Gundagai

sidewalk and his name ran in a banner along both fronts of the building. But the doors were shut, it was outside licensing hours.

'That's all right,' said Dad. 'Les'll let us in.'

'Are we going to have a drink?'

'We might.' He pressed a white enamel button at a small side door. 'What do you fancy?'

'Sarsaparilla soda.'

'I think Les can manage that.'

The door opened carefully and revealed a tall man with a florid face, a large Roman nose, a shock of receding curly hair in a Vee and a big pot. He was in his shirtsleeves and he bent on us very large shrewd liquid brown eyes.

'Hullo George,' he said, and his voice was curiously soft and silky. 'Better come in off the street; bring the nipper.'

'This is my boy Graham, Les. This is Mr. L. G. Watson.' It sounded funny with the initials like that. Mr. Watson told me to shut the door and we followed him down a dark passage and into a small private bar. He picked up a napkin, draped it over his shoulder and went behind the counter.

'Well what'll it be George?'

'A whisky, thanks, Les.' (five-eighths of an inch?)

'What about you, boy?'

'A sarsaparilla soda please.'

'Boy shows good taste,' said Mr. Watson unscrewing the bottle and pouring in a generous dollop. 'Don't like to see youngsters drinking.'

'Neither do I, Les,' said Dad piously.

The room was very dark and cool and sickly-sweet. Far off a clock ticked. Dad seemed to have shrunk slightly in the presence of the Neronian Mr. Watson who poured himself a tiny glass of beer.

'Just a pony,' he said. 'Well George, how's it coming?'

Dad cleared his throat. 'The firm needs another thousand of working capital. I was wondering . . .' he twiddled his glass and looked up at Les in the sickly-sweet gloom. Les looked at me. The clock in the far-off room seemed to tick more loudly and super-imposed on it with sudden and remarkable sonority was the purring of a cat.

'Perhaps the boy would like to pay a visit to Toby while we're talking. Eh boy?'

Once again I found myself alone but this time with a very large tortoiseshell Tom who purred like a power station with one turbine on the loose. When I became used to the stertorous purring I found that by some trick of acoustics I could hear the conversation in the private bar. I wondered if Mr. Watson knew this. It seemed to me inconceivable that he didn't. So I listened carefully without any guilt about eavesdropping. Most of the talk was too technical for me but I gathered that Les Watson and Harry Haines and Dad were going to be respectively Chairman, Works Manager and Managing Director of the new company. There would also be other directors. I heard the cryptic names 'Pip', 'Toc' and 'Denny'. It appeared too that some of the men like Bill Hilliard and Don McFadzean were to have shares. This must be what is meant by floating a company, I thought. Presently Dad called, Mr. Watson gave me half a crown, much to my surprise and delight, and we began to drive home.

'Dad, what's your contribution to TAMECO?'

'My contribution?' (I thought so: he's stalling.)

'Well, I mean, (I didn't want to let on that I'd overheard) Mr. Watson's giving money, isn't he?'

'You bet he's not *giving* it!'

'What about you?'

'Ah my boy,' he said, bouncing the heel of his palm on the wheel. 'I'm contributing skill.' I digested this in silence.

'Anyway, one thing TAMECO's going to do is get us a new car.'

'Oh Dad! Gee that's bonzer. What make?'

'I'd thought of a Chrysler. Of course Les Watson would have a Chrysler Imperial.'

He swirled the wheel a bit in his jubilation and instantly all delight at the new car was obliterated by an unexorcised horror of his driving habits. He was not the worst driver I ever knew; but he was the most unnervingly flamboyant. He drove with a kind of spurious unnecessary élan, making of quite simple gestures extravagant sweeps and flourishes. He couldn't even advance the spark or pull out the choke (in those days both on the steering wheel) without making a straightforward movement into a contortion of baroque complexity. He also fancied himself as a speed merchant and drove our sober domestic sedans as if they were sports cars. Of course it was quite harmless, even the leather helmet and the Auto-Reelite spotlight (strictly illegal) and the souped up carburettor with ethyl in the cocks: provided you weren't with him in the car. If you were, your foot was through the floorboard half the time. On mornings when he said, 'Come on, I'll give you a lift to school' my heart went to my boots. For it meant not only hanging about in a frenzy of impatience until he was ready—and he was the least punctual of men—but then a fearsome dash along Glenferrie Road, partly to make up for lost time, partly to show off to the schoolboys clinging to the laggard tramcars as we rocketed by. They thought he was quite terrific and I gained much kudos at school for having such a daredevil Dad. But they didn't have to ride with him.

The Road to Gundagai

Just how unnerving it was becomes apparent if one goes back over Dad's bikes and cars and traces his Toad's progress from a solo motor-bike to a Chrysler 75 in five cluttered years. First came the twin cylinder M.A.G. christened 'Humphrey' by Mother on the basis of a similar nickname bestowed on a motor-bike in a series of comic sketches appearing in *Punch*. Humphrey bucked like a bronco and spurted flame, shattering the neighbourhood with bursts of gunfire. Dad garaged Humphrey on the front porch where he soon deposited a large pool of oil and grease directly beneath the drawing-room window. By this time Mother had had the stained glass vitrified mucous porthole removed and replaced by a large oblong sash window—the only one in the house, the rest being casement or clerestory in the Melbourne suburban manner. The easiest way into the drawing room was to climb through this new window. Humphrey's pool of oil made this caper *streng verboten* under pain of the most awful penalties. 'I don't *like* the drawing room looking like an Irish cabin,' said Mother, 'but I can put up with it. What I will not put up with is oily greasy marks on the furniture.' This seemed reasonable, even to us.

Less reasonable was Mother's absolute proscription on pillion riding, despite Dad's siren beckonings. We fumed at this restraint but very soon relief appeared in the form of a side-car. This was made of wickerwork and was in the shape of a sedan chair in which one sat bolt upright. It was against local bye-laws to leave a motor-bike and side-car on the street, though heaven knows why, for in the early Twenties Melbourne suburban streets were as innocent of parking troubles as a mediaeval village. Dad solved this problem by removing our wooden front gate and inserting a wire-mesh cast-iron double gate. The problem of a driveway he solved by running the bike up the front path and the side-car on the front lawn or occasionally the rosebeds. We were supposed to open the gate for him as soon as we came home from school and if we didn't, a long drawn out Ahhrr-oooo-ah; Ahhrr-oooo-ah on the Klaxon soon brought us scurrying out. Dad's favourite manoeuvre, if the gate were open, was to approach the house at high speed, declutch, shift into low, swing in a sharp dextrous curve across the gutter and then gun the bike roaring down the front path and the rosebeds and brake it to a spectacular stop within inches of the drawing-room window. Then off with his shoes, on with his slippers and five eighths of an inch.

Although he took Mother to Government House in the wicker side-car Dad soon realized that it didn't exactly cut a dashing figure. The wicker basket disappeared and in its place came a long, low wicked looking side-car shaped like a bullet and painted bright green.

224

Central 434, Please

I had some fearsome rides in that bullet. Twice Dad took me in it up to the Dandenongs and once on a hair-raising trip down the Bay to Sorrento. For this outing Dad wore leather hip boots and jacket, goggles and a cap with its peak at the rear like an old-fashioned newsreel movie cameraman. The Ton-Up kids on the M1 had nothing on him. We scorched up the tarmac through Frankston, Rosebud and Rye to Sorrento, passing everything in sight. For me it was a day of alternate gut-churning dread and the sheerest exhilaration punctuated by a swim in a deep ocean rock pool on whose sandy floor crayfish walked on hairy stilts twenty feet below, and seaweed fronds floated lazily as if in mid-air.

At this point there comes into the story Sir Aurelian Ridsdale. He was the brother of Stanley Baldwin's wife ('Aunt Cissie') so when he was in Melbourne on business what more natural than that he should call on his rather distant cousin-in-law, and ascertain (primed no doubt by my grandmother) how she was getting on among the barbarians? He took the parents to lunch at Menzies Hotel and he himself came to visit us at 4 Grace Street. I must have made a favourable impression (or else Mother must have interceded on my behalf) for there on my birthday, gleaming with unearthly beauty, was a bicycle with a note on it in which Sir Aurelian wished me good luck. It was one of the blinding high points of boyhood; a glimpse through the gates of paradise and a feeling that one was larger than life and buoyed up by jingling balloons. Once I'd mastered the gleaming sensitive creature its uses became endless.

Vistas of intoxicating freedom opened up, but less than a month later I emerged from behind a tramcar looking in the wrong direction. There was a shattering impact and I was on my back with a circle of concerned faces peering down at me and blood coursing from my legs. Under a nearby Morris Oxford with steam jetting from its radiator lay the twisted mangled remains of my beautiful bicycle. When he heard the news—and this *is* miraculous—Sir Aurelian sent Mother a cheque to buy a new one! I suppose that to a well-to-do businessman ten pounds was little enough, but it was a gesture of astonishing rightness and perception. I never met this Maecenas. I wrote of course a fulsome letter of thanks to which he sent a brief quizzical reply. Years later when I was a young man he invited me to stay with him at his villa outside Algiers, but I was too busy and too poor to go.

The 'new' bike was secondhand from the emporium of Bruce Small in Malvern. Mother had prudently decided not to run the risk of another brand new bike being smashed up and the balance of the cheque went into my savings account. The effect of this was to make the whole business of bicycling fade into the light of

The Road to Gundagai

common day. Instead of being a wonder, the bike was now a necessary tool. But it was worth it for the prestige of dealing with Bruce Small, who was one of the men behind Hubert Opperman. And who was Hubert Opperman? Don't I mean Robert Oppenheimer of atomic fame? Ah, it's clear you weren't a bicycle fan in Australia in the Twenties. Oppie was the idol of all, boy and man, who could 'push a mangle'; he was, simply, the greatest wheel in Australia. He first came to prominence through spectacularly lowering the time on the annual Warrnambool to Melbourne road race. This was 165 miles of gruelling dirt, gravel, metalled but hardly any paved road. Now Oppie was ready for the Tour de France.

Never had we read or learned so much about that miraculous country. The newspapers were full of France—its scenic beauties, its incomparable wines, its charming women, its majestic history, (almost, if not quite, the equal of Britain's, though of course we had won, *in the end*) its friendship for Australia. Its ties with Australia. Historical heads were scratched and out came the encounter between Governor Phillip and Admiral Bougainville, the explorations around Tasmania by Bruni d'Entrecasteaux, the dramatic meeting of Captain Baudin with Captain Matthew Flinders (omitting the subsequent imprisonment of Flinders by the French Governor of Mauritius). Professor Scott, Head of the History Department of the University, wrote articles for the *Argus* on Franco-British co-operation, ending up with the Anglo-French Condominium over the New Hebrides, field of Australian missionary activities. We discovered a string of romantic French names on the map of Australia: Recherche Archipelago; Freycinet, Cape d'Entrecasteaux. Meanwhile the map of France became better known to Australian youngsters than it ever had been to their fathers who fought on the Somme. The gruelling route of the Tour de France was displayed in Bruce Small's window and we knew the names of the key points by heart: Rennes, Nantes, Bordeaux, Toulouse, Narbonne. . . . The French consul M. René Turcq was a popular figure not only with Melbourne society but with Melbourne sports fans.

As for the Tour itself, Oppie would win. There was no question of that at all. He himself was modest enough; in a final press interview before his departure he promised only to do his best and expressed the hope that he would not let Australia down. 'Good on you Oppie!' shouted the crowds and off he went. To those of us who'd actually seen him in Bruce Small's bike shop, had devoured the knowledgeable bike talk, hung on his creased smile, envied the impeccable 'brushback' hair, and cadged autographs, it was a memorable day as the streamers tautened and parted in curling clusters between his ship and Port Melbourne pier.

Central 434, Please

Oppie didn't win the Tour de France. The course, it appeared, was not only gruelling but unfamiliar; he at first lacked team-mates to pace him (this was remedied later); and the crafty Europeans, whom we'd regarded as decadent and old fashioned, revealed unsuspected sources of stamina, organization and cunning. Oppie, Opperman, 'le jeune Australien aux cheveux en brosse', came in seventeenth. Never mind: A Great Effort! Good Old Oppie! Better luck next time! Australia will be there! At Bruce Small's when he returned, he was the same old Oppie. And just at this time Dad removed the teasing motor-bike and garage problem once and for all by announcing that we were going to have a car. A great whoop went up from the dining table.

It turned out to be a four-cylinder 1924 Overland 'tourer' with a folding canvas roof and a body painted bright blue. Mother christened it Billy, rather archly, because of Willys-Overland, and the name stuck. Unlike most cars, which curved smartly inward at the rear (with or without a spare tyre clinging on behind) Billy prefigured in crude form the cars of twenty years later by presenting to the highway a protuberant bum or bustle which bulged out far beyond the rear seat and which housed the petrol tank and the tool kit. Though monopolized by Dad on weekdays it liberated the family on Sundays when it took us 'touring' down the Bay and into the hills, and we enjoyed the immense exhilaration of tearing through the countryside, whipped by the wind, at speeds sometimes in excess of forty miles an hour.

But 'Billy' brought chores with his freedom. The old garage-and-gate problem was not solved but merely shifted three doors down the street, and the evening ritual of honking and gate-opening continued unchanged. Added to it was the exasperating task of cleaning the car on Saturday. Dad would supervise or tinker with the motor, but never descend to a pail of water, a rag or a 'shammy'. Even more exhausting and time-consuming was the cartage of the petrol. It was admittedly in the early days of petrol pumps, but we never could understand why Dad preferred to buy petrol by the tin and store it in the workshop right next to the outside lavatory. This highly combustible and, come to think of it, illegal freight, was offloaded from a truck at the front gate. It was our job to carry the tins of petrol a hundred feet or so down the side alley and store them in the workshop. Each tin contained four gallons and only a small iron handle which bit deeply into the finger. By the time you'd handled two dozen of these cans and stacked them neatly, you certainly knew it. But it was fun, of a sort, filling the tank. You pierced the tin with a sharp hollow spike. The tin buckled smoothly and the curved metal spout fitted snugly on its rubber

The Road to Gundagai

collar. Then, gurgle, gurgle, in it went. Pretty soon Dad came out, his leather helmet forsaken now for a grey Homburg which, since he wore it on the back of his head with the brim up in front, made him look rather less like Anthony Eden than a stockyard outrider. The door slammed, from Billy's protuberant blue bum came a great fart of rich mixture, and away he zoomed to distant parts.

But now it was to be a Chrysler: to Mother, inevitably, 'Fritz'. It was the most glamorous car we'd ever seen. Fritz was a sheeny pearlish green and had a pair of flaring wings on his radiator cap. He was fitted with 'side curtains' attached with press studs. Almost a saloon in fact. Dad drove him with ecstatic belly-hugging love and abandon, and it was an honour—at first—to be allowed to clean him. Fritz's arrival also marked, thank God, the end of the petrol tins stored in the workshop next to the outside lavatory. Dad now embraced the petrol-pump so that he could show off Fritz to the garage attendants.

* * *

Meanwhile the tedious visits to The Works went on and on. A day there was spent essentially in hanging around until Dad was ready to go home. Left alone but not permitted to leave the premises I would mooch about the building, get in the way of machinists at their lathes, ask timid inane questions. The men half tolerated, half resented me. Talk was apt to dry up when I appeared; I might be a spy for the Management. Or else it would become effusively matey. 'Har, there, Graham. Like to run the mechanical saw for a while? Okay. Here's how you do it. Watch the pitch and speed eh? Make sure to keep the coolant flowing over the cut. That's the boy. We'll make an engineer of him yet.' Or else offensively proprietorial. 'Har, there, Graham. Mind emptying this bin of filings for me? Tar. Watch yer fingers, they're sharp. And when yer through, how about popping across the street and bring me back a meat pie? Here's sixpence.' But most of the time I just mooched around, supplied with odd cups of tea by the kind Mrs. Green, until Dad was ready to take me, perhaps home, perhaps to Les Watson's pub, but more likely to The Club.

* * *

It was the Naval and Military Club in Alfred Place off Collins Street, and I must have spent longer in it, and even longer waiting outside it than in or out of any institution in my whole boyhood.

Central 434, Please

Dad was prodigal, indeed profligate, in his use of The Club. His bills, he once told us with pride, amounted to about £40 per quarter. Since his income at this time was £520 per annum, it can easily be seen that his pursuit of the dear dead days of his wartime youth with 'Oz' and 'Pip' and 'Toc' and 'Dony' bit quite a hole in his finances. In fact it was just as well that Mother did have a little money of her own.

I was not allowed inside The Club until I was thirteen and at first, my acquaintance was limited to long waits in the car, while brisk couples passed by on their way to The Embassy, Jennie Brennan's School of the Dance, and I gingerly shifted silent gears and pretended to drive Fritz at high speed right through the Embassy and out the other side. Gay the lilt of the saxophone and the plunk of the banjo from The Embassy, and gayer the gusty male guffaws loosed on the night air of Alfred Place as the front door of The Club opened to exude yet another revelling Anzac veteran. But gloomy indeed the boy, or boys, or Lady Helps and occasionally Mum herself sitting in the cold and waiting endlessly for Captain Thirkell.

Another ritual was more agonizingly familiar; it emanated from 4 Grace Street, to be exact the drawing room (i.e. living room) in which, on top of the bookcase near the Bord Piano, sits the telephone. It is six p.m. Mother's voice from the kitchen:

'Graham, see if you can get Dad.'

'Okay, Mum.'

'Don't say okay.'

'Very well Mother.'

We had an early automatic dial, but Central, the exchange for the Club, is manual.

'Central 434 please.'

'Naval and Military Club.'

'May I speak to Captain Thirkell please?'

'One moment please.'

Obviously the flunkey has put the 'phone down and gone to look for Captain Thirkell. His steps clunk into the distance with that anonymous, sinister, slightly metallic sound which feet have on the telephone, whether over parquetry, linoleum, wall-to-wall carpet or cement. The steps die away and all that remains is a little static, a faint humming sound, an awareness, as of a movie screen when the censor's certificate precedes the main title assembly; a slight expectant hiss, and beyond it remote confused talk and laughter which might be coming from the bar at the Naval and Military Club, but which might equally be coming from other lines somewhere in the depths of the Central exchange, or from Mars.

The Road to Gundagai

I settle down to wait, and my left ear grows bigger and bigger. When it is the size of a football bladder Mother calls.

'Have you got Dad yet?'

'I'm waiting for him.'

'Tell him to hurry or supper will be cold.'

'Very well Mother.'

Ah-ha, approaching footsteps. They are coming over an immense distance, clanking up the sewers beneath Vienna streets, clumping up the corridors of Lubianka prison. They stop; a shattering jangle in my ear; it must be Dad picking up the 'phone at the other end. Clumsy fellow. But the voice is not his.

'Are you there sir?'

'Yes.'

'Sorry to keep you waiting. Captain Thirkell is unable to come to the telephone but he asks me to tell you he's leaving the club immediately.'

'Thank you very much. Hey Mother!'

'Don't *shout*. Come and tell me.'

'Dad says——'

'Did you *speak* to him?'

'Well no, not to him but to the fellow at the Club, he says Dad is leaving the club immediately.'

Mother snorted. 'That means he won't be home till eight. Come and have your supper.'

This lugubrious ritual was repeated on most week nights. We would be home from school, the garden chores done, the chips chopped for the chip-heater, and ravening for our evening meal. Mother would look up from the stove, face anxious, wisps of hair falling into her eyes.

'Go and see if you can get Dad on the 'phone. Find out if he's going to be in for supper.'

'Central 434 . . . May I speak to Captain Thirkell please. . . ?'

As I grew into my earliest teens Dad used to take me into the Club on his way home from The Works and I learned what it was that kept him so late. It was not, as Mother sometimes hinted, Demon Rum or even its more probable Australian equivalent, Foster's Lager, Carlton Ale or Melbourne Bitter. It was, rather, the Anzac Dream. This particular Saturday was typical of many. Dad parked the car in Alfred Place, told me to look after it, clomped up the white steps and through the burnished mahogany door and vanished. After watching the passers-by for half an hour, including a surreptitious peep round the corner at the traffic on Collins Street, I mounted the steps myself and rang the bell. The Club Porter, in brass buttoned tails, a pink and white striped shirt, a wing collar and a bow tie, came out from behind a glass windowed rabbit hutch. His initial glance was cool but when I said. 'I'm Captain Thirkell's son,' he thawed.

'Your Dad inside?' he asked. I nodded. 'And you want him to come out? All right. You just wait here a moment.' The porter eased himself down the tiled hallway swinging a game leg as he went. A roaring babel of men's voices surged in a gust up the corridor and then died away. I waited, gazed at the steel engravings of Lady Butler's *The thin red line at Waterloo, The sinking of the Birkenhead, The meeting of Wellington and Blücher*. The babel surged and ebbed once more and the porter came stumping back.

'Captain Thirkell would like you to join him in the bar; I'll show you the way.'

'Is it all right for me to go there?'

He bent a severe glance on me. 'Naturally, sonny (how I hated being called 'sonny'); this is a private club.'

I followed him down the tiled corridor to a large double door; he pushed it open and I was engulfed in the roar which from my height and age appeared to proceed from fifty giants with reddish faces, straining necks and bulbous pots, all talking at once. Each man had in his hand either a glass or a silver tankard. Their mouths roared open with meaningless ferocity and frightening geniality as they bellowed at each other across their drinks or broke into cannon roars of gusty laughter. They shouted across each other's speech, drowned each other out, listened not at all, kept up the continuous barking and caterwauling while I stood warily in a corner searching for familiar islands in the sea of noise. Soon I detected 'Donie' Joynt, the V.C., and made for him like a ship in a gale. When I touched his sleeve he looked down, at first with an expression of wondering irritability; but then a smile cut his lean face.

'You're George Thirkell's boy, aren't you? Wait here. I'll see if I can find your Dad.'

'Like a drink son?' A bronzed and grizzled veteran with a beaky nose and a zig-zag red and blue artillery tie leaned over me. It was 'Oz'—otherwise Colonel H. O. Caddy, D.S.O., V.D.—one of Dad's cronies who lived mysteriously in a flat in South Yarra cared for by a maiden sister with the identical beaky nose, though minus the tie. I said I would like a cloves.

'We'll see if we can find your Dad,' he said.

The drink arrived and as I sipped it through a straw, mostly unregarded in a corner by the fireplace, I took secret stock of the seething mass of men. They were all veterans with the R.S.S.I.L.A. badge in their lapels, but their talk was of current matters: the races, who to back for the fifth at Flemington, personal gossip, politics, whether

The Road to Gundagai

the present Prime Minister S. M. Bruce was a smart fellow or just a tailor's dummy, whether Billy Hughes the war-time P.M. would ever make a comeback. But underneath it all lay a lazy sense of camaraderie, of some secret shared in common and which excluded me, not only because I was of another generation, but because I had not been 'over there'; because the names Gallipoli, Gaba Tepe, Mudros, Anzac Cove, the Somme, Passchendaele, the Ancre, Villers Brettoneux, held for me no common memories softened by time but only the monstrous overtones of fearful shapes looming through the mists of myth and somehow unrelated to the bawling and shouting here in the unfamiliar club. I was on my own island; with the noisy sea of talk but not of it.

I dipped my nose into the cloves and ruminated on the club trophies: brass shell cases from French 75's on either side of the unlit fire, and over it, crossed Mauser rifles from the Boer War and the noble tattered remnant of the Jack carried into Jutland on Jellicoe's *Iron Duke*. On the wall nearest the fireplace was the famous map showing the Western Front in May 1918 with the disposition of allied and enemy strengths. The British divisions (and Australian and Canadian; in those days of rousing Empire no one discriminated) were of course coloured red; the French horizon blue, and the Germans field grey. It was noticeable that on either side of the thin wavy line, stretched from the North Sea to the Ardennes, the German divisions were grouped most densely opposite the British (and Australians and Canadians); but over in the Meuse-Argonne area, held by the Americans, they were thinly grouped. This map was always invoked whenever visiting Americans were too boastful or Australians wished to reassure themselves after some particularly spectacular American victory in the sporting field. Finally, through the press, I saw Dad easing his way towards me.

* * *

The Naval and Military Club included the rising airforce and I encountered many pioneers of the R.A.F. and R.A.A.F. around the bar, including Geoffrey De Havilland who was in Australia organizing his firm's contacts in civil aviation, and Wackett, at that time a Squadron Leader, later to become famous as the pilot of the wonderful Widgeon. The alliterative value of Wackett's Widgeon to a headline writer needs no comment. It was through these bold fellows that I had my first flight at Essendon airport in an old Fokker bi-plane.

The giants who operated these tiny aircraft and filled them with petrol from an ordinary bowser were up to their eyes in the development of pioneer flying. The exploration of the route from London to Melbourne reached heroic heights. Ross and Keith Smith, ex-A.I.F. brothers, opened the way in 1920, picking up a couple of knighthoods in a series of hedge hopping excursions that took the best part of two months. Then followed Parer and McIntosh whose incredible venture took over ninety days and landed them in Darwin as the originators of all tall stories about planes being held together by baling wire and string. Four naval flying-boats made the trip under the command of Group Captain Cave-Brown-Cave, and Dad attended a dinner at The Club to the intrepid airmen who had in fact pioneered the route for Imperial Airways via the Mediterranean, Iraq, the Persian Gulf, India, Burma, Malaya and the Dutch East Indies. A little later the Italians sent out Count de Pinedo and his navigator Campanelli to noise abroad the achievements of those latterday Renaissance figures, Mussolini's airmen. Their signatures too adorn a programme in the autograph book.

Next to make the trip was Sir Alan Cobham and he chopped several days off the previous record. We followed the drama of his progress in the *Argus* day by day: Basra, Bandar Abbas, Bushire, Calcutta, Alor Star, Singapore, Atamboea, Timor, Darwin. He'd landed; he was in the Northern Territory! The excitement was so tremendous and the feeling of Britishness so overwhelming that when the *Herald* sponsored a competition to make a slogan out of the call letters on Cobham's aircraft, GEBFO, the winning entry read 'Greetings! Every Briton's fist outstretched'.

But Cobham was soon eclipsed by 'Australia's Own' Bert Hinkler, the boy from Bundaberg, Q, whose solo beat all previous records and who established himself in Australian eyes as the equal of Lindbergh. The American had just astounded the world by flying solo in the single engined *Spirit of St. Louis* from New York to Paris. Our local tunesmith, Jack O'Hagan, author of *Gundagai* and other hits, hurled into the market place, through records and sheet music, the immortal national song *Hustling Hinkler*:

> Hustling Hinkler showed them the way
> And he's the hero of the day

The *Herald* didn't run a competition for the call letters of Hinkler's plane, which were GEBOV. But I thought I'd done pretty well in volunteering (stamped self-addressed envelope enclosed for reply) the phrase 'Greetings, Eagle Bundabergian of Vim'. Another batch of intrepid birdmen, as they now came to be called, was soon winging its way south and east, led by Amy Johnson, the girl from Hull, of whom it was reported by a school wag that when she finally flew

The Road to Gundagai

over Sydney Harbour bridge, which was still under construction, all the workmen raised their tools in her honour.

* * *

'Time to go now,' said Dad draining his pot. 'Want a lift Pip? Toc?' Fortunately not this time, and so we zoomed home alone to 4 Grace Street through the rushing twilight and after a hastily gulped dinner of scraps under Mother's disapproving and long-suffering eye, he dived into the study and the stamp collection. When he wasn't pruning standard roses Dad spent hours poring over his stamps, mostly in the evenings or on rainy Sunday afternoons in the brief but wet and chilly Melbourne winter. Dad specialized in British Empire Stamps and particularly in that part of it which stretched from Malaya to New Zealand. He had wonderful sets of Federated Malay States tigers, leaping out from red and blue backgrounds; portraits of turbaned sultans from the Straits Settlements; Australian stamps surcharged 'Cocos-Keeling Islands'; New Zealand exotic shrubs and of course the whole range of Commonwealth of Australia stamps, both new and used. The Commonwealth in those days was not much more than twenty years old; its temporary capital was still Melbourne, and the former separate colonies still thought of themselves very much as the independent and highly individualistic states which they had so recently been. This was reflected in their stamps. The Commonwealth design was a dull heavy portrait of Edward VII and later George V flanked with meaningless curley-cues and great swags of iron-hard wattle blossom. The stamps of the states were much more varied and interesting: the black swan of Western Australia; the neat portrait of the Queen for Victoria, ageing gradually from young woman with Chopin-smooth hair to the imperial dowager who glared with small disapproving eyes from heavy folds of veiling topped by a tiny crown. Best of all was the Tasmanian group with scenes of Hobart from Bellerive in purple, Russell Falls in gamboge, and Fern Tree Bower in red.

But the star of Dad's collection was the set from Australian-administered New Guinea, or Papua. The design was a simple Papuan native dug-out canoe with triangular sail hoisted; but it was beautifully positioned and the upper values of the stamp were printed in two colours. Dad had completed double sets, both new and used, and simply to contemplate them on the empty white page, gave endless joy. The only stamps that could compare with Papua were those of the Sudan Postal Service which, vertical as opposed to the Papuan horizontal, showed the burnoused postman mounted high on a camel and streaming across a desert edged with notations in piastres and milliemes. Of this stamp Dad also had complete used and unused sets; their frames black, their centres in green, red, magenta, light blue and orange. To me it was of course Papua that led the race, and when Sir Hubert Murray, administrator of the territory, came to visit us and called it Papooa, I was greatly disconcerted. Sir Hubert, a brother of Professor Gilbert Murray's, was another dividend from the rich capital stock of dons and distinguished elderly gents furnished by my grandfather, and I stood in some awe of him. Not so Dad. When I told him what Sir Hubert had said, he replied blandly, 'He's just an old goat; of course it's Papua' and went on with his stamps. Dad rose considerably in my estimation.

Dad had also taken over Mother's stamp collection which was a schoolgirl's eclectic grab bag supplemented by two valuable gifts. One was the immortal triangular Cape of Good Hope penny red which had, deservedly, a whole page to itself from which it glared with Euclidian hauteur. The other was a very mysterious stamp from Serbia. It had been made from a black and green plate and showed the present King and Queen of Serbia. But if you turned the stamp upside down the faces became the single head of the murdered former King of Serbia. There were supposed to be very few of these stamps in existence, for when the device was discovered the dies were destroyed and existing stamps called in. The engraver had meanwhile gone into exile to pursue his own labyrinthine course through the interminable intricacies of Balkan politics.

* * *

When he could be torn from his stamp collection Dad's hobby was the garden. Our lot was only 50 feet by 150 and didn't give much scope for originality, but Dad's garden in Hobart had been even smaller, so that 4 Grace Street must have seemed a whole manor of lordly acres. He was not interested in chores; these he left to us. He was interested only in the general direction of garden affairs, except for standard roses and citrus trees in which he took a consuming and to us quite incomprehensible interest. It was we who, under his direction dug out, uprooted and carted away two great ugly cotton palms which kept the daylight out of the house. It was we who demolished and chopped up an unsightly trellis and removed, in a labour unequalled since the cleansing of the Augean stables, a tangled heap of briar, vine and creeper. It was we who, much against our will, performed the deadly corvée of weeding. Those interminable Melbourne weeds; how they flourished in the light sandy loam backed by the tough yellow clay! How intractable

The Road to Gundagai

they were; how unwilling to submit to extermination whether by hand, hoe or shovel. We tried everything, in an endless series of Saturdays when we should have been disporting ourselves in the St. Kilda Baths: painful uprooting by hand; forking and turning over in the hope that they would grow downwards into the earth and suffocate; spading up and shaking out the sods; hoeing and then raking off the top layer of weed. Nothing availed and, since this was long before the days of D.D.T., the weeding never ended.

Into this scene of sweating grunting boys, spreadeagled on their hands and knees as they wrestled with the accursed weeds, strode Dad lordly in his Sunday morning dressing-gown with a cigar in his teeth and a pair of secateurs in his hand. He wandered around the garden snipping at his roses with desultory good humour, leaving us to pick up the thorny tit-bits scattered on innumerable small circular beds. For it was one of Dad's fetish beliefs that every standard rose should have its own little bed and as his collection increased with the years, the lawn gradually began to look like a sheet of paper on which a small boy has been disporting himself with the office punch. To my brother and myself, who had to mow the lawn once a week, *and* cut the edges, the proliferation of these holes was maddening. Puffing and panting, we slewed the hand mower round endless dinky little circles, ellipses and curves both concave and convex. Nothing was simple: there were no straight lines and our little front garden (50′ × 30′) became like an old curiosity shop. New roses we greeted with abhorrence; we were equally blind to the charms of the red Chateau de Clos Vougeot, the delicate rose of Kitty Kininmonth, even the ineffable apricot petals of Madame Edouard Herriot. We loathed them all. Dad pampered his precious charges as if they were orchids. His principal enemy was the aphis or 'the thrip' as he called it. He would tenderly inspect the young shoots and at the first sign of the multitudinous tiny greenish milch cows for the local ants we (not he) went to work.

'Okay boys. Tobacco juice!'

Dad had brought home sweepings and dry yellow sticks of tobacco from Dunhill's warehouse (courtesy Les Watson) and instructed us how to prepare the horrid brew. The tobacco was soaked in an old petrol can full of water and very soon began to give off a harsh and bitter effluvium. This was the signal to drain off the water into a second can and let it stand for a week or so. Dad directed operations but wouldn't touch the stuff himself. The Sunday morning selected for the attack opened with a reconnaissance in force. I followed Dad in his trailing bathrobe and heel-flattened slippers from bush to bush. He would show me where the infestation was heavy, his favourite method being to run his thumb and forefinger up a particularly badly damaged shoot, pulling off a nice greenish goo of crushed aphises—aphides. Then he handed me a brass garden syringe, told me to go ahead and returned to his stamp collection in the study, and to his five-eighths of an inch. It was a dismal occupation, for the tobacco water stank, the syringe leaked and backfired. I'd been specifically warned against blasting the aphis off the roses; but since, if gently syringed, it took them several hours to die, I was conscious of no progress, no sense of achievement. By the time the aphis started to drop off it would be Monday morning and I would be at school. Often I used to pray that the aphis would utterly destroy the rosebushes, but they never quite did and the niggling mowing and clipping continued.

Dad thought next that the rose bushes ought to be thoroughly manured—by us, not by him. He would confine himself to purchasing the manure and seeing that it was delivered. To those who have grown up in the horse drawn era there is something particularly satisfying in its neat little sandy dollops. The prospect of scattering it over the rose bushes was not unattractive. But returning home from school one evening my nose was assailed by an unknown but powerful and acrid stench. It hit me long before I reached 4 Grace Street and indeed it never occurred to me that it came from our house until I saw, piled in the front garden, a most enormous pyramid of muck swollen to immense proportions by an interlining of scabrous straw. It looked as if a passing giant had defecated from on high. Could this be manure?

Indeed it was. Dad had struck a bargain—or been sold a pup. A neighbouring milkman who kept pigs had offered to sell him two yards of pig manure for less than the cost of one yard of horse manure. Dad fell for it hook, line and sinker and the scourings off the dairyman's sties now sat in a pile on our front lawn stinking out the neighbourhood. We were at once charged with its demolition and spreading. Unlike horse manure, which is neat, fresh and manageable, pig manure is grotesquely untidy, comically tangled and tacky. Forkfuls looked like enormous sticky stinking birds' nests, and the heavy straw content prevented it from spreading properly. Finally a merciful rainstorm did more in a few hours than two boys with garden forks could have done in two weeks; and the following day Dad strolled slowly through the morning dew, his nose wrinkling happily at the mingled scents of pig dung and Madame Edouard Herriot.

Breaks in the endless round of garden chores were few indeed on those dreary weekends, but one sure-fire diversion was the arrival of the Chinese market gardener with his horse and four-wheeled covered cart full of fresh vegetables. Dad delighted to haggle with

The Road to Gundagai

these mysterious orientals—known to my brother and myself as the inscrutable enemas—and to bandy facetious pleasantries across the gate. Nothing delighted him more than to be able, as he fondly imagined, to beat down these wily hard-working vendors. He invariably addressed them as 'Chong', and the final unsmiling 'All li, tuppen ha'penny for you, boss,' made him King of the Castle for the rest of the day.

There were several of these Chinese gardeners and they all had names which hit our funny bones: H. Cooey Lee, Tom Lim Out and Harry Thin Coon, who was our favourite. Mother said they invented the names to undermine Dad's sales resistance with unseemly mirth; but no such aid was needed, for he was an absolute sucker for a 'bargain'. Trit-trot-trit-trot went Harry Thin Coon's cart and as it slowed opposite 4 Grace Street we leaped from our weeding with cries of 'The Chinaman, the Chinaman!' Harry tied his horse's reins to a small gum sapling on the verge of the pavement and disappeared into the rear of his covered cart emerging in a few minutes with a yoke across his shoulder from which were suspended two wicker baskets. He then laid out for our inspection the fruits of the unremitting labour by which he and his fellow exiles had transformed the bottom lands of suburban Gardiner's creek from muddy washes and swamps to neat strips of endlessly tilled vegetables. The following conversation would then ensue.

'How are you today, Chong?'
'Velly good.'
'You got any French beans?'
'Flench bean velly good. Tlippin.'
'Threepence? You'll have to do better than that, Chong.'
'No boss, Tlippin.'
'Nope (turning away) too much money Chong.'
'All li, tuppen ha'penny for you, boss.'
'Right! I'll have ten pounds.'
'But George! (in anguish from Mother) we don't *need* ten pounds.'
'Oh let it go, it's a real bargain; ten pounds Chong.'
'Velly good boss.'

Down came the basket and Harry Thin Coon ladled out French beans onto discarded copies of *The Herald*, soon to be followed by tomatoes, nectarines, plums, and great cumulus cloud cauliflowers. After Harry trundled back to his cart, the braver spirits among us would essay a daring climb onto the rear step and thence into the cart to filch a tomato or a nectarine. While one boy tackled this hazardous task he would be 'covered' by the rest of the gang running along beside the cart and crying out:

Central 434, Please

'Ching Chong Chinaman
Velly velly sad
Allee gleenee peaches
Go velly bad.'

This little ditty invariably aroused Harry Thin Coon to a sly and well calculated backward flick of his whip. If it failed to connect with the pilferer in the rear it usually scared him into dropping off. Harry was a mild man but there were horrendous tales of his rival, H. Cooey Lee, who was supposed to brandish a knife in his teeth and to wreak unmentionable damage on small boys.

The baiting suffered by all who, in our quiet suburban street, differed ever so slightly from the norm was fearsome; and it was rarely visited by any punishment. Those who suffered most were the Salvation Army, or the Salvoes as they were known to us. Our merriment was shared by Dad who, far from reprimanding us for impertinence when we followed the Army on our bikes making rude noises, surreptitiously encouraged us with the scatological ditty:

A Salvation Army, free from sin
Sailed down the Yarra in a kerosene tin.
One had a kettle and the other had a drum
And another had a pancake stuck to his bum.

My own relationship with the Salvoes was one of the classic love-hate. When the distant wail of the euphonium, slobbering upward into the antipodean sky, came wafting in on the breeze, I would instantly stop whatever I was doing and follow the sound until I caught up with the band. They often formed their little circle either in the bend of Grace Street where, in those blessed far off motorless Sundays, they were likely to be undisturbed.

The navy blue red-edged flag which had been carried at the head of the pitifully small procession was furled, and the contingent, usually five to six men in navy blue uniforms with silver buttons, and peaked caps, and three or four women, mostly middle-aged and in those atrocious black straw poke bonnets with a hole cut behind for the 'bun', formed their tentative circle. The bandsmen grounded their instruments while the leader waited for a few moments in case a crowd should gather. It never did and so he usually started off with a rousing melancholy evangelical hymn, redolent of the hopelessness of murky fogbound northern cities, and off we went. My favourites were *What a Friend We Have In Jesus*, which gave splendid scope to the euphonium, and *Yield Not to Temptation for Yielding is Sin*, a brisk dashing 6/8 to which the fellow with the small snare drum contributed plenty of bite.

The Road to Gundagai

By now a desultory group of onlookers had formed. They were rarely more than a dozen and the majority were kids like me who skulked on the outskirts rather than take part in the performance. There would usually be a couple of Mums with prams and string shopping bags, a loafer or two, the occasional 'Yuk-yuk'—our name for adolescent youths—ready to poke fun, and possibly a well-dressed couple in the offing. Who or what they expected to comfort or convert in sober middle-class Malvern remains a mystery. They should have been patrolling the wilds of Footscray, the wastes of Collingwood or the jungles of South Melbourne. We thought they might be scared of the toughs, but it's more likely that they hoped for a heavier collection box. The leader would call on Brother Jones or Sister Mary to say a few words. This was the signal for a high-pitched harangue to the empty Sunday street on sin and redemption. Sister Grace was my favourite. She had a lean nose, rimless glasses and a delivery so ferocious that it shook her from stem to stern. One afternoon, looking, as I thought, sharply at me, she began a rancorous tirade about people who spent Sunday working in the garden. Her peroration was memorable: 'And as I passed by these good people digging up their gardens, I thought how much better they'd be employed in digging up their souls!!!' One up to Sister Grace! I could scarcely forbear to clap, for here was obviously *the* argument to use with Dad to put paid to weeding over the weekend. I expounded Sister Grace's theory at supper that night. Dad's reaction was disappointing.

'Those Salvoes are a bit too bloody helpful.'

The end came sharply one very quiet sunny Sunday morning. It had been a particularly stirring performance with a blood-rousing rendering of *Yield Not to Temptation*. Off they marched, instruments slung silent fore and aft, flag flying at the head of the file, and the motley collection of kids and dogs with myself wheeling in and out of the throng on my bike. I was close up behind Sister Grace when someone in the rear started to sing, *sotto voce*, the opening bars of 'A Salvation Army Free From Sin'. I started to titter. Sister Grace whirled on me with unexpected savagery.

'I should think you boys would have something better to do than make fun of the Army!' she blazed. I fell off my bike with astonishment and shame. She stood over me in the middle of the road like an avenging angel while the Army marched away into the distance and the kids and dogs and bicycles scattered to the four winds. I rose slowly to my feet. She was trembling with rage and indignation. The rimless glasses on her lean nose shook in the wind of her passion and the straw bonnet became a bat's wing. I crawled silently away from the intense gaze of her watery pale blue eyes. 'I should *think* so!' she hissed and without another word turned and marched off to rejoin the little pilgrim band. That was the end of the Salvo-baiting.

* * *

All this was in the halcyon days before The Depression, when Australia was 'riding high on the sheep's back'; before the conspiracy to oust Dad from TAMECO; before the fire of the marriage had cooled to clinkers. Life was warm and comfortable for Dad, and the Twenties rolled on and on in a series of long sunny afternoons. The pianola tinkled across the street: *California, Where I Met you at Dew Time; Annabelle, You Made a Wild Man out of Me; Chong, he Comes from Hong Kong*. Of Dad it might be written, as Scott Fitzgerald wrote of the Great Gatsby: 'So we beat on, boats against the current, borne back ceaselessly into the past'. And as the golden days moved all unsuspected towards the bleak abyss of 1930, so his generosity flowered. Especially in the little things; the important unimportant things.

One day I was cycling back from school having stayed late to dig with a volunteer detachment on our new swimming pool. Sir John Macfarlane, an 'old boy', now Vice-Chancellor of the University of Melbourne, had given the school £1,000. The Head had announced that since a pool would cost £1,700 he hoped that we boys would supply the volunteer labour. In common with a dozen school-fellows I'd dug into gooey clay, carried clods away in a barrow and generally exerted myself for the common good. Tired with honest exertion I had mounted my bike for the long (uphill) pedal home. But at the Kooyong railway gates I was stopped by an odious plainclothes John Hop.

'Where's your light?'

'My light?' The western sky was still tinged with orange and I looked at my watch.

'Lighting up time's six-ten,' said the cop. My watch said six-twenty. I fumed with a sense of injustice and gave a heated account of my activities during the past hour. The cop was unimpressed.

'What's yer name and where do yer live?' By the time he was through with this hateful process it really was getting dark.

'What'll I do if another cop stops me?'

The man gave a bleak little smile. You can just tell 'm yer name's been taken already.'

I cycled home full of rage and unburdened myself to Dad. (It was no use, on these occasions, seeking Mother's sympathy. She was as likely as not to say, 'It was probably your fault anyway.') Dad was

The Road to Gundagai

sensible and vaguely sympathetic. We were to wait and see what happened; perhaps nothing might. But three nights later a uniformed John Hop with a tall patent leather helmet rang the bell and handed me the dreaded 'bluey', the summons for riding a bike without lights.

At this point Dad took over. He telephoned the police and found out when I would have to appear before the magistrate. It was a Saturday but instead of going to The Works he accompanied me to Malvern Town Hall and when my case was called, spoke eloquently in my defence. Here was a boy who'd stayed late at school to do his bit in a great volunteer effort—a boy who'd given generously of his time and muscle in a great cause. Through so doing he'd started his weary way home just before lighting up time. And while slowly pedalling back to a well-earned supper he'd been stopped by the witness for the prosecution, ten minutes—a bare ten minutes—after the official lighting-up time, with the sun hardly set, the sky still blue, half an hour's daylight left, in which, had he been permitted to proceed unimpeded, this noble hard-working boy could have been home, safe and sound eating the evening meal he so richly deserved! He had great respect for the police, but surely they had better things to do than split hairs with innocent boys over lighting-up time while robbers escaped from Pentridge Gaol, and 'Squizzy' Taylor was still at large.

The magistrate banged his gavel at this and called for order. Would the witness kindly confine himself to the subject. Dad bowed and was silent. There was a slight pause during which I was conscious of heads turning towards me. The magistrate cleared his throat. 'Discharged upon payment of five shillings into the parish poor box.' I could hardly believe my ears. I saw Dad grin quietly at me across the court while the magistrate barked, 'Next Case!' He paid the five shillings to the clerk of court and I was a free man. Dear feckless Dad, if only all his problems had been as simple.

Chapter Fourteen

UP RODE THE SQUATTER, MOUNTED ON HIS THOROUGHBRED

DUE of west Melbourne the green pasture and the flat neat farms along the Werribbee River died out against a long blue line of scarp. At this point road, rail and river, either by a wild leap to freedom or a painful tortuous descent, quit the plateau fifteen hundred feet high in the middle of which lay Ballarat, the magic city. This was the land of the 1851 gold rush, the site of the Eureka Stockade where the enraged miners raised the flag of the Australian Republic in 'our own little rebellion'. Above the lavas and congealed basalt rocks of the Western District extinct volcanoes had been clothed with bush; and on the outskirts of the city itself tiny man-made volcanoes—earthworks, lodes, pits, scrapings, scrabblings and diggings—were likewise covered with grass and shrubs. They looked now curiously quiet and harmless and gave only the mutest evidence of the frenzied gold fever which produced such unbelievable fortunes as Welcome Nugget and Welcome Stranger, each containing well over two thousand ounces of pure gold.

It was to this area that Nell and Basil Hall had moved, and our holidays with them; so that the long carefree days among the hot yellow orchards of Panton Hill now continued under conditions approaching those of the gentleman farmer: *La Côte*, incongruously named homestead for seven hundred acres of rolling sheep country near Ballan, the country town for a large stock and farming area. The sheep stations were not the magnificent twenty thousand acre properties of the fabulous Western District. Ballan lay just on the border line between the sheep country and the farm country and the stations were of more modest acreage. But there was nevertheless a subtle change in the status and bearing of the neighbours, and one quickly discovered, even in democratic rural Australia, that two classes existed. On the one hand, were the station owners and their town guests, the professional men from Ballan, the doctor, the lawyer, the engineers of the local wireless transmitting station and one or two marginal farmers who went in for mixed sheep and wheat or fruit, and were therefore considered on the verge of being respectable. On the other hand were the roustabouts and boundary riders from the sheep stations, the railway folk, the workers in the little town and the local phenomenon known as the 'cocky' farmer. This really meant, in European terms, a peasant yeoman, although no Australian would ever admit it. He was usually a dour independent cranky kind of fellow whom one saw with one foot up on a wire fence peering morosely into the middle distance with a short pipe stuck between his teeth.

Ballan itself was ungracious and unlovely. There were two streets: one was the main Melbourne to Ballarat highway and the other ran at right angles up to the railway station. The prevailing impression was of openness, dissonance and a ramshackle unplanned confusion as if the town had been thrown down in a hurry from a passing aircraft and somehow taken root. Though pollarded planes lined the road to the station two blocks long, the main drag was treeless and disconcertingly gaunt. On either side of the black tarmac were wide dirt verges, beyond them bits of vestigial sidewalk, sometimes cement outside the butcher's or the chemist's, sometimes duckboard over a culvert, mostly simply a dirt footpath between the fence and the highway. You can see drier and more desiccated versions of such towns in the outback paintings of Russell Drysdale and Sidney Nolan. For Australia, Ballan was quite well-to-do and indeed well treed, especially south of the main road around Miss McCoppin's Guest House with its tall pittosporum hedge bedded in a nest of pine trees. But if you were used to the little Gippsland towns sheltered from the heat by tall gums, Ballan seemed terribly empty and windswept out on the bare plateau. There are a hundred towns like it in Western Canada. Indeed Ballan was essentially a prairie town with two differences: few false fronts, and plenty of deep verandahs usually supported on hitching posts. To these the local ponies, brumbies and hacks would be tethered while their owners visited the feed-and-grain store or the loan company or drank beer in the cool sawdust-strewn recess of the local pub. From Ballan, roads radiated out not only to *La Côte* but to *Bungeeltap*, *Yaloak*, *Darra* and *Ballark*; and behind these harsh aboriginal mouthfuls of consonants lay hospitable homes in secret clefts in the plateau where the minor Australian squattocracy rode out the roaring Twenties on the sheep's back.

First then to *Bungeeltap*, the home of Mr. and Mrs. William Rhodes where gin and geniality flowed free down the valley of the Moorabool, an eroded stream sinking slowly below the bare plateau with the rims of its deep cleft outlined by great tors like a dry and

Up rode the Squatter Mounted on his Thoroughbred

windswept Dartmoor. Rhodes had made his pile in Western Queensland where he'd owned one of those enormous semi-desert stations, a sheep to four acres. A lean, knuckle-nosed and melancholy man, he was highly respected by the squatters on the rich sheep-to-the-acre country around Ballan, for Bill Rhodes had 'beaten the drought'.

Far beyond Longreach, itself at the end of a perilously thin and lonely finger of railway pushing four hundred miles in from the Queensland tropical coast towards the dead heart of Australia, Bill Rhodes had his station. One can see it frying in the sun: desolate flat plains studded with dwarf mulga; an endless burning horizon too sharp for the eye to gaze at; and in the middle, sheltered under a few scrawny gums and pepper trees, the four-square stocky wooden homestead with a tin roof, a verandah and tanks for the house. Out in the distance were open sloughs or playas which filled with water in the rainy season, but around Longreach the rainy season might come once in two, three or five years. Bill Rhodes hung on for six consecutive summers without seeing a drop of rain. What saved him was a small artesian bore. He was just on the edge of the great Queensland Basin, and it had not 'gone brackish on him'. When the rain finally came, turning the baked ocherous vistas and the mournful sunbitten plains into a riot of unexpected greenery, Norman who was seven and Jean who was five, nearly went out of their minds at the rattle of the rain on the tin roof. They had grown to that age without hearing, seeing or smelling rain.

While his neighbours went under, Bill Rhodes hung on to his own land and sheep and in the post-war boom made a killing which no country Australian would ever have begrudged him. This lean and ropey man with neck tendons like strings then came south fifteen hundred miles into the Moorabool Valley and there he found an old stone farmhouse built at the time of the gold rush. He bought it and he and his wife between them turned it into a generous, jolly, comfortable, well-to-do Toorak mansion set in the bush. The orange terra-cotta roof, so disconcerting in these surroundings, beckoned across the valley to tennis parties from twenty miles around every Sunday. Bill Rhodes himself remained moody and introspective, lurking uneasily in the background at his wife's parties or discovered slouching through the home paddock kicking up tussocks with his knee boots. Not for him the tennis parties and the buffet suppers and the uproarious weekends. He contented himself with mournful sauntering over his property and driving fast, expensive cars.

The diffident men of *Bungeeltap*, though Bill Rhodes held within himself suppressed thunders of appalling dimensions, were more than

The Road to Gundagai

compensated for by the gay and jolly women. Mrs. Rhodes and Jean, then in her early twenties, were not simply the life of the party, they *were* the party and the party was endless. Mrs. Rhodes had been gay and stoical in adversity, now she was gay, plump and extrovert, enormously kind and friendly.

She turned *Bungeeltap* into a permanent open house and she surprised us with a silver flask of gin even at a picnic in a most inaccessible and unlikely spot. Her lavish hospitality was never imposed upon, and she had more energy at fifty than most women have at thirty, as well as the proverbial heart 'as big as a whale'.

Jean Rhodes had black shingled hair laid sleek against one cheek in the currently fashionable kiss-curl. She Charlestoned brilliantly in a bead-fringed knee-length evening gown. She had a friendly sardonic, magenta mouth, a prominent aquiline nose, a voice of singular penetration, and a never failing generosity.

She summed up for most of us the Roaring Twenties and Our Dancing Daughters. She was a firefly will-o'-the-wisp utterly and entirely fastidious; no breath of gossip ever touched her yet she was always in the middle of whatever shenanigans were in progress. Like many Australian country girls she unleashed a terrific forehand drive, just casually thrown away as if there were nothing to it, and a line of tough sardonic humour in delightful contrast to her showy dress and makeup. Her Homeric cackle floated across the valley of the Moorabool and when they were whooping it up at *Bungeeltap* she was the wildest and gayest of them all.

Up to the minute in all things the Rhodes' had done away with the dreadful chore of gate-opening. Instead of stopping the car and letting a youngster run ahead, all Uncle Basil had to do was direct the front wheels firmly at a tread in the ground. There followed a sharp clack, the gate whipped itself open and slammed itself closed behind us as we went over another tread.

Then a series of hairpin descents and over a ford, and into the friendly grey-cement barracks of *Bungeeltap* with the wide-eaved frowning terra-cotta roof something like an early Frank Lloyd Wright. Six or eight pairs at tennis with tea served at the nets lasted out the afternoon, but when the long summer evening began we all trooped to the main living-room—the lounge as it was called—of *Bungeeltap* and while Jean and Mrs. Rhodes assisted by the deferential Norman, passed the drinks, someone sat down at the pianola.

The mechanical player-piano dates one more surely than any piece of apparatus ever invented. It reigned supreme for a generation and died only in the early thirties with the development of radio and of electric recording on large bass-oriented phonographs. The pianola at *Bungeeltap* was as the exemplar of the type. It was an

Up rode the Squatter Mounted on his Thoroughbred

upright which, when not in use, resembled a rather heavily-built cottage piano.

But with two swift movements rubberized pneumatic treadles fell out over the main pedal assembly, and mahogany veneer shutters flipped aside to reveal, set in its zinc lined cabinet, a long bar of metal pierced like an oversized mouth organ. From the cabinet at the side one selected the appropriate roll: it might be *Ramona*, or the *William Tell Overture* or the *Doll Dance* or *Who?* or Handel's *Largo*, depending on the mood. One inserted the roll into the sockets like a jumbo film into a camera, pulled it down over the mouth organ, hitched it to the bottom roller and started pedalling. Wow! What a cataract of jumping, jerking, jiving mechanical sound came out of that wonderful instrument. If you were lucky you had a model which depressed the keys from the inside so that ghostly fingers appeared to be playing impossible chords: great tenths walking up and down the piano like a ladder, enormous arpeggios, broken fifths and thirds and the rhythm never varying by one hair's breadth.

The comic character of the period was, of course, the man who pretended to 'play' the pianola. All it needed was for drinks to circulate freely and the mahogany veneer shutters to be closed. Then the character (it was often Uncle Basil) seated on the stool with a drink near at hand would allow his fingers to roam lightly over the keyboard and to imitate, to an admiring throng of shrieking girls, the gymnastics of Zez Confrey, Lee Sims or the early and pre-*Stardust* Hoagy Carmichael.

'Who - - - ooo - - - ooo - - - ooo stole my heart away
Who - - - ooo - - - ooo - - - ooo makes me dream all day . . .'

Thus the tattered pennons of Jerome Kernish jollification swept out of *Bungeeltap*'s windows and across the valley and over to the residence of V. V. Mogg, the elderly and eligible bachelor of the district who was the darling of all the Ballan ladies and who would come creeping downhill to the ford in his creaky Austin. Mogg had thick grey hair parted in the middle and smoothed down with brilliantine into thatched eaves over a ruddy face as big as a pie. To hear him give with *Come to me, my Melancholy Baby* was the essence of *Bungeeltap*.

This activity was viewed with indulgence, but as essentially frothy, by the real power in the area: J. M. Molesworth of *Ballark*.

The Road to Gundagai

With his portly paunch, his leathern gamecoat, florid face, and battered old stockman's hat; his thatch of white hair, and multitudinous family, enormous mansion, itself squatting close to the ground in the middle of several thousand acres; his wife's and daughter's trips Home; and finally his large town house in Melbourne and his summer place at Barwon Heads one came finally face to face with that pillar of the Australian establishment: the squatter.

Molesworth was an eighteenth-century figure; a genial latter-day Squire Trelawny in moleskin breeks; a Justice of the Peace ready to dispense summary justice; a feudal father-figure. And yet he was subtly changed by the hard white Australian light, and the hard bright incisive social pressures, into a democratic institution. Though he might speak *de haut en bas* to a young fellow 'up from town' or to one of his social equals whom he happened to dislike, he was on terms of a free and easy yet dignified familiarity with the stockmen and the boundary riders and even with the itinerant shearers, that roaming band of desperate, desolate men who imprinted on the Australian outback the image of social warfare which at first seems so alien to it.

Everyone knew that J. M. Molesworth was the boss, that he lived in an enormous homestead and that he was worth a hundred thousand pounds or so. He himself did not pretend that any of this was untrue, but to see him burning a break, dipping sheep or leaning over a wire fence talking to a stockrider, was to recognize a grazier's hierarchy in which everyone was equal because everyone had his place. In the land of the freeborn, Molesworth and the boundary rider conversed as equals, not monetarily of course, but as men engaged in a co-operative activity. The bulk of the profits went to the boss, but he provided the men with a hard, free, open life in which they acknowledged few equals and no superiors and out of which came the extraordinary Australian sense of 'mateship'. Neither Molesworth nor his men would let each other down. The men knew that Molesworth's daughter Maroa (named for an earlier sheep station) with her beautiful profile and exquisitely thin hands, took trips 'Home', but they didn't resent this because it never occurred to her to flaunt it. They rode with her to far-off paddocks and there was a certainty in their relationship that was wonderful to see. Stability, security; these were conferred not simply by wealth but by the land itself, by the homestead and by the forging of common traditions even in the short space of eighty years.

Those of us who came up from town envied Molesworth's men, no less than we envied him for the apparent serenity, shared by them all; for their rough good nature and perfect understanding.

Up rode the Squatter Mounted on his Thoroughbred

This may be a romantic view of the squatter, but once the Shearers' Union won their big battle in the 1890's the squatters were never the object of the massive resentment directed against the city industrialists. The class struggle, bitter in the cities, hardly touched the country. The further west one penetrated beyond the tangled volcanic hills near Ballarat down onto the great lava plains of the Western District, the more entrenched the squatters became; but they remained within a structure both egalitarian and paternalistic, a conservative force that was not reactionary.

What impressed us most, I think, was the impeccable natural good manners of the Molesworth family. Besides Maroa there were four boys, Dick, John, Bob and Ted, and a little sister. The boys went to Geelong Grammar and they all moved graciously and steadily through the hectic Twenties with a good-nature and courtesy to which I could never have attained. I suppose their serenity came from security, and this was something to envy as well as admire. At the enormous multi-family picnics that took place on the banks of the Werribbee it was always the Molesworth boys who moved softly and with exquisite courtesy among the rugs and palliasses spread on the tough springy grass and myriad dead leaves. Dr. Clark, the local saw-bones, was more sardonic in his conversation; Jackson Adams, the bank manager's son was more knowledgeable; but how was it that the Molesworth boys, with their red calloused hands and large feet, nevertheless always managed to give an impression of strong serenity and smiling good nature? One must put it down in the end to breeding.

Ballark had nothing skittish about it, and gay weekend tennis parties were not for that part of the world. Country cricket matches were *Ballark*'s great speciality, with Molesworth heading one team and Dr. Cordner from far-off Diamond Creek, heading the 'townies'. Cordner was a magnificent hitter and once knocked up seventy in an hour against the country team. I was usually last man in or sometimes twelfth man; my score either one or else nought not out, though once on an unbelievable occasion when the 'townies' faced defeat so certain that each man on the team was allowed to bowl, I secured two wickets with two successive balls.

The annual dance at *Ballark*, attended by friends from the entire district, also brought relatives of the Molesworth's from England and from Melbourne. Cousin Norman Bayles, an elderly exquisite with lemon gloves, a tweed suit with hacking vents and a paisley bow tie, arrived at *Ballark* in a canary coloured Bentley convertible. His niece, Ayliffe Neale, electrified the party by wearing an anklet on the dance floor from which depended a small heart on a chain. Both Bayles' exquisiteness and Ayliffe's frivolity were known and admired rather than resented or reproved by the men who worked for Molesworth at *Ballark*. They and their women were largely responsible for preparing, under Mrs. Molesworth's direction, the enormous cornucopias of food. In a kitchen the size of a railway station fruit salad was mixed in barrels and tubs; meringues rose in tiers like the cans balanced in patterns in a supermarket; huge haunches of glazed mutton and ham made the dark sideboards sag. Generous silver bowls of punch, illuminated by candlelight, lay under the big Sheraton mirrors; and out on the verandah—one of those wonderful broad sweeping Australian verandahs of polished red gum, fifteen feet wide and sixty feet long—couples danced beneath Japanese lanterns. Those who were too young or too old or too clumsy-footed sat in a corner and listened to the *Two Black Crows* in their immortal duel on Columbia. The amount that was eaten and the energy consumed at these enormous bean-feasts was quite fantastic and of course most people were young enough to 'see the clock around'. Gay parties from Melbourne would stay up for the whole weekend, breakfasting off hair-of-the-dog and bacon-and-eggs at eleven o'clock on a Sunday morning before being bustled off rigorously and severely to the little wooden church whose rector was Mr. Kaneen.

Uncle Basil was regarded as a godless man by Mr. Kaneen who once bicycled four miles out from Ballan on a sizzling January afternoon to remonstrate with him. The squire, who was in the kitchen garden, saw him coming and retired to the gun room giving strict orders to his wife that she was to tell Mr. Kaneen that her husband was from home. When the poor sweltering clergyman in due course appeared, in his black velours hat, his wilting dog-collar and his black alpaca coat stained to a deeper soot with the sweat of his own shoulder blades, Aunt Nell did her duty and told him that her husband was indeed from home. Unfortunately the children had not been briefed and a piping voice revealed that father was in the gun room. Uncle Basil, flushed out of his retreat and flushed with annoyance was forced to make an appearance. The exchange that followed was memorable and raised him higher than ever in our estimation.

Mr. Kaneen: 'I've not seen you in Church lately Mr. Hall.'
Uncle Basil: 'Well, damn it, man, you haven't looked!'

The wonderful summers at Ballan came to an end when the Halls decided to take *their* trip 'Home'. It was lucky that they left when they did for they were able to take the entire family round the world just before the Wall Street crash knocked the bottom out of the wool market and engulfed everybody, including the Halls and ourselves. Only the very wealthiest squatters escaped; and to

Up rode the Squatter Mounted on his Thoroughbred

meet these fabulous beings one had to penetrate somewhat further west and south of Ballan.

* * *

Through his Shuter mother, Uncle Basil was connected with some of the older Western District families, and this together with Mother's admirable tenacity and brass, secured two suburban boys in ragged sweaters and gym shoes an unexpected entry into a world where a 16,000 acre station was an every day occurrence and where the really big people, like the Russells at *Barunah Plains*, boasted stations of 40,000 acres: stations so limitless that when you stood at their homestead everything that you saw, apart from distant mountains, belonged to them.

One September holiday the Halls were unable to have us because they themselves were going to the Western District to stay with the Kininmonths at *Mount Hesse*. We were greatly cast down, but later astounded and sceptical to learn from Mother that we too were going to *Mount Hesse*. Mother, desolated once more at the prospect of having two boys eating their heads off around the house for three weeks, had actually had the wonderful effrontery to telephone Aunt Nell, a guest at the Kininmonth's sheep station, and say that we would like to come. This put Nell in an awkward position, but she and Mother had both counted without the party line. At *Mount Hesse* there'd been five or six rings, but a lot of 'phones had lifted stealthily off the hooks like kites sharpening their beaks and Mother, unknown to her, had a large and admiring audience. When she'd finished describing the virtues of her two boys to Nell (including the cherished education and the artistic antecedents) one of the three Kininmonth sisters cut in on the line and said, 'That's all right Mrs. Thirkell, we'll be glad to have them for the holidays.' We didn't know this at the time, nor of the slender thread on which our welcome might hang. All that mattered was that we were off on the *Geelong Flyer* from Spencer Street Station, where all the exciting trains started from.

South west lay the lava plain, flat, melancholy and studded with small volcanic hills bursting up like fingers thrust through a canvas. Seaward the plain was bounded by the Otway Ranges, the more conventional tree-clad bushy hills fringing the Southern Ocean. To the north rose the great Ballarat escarpment and the Grampians. Between these two ranges, and beginning almost as soon as you left Melbourne into the sunset, lay a great sweeping largely treeless plain, strewn with chocolate-brown basalt boulders carefully gathered into dry-wall fences to separate the paddocks. In the

The Road to Gundagai

shallow depressions of the plain lay lakes both salt and fresh, some blue, some green, some a dirty brown. The fresh lakes teemed with abundant bird life and carried a lush fringe of reeds. The salt lakes lay curiously remote and bleak; as improbable as a Martian landscape. They ranged from small sloughs to large circular fresh water sheets, such as Lake Colac; from sad, shallow depressions, such as Lake Merdeduke, to the salt playa of Lake Beeac around which, when it dried out, crazy men on motorbikes raced madly along the blinding salt. The monster of them all was Lake Corangamite, almost twenty miles long and barely ten feet deep, a lost and lonely expanse of water onto which you looked down from tiny grass-filled extinct volcanoes.

This was the Western District. Between Geelong in the east, the South Australian border on the west, the Otway Ranges in the south, and the Grampians to the north, lay the heart, core and marrow of Victorian squattocracy. Their daughters went to Clyde, their sons to Geelong Grammar. They bought their suits at Gieves', their wives' jewellery at Asprey's, their hats at Locke's, their guns at Wilkinson's, their tea at Fortnum and Mason's and, when mortgaged, as some of them were, their credit at Goldsbrough, Mort, Dalgety's or the Bank of New South Wales. The women took a trip 'Home' to England every two or three years, and the young scions, from the most Byronic of face to the thickest of skull, went to Oxford and Cambridge where if they didn't finish their course they often ended up stroking the eight or captaining the eleven. There may have been few double firsts, but there were many double blues. Into this land of horsey privilege, smelling of saddle-soap, dubbin and the sweet-sour odour of sheep-dung, but magnificently housed in mansions that proclaimed a crude cousinship with Longleat or Audley End; into this land, mouths agape, went the boys from suburbia.

At first the taste was almost too rich for our blood: cream, real cream on the porridge; an eight valve super-heterodyne wireless set; a drawing-room with a twelve foot ceiling and a Bechstein grand; 'peace-loving' horses of our own; a willow-fringed dam to row on and to swim in. The initial approach was unlikely enough. The train rumbled out of Melbourne into the setting sun across the Maribyrnong River on a high lattice girder bridge with the delicate Footscray smell of slaughter houses and tanneries followed by the roar and blaze of the Victorian Railways' workshops at Newport. But west of Newport the landscape suddenly opened out. The hills receded into the distance; the trees became sparse, their place being taken by the artificial windbreak, a dark soldierly row of man-planted red gums or pine trees beneath which sheep and cattle

Up rode the Squatter Mounted on his Thoroughbred

could shelter in the summer heat. The You Yangs thrust their queer conical spikes up into the sky and we reached Geelong.

So far the territory, though unfamiliar, was not unknown, but beyond Victoria's second city we plunged through a tunnel and emerged into the Western District proper. It was September and on the heels of winter, night still fell early. We were bound for Winchelsea and presently the conductor in peaked cap and with deep creases from nose to chin slid open the door of the second-class compartment and called the station. The train shuddered as it slowed on a hard curve, and jerked to a stop. The door slammed and in a few moments we watched a receding tail-light curving out of sight into the gloom and were alone on a tiny wooden platform with half Australia at our backs. It was not yet entirely dark and a smear of slatey yellow lay along the horizon. A wind whipped round the little shed and the oil lamp at the deserted station master's office guttered. They must have forgotten us; maybe we really aren't wanted. But at this moment came a reassuring clomp-clomp of steel-nailed boots echoing on the wooden platform.

'Are you the boys for *Mount Hesse?*'

We said we were. The voice was gruff, gravelly and friendly but somehow remote, speaking with the confidence of broad acres.

'I'm Jim Kininmonth. You'd better hop in the car. We've fifteen miles to go.'

Fifteen miles! This in itself was a dramatic enormity. Imagine people living fifteen miles from a railway station! The car sped along the dirt road through the dark between long rows of tight straight gum trees. Occasionally a gate reared up in the headlamps and as we dashed down to open it scores of rabbits scurried for cover. At last, when it was quite dark, the car swept by a lodge gate, past laurels and rhododendrons, past a group of sleeping peacocks huddled on a stone parapet. We scrunched round a broad carriage drive and stopped in a flurry of gravel before large freestone steps at the top of which stood a very small woman who looked at us as if we were two forlorn imps and said, 'You'd better call me Aunt Mary.'

I awoke next morning in the largest and best appointed bedroom that I'd ever seen: striped Regency wallpaper, tall ceiling with plaster cornices, glassed tall-boys, a fireplace like a cave and two long windows festooned with cretonne curtains. On the bed-table was a paperback copy of *The Memoirs of Sherlock Holmes*; in the room hung the faint odour of acetylene gas from the home lighting plant, and out of the window lay the endless melancholy plain. It flowed forever in all directions, engulfing us like a sea. In the distance were dark windbreaks and small lonely buildings smothered in trees, like a stone in a heap of tussocks. These were as ships moored or becalmed in this enormous ocean of land which swept majestically upward towards Mount Hesse itself, scarcely a mountain, more a low ridge, and in another landscape scarcely a ripple. Before us the plain stretched out four or five miles to flow round the base of an abrupt humpy extinct volcano. This was Mount Gellibrand on the hither side of which, barely visible in its flurry of trees, was *Turkieth*, the home of the Ramsays, whose mother had been a Kininmonth. On the other side of Mount Gellibrand, hidden from us, was *Mooleric*, home of other Ramsay cousins. If you craned your head out of the window and looked far away to the north you could just make out the hulk of *Barunah Plains*, home of the Russells.

In all this vast and melancholy expanse there was no one else to see, nothing but sheep huddled in the corners of empty paddocks, the stippling of wire fences or the thin line of a basalt wall separating paddocks hundreds of acres in extent. But then, to look down into the busy forecourt of the homestead itself with cats and dogs, horse champing in the stables and cattle to be milked, to hear the banging of screen doors, the whining of the cream separator and somebody cracking a stockwhip, this was to realize that we ourselves were adrift on the same sea looking down from the fore peak of *Mount Hesse* onto the busy decks below with the land waste all around us. The landscape induced a romantic desire to quote and I intoned softly, 'To fade into the universe and with it be a part, a phrase, a harmony.'

'What's that,' said Colin from the bed. 'What are you mumbling in your beard?'

I repeated the rubric and gestured expansively with my arm which hit the casement window. It flew open violently, banged against the bluestone wall and shattered. Shards of glass cascaded down the tin verandah roof and came to rest in the eavestroughs. Below in the courtyard a cook's yellow face, mottled in fury, gazed skyward and someone shook a fist. Not an auspicious beginning. Yet the weeks which followed were as near to heaven as a boy can come, though punctuated by lateness for meals, forbidden birdnesting, surreptitious singeing of a celluloid comb, sliding reproved down the banisters and reckless burning out of the gramophone motor. But this was simply the rough blurred edge where the two worlds met: suburbia and squattocracy.

The homestead of *Mount Hesse* was built solid and looked uncompromisingly Scots, its arcaded windows set in two storeys of frowning bluestone with thick walls and a slate roof. It was very nearly, though not quite, a mansion. The heavy door opened into

Up rode the Squatter Mounted on his Thoroughbred

a large hall with a stained teak floor on which were Indian numdahs, Persian scatter-rugs, and heavy oak chests. At the entrance to the corridor a row of pegs supported the riding equipment the Kininmonth sisters had brought back from a trip to Argentina: gaucho chaps, an alligator-hide stockwhip, flat brimmed hats with chin draw-strings of Kangaroo hide lace and, unaccountably, an hour-glass. To the left was the 'study'; in reality a sitting room for since *Mount Hesse* was owned by the three Kininmonth sisters, Mary, Daisy and Kitty, there was no man in the house. The property was run by Mr. McCallum who lived in the Manager's house down at the gate and nearer to the outbuildings dominated by the gargantuan barn of the shearing shed. The true study was therefore in Mr. McCallum's house. In the sitting-room were the usual bound volumes of *Punch*, the *Illustrated London News* and the *Tatler*.

Across the hall the door opened into a magnificent drawing-room in the grand style, thirty feet long with a high ceiling from which drooped a glittering chandelier. A large triple tier gilt mirror covered a marble fireplace. A sweep of windows almost from ceiling to floor gave onto a rough attempt at a formal garden. The Bechstein grand and the phonograph, on which we played ad nauseum, *What'll I Do?* stood in twin corners. At the other end of the drawing-room folding doors opened into a vast dining-room. Here was the country home of the novels of P. G. Wodehouse and the plays of Ralph Lynn and Tom Walls. Osbert Lancaster has aptly described it as 'Aldwych farcical'. An eight-leaf mahogany table, equally good for playing blow ping-pong as for an eighteen place dinner, sat solidly on a thick Turkey carpet. Over against a wall of dark thickly mullioned magenta brocade was the classic sideboard and chafing dishes. You came down to find the kidneys, the eggs-and-bacon, the kedgeree, the kippers, the porridge, the chops. Having helped yourself in this atmosphere of unnatural luxury you could listen, if you were very lucky, to Daventry on the eight-valve super-heterodyne.

Yet as the days went by it became clear that the wealth and the comfort were, for us, earthbound and democratic rather than exclusive and hierarchical. We had been admitted to the magic circle because we were recommended by Basil Hall and therefore the standards applied to us were not those which squatters would normally apply to suburban Melbournites. They were their own standards. To the extent, therefore, that we fell short we were judged on their terms rather than on ours. While this made for some misunderstanding it helped us to preserve our dignity.

There were five Kininmonth sisters but two had married and lived off the station, one in Scotland and one 'next door', (four miles off) near the foot of Mount Gellibrand. The three remaining were spins-

The Road to Gundagai

ters: Mary, Daisy and Kitty. Mary was small, brown and spare with penetrating eyes and wispy hair. It was she who ran the house and to whom we, as visitors, were ultimately responsible. It was she who chilled us with reproachful more-in-sorrow-than-in-anger looks over burned combs, raped birdsnests or lost rowlocks from the rowboat. Fortunately it was also she who kept our return tickets. Daisy was the middle sister, younger, sunnier, more open-faced and freckled. She wore big straw hats which cast a wonderful Renoir-like glow on her broad forehead and cornflower blue eyes. The youngest was Kitty, an ash blonde with a high-pitched exciting voice, which spoke of laughter in the next room. They were at their best on horseback. Each had her special mount and they rode in breeches and blue open-necked blouses or else in smartly cut covert coats. It was poetry simply to watch them cantering across the home paddock towards the stables with a great wind out of the west fanning the horses' tails.

We boys became horsemen of a sort. Colin was allotted a twelve-year-old white gelding named Punch; for me came a grand-fatherly twenty-year-old pony named Nelson. We rode, as at *Fairview*, on sheepskin saddles, barefoot and without stirrups, with a halter for a bridle. It was nervous work. Though the horses were old and sure-footed the apparently flat country was treacherous for cantering, for it was pitted with rabbit holes often hidden among the tussocks, and over the plain lay scattered black pock-marked basalt rocks which had not yet been gathered into dry walls. But we soon acquired the proficiency to ride three or four miles across the mournful prairie to a distant windbreak for birdnesting. We would tether the horses to the boundary fence and go in amongst the trees, climbing the pinus insignis with its wonderful hand and foot holds and its sharp spiky branches covered with sticky resin. We had to be mindful not only of magpies, whose savage beaks belied their golden gurgling song, but also of hawks, much fiercer; and even, in the spring time, king parrots.

We were not allowed guns, being considered too young, so that rabbiting had to be pursued by other methods. The *Mount Hesse* equivalent of the ferreting at Kangaroo Ground was to hunt down rabbits on horseback, or from a souped-up stripped-down Baby Austin. If this sounds barbaric one has to remember that these were the days before the discovery of myxamatosis and rabbits were a fearful pest to the squatters, ruining pasture and destroying fences. Many were the methods tried to get rid of them. The State of Western Australia built a rabbit-proof fence one thousand miles long to protect it from the slow lemming-like surge of rabbits across the great sandy desert from the east. On a nearby station to *Mount*

Up rode the Squatter Mounted on his Thoroughbred

Hesse they fenced an entire warren, blocked up all the holes and backed a half-ton truck into the remaining entrance. Fitting a rubber hose on the exhaust pipe they inserted it down the burrow and while the truck roared and back-fired many thousands of rabbits were methodically gassed. Because they were a pest we were allowed to hunt rabbits to exhaustion on horseback and this was not as hard as it sounds. Provided you could come between the rabbit and its burrow it grew confused and could be hunted until it lay panting and bewildered on the ground, easily despatched by a 'rabbit killer' with the heel of the hand on the back of the neck. The souped-up Austin was much more exciting. It was the invention of Harry Laing, a cousin of the Kininmonths, who had come out to do a spot of desultory jackarooing. He was tall and lean, of a Gary Cooper ranginess, and had a head of curly blonde hair coming down in a widow's peak to which ladies were highly susceptible. Harry rode well and did, one supposed, a certain amount of work around the station; but his principal job to us seemed to be hell-raising. He had a motor-bike on which he scorched around the salt pans of Lake Beeac, and it was he who took the windshield and the hood off the baby Austin and drove it hell-for-leather across the plains, twisting this way and that to match the frenzied twisting of the fugitive rabbit. Harry of course did have a gun and sometimes despatched the rabbit in this way.

* * *

In the roasting summer, bush fires were a severe hazard. The Otway Ranges showed blue through a purple haze of smoke, and on the treeless plain there was always the danger of a grass fire, which could sweep across the prairie like a wind, engulfing all before it. Kininmonths and Ramsays decided to protect *Mount Hesse, Turkeith, Mooleric* and *Nangana* with a fire break one chain wide. The burning of this break required an army of beaters organized by Jim Kininmonth, while the elaborate commissariat was under the direction of Mr. McCallum. We set off early in the morning towards the boundary fence: two score men on horseback followed by a couple of four-wheeled wagons with the tea billies, the canvas water-bags, deliciously cool in the heat, and great mountains of crude satisfying sandwiches filled with mutton and chicken and wrapped in old copies of the *Argus*. The main encampment was in the lee of a windbreak, and the deployment of the burners began. Each of six men trailed behind him a brass pipe shaped like an inverted walking stick. It was hollow and filled with kerosene. The end had a wick and from it burned a bright yellow flame. As the six marched slowly forward on a broad front of sixty-six feet each left behind a little trail of flame which quickly spread and sputtered until the whole broad band of grass flamed and burned. In their wake, along either edge of the break, came the beaters wielding long poles to which had been attached triangular strips of cow hide. Most of the time all they had to do was beat out flames along each edge of the break. The fires tended to spread inwards until they met in a blackened waste leaving behind a pitiful desolation of roast lizards, fried snakes, broiled goannas and singed and blinded rabbits. But sometimes a gust of wind from the western oven would roar across the break and then the man-made fire would rage momentarily out of control while beaters belaboured the ground frantically to put it out. Once, the flames leaped upward into a copse of blue gums which immediately became pillars of searing fire, shooting skyward in the heat.

Following the beaters at a distance came the commissariat, now walking slowly over a desert of grey ash and crunchy blackened grass. At one thrilling moment a snake which had lain in a rabbit burrow while the fire passed over rose up on fully a third of its length and advanced swaying towards Mr. McCallum's horse, its wicked bluish tongue darting like an arrow between open fangs. The horse shied violently and almost threw its rider, but up came Harry Laing with a mattock and despatched the snake in one swoop from the horse's back as if he were hitting a ball with a polo stick. At the end of the day we'd burned almost four miles one chain wide and in succeeding days the break was continued until it encircled the whole of *Mount Hesse* and its neighbours, a distance of over thirty miles.

One of the five Miss Kininmonths had married a Ramsay of *Turkeith* and there were three daughters, Betty, Catherine and Paddy. We were all at the tomboy age and mingled indiscriminately, whether on horseback, rowing the little boat on the willow-fringed dam, swimming in water holes or jouncing across the bumpy plain in the souped-up Austin singing *You're the Cream in my Coffee*. All three nieces were tremendous horsewomen (or horsegirls), sportswomen and athletes, but they didn't make life difficult for us on that account. When Mother returned from her visit to England she brought me, unwisely perhaps but with a mother's fond excess, a Fair Isle sweater, a complete suit of plus fours in heather-mixture tweed, golf socks with green garter-tabs, a basic set of clubs with a bag, and a pair of sturdy brown brogues with crêpe rubber soles. I had at this time scarcely hit a ball save on the nine hole public course near our suburban home, but when I arrived at *Mount Hesse* magnificently accoutred it was obvious to everyone that I must be a champion. I was therefore paired with Betty Ramsay to go round in a Canadian foursome at the *Mooleric* course. On the first tee I faced

Up rode the Squatter Mounted on his Thoroughbred

up to the ball with my driver and by a piece of outrageous good fortune hit it swift and true for one hundred and forty yards down the fairway. The rest of the eighteen holes were a miserable exposition of foozling, duffing, lost balls and tempers, and a measure of my undoubtedly true worth as a golfer. Throughout this agonizing performance which lasted a whole afternoon there was never a word of reproach out of Betty or her sister.

Well, if not a golfer I could at least be a caddy. I persuaded 'Aunt' Kitty to let me go with her to the open tournament at the country town of Colac. Unfortunately I hadn't been told, or was too naïve to know, that if you caddy for a man for eighteen holes he should give you a tip; accordingly I worked like a dog all day and at the end received nothing. The days of *Mount Hesse* appear to have been entirely spent in these wonderful pursuits of break-burning, horse-back-riding, golfing, rabbiting and playing *Cock-a-doodle, I'm off my noodle* with Harry Laing in a four-handed duet on the Bechstein grand. Yet the station was after all dependant entirely on sheep, and it would be odd to leave it without some account of them.

* * *

The shearing shed was by far the largest and most impressive of all the station buildings. It was an enormous barn-like structure about one hundred and forty feet long and thirty feet high and at shearing time in September it became a centre of the most tremendous activity. The shearers arrived from the next station, some on their own horses, but most of them in one-ton trucks; and the sheep were herded into pens to await their turn at the shears. Around the milling animals barked the dogs, yelping and nipping and keeping their woolly charges in a state of terror, and so close packed that the dogs could walk across a herd on its back. The roustabout opened the slip rails, gave the lead ewe a kick and she leaped up and dashed towards the funnel that led into the shearing shed. Behind her each of her silly followers leaped over the same non-existent slip rails and a blurred scatter of innumerable trotters rushed through the gate in a cloud of dust, flies, sweat and sheep-dung. I was foolish enough to ask Harry Laing how he could count the sheep so accurately as they streamed through the slip rails. 'Oh,' he said, 'that's simple. We just count the feet and divide by four.'

Once inside the shed stalwart shearers grabbed the sheep under the armpits and plonked them down on the rear between their knees while they bent over the resigned animals and removed the fleece with incredible skill and rapidity. Mechanical shears were coming in at this time but the sheep were still shorn mostly by

The Road to Gundagai

hand. The speed with which the fleece was clipped clean and close and then thrown on the sorting table was as remarkable as the sight of a shorn sheep staggering across the floor on its way to the dip tank. These were mostly high-class merinos mingled with a few cross-bred or come-backs, and they had great folds of dewlap wool around their necks and shoulders. The fleece was so deep that when you put your hands on the rough exterior and parted it you revealed three to four inches deep of pure white wool as soft as silk and as strong as sisal. A good shearer could snip close around the sheep's eyes, horns, tail and testicles without so much as causing a single nick. There developed tremendous competition amongst the shearers as to who could shear the most sheep, and being Australians they held a book on it at the end of the day, and at the end of each week.

The home paddocks now filled with miserable forlorn goat-like creatures, all white and skinny; the lambs were the only unshorn creatures, long tails dragging on the ground, and most of them not as yet 'dagged'. Dagging, which is the castration of baby rams with a dagging knife, was no pastime for the squeamish. The first time I was invited to observe a dagging ceremony one of the shearers, in a gesture of skill and bravado, performed the act with his teeth. They were enormous fellows, these shearers, working all day in old flannel singlets and a pair of corduroy dungarees and sustained by innumerable huge white enamel mugs of piping hot tea and dozens of broiled lamb chops. They lived like kings and at the weekend they went off to the nearest town—which wasn't very near, at least fifteen miles off—to drink a beer or two, or as they frankly put it, 'to get shickered'. But whatever the shearer's Saturday night, he showed up blear-eyed, but efficient and on time on Monday morning. Then just as suddenly as it had begun, the work was all over, and like a plague of departing locusts the shearers took off in their trucks and wagons to the next station and we wouldn't see them for another year.

Now came the time for the squatters to relax. 'Shearing's over' and those who couldn't afford the trip Home went 'down to Lorne'. The seaside resort of Lorne, on Loutit Bay, was pre-eminently the squatters' riviera: a mile or two of broad yellow sandy beach backed by low eucalyptus-clad hills and fronting the Southern Ocean. Here the fashionable gossip writers came to find out what the people who sustained Victoria were really up to in their leisure hours, and fill the social columns of the *Herald*, the *Australasian* and the *Bulletin* with their doings. These, though costly, were simple: bathing, surfing, drinking, mostly beer and in enormous quantities, tearing around the little town in fast Lancias or Bentleys, dancing, sun-tanning and drinking again. Everyone knew everybody else, each knew what his

Up rode the Squatter Mounted on his Thoroughbred

neighbour was worth and all knew that each of them was worth more than all their non-squatting co-citizens put together. They seemed friendly extrovert snobs, in a wonderful world of the senses and emotions, of golden brown bodies on golden brown sand and no thought for the morrow.

* * *

Lorne was the essence of squattocracy; so was Barwon Heads. Yet Queenscliff, also a seaside resort and also, at least technically, in the Western District, was a rank outsider. Port Phillip Bay opened onto the Bass Strait through a narrow three-mile passage known as The Rip which lay between Point Nepean and Point Lonsdale. At The Rip the great curving arms of this sheltered sheet of water, forty miles across, almost linked hands, but they presented a striking contrast. Point Nepean was a long, thin, spiky promontory between ocean and Bay, tufted with enormous sand dunes. Point Lonsdale, being an outlier of the Western District, was made of dark brown sandstone cliffs backed by the usual rocks of pitted basalt. Just to the north of Point Lonsdale lay Queenscliff, a holiday town perched on a steep bluff combining the pleasures of the metropolis with sea air. The courting couples could parade up and down Hesse Street instead of 'The Block'; there were movie houses, a legitimate theatre, a golf course and above all The Ozone.

The dedication of Australians to sunbathing and their love of bronzed bodies and burning sands, made Queenscliff an anomaly. The beaches of Point Nepean, like those of Lorne, were covered with half naked men and women who, in that censorious era, braved the beach police by refusing to wear the regulation 'neck-to-knee' bathing togs. Behind the salty bushes, rakish summer cottages lay half hidden. Behind the dunes, in the ti-tree scrub and on the streets of Portsea the fast set disported themselves, and gin was as popular as beer. Yet across The Rip in Queenscliff all was sedate, beery and middle-class, the very epitome of an antipodean cockney paradise. Queenscliff had a 'Front' and you bathed primly and undressed carefully in sandstone caves hidden from view. Instead of burning sands there were secluded inlets. Though it was not impossible that a man might bring someone else's wife from Melbourne to Queenscliff for weekend, he would need to be extremely circumspect. In Portsea not only would it have been known, but the knowledge would have excited scarcely a ripple. On the treeless rise of Hesse (pronounced Hessey—unlike *Mount Hesse*) Street were worthy shop windows and one or two enormous beach hotels with triple storey verandahs and balconies and a tall tower with a mansard roof. In Portsea jazz

The Road to Gundagai

blared from the panatrope. In Queenscliff the municipal band played in the local park. In Portsea couples paraded up and down in swimming togs; in Queenscliff they dressed in open-necked shirts and baggy trousers, usually with a brace of kids in tow. Portsea was exciting, forbidden and fashionable; Queenscliff was pedestrian, respectable and family. It was in fact the 'Southend' of Melbourne.

For a boy these things didn't matter and the dramatic fact about Queenscliff was that you went there by paddle steamer. Though paddle boats have come back into vogue today, particularly as river steamers on the Mississippi and the St. Lawrence, these are of the prosaic stern-wheel pusher type. The pleasure steamers that plied from Port Melbourne to Queenscliff—the *Weeroona* and the *Hygeia* —were old-fashioned side-wheelers. Seen end-on they appeared monstrously clumsy and of immense girth; but when you were aboard and watching the great paddles churning through the water in a massive circular sweep, swishing the sea out behind them and pulling great bucketfuls of it up under the enormous semi-circular guard, you were conscious of an awesome surge of power. Equally dramatic was the way a stern-wheeler could reverse, one paddle full astern and the other full ahead, to 'turn on a sixpence'. The trip down the Bay took about two hours and the only land seen on the whole stretch was a group of undistinguished low sandbars known as the Mud Islands off which lay a mysterious fort. Tiger Webb's parents took me down to stay with them at Queenscliff and once away from the family atmosphere and respectability of Hesse Street there was a whole world to explore.

The Webbs rented a single storey wooden house facing a dirt road and the railway track that led across arms of the sea to the military firing range on Swan Island. A less prepossessing outlook for a summer cottage would be hard to find, but in Queenscliff there were no private beaches as there were at Portsea and you swam as you still do in many seaside resorts in England. You took a towel and bathing togs wrapped up in a neat sausage under your arm and walked half a mile to the beach, there to change in the threepenny bath house, or surreptitiously, if you could avoid the eye of the beach attendant, behind a rock at the foot of the cliff.

Tiger and I did a lot of this but most of the time we spent fishing. The dirt road and railway track onto which the Webbs' little summer cottage faced with its thin strip of trampled herbage, its cabbage palms and its inevitable backhouse, led to the viaducts which crossed the arms of Swan Bay. The tide raced seething in and out beneath these trestles. The water was pellucid and the bridges made wonderful fishing positions for old and young. Right after breakfast you rushed to the middle of the trestle to get a position

Up rode the Squatter Mounted on his Thoroughbred

and hung on to it all day, draping your lines over the railing and letting them trail in the tidal surge below. Spiny leather-jackets, whiting and small striped bass were easily come by and with luck you might spear a flounder from a flat-bottomed boat. The big fish, the schnapper and barracuta, cruised outside in the Bass Strait.

At last the Webbs decided to take a look at Sodom and Gomorrah across The Rip and we climbed into the little launch that plied to Portsea. Children are not usually as scarey as grown-ups. They know so little of what may happen that it never occurs to them to expect the worst. However a glimpse of Mrs. Webb's face as we squeezed the last of fifty or sixty people onto the launch made me wonder. Out in the middle of the stream the engine failed and we were left wallowing in The Rip and its shark-filled waters. The moment of alarm had come. The captain sent up a flare and after an hour of very uncomfortable tossing we were rescued by a police cutter and towed back to Queenscliff. The most poignant memory is of picnickers climbing, green-faced, from the launch onto the deck with all the costly freight of cucumber and chicken sandwiches, fruit salad and beer left uneaten and undrunk.

Chapter Fifteen

ANGELA (SUI GENERIS) THIRKELL*

Returning full of joy and sunshine from the country and skipping down the platform with my kitbag I saw Mother's face staring at me from behind the ticket barrier and at once divined the horrid truth.

'Did you have a good holiday? I'm taking you to the dentist.'

Mother was rigorous in these matters and sent us to the dentist at the end of every term. If only her assiduity had been matched by my heredity, or her diet. No man ever laboured in a vineyard to less purpose than our poor dentist, Dr. Shuttleworth; by the time I was twenty-five half my teeth had gone. But in other fields Mother's successes were less transitory. One afternoon I brought home from school a boy named Nelson, destined to be the most long suffering of mates. Just as we rose from the supper table to dash from the room for a game of twilight football among Dad's citrus trees in the back garden, Mother said: 'You have five minutes before Reading Aloud.' This stopped me in my tracks, while Nelson stood his ground and tried to mask his mistrustfulness with a nonchalant neutrality.

'Reading aloud?' I said.

'Yes, stupid,' said Mother. 'You know perfectly well we have it every night.'

'But what about Jim Nelson?'

'Jim Nelson can listen to *Little Dorrit* if he wants to,' said Mother. I slouched moodily into the back yard with my hands in my pockets followed by the perplexed and wondering schoolfriend.

'What does your Mum mean?' he asked. 'And who's Little Dorrit?'

With a strangled grunt, I threw him a ball. 'Catch.' He caught the ball but, 'I wouldn't mind hearing about this Little Dorrit,' he said. Deserted, even by my friend. We had five minutes of catch,

---

* The phrase was written in his own hand on the title page of his *Short History of Australia* by Professor Sir Ernest Scott, a friend and admirer.

Angela (Sui Generis) Thirkell

and then repaired to the 'study' (Dad was out) and Jim Nelson lay solemnly on his belly on the floor with his chin cupped in his hands and his elbows on the ground before him, while to the accompaniment of gurgled sips of after-dinner black coffee and their dramatic rumble down her gullet, Mother read us an instalment. Nelson came back the following night at his own request just so that he could catch the next episode in the cliff hanger; but thereafter he said he'd rather play football with the other fellows: reading aloud was a bit 'queeny'.

This ritual was part of Mother's insistence on maintaining standards amid the alien corn. It was for her the intellectual equivalent of dining in a dinner jacket in the jungle. What it amounted to essentially was re-reading to us the books which she had enjoyed in her own girlhood. The sole exception to this rule was John Buchan's *Mr. Standfast*. Mother had conceived an admiration for Buchan based on his exploits in South Africa as a member of 'Milner's Kindergarten', in the days immediately following the defeat of the Boers in 1901. She regarded *Mr. Standfast* as simply the latest in a series of Buchan adventures and was quite unprepared for the eagerness with which we grasped this tale of intrigue and upper-class stiff upper lippery during World War One. But, of course, it was a Richard Hannay book, the successor to *Greenmantle*, and therefore it exuded the atmosphere of the 'establishment' in far-off England as well as the true thunder of guns on the Western Front to which Dad had accustomed us. There was Blenkiron, that highly improbable American; the quite preposterous German spy, Graf von Schwabing, masquerading as a Rotarian in Biggleswick; and the prissy and too-clever-by-half Mary Lamington (her name moved us to mirth since it suggested to us a sponge square covered with chocolate and grated coconut). Altogether, a most unlikely story. But it held us mesmerized and it was the only book which we literally snatched from Mother's fingers because we wished to finish it ourselves faster than she could read it aloud.

Buchan was all right, because he was a gentleman; other contemporary literature was frowned upon. Mother herself might conceive a passion for *A Passage to India* or *Babbitt*, but they were never read aloud to us; nor did she ever read to us any of the spate of novels which her brother was at that time actively producing and which culminated in *Greenery Street* in 1925. What she read was an extraordinary grab bag from a treasure chest of girlhood memories. Over a period of seven or eight years we listened to the entire works of Dickens with the exception of *Barnaby Rudge* and *Master Humphrey's Clock*; to most of Scott's Waverley novels; to Thackeray's *Henry Esmond*; to the *Memorials of Edward Burne-Jones*; and to

The Road to Gundagai

curious private anthologies edited by Lady Glenconner. We were also encouraged to read to ourselves such ancient children's classics as the books of Charlotte M. Yonge and Mrs. Molesworth, Charles Kingsley's *The Water Babies* and the fairy stories of Grimm, Hans Anderson and Mary de Morgan.

The evening ritual of reading aloud was absolutely rigid. Nothing was allowed to interfere with it—at least, no activity of ours. From it there gradually spread over us a network of fine filaments labelled 'conduct'. This code of conduct, since it was derived from books, was essentially literary; the acts which our exemplars and hence ourselves were and were not allowed to perform. These had nothing whatever to do with ordinary human relationships. We did not learn how to deal with, much less to live with, our fellow man. What we learned were basically literary postures to be assumed in fictive situations. It was a code of highly articulate cleverness rather than of intellectual honesty. The emphasis was on the skills required to solve acrostics, word games, dumb crambo, crossword puzzles. Familiar quotations, including 'capping' one's rival, were a favourite. Literary allusions encouraged the kind of conversational gambits which pass for brilliance before the less educated, but which in fact depend entirely on a retentive memory and on an unwritten law (known to you but not to your interlocutor) that those who know more or who can parrot more (irrespective of how deep their knowledge goes or on what it is based) have the right to be rude to others and to say cutting things to them.

It will readily be apparent that for a boy to assume such postures in democratic Australia would have earned him a good kick in the backside. The postures, when adopted by Mother, were less likely to be so rewarded; but her essentially literary conception of life made her dealings with Australians, and particularly with local trades people, a long cantankerous running battle. Several scenes recur. almost all with Mother at the centre being rude to someone, no doubt often with justification. There was Mr. Young the butcher, proprietor of Young's Meat Emporium. He had smarmy 'brush-back' curly hair, a wax moustache, a pair of evasive eyes and a bogus bonhomie which wouldn't have fooled a three-year-old. His inevitable greeting to Mother was 'Good morning Mrs. -er-um—baby's looking well today.' Her reply was, 'When you can address me correctly you may take my order.' Mr. Young wanted the business but he was an ex-Digger who had fought in the A.I.F. and this kind of language made him apoplectic. He cursed under his breath and got on with the order, but he took it out on us boys if we went alone on a Saturday morning to pick up the goods.

'Here comes little Mr. High-and-Mighty' was a favourite locution.

Angela (Sui Generis) Thirkell

On one occasion the brass letters fell off his plate-glass window so that instead of reading 'Young's Meat Emporium' the legend was 'You g's M at Emporium'. Mother's gambit as she entered the shop was, 'I see you believe in truth in advertising.' There was Mr. Coughlin the milkman whose milk she found undrinkable, the clerk at the Post Office from whose precincts she would often stride forth into the street muttering 'Sold again!' There was the chemist with the respected but improbable name whom she greeted, on finally meeting him, 'Good morning, Mr. Golightly; I was beginning to wonder whether you existed.' There was also the supreme occasion when we were sitting on the dummy of a cable car, and the man in the next seat cleared his throat and spat on to the street. As the globule (known to us as an oyster) arced over her and fell with a resounding smack on the pavement, Mother said in a loud voice, 'If you do that again I shall scream!' 'That's all right, lady,' said the culprit. 'Just you watch this.' He cleared his throat and spat again but it was into the wind of the onrushing car and the debris sailed back on to his own overcoat. Fortunately it was not Mother's, but she did scream. The brakeman stopped the car and we got off, purple with shame.

She met her match, though, in a tight-lipped tram conductor whom she had the hardihood to tackle on his home ground.

Conductor: 'Fez please! Hurry along there!'
Mother: 'Kindly don't push!'
Conductor: 'I ain't pushin'.'
Mother: 'And don't speak to me like that!'
Conductor: 'What's wrong with it?'
Mother: 'For one thing it's not good English.'
Conductor: 'It's good Australian; that's enough for me.'
Game, set, match and rubber.

Broadly speaking Mother looked on Australians, with few exceptions, as members of the Lower Classes. She agreed heartily with an English visitor who once told her (within our incredulous hearing) that Australia was 'a wonderful country for Warrant Officers'. The social attitude implicit in such a statement troubled her not one whit. The whole of this great grey sun-baked continent she regarded much as if it were Hornsey or Tooting Bec, and she a Kensingtonian of high degree. What made it unbearable on both sides was that in those distant days there was just enough truth in it to hurt. Mother *had* been a Kensingtonian and though never belonging to the 'establishment' had been able to arrogate to herself something of its attitudes, based on the genuine distinction of her grandfather and her father. The Australian big towns of the Twenties did bear a superficial resemblance to London suburbs and what riled her was to find suburban types and members of the Lower Orders actually running the country. It never occurred to her that she was a guest in their house, nor, I think, did she really grasp the nuggety toughness of the city dweller or the rangy, loping, deep-eyed stare of the country dweller, both of which spoke of hard horizons and a land where the sunshine got into your bones so that a runty fellow from Nottingham or St. Helens became in two generations a 'white Zulu'.

On the other hand this determination to preserve literary standards did earn her a deserved reputation as a remarkable intellectual eccentric in the essentially semi-colonial society of those days. Who, without supreme confidence in themselves, could have held a literary tea-party for fifty women—artists, musicians, writers, dancers, professors' wives—in a small suburban house, and dared to mask the presence of the outside lavatory and other amenities by hanging carpets on a clothes line propped up with a stringy-bark sapling? Such brilliant improvisation argues character, and though she didn't live in Toorak or South Yarra, those who made the pilgrimage to the funny, ugly little house on Grace Street included many of the leaders of academic and cultural life in Melbourne. She even achieved the dubious honour of being invited to dinners by Mrs. Willy Byers, a preposterous but lovable woman who aspired to create a genuine *salon* in darkest Melbourne. She had unlimited funds at her disposal and an overwhelming bosom beneath which cowered a barely visible husband (who provided the money); and she was an unabashed and indefatigable lion hunter and headline grabber. Her lisp—imitated by students who were bidden to her literary teas, as an unctuous, hand-wringing 'Pawis! The Spwing! The Twocadewo!'—was no impediment to her social advancement. She was the queen bee of a curious mixture of semi-colonial café society and bohemia, no doubt all secondhand and much of it second-rate, but a lot of it fun.

Dragging an unwilling Dad with her in a boiled shirt, which he hated, Mother attended Mrs. Willy Byers' evenings and because of her allusive, elliptical, firecracker conversation, heavily larded with quotations and literary references, she was a nine days' wonder. But she was also distinguished in her own right. She was a member of the Classical Association and read before them *in Latin* papers on Virgil and Horace which excited the admiration of school headmasters and professors. She was a member of the Lyceum Club where ladies with artistic propensities gathered for tea and discussions on Wednesday afternoons. Most interesting of all it was through her own magnetic if acid personality, and the grape-vine stretching back to England, that our little house held within its bounds such a host of local and visiting celebrities.

To dinner came Sir John Monash, leader of the Australian Imperial

Angela (Sui Generis) Thirkell

Forces. My brother has written of him as 'Joshua Reborn'. To me it was entirely miraculous that this legendary commander should be in our house. He came in a white tie and tails, his chest covered with miniatures. This was disconcerting, because at school we sang a song, the refrain of which was:

'Hi, hi, hi, for Generals Monash, Smith, McCay'

and one imagined him stomping up and down the Western Front, his Sam Brown cinched round his noble pot and his cavalry boots squelching in the mud. But even in civilian dress he was impressive enough: not tall, but with a large and powerful head, a high domical forehead, bushy eyebrows, purple pouchy bags under his eyes which were a penetrating, probing brown. There was something brooding and aloof about the face with its pendulous nose and moustache clipped to the point where it blended with the olive skin. He was at that time chairman of the Victorian State Electricity Commission and I still have in my autograph book his letter to Mother which courteously warns her in advance that there may be 'labour troubles' at Yallourn and that, should he have to leave early, he hopes she will understand.

Every year on April 25th the veterans of Gallipoli and the Somme paraded down Swanston Street ten abreast, Monash at their head, flanked by half a dozen bemedalled generals. It was a ceremony of extraordinary impressiveness, entirely undiminished by the fact that each year the band of veterans necessarily became smaller. The last time I saw Monash lead the parade was when I was almost grown up in 1930 and a year later he died. For us at school he had a special significance because he was an Old Boy, and it is typical of this great Australian Jew that when he was asked to suggest a motto of the House which had been named after him he took a Scots or Gaelic one: *Mak' Sikker*, make certain.

To suburban 4 Grace Street came Dion Boucicault the actor-manager and his wife Irene Vanbrugh, presumably guided there as part of the network operated by Mother's brother in England and which at that time included Barrie and Cynthia Asquith. Another visitor was the celebrated diseuse Dorothea Spinney, who wrote in my autograph book 'Good luck to arithmetic' which suggests the more painful preoccupations of those years. Because of her, Mother decided that I had a voice and began to teach me simple ditties, with herself as accompanist at our little Bord cottage piano, such as *Orpheus and his Lute* and *The Kerry Dances*. But no more than a husband can teach a wife to drive a car can a mother teach her son to sing. The lessons were a lamentable failure with Mother's piano accompaniment continually getting out of phase with my singing.

The Road to Gundagai

They generated on my part an uncontrollable irritability with her lack of understanding (as I imagined) and on her part an uncontrollable impulse to laugh at my breathy voice. I think she hoped to catch me before my voice broke so that I could emulate the boy sopranos in St. Paul's Choir, but she was about six months too late. She never, during these lessons, alluded to the fact that my father had been a distinguished lieder and folk singer in his day. In fact she never alluded to him at all, and forbade me to do so. Nevertheless I think she hoped that out of the wreckage of her first marriage could be rescued some remnant of the combined talents which had presumably gone to making up my own genes. What if the boy should have a voice? Unfortunately the boy did not, and when his Mother told him that *Orpheus with his Lute* sounded like 'Orpheoo, wih hih Loo', there was nothing to be done but for the lessons to break up, or break down, in tears and recrimination.

Mother's rigid code of manners was severely undermined by the visit of Mrs. Casey who lived in an enormous house at the top of a hill in South Yarra and who was the mother of Australia's future Foreign Minister, Richard G. Casey. There was some suggestion that Mother was being 'looked over' because Dad at that time was doing a metallurgical job for the Broken Hill Proprietary Company in which the Caseys had an interest. Mother had prepared for the arrival of this *grand dame* by purchasing from Herbert Adams' Rich Cakes Limited a large square 'rainbow'. This was a most unusual treat and we looked forward to gobbling up the leavings, for the cake consisted of three layers of coloured sponge interspersed with cream filling and clothed in marzipan and chocolate icing. We were allowed to sit at the table while Mrs. Casey picked at her bread and butter; then along came the rainbow cake. Would Mrs. Casey care for a slice? She would indeed! Before our unbelieving and admiring eyes she carefully separated the icing and cream filling and popped it into her capacious mouth leaving all the sponge on the plate. For months afterwards whenever we were enjoined not to be greedy we virtuously cited Mrs. Casey.

Into the little suburban house came Ernest Scott, Professor of History in the University of Melbourne. He was a portly fellow with a small walrus moustache and a bubbly fund of humour and tart anecdote. He had been a Hansard reporter at the time of Federation in 1901 and had hob-nobbed with Alfred Deakin, Edmund Barton and the other architects of Australian Federation. He lacked higher education and his appointment to the Chair of History caused a sensation; but he held it until his death in 1940, honoured by generations of students to whom he transmitted his sense of perpetual curiosity, his determination to probe to the bottom of things, and his admiration for the apt phrase provided that it was not a short cut which neglected the true byways of history. It was always a pleasure to his students to see in any professorial list, among a peppering of degrees both earned and honorary, the single unadorned entry: Ernest Scott.

His wife Emily (she became Lady Scott when he was posthumously knighted) was an entirely different person, whose brother was a mysterious financier with an imperial and a perpetual cigar. She had been a Miss Dyason and had a kindly though acidulous face clamped tight by a pair of pince-nez; a breathless rapid-fire vocal delivery and a love of music, or perhaps of the accoutrements and paraphernalia of music, equal to Mother's. Emily Scott held Sunday afternoon *salons* at their rambling house in Brighton to which the young people were sometimes invited. One could have preferred to have been in the library with 'Scottie'. There, three of the four walls were solid books from knee height to the ceiling; they were entirely uncatalogued and he knew unerringly where each volume lay. But one was forced into the drawing-room next door where music was in progress and where Emily's terrifying habit of shifting people around after tea was horribly unnerving to all those under fourteen. One summer a grotesque but hard-working trio was formed, consisting of Emily on the 'cello, my Mother at the piano and Norah Streeton on the violin. Norah Streeton (nee Clench and born in Cobourg, Ontario), had been a concert violinist and was hence the only true professional of the trio, but they had a great deal of fun and it was fun too for me to listen to them; to hear Mother saying:

'No, Emily, it isn't like this, it's *one*, two three, one *two*, three ...' Most deliciously ecstatic of all was to hear Mother being contradicted by Emily. 'No, Angela, it's just that you aren't reading properly.'

Norah's husband was Arthur Streeton, the Australian impressionist landscape painter and senior member of the so-called Hiedelberg School. Streeton is as out of fashion today in painting as Scott is in history. But while one may deplore the sentimentality of such a title as *The Purple Noon's Transparent Light*, one of Streeton's most famous paintings of the Yarra Flats looking towards the Dandenong Ranges, no doubt Drysdale, Boyd, Nolan and Dobell would acknowledge a debt to him. He pulled Australian painting out of the colonial brown gravy period and created, at a time when it was nationally as well as aesthetically important to do so, an authentic vision of Australia's harshnesses and limpidities. The Streeton's boy Oliver was our contemporary and was looked down on because he collected fossils.

Another artist friend was Thea Proctor, the Sydney water colourist, whose delicate, though rather anaemic art nouveau drawings were much in demand among the social set. She worked in water colour

The Road to Gundagai

and in lithograph and some of her drawings were in the shape of fans. She did a quick sketch of Mother in pencil and wash. Of course it couldn't compare with the Collier portrait. This was a full length painting of Mother in a blue dress and a black hat with a great curving red ostrich feather coming down over one cheek. It is now in the National Gallery in Melbourne. Nor could Thea's compare with the famous Sargent portrait. This was a charcoal sketch of Mother when she was twenty-five by John Singer Sargent. The American's brilliant virtuosity distilled on paper in less than two hours and through the sole medium of charcoal, the essence of such different textures as soft hair, a young woman's flesh, seed pearls and ruched muslin. He made Mother's neck one-and-a-half times as long as her head, but apart from this artistic licence it is a vibrant likeness. 'Her neck is like the swan,' said the egregious art critic of the *Herald*, in reproducing, without Mother's permission, the Sargent portrait. She never spoke to him again. Not that this was the solution. Throughout her life Mother was 'never speaking to people again' and all it did was to isolate her progressively from the outside world. But though Thea's little portrait lacks the audacious, indeed aggressive bravura of the Sargent picture and the larger-than-life society sheen of the Collier picture, it is the way I remember Mother; the way I most like to remember her.

Lord Forster, the Governor General and his daughter Mrs. Pitt-Rivers, came to tea. So did Murray, of Papua, Sir Aurelian Ridsdale with his cheque for the bicycle; Sir Hugh Bell of Dorman Long, with a musical watch that played *Rule Britannia* when it struck twelve. Dorman Long had the contract for the immense and noble arch of the Sydney Harbour Bridge, and Sir Hugh was in Melbourne to look into its finances; for Melbourne, not Sydney, was, to the rage of Sydneysiders, the financial capital of Australia. He was a brother of Gertrude Bell of Arabia and came to 4 Grace Street through the Mackail network; and here we come inevitably to the Mackails.

In 1923 my grandfather was offered a series of lectures at the principal universities of Australia, and in public auditoria in the large cities. The prospect of seeing their exiled elder daughter and her children was enough to make my grandfather, then in his middle sixties, agree to undertake the longest sea journey in the world. It was a considerable triumph for the local Classical Association, the Royal Society, and the universities, for he had previously declined invitations to address the Rice Institute in Houston, Texas and to lecture in India and South America. So the Mackails took ship at Tilbury in the *Orsova* and in due course, arrived at Perth where the first lecture was delivered. What they thought of Australia, and particularly 4 Grace Street, had to be inferred by their grandchildren from their remarks. My grandmother was loud in her praise of the beautiful poinsettias in Brisbane, and she thought that Sydney Harbour was wonderful (she'd better: no visitor who failed to comment on Sydney Harbour would have left the country alive). But she found the hugger-mugger of our little house nearly intolerable, particularly as all three children came down with 'flu during the visit. My grandfather, as befitted a man of years and dignity, was lodged far away from all this family squalor. Suitable rooms had been found for him with Sir William Irvine, the Chief Justice of Victoria; but my grandmother mucked in with us.

She was really appalled by my accent. She made me stand each morning for ten minutes at an open window saying 'round' fifty to one hundred times until I got the diphthong the way it would suit her. But once she was out of the room I lapsed into the protective colouring of the local argot. It was *our* winter when they came and my grandmother, though herself a frugal housekeeper, was dashed by the full horrors of Melbourne suburbia, including the interminable ritual of fire lighting in the drawing-room and the endless comedy (if you had a sense of humour) of the chip-heater. What the house needed was a large brick open hearth with a log burning merrily in it. What it actually had was a small Victorian grate which had to be 'blacked' with a brush and (since there was no housemaid) by me on my hands and knees. The fuel, once one had bedded down old copies of the *Herald* or the *Argus* and chips laboriously chopped in the back yard, consisted of brown coal briquettes and mallee roots. Given a shimmering bed of coals at a temperature of say 300 degrees centigrade, brown coal briquettes and mallee roots make a wonderful fuel; but to try and get them started from a piece of paper and a few chips, even when supplemented by what was called a 'firelighter' (a little cube of sawdust, kerosene and resin, sold by the local hardware merchant) was very nearly impossible. The favourite method was to cover the grate with a newspaper, thereby inducing a draught, but the flame scorched away the centre of the newspaper and headlines of murders and ads for female underwear disappeared with a whoosh up the chimney and you were lucky if you didn't start a soot fire. Drenching with kerosene was strictly forbidden but was the artifice most often resorted to, and some horrible smells and burned carpet edges resulted.

The bathroom was even more fantastic. The heating unit was a chip-heater and when you wanted a hot bath you put in paper and chips from the wood shed, lit them and hoped for the best. In due course a mean trickle of warmish water would emerge from the spout which somehow seemed in keeping with the bathroom itself that contained no lavatory and in which logs, chips and a small sack of coal had to be kept. However my grandmother survived and so did we and shortly after she left (indeed, as I understood later, thanks to a cheque from her) we graduated from a chip-heater to a gas-heater, forerunner of the modern Ascot.

Apart from the sullen and difficult Lady Helps there were still no servants at all. Mrs. Robotham may have assisted with the copper and the scrubbing board but there was no one else. We boys did our best. We not only cooked and washed up and mowed the lawn and weeded the garden and emptied the garbage and chopped the wood and fetched the bread and milk and painted the front fence but we also, of course, made our own beds. Australians were great believers in the 'sleep-out'. They partook, with their English cousins, of the belief that unless you were in a draught while you were in bed it was unhealthy. The windows must be flung wide open and on no account must there be any fires or radiators in the bedrooms. We achieved this in good measure by sleeping on the front porch without sheets (since this would have raised the laundry bill) and sometimes without pyjamas, in the raw, but well tucked in with one of Dad's old Western Front army tarpaulins to keep the rain out. At night before going to bed I did my homework with one small bar from an electric heater glowing a dull cherry red in the surrounding chill. A Melbourne winter night could be every bit as unpleasant as its equivalent in Surbiton or Walton-on-Thames. In fact though I suffered greatly from chilblains as a boy they never recurred again until, as a middle-aged man, I spent winters in Britain. Did we mention whitlows, boils, blackheads and pimples? If so, we should certainly have added chilblains.

But there were compensations, for on the 'sleep-out', at least the front one, you could hear the neighbours' goings on. From the back porch all you could hear was the occasional flushing of the outside lavatory, but from the front, why, the whole street came alive! From the Birts' opposite came the tinkle of the pianola pounding out such popular favourites as *Why did I Kiss that Girl* and *Poor Butterfly*, while the teenage Birts danced and Charlestoned, and the light-fingered gentry, skulking behind the cotton-palms, leaped deftly over the low window sills in the bedrooms and made off with all the ladies' furs. From the Bridgemans next door the most frequent sound was the clacking slam of a screen door, the click of high-heeled shoes on an asphalt walk, a giggle, a car door crashing shut and a terrific gunning of the motor in the night, before taking off down the street. At this point the bedroom window of the Lewis's next but one would rise while he shouted into the uncaring night 'Stop that bloody row and let a fellow get some sleep.' Even more dramatic was the appearance of Mr. Capuana. It was of course an unlikely name, but then he was an unlikely man. He sat alone in a single-seater convertible, he wore a Homburg hat and yellow kid gloves, yet he was a roomer with the Hambleys next door but one. Why should a man so obviously reeking of opulence be (a) without a girl and (b) a roomer with the Hambleys? This was something we never learned. Mr. Capuana remained a mystery. Around midnight the suburban street shuddered into silence or perhaps a lovers' whispered colloquy outside the gate, the import of which was vaguely disturbing but entirely inexplicable.

* * *

Mother continued to hold us together in the midst of all her activity; doing her own cooking and lighting fires with mallee roots; supervising the erection by Dad of a network of naked wires festooned across the drawing-room ceiling; coping with sullen or sulky lady helps; feeding, washing, educating, darning and mending for three rowdy boys. She nevertheless managed not only to conduct her *salons* and to have her dinner parties in these bizarre surroundings, but by sheer force of personality kept her desk to herself. It was at that desk, surrounded by the noise and brawl of a husband and three boys that, like Jane Austen with her observant silences in the rectory drawing-room, she began the satirical essays and short stories which ultimately led to the great flow of novels that poured out during the last thirty years of her life.

The desk stood in a bay window in the drawing-room and looked out across a board fence to the blank brick wall of Mr. Muir the accountant, next door. But I'm sure that Mother's eyes were unseeing. Already in the early Twenties she was writing articles on life in Australia for the *London Mercury*, the *Cornhill* magazine and *Blackwoods*. Anonymous 'middles' on literary subjects were in constant demand from her by the editors of the *Argus* so that when the crash came at TAMECO and Dad's earnings dried up to nothing, she was able to help to support us by a stream of articles and broadcasts. When I think how meagre, how miserable, was the pay for this casual work in the late Twenties—a penny a line from the *Argus*—three guineas for a fifteen-minute broadcast from the ABC —I am lost in admiration at her singleness of purpose and the force of her personality. Around that desk she built her own little sea-wall to keep out the roaring family and the unfriendly Australian. At that desk she gained the initial journeyman skill which from 1931 onwards enabled her to produce no less than thirty-seven novels; whatever their content, an astonishing achievement: *The Brandons, Wild Strawberries, Before Lunch, Northbridge Rectory,*

The Road to Gundagai

Miss Bunting, Love Among the Ruins and so on until the final *Three Score and Ten*, posthumously completed for her by Caroline Lejeune. Nevertheless filial admiration is rarely wholehearted and I am left with a weird sense of frustration and sometimes of anger at the codes of conduct which she imparted to us. *She* might consider herself superior to the Australians; *she* might be able to high-hat the neighbours; but we did not, did not wish to and never could; and it was demoralizing to be taught that we should.

I think the only time Mother ever really came to terms with Australia was when Emily Scott took her to a small country cottage she rented at a little village with the wonderfully tuneful name of Wandiligong, high in the not so romantically named Ovens Valley in the foothills of the Australian Alps. There she went with young Lance, who was by this time four or five, and spent idyllic weeks by pellucid streams full of brown trout, among water meadows and foothills, and high above, the great massif of Mount Bogong towering 6,000 feet into the cryptic Australian sky. Lance was another family, he was nine years younger than me and seven than my brother, so that it was really like having a baby to play with. Come to think of it, we exposed him to the most hair-raising dangers. His two-wheeled go-cart with the long handle we lashed behind a bicycle, and then careered downhill at a smart fifteen miles an hour with baby brother bouncing behind.

Once someone slammed a window sill on his finger and with great presence of mind we jammed on the top piece and held it there until Doctor Gutteridge arrived. For Mother with Lance at Wandiligong it was a calm period when she came to terms with that harsh, greyish-olive continent, around the edges of which, like ants on an upturned saucer, clung six million people.

Yet her patience was severely tested when her Mother-in-law came to stay. Rumblings of this impending event reached us by illicit means, for we overheard a flaming row between Mother and Dad as to whether Meo should come over from Tasmania for the wedding of Edna Tabart, Dad's niece. Mother said she didn't mind Meo coming if she stayed at a hotel.

Dad said Meo couldn't possibly stay at a hotel; this would bring permanent disgrace to him and send him down with grey hairs in sorrow to the grave. Mother's reply was that she was not going to cook and wash up for any more drones, at which point Dad cunningly suggested that my brother and I would be very helpful. I was very much astonished at hearing myself grudgingly praised by Mother for my ability not only as a cook (be it only of flap-jacks, and other scout-like recipes) but also as a washer up. Yet as I preened myself in the wake of this genuine and unexpected praise, my heart sank at the thought of the extra work we would have to do.

There followed a trial by letter across the Bass Strait. It was beautifully done. Mother wrote saying how nice it would have been to have had Meo for Edna's wedding, but unfortunately she could not put her up. Meo replied that she would like to come anyway, and wouldn't mind staying at a temperance hotel in South Melbourne. This naturally caught Dad on the raw. It was a disgrace that his Dear Old Mother should have to stay at a hotel, let alone a temperance hotel or 'coffee palace' as they were known. Mother wrote back saying that she would pay for putting Meo up at a hotel. Meo replied that she was coming to 4 Grace Street and in fact such was the speed of the S.S. *Loongana* across the storm-tossed Strait, that she actually arrived before the letter. Mother put on a very bad face and we were a bit ashamed at the poor mouth she pulled, though she brightened up when Meo said she would only stay for a week. The week of course turned out to be one of those metaphorical excesses which are permitted to Mothers-in-law. She stayed for seven but, in the end, it was not an unmixed blessing because Mother turned the tables on her by leaving her in charge of us while she went off to Wandiligong with Emily Scott and Lance.

Dad soon got very tired indeed of *his* Mother and it electrified us when he argued openly with her. On such occasions he refused to call her 'mother', addressing her, most daringly we thought, as Em, which was short for Emma. Her full name was Emma Alicia Genevieve, a wonderful Victorian combination. Dad would be in the study peering over his stamp collection and his five-eighths of an inch. Meo would enter unannounced and without knocking. Dad's face would remain glued to the lens through which he looked at his precious stamps. The following conversation would then ensue:

'George.'

No answer.

'George, I'm speaking to you.'

A grunt.

'George,' with a long sad sigh. 'Why don't you write to me more often?'

Dad, also sighing and as it were brushing away a tiresome insect: 'I do write to you.'

'Yes, but not very often. You don't write as much as Winston used to.' Winston was Dad's elder brother.

Dad, stung to reply: 'Damn it. Winston lives right in your house. Why should he bother writing?'

Meo, very pained: 'I don't think that's at all a nice way to talk.

Dad, suddenly rising in dudgeon from his stamp collection and

The Road to Gundagai

grabbing his mother by the shoulders: 'All right, come along, Em, I've had enough of this!' And he would push the expostulating Meo before him into the passage and slam the door. To us kids this was high drama. Meo would stand in the corridor outside Dad's study, bosom heaving, breath sucking in through her store teeth.

'I've never been spoken to like that in my life! I don't know what's come over your father.'

Ignoring the fact that he was not our father we would placate poor Meo with another cup of tea.

Finally Edna, who had emerged from a long-legged gangling Charleston-kicking hoyden into a mischievous young woman of Junoesque proportions, was taken to the altar and a few days later Meo was taken to the docks by Dad, and placed firmly aboard the s.s. *Loongana*. We didn't stop waving until she was out of sight down the long silver sliver of the Coode Canal. Even then, Dad said he was going up to Essendon Airport, hire a plane and follow the ship down the Bay to make sure that it cleared Port Phillip Heads and was well and truly on its way back to Tasmania.

* * *

Despite all these distractions Mother still taught us to read widely, and continued to impart values of a 'literary' type. She encouraged any capacity we had for hard work: but as to how to deal with human beings, this she was unable to impart to us because she herself never learned how to do it. Or perhaps it was not a case of learning how. She was not able to 'give'. An intelligent woman, she nevertheless confused cleverness with intelligence, literary allusions with the give-and-take of conversation, calculated rudeness or 'capping' with wit. Hers was the tragedy of the inarticulate heart. The one she had was warm but it was deeply buried and it was terribly difficult for it to come out. It was like a small animal crouched in a burrow peering with frightened beady eyes at the intruder; and when it put out its tongue, as you thought in affection, woe betide the hand that reached for it. Instead there would be a snap and a raising of lizardly hackles. She could 'give' on paper. I have wonderfully amusing, witty and loving letters from her; but to be demonstrative, in person, ah! that was different.

In a book of fairy stories by Mary de Morgan, recently reprinted, there is a tale called *The Heart of Princess Joan*. It is the story of a girl who was left without a heart and who was cold, not as the obverse of hot, nor because she willed it, but because she couldn't help it: she knew nothing else. Her heart had been stolen from her by a wicked fairy at birth as a punishment for her Mother's arro-

Angela (Sui Generis) Thirkell

gance. Because of this, Joan could never cry and could never be kind. One day a prince came to the palace where she lived and asked for her hand in marriage; but he realized that only if he could find her heart could he truly have her for his wife. For years he wandered through snowy wastes, among bleak crags on the edge of the northern world and finally came to the Gothic castle where lived the old witch who kept the heart. He bargained with the witch, took the heart—a tiny pincushion with pink fluffy wings—and carried it back in a little cage at the pommel of his saddle. After many years he returned to the city and learned that Princess Joan was now betrothed to another. Flung into prison for his importunity, he opened the little cage and waited. The heart rose in the air, hesitated, darted hither and yon and finally flew out through the barred window in the wall of the prison. A moment later, to the utter surprise of ladies-in-waiting, Princess Joan burst into a flood of tears, left the marriage procession and through the barred window embraced her lover. She married the prince and they lived happily ever after. Princess Joan was my Mother; it was her ill luck that two marriages failed to bring her the fairy prince.

Chapter Sixteen

THE BUGLES OF ENGLAND

THE Australia of my boyhood conveyed the piercing sense of a lost heroic age. People of Dad's vintage looked back to an era when men were giants and deeds doughtier than in real life. This may have been due to the difficulties which followed the achievement of Federation in 1901. In the 1890's a generation had grown up passionately proud of being Australian. There was still a fierce loyalty to the Crown and the Flag (the Union Jack); but an equally fierce loyalty to The Southern Cross was now felt to be entirely compatible. The new national pride found expression in the ballads of A. B. Paterson, the paintings of Streeton and Longstaff, the stories and poems in the *Sydney Bulletin*, the earthy folk-poetry of C. J. Dennis and of course in the final culmination of years of political effort. When in 1901 the Duke of Cornwall and York, later George V., stood beneath the enormous towering wooden dome of the Exhibition Building in Melbourne, worthy, despite its spindly shape, of the talents of some latter day antipodean Bramante, there was a tremendous sense of achievement.

Then during the next decade the new nation floundered along in the uncertainties of the new federation. The men who had left their States to go to the Federal sphere quarrelled amongst themselves. Governments changed with lightning rapidity, even granted triennial parliaments. Those who had stayed behind in the bigger States began to play politics against the centre. The haves—New South Wales, Victoria and Queensland—were accused of ganging up against the have-nots—South Australia, Western Australia and Tasmania. And then suddenly, as if to resolve it all, came Sarajevo, the march through Belgium, the 'scrap of paper', the mobilization call of August 4th, The Empire is With You, Kitchener's enormous portrait with the massive walrus moustache obscuring whatever lay behind, and the finger pointed: 'Your Country Needs You'. Australians of that far-off day never doubted which country it was that

The Bugles of England

needed them: it was England. Yet paradoxically they would prove their Australianism by rallying to England's defence.

In common with their English cousins the Australian entered the war with what now seems to have been an unbelievable light-heartedness, as a contemporary school jingle suggests:

Some days ago a peaceful world received a sudden shock;
Der Kaiser Wilhelm he will give der universe a knock.
He rushed at little Belgium and he made a passage through;
Great Britain said 'Now German Bill this really will not do!'

It was all a big lark, but soon the Australians found themselves helping to make a myth at Gallipoli which was to dominate their land for a generation and to give them and the world ANZAC and the Anzac tradition. Australia grew towards nationhood in the political ferment of the nineties culminating in Federation; but the new nation was proven by the exploits of the Diggers in Flanders and at Suvla Bay. The ironic thing is that although this terrible baptism of fire helped, as perhaps nothing else did, to create the Australian national spirit, it was to England that the young men looked as they enlisted. England was still Home; it was the 'there' where Australia was to be in *Australia Will be There*. In the chapel at Scotch College hundreds of reedy voices rose in unison towards the rafters as they sang another song which catches forever the extraordinary mood of passionate love for a distant Mother Country. This song had the added merit in our eyes of having been written by a Scotch Old Boy, J. D. Burns (as if the dice weren't already loaded in his favour without the overtones of such a name). Burns had enlisted with the AIF in 1914 as a second lieutenant and had been killed in France. He was one of the many Scotch collegians who gave their lives, but to us his poem *The Bugles of England* irradiated him with the same magical light as Rupert Brooke. It was set to music in mournful minor cadences and it is impossible to hear it in the mind's ear today without a constriction of the throat. The boys who sang it often wept unashamedly for its nostalgia, its innocence and its heartbreaking might-have-been:

The bugles of England are blowing o'er the sea
Calling out across the years, calling now to me.
They woke me from dreaming in the dawning of the day
The Bugles of England; and how could I *stay*?

The banners of England unfurled across the sea
Floating out upon the wind beckoning to me.
Storm rent and battle torn, smoke-stained and grey
The banners of England; and how *could* I stay?

The Road to Gundagai

Oh England, I heard the cry of those who died for thee
Sounding like an organ voice across the wintry sea;
They lived and died for England and gladly went their way
England, oh England, and how could I stay?

There is in this song no mention whatever of Australia or the fact that in rallying to the flag these young men were defending Australia and creating a nation. It was sufficient in those days that the Mother Country was in trouble. And there have been baser motives: the call of the Anglo-Saxon or Anglo-Celtic bloodties, was the call to the heart and the mind of the unseen yet well loved Homeland. This ship of state, sailing on through Australian hearts, heavily barnacled with innumerable individual emotions, dragged these young men in its wake as surely as if they had been tied with cords. The emigrant vessel was coming home; *The last of England* was to be the first. Of course many young men joined up for the fun, and as a boy one heard a great deal about the fun they had: in ports, on leave, in estaminets behind the lines, in the gay, ferocious abandon of such songs as *Inky Dinky Parley-Voo* and *Carry me Back to Blighty* which were as much Australian property as English.

To have fought in Gallipoli conferred a special cachet. Flanders Fields: that was fine and you were a good fellow and a Digger and a mate. But those who had fought at Anzac Cove; who had swum their horses naked in the sea under the pounding fire of Turkish mortars; who had camped in a sort of Old World version of the Ballarat fossickings under the shoulders of Gaba Tepe; who had in their democratic lordliness treated the pink-cheeked British 'pommy' officer with ribald contempt; who had participated in the withdrawal by night, leaving a ·303 rifle with a string attached to its trigger and the other end to a punctured billy from which the water would slowly drip so that the gun would fire long after the man had gone: these men had seen something fierce and tough and precious and holy. Those who stormed Cape Helles and who crept out of the Dardanelles in the evacuation were united in a band of comradeship which was tremendously impressive for a youngster to behold.

The sense of national sacrifice engendered by Anzac was very strong indeed. The Anzac Parade down Swanston Street every 25th April was inexorably noble. The enormous mausoleum-like war memorials erected, particularly in Melbourne and Canberra, these monuments to the fallen, filled us all with awe. *Dulce et decorum est pro patria mori* was something we believed in passionately. The emphasis on blood, on redemption through sacrifice, on the washing away of sin, became somehow mingled with our own Presbyterian *angst* and slopped over even into Sunday School which we attended

The Bugles of England

in an ugly red brick spireless church with the legend A 1906 D on its gable. Both the Anzac myth and the reality have been wonderfully captured by Alan Moorehead in *Gallipoli* and by Sidney Nolan in his paintings: the myth rider in an Australian lancer's hat with the emu feather become one with his horse; the Australian bronzed young man become one with the Greek god; and the whole merged, along with the unblinking stare of the lizard on the sun-baked rock, in what Moorehead has well called 'the timeless dream'.

In church, particularly on Anzac day, we had the impression of participating in a national ritual sacrifice. Bereaved mothers, as stern-faced as Volumnia, attended service standing erect and dry-eyed their bosoms stitched with their dead son's medals. Those maimed and crippled sat in chairs or hobbled on crutches. The veterans themselves had that sober, slightly worn-away but tremendously innocent and worthy air that is shared by those who have been prepared to lay down their lives for their country. That of course is why the soldier is to be honoured. Some recent plays and television shows have suggested a way in which Anzac memories were exploited, simply as an occasion for old sweats to bite on their milk teeth and let the whole thing degenerate into a booze-up. No doubt there was as much boozing then as there is now; but after all, an Anzac celebration in those days was a wake, and traditionally at a wake one drank to forget.

The feeling of blood and sacrifice and the spectre of sudden death lay heavy over the generation which just escaped the war. Every schoolmaster had his row of miniatures; all were members of the R.S.S.I.L.A.; our school chaplain had served in France; and at that time we still had compulsory military service. The mingling of war and religion and Empire—the three seem in my memory to have been indistinguishable—gives the era in retrospect a certain fierce and formidable pride. We felt it in the scouts as well as at school, and at home I had a reproduction of Will Longstaff's 'The Menin Gate' and during the brief period of religiosity through which most youngsters pass, I used to stand in front of it every night reciting Laurence Binyon's 'To The Fallen'.

* * *

I joined the Presbyterian Sunday school principally because Tiger told me that anyone who had been in Miss Davies' class for more than a month was entitled to go on the annual picnic. This was held at Edithvale on a burning stretch of yellow sand and when it was over I told Tiger that I was through with Sunday school. Mother overhead this supposedly whispered colloquy and insisted that, having

The Road to Gundagai

joined, I must see the year out. This was not so bad as it might have been because years of Presbyterian morning chapel and following the Salvation Army on a bicycle had given me a rousing repertory of evangelical hymns. Furthermore the Sunday school classes were mixed. This at first meant nothing to me at all; but during the course of the year certain inevitable changes made me aware for the first time of one of the girls across the street with whom I'd been merrily playing in tomboy fashion for ages. Coming home from Sunday school and choir practice late one evening she put the wicket gate between us and then suddenly reached up and kissed me. She smelled strongly of washing-up but it was glorified by the first touch of a girl's lips; and here, obviously, my Australian boyhood comes to an end.

* * *

And yet, perhaps a brief postscript is required. The 1929 crash brought TAMECO down in ruins and Dad was eased off the board by what he described as the 'treachery' of two officials, whom he would identify as 'Judas' and 'Pilate', together and the pusillanimity of directors such as Les Watson and 'Denny' who had let him down, as indeed, it appeared, had Harry Haines and Bill Hilliard and Don MacFadzean and Old Uncle Tom Cobleigh. Mother kept repeating: 'It's just like a bad American novel'. At any rate Dad's income ceased except for the odd commission on the sale of gudgeon pins, bushes and tappets; and Mother, giving thought for the morrow and her bairns, decided on a bold strategem.

In those days a husband's written consent was required before a wife could obtain her own passport. Mother procured Dad's consent on the not unreasonable ground that it was time for her to take another trip 'Home'. Apart altogether from the fact that he wasn't being asked to contribute, Dad, as a non-earner, was in no position to refuse. One day Mother returned the rented Thürmer piano (the Bord had long since packed it in), plucked the Sargent portrait from the wall, put the silver in the Bank of New South Wales, picked up young Lance and took ship for England. She never came back. Though the complete sets of Dickens and Thackeray, and the peacock fire screens and the round convex mirrors with gilt frames, and the dragon china and the lustreware vases remained at 4 Grace Street, Mother's presence gradually ebbed away, and one day Dad said to me over a lugubrious lunch at Scott's Hotel, 'I don't think your Mother's coming back.' I told him with blazing sincerity and complete naïveté that I was quite sure he was dead wrong. She would never do such a thing. 'That's all right,' he said, 'have another plate of oysters.'

The Bugles of England

Though I didn't realize it at the time I was the unwitting instrument of Mother's departure for I had gained scholarships to the University of Melbourne which would make me self supporting for the next four years; and thus her worry about what to do with the 'grown-up son' had vanished. Lance she took with her, Colin followed her to England a few months later, having secured the final exhibition in Economics in the school leaving examinations. I myself went into residence at the University where, in my final year, I met my future wife, undoubtedly the best thing that happened to me during my entire Australian career.

Then one day, with the memory of Dad's mournful face receding among the girders and grimy glass of Spencer Street Railway Station, and his parting gift of a steamer rug in my third-class cabin, I found myself staring down into the threshing greenish sea behind R.M.S. *Aorangi*. Sydney Heads, crowned at this distance by the great arc of the Harbour Bridge which had pulled itself up out the ocean, fell slowly astern. I was on my way across the Pacific to join my own father in far off Canada; and so the story ended as it had begun, with a steamer's wake: that eternal symbol of aching horizons, hopeful dawns and golden dreams.